Scenery: Draughting and Construction

for theatres, museums, exhibitions and trade shows

John Blurton

A & C Black • London

First published in 2001
by A & C Black (Publishers) Limited
37 Soho Square
London W1D 3QZ

© 2001 John Blurton

ISBN 0-7136-5684-0

A CIP catalogue record for this book is available from the British Library.

Printed in the United Kingdom by Butler & Tanner Ltd, Frome, Somerset

Contents

Preface

The business of arranging a production for a client involves many individuals and groups representative of an extremely diverse skills base – this industry is a broad church. Productions can be in the theatre, taking the form of plays and shows, or in museums, creating their sets and settings. Exhibition stands and sets range from the humble 'point-of-sale' podium to the Expo-type edifice and the giant theme park – from the prosaic to the baroque. Trade shows are produced in a multitude of venues that may or may not have been designed to hold a show; they range in size from the small conference set to extravagant corporate 'product-launches' – car launches, for example, that can dwarf most theatre productions.

It is common for people to work across the whole range of the business, the skills required for each type of production being so similar. Each trade and skill is inextricably linked to the other: a symbiotic relationship exists between all the professions involved in show production. No participating trade is an island, but each is a part of the main – the production.

The aim of this book is to crystallise and place into one volume some of the information used by these trades. A successful production is achieved through the medium of the draughtsman, the person who gathers and collates the various threads of data and places and fixes them on paper. The draughtsman is a conduit through which information is diverted in order that it be rationalised and consolidated into the form of an approved drawing – a drawing that meshes the requirements of the numerous interests in the show. It is *not* a book that attempts to teach technical drawing in itself, no more than it teaches geometry, or carpentry, or engineering as complete subjects. Existing books perform that function. However, it does try to gather technical information from many sources in a fashion that can be quickly referred to by anyone in this business. It attempts to be a 'one-stop' shop, containing numerous pages of data that would normally be scattered among dozens of volumes.

Therefore, although this book is intended to be *most* useful to the draughtsman, the information it contains has been deliberately compiled to be of use to anyone whose professional life involves him or her in scenery, sets and the stage.

The four parts of this volume fulfil different functions. For a full understanding of the subject, each part ought to be read in numerical order; however, it will be seen that the four divisions are designed to allow the book to be used as a quick reference guide, as and when required.

Part One concentrates upon the drawings themselves and the processes involved in completing a successful package of drawings. Drawing equipment and the types of materials commonly used in our industry are included here ... as is the crucially important subject of surveying.

Part Two consists of eight chapters describing basic scenic construction, each chapter dealing with the main parts of a set: walls, floors, staircases, etc. For ease of reference, these chapters have a more clipped text style: issues are discussed that need to be read in conjunction with the illustrations supplied. Each chapter has text and drawings that describe conventional methods of construction and most have examples of more complex uses of these conventions.

Part Three includes an example of a complete *design*-drawing package. The small production illustrated here consists of only four drawings, but the accompanying text is intended to show how the issues raised in Parts One and Two – the bulk of the book – are put into practice. (A complete *construction*-drawing package could not be included – dozens of A1 drawings reduced to A4 would be unreadable and consume too much of the book.)

Part Four contains useful reference data. This information is usually scattered among various types of books or brochures ... here, it has been gathered together for convenience.

Dimensions are in metric throughout the book, but imperial equivalents are shown in brackets where appropriate. For clarity, the drawings only include imperial equivalents when necessary for the understanding of the issues under discussion, or to give a sense of the scale of the item in question. It is normally the case that the *actual* dimension size is irrelevant to the points being made – and it is for this reason that many of the dimensions are too small to be read with any ease: it is only important to understand that a dimension would have to be indicated where shown ... what that particular dimension *is*, will change from job to job. Again, for clarity's sake, most drawings have been stripped of the full amount of dimensioning necessary on a drawing issued for construction (here, only A4 is available; in real life, A1 and A0 paper sizes would be used).

Finally, the subject of correct grammatical gender has proved problematic when attempting to describe complex issues in a clear fashion. Being a technical book, the primary aim of the text is clarity and the introduction of too many 'he or she' inserts only serves to muddy the waters. Clumsy, artificial words such as 'draughtswoman' or, even worse, 'draughtsperson' are an anathema not only to me but also to lucid English, so they have not been included. I freely apologise for any offence caused and would stress that none is intended. To its great credit, this industry has long been blessed with an indifference to gender – in fact, all human life is here, openly displayed.

Acknowledgements

My wife and business partner, Margaret, produced this book with me. As with every project that we embark upon, she shared the workload equally with myself. We have drawn all the drawings contained here; many have been imported from drawings that we supplied to specific projects and have been adapted to suit this medium, while others have been drawn specifically to illustrate points contained within the book.

Two drawings – those relating to stage revolves – have been 'cannibalised' from drawings kindly supplied by *WeldFab Ltd* – an engineering company based in Norfolk. Due credit must be fully acknowledged to the following set-building contractors, all based in South East England: Alan Walker of *Kimpton Walker Ltd*; Philip Parsons of *Steeldeck Ltd*; Kevin Martin of *KP Martin Ltd*; Paul Stroud of *Versatile Ltd*.

Thanks also to the designer and construction draughtsman, Will Bowen, whose companionship over many years has been treasured and whose impeccable knowledge of mathematics has been imparted with such generosity.

Where relevant, the designer of the show has been credited on the drawing itself. *Imagination Ltd* has been the designer and prime mover of several of the productions whose construction details are drawn. Thanks also to Neal Potter, the museum designer and head of *NPDA Ltd*.

The Royal National Theatre has been of constant help in producing this volume. From David Roberts, the Head of the Technical Department, to the Production Offices that run the three auditoria within the complex, all have been generous in their support. Particular thanks are expressed to William Dudley, the designer of *All My Sons* for the RNT, a production that is featured in numerous drawings included here.

I apologise for any omissions – if they exist, they are entirely unintentional.

Finally, this book began life as a series of proposed lecture notes, commissioned by a training organisation that is physically based within the Royal National Theatre and arranges training courses throughout the UK's major theatres. Unreserved gratitude therefore, to Tony Bond who runs this organisation, the TTTS, or *Theatre Technical Training Services Ltd*.

John Blurton
December, 2000

Part One: DRAWINGS

Introduction

Providing drawings for the entertainment industry is a most satisfying occupation: there is a huge variety of non-repetitive work in which to immerse oneself – it can be said that one is re-inventing the wheel every week. Each project is virgin territory in the sense that, almost by definition, no two shows are identical; many shows are similar, or of a similar type to others, but they will almost always be unique in their own way.

Boredom, therefore, is not a familiar emotion to those who draw shows (projects may often be referred to as 'shows' – a familiar colloquialism, frequently adopted, regardless of whether or not the project is a true 'stage show'). Unlike many professions, it is usually impossible to say exactly what job you will be doing in six weeks' time: the fast turn-around of productions and the varied nature of those productions guarantee this variety.

Satisfaction, however, *is* a familiar emotion experienced by the draughtsman: when the completed project is seen in all its glory, fully lit, properly rehearsed and functioning as designed, only the draughtsman is fully aware of the decisions taken along the way in order to achieve technical excellence. **Technical excellence is the aim of the draughtsman.**

Whether one is working for theatres, museums, exhibitions or trade shows, or is lucky enough to work across the whole entertainment spectrum, the basic principles of drawing still apply. Each seemingly intractable problem presented, once solved, is stored in the brain and will almost certainly be dusted off and used again in later circumstances – and it is surprising how often those solutions can be applied to areas that bear no relation to the project that originally generated the problems. In short, experience gained in the theatre, for example, will be of the same value to you when and if you cross over to a different discipline – a scene within a museum complex carries within it the same inherent problems as a scene in the theatre. **Flexibility of mind and a developed sense of lateral thought are therefore vital attributes for the draughtsman to acquire.**

Part One of this book provides a broad outline of the scenic draughtsman's profession. It explores the following points:

- *The function of the drawings*: the reasons for having the drawings commissioned.
- *The first principles of drawing*: how to ensure that the drawings are of value.
- *The types of drawings used by our industry*: drawings come in many forms and have to fulfil various functions and invoke different disciplines.
- *Drawing equipment*: the draughtsman's tools are discussed.
- *Construction materials*: a basic grounding in the use of materials most commonly used by our industry in scenic construction.
- *Surveying*: a guide to on-site surveying.

1 • The Function of Drawings

Drawings perform many different functions and fulfil various needs. The different types of drawings are discussed later, but it is vital that when drawing any kind, it is the ultimate function of that drawing that needs to be kept uppermost in the draughtsman's mind – what is this drawing for? Why is somebody paying me to draw this?

This may all sound rather obvious, but it is surprisingly easy to forget this basic priority and to let the drawing wander off into realms that have little bearing on the real reason for attempting it in the first place. A set contractor may ask for a basic drawing of flattage so that his carpenters can begin construction. He is not asking for a beautiful piece of work that he can frame and hang upon his wall – he wants a clear representation of the job to be built and he wants it to be draughted economically. Alternatively, a trade show production company may well request drawings of a proposed set that will illustrate to their client simply what the set looks like; in this case they do want an attractive drawing, and may not necessarily be interested in exact dimensions or construction details. **In short, listen to your brief!**

The main functions of the drawings can be listed as follows. They are to:

1 Save money for the production

A) The main function of the drawings is to save money for the production – do not forget this simple fact! If shows could be produced without the cost of drawings, then they would. One hour on the drawing board can save a dozen stage crew from wasting an entire eight-hour shift. One extra hour spent simplifying a piece of scenery can save the set-builder from having to spend thousands of pounds of the production budget. One extra hour spent confirming screen sizes in relation to projection 'throws' can save the whole show from being a disaster.

B) If the above were not true, nobody would pay us to produce the drawings at all. Drawings are not just pretty pictures, they are a means to an end – and that end is more important than the drawings are! We produce vital tools, without which the shows could not function.

2 Ensure that the set fits into the venue

A) Regardless of all else, if the set does not fit into the venue then the job has failed from a technical point of view. It is of paramount importance to ensure that the set does not have to be cut down or altered in any unforeseen way when the job 'fits-up', either in its first venue or, if touring, in any future venue.

B) Always obtain as much information about the venue as is possible; a survey is obviously ideal (*see also* Chapter 6), but photographs are useful, as is speaking to key permanent staff. Most venues (not all) have their own set of drawings – usually a ground-plan and sections – but treat these with healthy scepticism until such time as you

have grounds to trust them (check details on-site, if possible). Many venues use drawings that are out of date and/or have been copied so many times that they are unsafe to scale from. Some provide computer-aided drawings (CAD) which appear to be very accurate, but which may have been 'put in CAD' from old, unreliable drawings (i.e. they have been drawn without a survey having been done).

C) When drawing a **touring show**, draw it to fit the smallest venue of its tour; this may seem obvious, but it is surprising how many times the designer, etc. concentrate solely on the first venue and let the rest of the tour look after itself. The production draughtsman must protect the interests of the whole of the show's staff – not just those of the designer. Draw the set to fit the smallest venue and specify additional units to be built for the larger venues. When sets are physically sawn or cut down onstage to fit smaller venues, both the artwork and safety issues may become compromised. Also, if that set then returns to a larger stage, it is almost impossible to disguise the joins in the artwork/décor.

D) Check the relationship between the stage floor and the **flying equipment** (flown bars or hoists). The key 'setting-line' (a line from which the setting of the show begins) of the show may well relate to a flown piece of scenery, rather than an onstage piece of set. Try and measure from, say, the upstage face of the 'iron curtain' (Safety Curtain – fire curtain) to one of the flying bars (any bar that can be easily flown in), then establish the (plan view) centre-line spacing of the bars, which are usually in batches of identical spacing. The bar's centre-lines are shown on plan and section of the venue's drawings (or should be!).

E) Check for any **get-in restrictions** (the 'get-in' is the door through which scenery is handled from truck to stage or stage to truck). The size of the get-in is of obvious importance, so measure the clear height, width and the diagonal of the get-in doors. Also, sketch any restrictions that would limit the length of scenery passing through. For example, a narrow alleyway may lead from the street or truck to the get-in doors: any bends in that alleyway may restrict the length of anything attempting to pass through. Some venues have restricted use of their get-in for reasons of noise pollution, traffic congestion and so on.

F) Check for any equipment that may be installed by the venue after your 'recce'/survey, but prior to the set being installed, e.g. air conditioning units. (The term 'recce' is used colloquially for 'reconnoitre' – a thorough look around the venue.)

G) Check for any **Health & Safety** restrictions that may affect parts of 'your' set. Each venue will have its own individual problems and, therefore, its own safety requirements.

3 Ensure that the designer's needs are met

A) Interpreting the design is key to the success of the drawings. Ideally, a bond of trust is established between the designer and the production draughtsman. Most designs become compromised to some extent, either for reasons of budget or for reasons of practicality. If in doubt, discuss the proposed changes with the designer – you will soon learn which elements are closest to his heart in each particular set. *Listen* to the designer, and try to get a feel for what it is that he is after. Aim for quality and practicality when making compromises.

B) Most designers are experienced enough to know that changes may have to be made to the set design; if a designer is 'difficult' about such changes, then simply refer the decisions up the chain of command. Someone will decide (usually the Production Manager and/or Producer – money is king, finally!).

C) Designs that have gaps in them (incomplete, in short) can be problematic. Establish *at the outset of the project* whether or not you are expected to draw these areas, subject to the designer's approval (by 'signing them off'), or whether the designer himself is intending to supply more information. Sometimes the former method is ideal (quicker) because the production draughtsman will normally be more acutely aware of budget implications than will the designer (but bear in mind that someone is now paying for you to do the designer's job!). Sometimes the latter method is correct, usually in a situation when nobody knows what is in the designer's head.

D) Remember that, if you interpret the design wrongly, your name will be cursed loud and long; but if you get it right, nothing will be said.

4 Prove sight-lines and maskings

A) **Sight-lines** need to be 'proved'. This means ensuring that all seats within the venue provide a clear view for the audience of what they *ought* to see, and that the set successfully masks what they ought *not* to see. Lines are drawn, on plan and in section, from critical seats (usually the extreme seats) to relevant pieces of the set (e.g. an audio-visual screen or an actor's entrance door). Remember to do this both on plan and in side section. The side-section sight-lines will show how low borders and other top masking can be set without obscuring the view of the set from, say, the Upper Circle. Equally, in side section, the sight-lines from the front stalls can confirm that the flown borders mask unwanted items in the grid, such as scenery that is flown out and stored. (Flying: 'in' means down, 'out' means up.)

B) Using these sight-lines, **maskings** can be placed with assurance. In plan, the side masking and legs can be placed. In side section, borders can be set, as well as the 'out-deads' of flown scenery, ensuring that when flown out, the scenery is no longer in view. ('Out-dead' is the height at which a flown piece is stored when flown out. 'In-dead' is the height at which a flown piece is set during the action of a show – when it is in use. There may be several deads for one piece, of course.)

C) The designer should do all this, but often doesn't. *It is for you to check! Note:* It is quite usual for the flown border heights to be fine-tuned on stage, towards the end of the fit-up, by the designer/production manager/lighting designer/crew. This is because the precise angles of the lamps on the lighting bars cannot be exactly predicted during the drawing stage (art does come into all this, after all!). The impedimenta attached to lamps cannot always be predicted either, nor such things as how vertical lighting stands may work. Obviously therefore, the final heights of borders are set onstage to ensure that optimum masking is obtained.

Simply remember that it is the draughtsman's responsibility to consider and draw borders and maskings in order that the pieces get made (or rented) in the first place and that bars, or positions, are allocated on the drawing for all to see. **If items are omitted from drawings, they often don't get made (or ordered).**

D) Rather than drawing the whole venue in plan and section just to establish sight-lines, it is perfectly acceptable to submit stylised (greatly simplified) drawings for this task, possibly at much larger scales (say 1:200). Only certain seats/points need to be plotted (extreme seats at the front and back of each level of seating): draw lines from those points to, say, the iron curtain line. If drawn accurately, these lines can then be safely transferred to your working main stage plan/section. Alternatively, pencil them on to the venue's plans and sections (if they are accurate!), and then transfer them to your own drawings.

5 Establish a flying plot

A) A flying plot is simply an indication – drawn to scale of course – of which particular **flying bars** are to be used in the production. These bars will always have a designated number (designated by the venue – see their drawings), and it is usual custom to show the bar's number and the title of the piece of kit which will be hung upon it. Stored scenery not used in 'your' show, perhaps from other shows in the repertoire, should also be indicated – again showing the bar's number upon which it is stored.

B) The flying plot may be drawn on the plan, the section, or preferably both. The section illustrates the heights of these bars – however, the height above the stage can be shown on the plan by using '+' dimensions – '+8000' being 8000 mm above the venue's stage. Do ensure that it is clear whether your height dimensions are given above the venue's stage or above the show-floor level! It is more useful to the crew to have heights given from the venue's stage because, often, much work has to be done before the show floor is set and it is easier to measure from an existing floor.

C) It is common practice to show the flying plot off to one convenient side of the ground-plan. This saves having to write information on the usually busy central area of the plan.

D) Flown scenery is usually indicated with dashed/dotted lines in plan view – if the piece does not always live permanently on the show floor.

E) Flying plots have to be drawn for each venue of a touring show.

6 Establish a setting-line

A) *Always remember the stage crew!* Where do they begin to build this set? Where should they start? Always establish a line that is relevant to both the venue and to the stage set, from which the crew can begin to build the show. If a show has its own floor, then let this setting-line relate to a suitable starting point from which to begin laying it.

B) Many venues have their own setting-line (often shown on their drawings) and, in theatres, this is frequently a line flush with the upstage edge of the iron curtain. Ensure that your set is given a relationship to this line (e.g. the show floor sets 1000 mm upstage of this line).

C) The setting-line may occasionally be a particular flying bar's position onstage if the first thing built is to be a critical piece of flown scenery. The rest of the set can be positioned from that flown piece.

7 Allow for accurate cost estimates to be made

A) Design drawings must be comprehensive enough for the set-builder and others to be able to estimate the cost of constructing the set. Many current design drawings are less than adequate, to say the least, and some designers rely too heavily on others to do their work for them. This, to be honest, is the fault of producers/directors who do not realise that such inefficiency can waste a considerable proportion of their production budget. If asked to produce design drawings, ensure that adequate information is given on those drawings.

B) Given that design drawings will lead to construction and setting-out drawings, ensure that they contain enough information for these next drawing stages to be achieved. If the design drawings do not contain enough information, the contractor knows that he must allow more costs for *his* drawing programme. Draughting costs money! The cost of drawing has to be included in all estimates.

8 Provide information for Stage Management

A) Stage Management staff will want to use the ground-plan for replicating the acting areas within a rehearsal room (usually by marking out the floor with coloured tape). Ensure that they can read this information with ease.

9 Form a basis for further drawings

A) The main drawings of the set – the ground-plan and section – will be used by the lighting designer to establish his lighting plot. He will produce his drawing from the information shown upon these drawings.

B) The sound technicians and the audio-visual technicians will do likewise.

C) It obviously saves much re-drawing if you are aware of the needs of the above people when first drawing the set. Where possible, talk to the other relevant people and agree on what everybody's needs are.

10 Indicate Health & Safety issues

A) Health & Safety issues are the responsibility of *everybody* involved in the production. This is the law of the land! You cannot duck the issue by claiming that you thought that somebody else had responsibility for Health & Safety.

B) If you spot a potential problem while draughting, always indicate your concerns on the drawing; nobody

will mind your being too careful. At the very least it will become a discussion issue.

C) Have the moral courage to refuse to draw what you know to be a potentially dangerous piece of set. (As a personal example, I have always refused to draw a staircase that has uneven risers because I know that people will trip on them. Uneven risers are illegal and will lead you into court if an accident ensues – it is as simple as that! Don't rely on the designer or the production team to always know about such matters.)

D) Explain any reservations that you may have to the designer, the production manager and the staff responsible for that particular venue.

E) Each venue will have its own rules individually tailored to that venue by the Fire Officer, the Local Authority or some other regulatory body. Make sure that your work is passed to them for their approval.

F) **Trade shows** usually have an invited audience and can therefore be officially classed as 'Private Functions', which can and do fall outside the remit of the fire and safety regulations governing 'Public Functions' (depending, of course, what country or city you are concerned with). However, it is extremely foolish to attempt to compromise Health & Safety issues on these grounds. Play safe; treat all shows as being governed by strict and sensible rules. In my experience, every venue's Fire Officer prefers his advice to be sought regardless of whether the event is officially classed as 'Public' or 'Private'.

G) Having made the above points, it is obvious however that some parts of the set may be 'allowed' to break the strict definitions of the regulations. An example may be a tall rostrum upon which an actor/singer will face the audience – it is unlikely that a protective handrail is wanted by the designer/producer/cameraman, particularly on the downstage edge. These matters should be aired by all concerned before a decision is reached.

H) Always flag-up Health & Safety issues *on the drawings* so that all relevant bodies are aware of the concerns. For example, actors may exit the stage with their eyes temporarily 'blinded' by the stage lights – therefore all get-off treads should have white nosings and, if necessary, crew should be on-hand with torches to see actors safely off the stage. Simply indicate this on the drawing.

I) Always indicate the **fire rating** of materials that are to be used in the show (e.g. Class 1 or Class 0). The venue will advise on this matter, as each venue has its own regulations.

J) **Pyrotechnics** (fireworks, etc.) are often used in shows and carry an obvious Heath & Safety risk potential. Steel pans and tubes are used to house them, linked by thin electric cable for ignition. The 'pyro' expert will usually deal directly with the Local Authorities, giving them a practical demonstration onstage prior to the opening day. Always discuss his needs before completing the drawings – and do what he says is necessary. On the aesthetic front, be aware that these effects can stain or singe adjacent parts of the set, so discuss positioning very carefully.

K) Always indicate the **clearway** required by the venue's Fire Officer. This applies particularly to exhibition and trade-show design. The clearway is the *minimum clear space* that must be maintained along a fire exit route. Do the same for the headroom.

L) Never block **fire hoses**, **alarm points**, **fire exits**, etc. with parts of the set. It is illegal. If you have problems with this, a compromise can sometimes be reached with the venue's responsible person (e.g. the show can pay for a Fire Officer to be on hand at the point in question). In truth, money can be thrown at most problems in order to solve them.

M) The 'golden rule' relating to these issues is, *If in doubt, ask. If still in doubt, keep asking.*

11 Position offstage technical areas

A) Most shows require spaces allocated for use as technical areas; these can be offstage or onstage, but because they are vital to the show it is important not to ignore them at the early planning stages of the project, as so often happens. Space is usually at a premium, so be aware *from the start* of all the requirements of the show.

B) Control is an area (or areas) from which the show is controlled and 'run' by the technical staff. It may contain, for example, the lighting desk, the sound desk, the audio-visual (AV) desk and the show-caller's desk (stage management). These have to be 'front of house' so that a clear view of the show's running may be maintained. Control is always required in trade shows and usually consists of a raised rostrum placed at the back of the auditorium, neatly surrounded by some sort of flattage. It is a good idea to allow the access to the control area to be separate from the public's access to their seats (in case, during the show, a member of the control team needs to dash backstage for some reason – it looks more professional if that can be done secretly). Always find out how much space will be required for this area and simply ensure that all the staff have an unobstructed view of the production. Note that at the back of a raked audience seating deck, the control may have to be very high up and have its own ladder access. Clearly, many purpose-built venues have control areas built-in and, if they are suitable, then the draughtsman need not become involved.

C) Camera positions need careful thought. Many shows (particularly trade shows) require camera positions, some front-of-house and some onstage (often hand-held). Hand-held cameras need little in the way of technical support on the drawings, but ensure that you are aware of their existence – they still need a clear view and some free space and may need a rostrum to achieve this. Fixed cameras will invariably require a rostrum (minimum 2440 x 1220 mm – 8' x 4') *which is not attached to any other piece of kit* for fear of introducing vibrations picked up from, say, an adjacent seating deck or follow-spot rostrum. This is important! Do not shove a camera into the control area, for example, without having a clear space all around the separate camera rostrum. Camera platforms may also require a handrail (1100 mm – 3' 7½" high, as regulations currently dictate), but always seek the camera operator's advice on this matter before beginning construction drawings.

On the subject of cameras, do bear in mind that if the camera's task is to show, for example, a head-and-shoulders shot of a speaker at a lectern, then give some thought to the *background* of that shot. Be aware that stark background patterns may distract from the speaker when seen on TV or screen. Also, if the camera is taking live-action shots of the speaker which are then relayed to an AV screen, a patterned background may cause interference patterns to 'jiggle' about on the screen. (This interference effect is recognisable to all of us through the shared experience of watching TV weathermen in jackets sporting patterns that cause the image to shimmer.)

D) **Follow-spots**, or 'limes', are the hand-controlled lamps that light cast members who are to move around the stage. They are front-of-house (in the auditorium, not in the stage areas) and may require rostra. Again, they may need separating from other areas, such as Control, to avoid vibration. The lighting designer will indicate where these are to be positioned: ask early, so that you are aware of them.

E) **Sound speakers** can be surprisingly large! Find out if any need to be hidden within the set. 'Sound translucent' cloth can be used to conceal them without compromising the sound quality – this cloth is simply the same material used to clad the speaker box fronts themselves. Decide whether the front-of-house speaker stacks need disguising in any way. Find out at an early stage all you can about proposed speaker requirements, because the sound department will put their kit in anyway – regardless of aesthetic considerations. It is preferable to have pre-planned how it will all look; if designers forget this fact, do remind them. Despite what they will often try and tell you, the sound department does have *some* flexibility as to the positioning of speakers (although it doesn't help your cause to tell them to 'just turn it up!'). Fight your corner on the aesthetic front!

F) Finally, bear in mind that the **cable runs** of sound equipment must usually be separated from the main power cable runs (I believe that this is to prevent interference). It is important to discuss cable runs at the planning stage, especially in venues that do not usually hold shows.

G) **'Dimmer City'** is a colloquial term for the area where dimmer-racks are to be placed (as well as other electrical kit). In most theatres and purpose-built venues these areas tend to be pre-existing, but for many touring shows (trade shows in particular) the dimmer-racks are toured and need placing somewhere. These areas do take up a lot of room, need decent ventilation or free-flow of air and cannot but help giving out a soft humming sound, which may distract from the show. Again, find out from the production manager how large an area is required and where it is best placed. Do this at an early stage.

H) **Projectors** may need a projection booth, rostra, masking, hanging points or constant access. Take advice, at an early stage, from the AV engineer as to the requirements and positioning of all projectors. As previously mentioned, be very aware of vibration contamination from adjoining areas and consider providing separate rostra for projectors. Film projectors can be very large (having a complex arrangement of film spools around them) and may require a purpose-built, soundproofed booth to house them. The booth will need a projection window made of optical quality glass (glass manufactured in such a way as to eliminate optical distortion), an available water point (for their cooling systems) as well as portable air-conditioning units (which will require an 'exhaust' outlet from the booth). The booth can be made of 'on-edge' flattage, say of 95 x 21 mm, (4" x 1" par) clad both sides with 4 mm (⅛" or ⁵/₃₂") or 6 mm (¼") ply that 'sandwiches' a thick layer of insulation material. Always ask the film technician for a dimensioned sketch of his requirements.

I)   Many of the above points may appear to be solely within the domain of the 'trade show' or 'rock and roll' side of our business. However, many theatrical productions tour to 'empty' venues (venues with no facilities supplied) and therefore much of the above-mentioned kit has to be brought in and positioned, just as in a trade show. Some touring theatres in the USA, for example, are empty on arrival - they have no cloths, lamps, sound equipment, etc.

12 Position the audience

A)   Many events are held at venues where the **audience seating** is brought in, as and when needed. Clearly, great care needs to be taken to ensure that an ideal seating lay-out is achieved, providing an uninterrupted view of the show from all seats while obeying the local authority's regulations concerning audiences.

B)   Other events may require that certain areas of existing seating shall not be sold for that production (the Royal Albert Hall is a prime example); this can be for many different reasons. Whatever the reason, choose the 'used' seats carefully to ensure that they all have an ideal view – check this both in plan and in section. The venue will use your drawings to guide the audience to the correct seats.

C)   The audience numbers for trade shows are usually decided *before* the set is designed – because the client wants a specific number of people to see each show. In addition, venues are frequently chosen before the design stage is reached and these venues often necessitate that seating be brought in and erected for a particular show. In these cases, the first thing one does when designing is to lay-out roughly a **foot-print** (plan view of maximum area required) of the audience block(s) within the venue. The stage area is then drawn to suit the available sight-lines. (It is no use trying to insist upon a certain, favoured design if the practicalities of the venue and audience blocks prove that it cannot be clearly seen by all.)

D)   Remember that during rehearsals, the director/producer will tend to be watching from the centre of the stalls and so have an 'ideal' view of the set. It must be part of the draughtsman/designer's job to ensure that the whole audience has a decent view. As previously described, this is accomplished at the drawing stage of the production, but when the show is fitting-up, always keep walking around to the extreme seats in order to confirm that the sight-lines and maskings are correct. The production manager should also do this during the fit-up as part of his job.

13 Act as a discussion point

A)   At the beginning of a project there can be so many varying factors affecting the show that it is difficult for everybody involved to visualise how it will work. In these circumstances it is best for someone just to begin work –

to begin suggested lay-outs (ground-plan and simple sections). These will only form a discussion point at this stage, since they are **proposal drawings** and not for construction. At meetings, each department will then input their own requirements and the drawings can be further developed from there. *This is a useful function and must not be considered a waste of time: do it often.* It is surprising how one drawing, however unfinished it may be, provides more information than can many hours of discussions at meetings. Drawings allow for problems to be *seen*.

B)   These early, proposal drawings may often graphically indicate that more information needs to be supplied by certain departments (who thought that everything was under control), or that the designer has made certain mistakes. That is the function of these drawings and must not be seen as a malfunction on the part of the draughtsman. In an industry that brings together so many different trades and crafts, it is not surprising if early assumptions are shown to be wrong when the first drawings are attempted. Sometimes errors have to be drawn, and highlighted as being errors on the drawing, before the various trades can see why their first assumptions were wrong. You, as a draughtsman, hold the threads of everybody else's knowledge and have to weave those threads into a practical and suitable format for the show.

14 Show that someone has considered the problems

A)   This may appear to be an esoteric point, but it is not. It is the key to what we do. In a busy industry, it is economically prudent to have someone – anyone, but usually a draughtsman of some description – who will sit quietly and consider the problems involved in the show. Thinking time is as important as drawing time. The draughtsman is ideally placed to spot the potential pratfalls in advance of the rest of the team: the simple act of drawing necessitates forethought.

B)   The draughtsman does need a peaceful and relaxed atmosphere within which to work. Distractions will fracture the thought processes, lead to errors and undermine the point made above.

Hopefully, the above list of the various functions of drawings in our industry, although not exhaustive, is longer than one would have at first imagined and has brought into focus the numerous considerations that must be borne in mind when attempting to draw a show.

I would strongly suggest getting into the habit of using the above list as a check-list to scan *before* drawing a production, noting the points that will apply to that particular production. Take your check-list to early meetings and ensure that all points are aired for discussion – the resolution of problems can follow, once discussed. In time, of course, each point will be firmly embedded in the brain and the list referred to less frequently.

2 • The First Principles of Drawing

Listing first principles, or golden rules, is a potentially dangerous process – since, by definition, the implication is that there are lesser rules which can be safely ignored, and that is not the case. However, we have to define the issues that *must* be kept uppermost in the mind of the draughtsman. Some may appear self-explanatory, but I make no apology for their inclusion; when investigating the cause of an error with the benefit of hindsight, it can often seem obvious how the error occurred – clearly, it was not that obvious at the time! Other points may have been touched upon earlier and some may be further developed later.

1 Clarity and precision

A) *All* drawings must be clear to those who will read them. A faxed sketch to a set-builder may be mumbo-jumbo to the sound department, but, as long as you know that the set-builder understands the technicalities of the sketch and it is only for his or her use anyway, then this may be adequate. Conversely, if a drawing is to be for the benefit of all and sundry, then go to greater lengths to ensure that an idiot could read it – many idiots will read it! In the trade-show world, some producers possess no understanding of anything technical and cannot read drawings (it may be their first show). Of course, their ignorance is not your fault, but you must 'go that extra mile' to attempt to make the drawings as clear as possible. In other words, **know your readership**.

B) Some drawings are inherently complicated and resist simplification. This does not present a problem as long as those who will use the drawing are experienced and professional enough to be able to read them (again, know your readership).

C) If a drawing is in danger of being too difficult to read, then attempt to break it up into **layers** – each drawing being representative of a horizontal layer of one area (I am referring to a plan view here). For example, layer one can be a drawing showing the mathematical setting-out of an object at ground level; layer two can show the construction details of that object at that level; layer three can be the setting-out of the object at ceiling level; layer four can show the construction at ceiling level, and so on. CAD drawings are ideal for this kind of work because they allow for easy 'copy and paste' procedures.

D) Having made the above point, my personal opinion is that it is usually more convenient for all concerned to have as few drawings in a package as possible. Certainly, for carpenters and engineers who are working 'on the bench,' it is far more convenient to have one A1 drawing to work from than to be given three drawings – which they must then cross-reference, etc. amid the dust and mess of a workbench. In many instances, this is very

easy to achieve: simply give sections at 1:5 scale, instead of 1:1 or 1:2 scale. Plainly, different jobs bring different circumstances, but in general, I feel it is more professional to keep the number of drawings down to a minimum.

E) Clarity can often be introduced into a drawing by simply adding a human figure, at the correct scale, to one side of the elevation. This is most useful to clients who are not experienced at reading drawings – they find that they can suddenly 'see' the scale. A stylised human figure is adequate.

F) **Precision** in drawings should be taken for granted. *Always draw to scale* as accurately as is possible – even though people should never have to scale from the drawings, because everything should be given dimensions. Scaling from drawings is unwise because the very act of copying drawings can slightly stretch or shrink the paper, rendering the scale irrelevant. When drawing by hand, if you draw accurately, **scaling** acts as a rough double-check when you are wrestling with complicated maths in order to arrive at a given dimension. For example, at 1:25, I can be sure that if my calculator gives me an answer that is more than, say, 30 mm different from that which I scale-off with the scale rule, then I ought to re-check my maths on the calculator. *Do get into the habit of checking your maths against the scale of your drawing!*

It is surprising how often somebody will mention that they found your drawing to be 'dead to scale' (accurate), even though you know that they need never have had to scale from the drawing because all dimensions were given. The point I am making here is that it is simply a better thing to remain accurate; it has universal human appeal. It is almost instinctive in human nature to want drawings to be completely to scale; people trust scale (even though they shouldn't). So, draw to scale.

G) **CAD** drawings are easier to produce on an accurate basis. But there are still a myriad reasons why/how even CAD drawings can be drawn wrongly ('garbage in, garbage out' is the familiar cry when such errors are found). I frequently check all the important dimensions with the measuring tool before going too far with a drawing. This also applies to angles – it is fairly easy to draw what one thinks is a perpendicular line, only to discover that an inaccurate assumption has been made. Precision cannot be taken for granted in CAD drawings – it has to be *achieved* by the draughtsman.

H) Precision leads to clarity in drawings. If you are drawing a section through tubular steelwork, for example, it is normal practice to draw the wall thickness of any steel tubes that the section is slicing through; if that is *not* done then the drawing will appear as a jumble of lines. The second that you do ink in the wall thickness, then all becomes clear.

2 Mathematical precision

A) All maths shown on your drawings must be precise. All dimensions, angles and working data must be accurate. This is the single most important aspect of our sort of drawing work. *Always* double-check all the maths. It is infuriatingly easy to fall into the trap of double-checking the difficult maths, but forgetting to check that a simple column of dimensions add up correctly. It is expected that anyone using the drawing will follow the dimensions given – so give the right ones! Inexperienced draughtsmen are frequently over-concerned with the *look* of their drawing and do not give dimensioning enough thought.

When drawing in CAD it is easy to think that the maths can be forgotten – because one simply draws what one wants and 'asks' the machine for dimensions. However, it is still very easy to 'pick' your required dimension from the wrong point without realising the error. Equally, in CAD one should use geometry to set-out the drawing in the first place, so accurate maths is still of major relevance.

B) Never write a dimension on a drawing without having first confirmed that the dimension shares a **mathematical logic** with the rest of the drawing. You will often see drawings by untrustworthy draughtsmen who pluck some figure out of the air (they may have scaled the dimension from their drawing) that is completely at odds with other dimensions given. The reason for this is that, sadly, so many draughtsmen are simply unaware of basic maths. Learn the maths, or give up now.

C) Beware of 'number dyslexia' – this is the cause of most of the mistakes that I have made! By this I mean simply writing a number down in the wrong order – for example, intending to write '2420', but actually writing '2402'. Daft, but we all do it! Try checking for this when the drawing is completed (that is when a final check should be made, just prior to *issuing* the drawing). CAD tends to eradicate this problem, as it 'reads' and prints the dimension for you, but your CAD drawing may still be based upon your hand-sketched, on-site survey – and that is where the dyslexia is most likely to occur.

D) Try not to give '**information overload**'. Provide the dimensions and geometry necessary to the drawing, without needless repetition. In other words, show enough maths, but no more.

E) Only show maths that is **practical** to use. It is of little benefit to a scenic carpenter to be told that a particular angle is 53.78657°: it is unreasonable, as well as idiotic, to expect them to fetch a calculator in order to decipher what that angle really means. In this particular case, it is simpler for all concerned to draw and dimension the three sides of a triangle (whose relevant angle is that given – i.e. 53.78657°), so that the carpenter can physically set out that triangle. The carpenter need not know what that angle is; but *is* expected to know how to set out a triangle when given the lengths of the three sides. It is often the case that it is useful to the draughtsman to indicate the exact angles of a triangle on the drawing (to make checking-back an easier task); there is no problem with doing this, but do give the other, more simple, information that is required by others.

F) When drawing large objects – a show's floor, for example – be aware that most workshops have limited floor space on which to do their setting-out. It is of little use to the contractor to be told that they must set out a curve of radius 9 metres if their workshop is only 6 metres long. Always consider this thorny problem and attempt to break down the maths of the whole job into smaller, more manageable sections if necessary.

G) It is quite acceptable, and on some jobs vitally important, to produce a '**maths and setting-out only**' drawing. Normally, this drawing would be the first to be done; it would lay down the maths of the key pieces of the set (usually in plan view) and establish an entire mathematical framework within which to work.

This drawing may not necessarily be used by the carpenters or engineers as a bench drawing, but is more likely to be used by other draughtsmen who may be working on the show. An example of this is when more than one contractor is involved in a job and each has their own piece of set to draw: it is obviously preferable for everyone to be working within the same mathematical framework. ('*So that we are all wrong together*' is a familiar, and wise, comment amongst contractors. The overall dimensions could be inaccurate, but all internal parts will fit together.) This drawing becomes the hymn sheet from which everybody sings.

At early meetings, try and establish who is best suited to provide this drawing (whom do we all trust?). Often, it is whoever can start the work first – so it could be you. I frequently draw a maths-only drawing merely for my own convenience, as a point of reference; if others want it, they can have it.

H) When **checking the accuracy of the maths** on completion of the drawing, try to do so by approaching the problem from a fresh viewpoint. In other words, don't use the same approach that you employed to establish the maths in the first place. This helps because, when one is working on a difficult job, the mind tends to become stuck in a particular groove of thought and so, if a mistake has been made, it will tend to be made again and again. In short, try to use different sorts of maths, based on different criteria, to check your work prior to issue.

I) When **checking the drawings**, try to clear your mind of what you already know and imagine being the person who has to pick up that drawing for the first time and begin setting it out. If you do this, it is surprising how often you will find that key dimensions have been left off in error.

3 Have a clear title block
(see figure 2-01)

A) The title block is very important in maintaining clarity and neatness. Its exact position on the drawing is a matter of individual choice, but try to ensure that when the drawing is folded the title block is still uppermost – and therefore in view. Do bear in mind that many paper copiers automatically fold the drawings as they leave the machine, and that if the title block is either in the top or bottom right-hand-side of the drawing, then it will be uppermost when the drawing is folded.

B) In our business, I would recommend that the title block contain the information that is listed below (point '**C**' onwards), although many productions like to show a 'cast list' of the designer's name, director, production manager and so on. I find this a pointless exercise – it is the

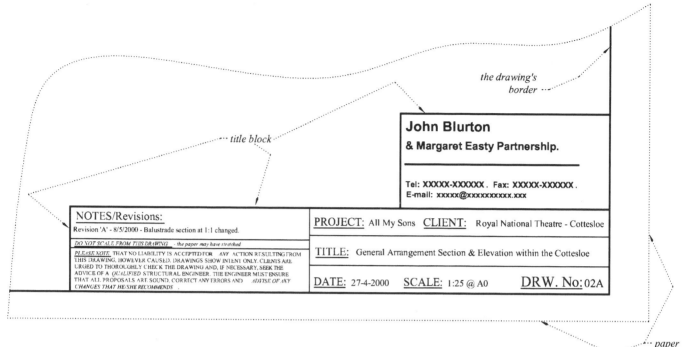

the drawing's
border · · ·

· · · title block · · ·

John Blurton

& Margaret Easty Partnership.

Tel: XXXXX-XXXXXX . Fax: XXXXX-XXXXXX .
E-mail: xxxxx@xxxxxxxxxx.xxx

NOTES/Revisions:	PROJECT: All My Sons CLIENT: Royal National Theatre - Cottesloe
Revision 'A' - 8/5/2000 - Balustrade section at 1:1 changed.	
DO NOT SCALE FROM THIS DRAWING - the paper may have stretched.	TITLE: General Arrangement Section & Elevation within the Cottesloe
PLEASE NOTE, THAT NO LIABILITY IS ACCEPTED FOR ANY ACTION RESULTING FROM THIS DRAWING, HOWEVER CAUSED. DRAWINGS SHOW INTENT ONLY. CLIENTS ARE URGED TO THOROUGHLY CHECK THE DRAWING AND, IF NECESSARY, SEEK THE ADVICE OF A QUALIFIED STRUCTURAL ENGINEER. THE ENGINEER MUST ENSURE THAT ALL PROPOSALS ARE SOUND, CORRECT ANY ERRORS AND ADVISE OF ANY CHANGES THAT HE/SHE RECOMMENDS .	
	DATE: 27-4-2000 SCALE: 1:25 @ A0 DRW. No: 02A

· · paper

Figure 2.01 *An example of a title block. NTS (Not To Scale).*

intended use of a title block to communicate vital information and, if useless information is included, people will ignore it and will therefore miss vital notes as a consequence.

A small but useful point: I prefer to see drawings which have a line drawn as a **border** around all four sides of the sheet, as well as around the title block. Firstly, it looks better (and that is a good enough reason), because it frames the drawing regardless of tatty or dog-eared edges that may appear on the copies. But more importantly, it proves to the recipient of the copies that they do indeed have the *whole* of the drawing copied in front of them. This last point is of growing importance because production managers will often copy a drawing and then slice it up for faxing, or, even worse, for distributing in separate pieces to those whom they feel do not need the whole drawing. It is sheer folly to do this of course, but it happens. A border will indicate to the receiver of copies that they have the whole of the drawing, or not.

C) 'Drawing number' should be prominent within the title block. Be meticulous in ensuring that drawing numbers are not duplicated on a production. Large jobs can have hundreds of drawings, and a rogue drawing number can cost plenty of money! Always add a letter to the end of the drawing's number if you have revised that drawing. For example, 'Drw.005' becomes 'Drw.005A' when first revised, and 'Drw.005B' when next revised.

Drawing numbers may frequently include a 'job number', a 'client number', a 'part number', an 'area/zone number', etc. – as well as the *actual* number of that drawing. So, the full number may be '4562/Brown/13/Z4/001A' – which is awkward to the eye, to say the least! Try to separate the drawing number off to the right (as in '4562/Brown/13/Z4/ . . . 001A'). Make it as easy as possible to find the drawing number.

D) A 'See also. . .' box is a good idea to include in, or near, the title block. It indicates the drawing numbers of other drawings relevant to the one in question.

E) 'Revisions' is an area that contains details of how many times the drawing has been altered. As pointed out above, remember that if a drawing is altered, you place a letter after the drawing number; if it is altered again, you replace that letter with the next letter in sequence. Many title blocks include printed lines that you can fill in with the revision letter, the revision date and some details of what has been revised. I tend to put this information in my 'Notes' box (*see* below). Whatever the case, ensure that these details are shown somewhere on the drawing.

F) 'Scale'. Remember that when designing a title block, you may have to enter three or four scales into this box. It is a good idea to add, after the scale, 'at A1' (or whatever paper size you are using). This ensures that all future recipients of the drawing can see if the drawing has been reduced – or not – by a copier.

G) 'Drawing title' is self-explanatory. However, if you are designing a title block, ensure that there is ample space for this as some titles are necessarily wordy.

H) 'Name of production' is again self-explanatory. Qualify the name with the location if the production will have separate drawings for different venues; e.g. 'Hamlet, Glasgow'.

I) 'Client' will be the name of whoever is paying you, or your employer, to produce the drawings. (Whatever you do, spell their name correctly!)

J) 'Date' should be the date that the drawing was completed and first issued.

K) 'Notes': leave a space in the title block for notes that pertain to that drawing. In this box, when relevant, give the fire classification of materials that are to be used in the construction of whatever your drawing represents, e.g. 'All Class 1 Materials To Be Used'. Strangely, people quite often do not even glance at what is in the 'Notes' box, so if there is something that you most certainly *do* want them to notice, then highlight it in some fashion (pencil shading, triple underlining, etc.).

John Blurton
& Margaret Easty Partnership.

Xxx Xxxx Xxx,
Xxxx Xxxxxxxx Xxxxx,
Xxxxxxxxxxx,
Xxxx, XXX XXX,   **Tel:**   XXXXX-XXXXXX
Xxxxxxx.   **Fax:**   XXXXX-XXXXXX

E-mail: xxxxx@xxxxxxxxxx.xxx

DRAWING LIST

PROJECT: **All My Sons**
CLIENT: *Royal National Theatre — Cottesloe Theatre*
DATE LIST ISSUED: **28th May 2000**

(Shaded cells = SUPERSEDED drawing)

No:	Rev:	Title:	Scale:	Fin:	Copies:	e-mail:	Disc	Comment
001		GA Plan In Cotts	25 **A0**	_	1	_27/4	_	
002		GA Sect/Elev in Cotts	25 **A0**	_	1	_27/4	_	s/seded
002	A	GA Sect/Elev in Cotts	25 **A0**	_	1	_8/5	_	
003		Set Finished Views	25 **A0**	_	1	_27/4	_	s/seded
003	A	Set Finished Views	25 **A0**	_	1	_27/5	_	
004		Doors	10 **A1**	_	2	_22/4	_	
005		Window sashes	10 **A1**	_	2	_22/4	_	
006		Top Flown House Unit	15 **A1**	_	2	_28/4	_	
007		- ditto - Construction	15 **A1**	_	2	_28/4	_	
008		Bot Truckd House Unit	15 **A1**	_	2	_30/4	_	
009		- ditto - Construction	15 **A1**	_	2	_30/4	_	
010		Black Side Flats	15 **A1**	_	2	_2/5	_	
011		Roof - GA	15 **A1**	_	2	_8/5	_	
012		Roof - Beams	15 **A1**	_	2	_8/5	_	
013		Roof - Flats	15 **A1**	_	2	_8/5	_	
014		Push-in Gable Ends	15 **A1**	_	2	_8/5	_	
015		Main Columns	15 **A1**	_	2	_8/5	_	s/seded
015	A	Main Columns	15 **A1**	_	2	_28/5	_	
016		Balustrading - GA	15 **A1**	_	2	_13/5	_	s/seded
016	A	Balustrading - GA	15 **A1**	_	2	_28/5	_	
017		- ditto - Construction	15 **A1**	_	2	_13/5	_	s/seded
017	A	- ditto - Construction	15 **A1**	_	2	_28/5	_	
018		Stair Unit	15 **A1**	_	2	_14/5	_	s/seded
018	A	Stair Unit	15 **A1**	_	2	_28/5	_	
019		Cotts Lift Rostrum	15 **A1**	_	2	_28/5	_	
020		Fascias	15 **A1**	_	2	_26/5	_	
021		Sub-floor & get-offs	15 **A1**	_	2	_23/5	_	
022		Top Floor and Boards	15 **A1**	_	2	_23/5	_	
023		Show-floor/Ramp	25 **A1**	_	2	_28/5	_	

Total drawings to this point: - *29 drawings supplied, 23 are current.*

L) **Personal details** are a matter of choice, in the sense of how much you include. It is always prudent for the name of the draughtsman to be in the title block and a contact telephone number to be included (and fax/mobile/e-mail, if desired). You may live to regret giving your home number here, unless you have an answering machine to protect you.

M) **Legal jargon**: most companies have some sort of legal jargon pre-printed on their drawing sheets. These qualifications – for that is what they are – are normally an attempt to stress to the client that liability is limited in some way. They may also mention copyright ownership. It is good and common practice to include the phrase, 'Do not scale from this drawing.'

4 Ensure that drawings are current

A) Whenever your drawings are revised, ensure that all relevant parties have and know about the new revision. Nothing is more infuriating than to find that one department or company has been working from the original drawing while the rest of the production team are working from revision 'E'.

B) It is the responsibility of the draughtsman to ensure that revised drawings are distributed correctly, either by posting them off directly or by nagging the production manager to do so. *Do* double-check this matter. E-mailing is perfect for sending these messages and drawings together, although many people tend not to read the e-mail message properly. Always telephone recipients of revised drawings to let them know that they exist.

5 Keep a drawing record

A) It is important to keep a list of drawings that pertain to a production. A simple A4 (portrait) list containing columns with the following headings is ideal: *Drawing Number*; *Title*; *Scale*; *Revisions*; *Date Issued/e-mailed*; *No. of copies*; and *Issued To*. An example of a show's drawing list is included on page 11.

B) Each time new or revised drawings are issued, photocopy the list and highlight the numbers of the drawings that are enclosed with the list.

6 Know the type of drawing that you are producing

A) The types of drawings used in our industry are dealt with in Chapter 3. The point made here is that you should always be aware of the type of drawing that you are being paid to produce. A drawing provided for a producer – illustrating an overall scheme, for example – will not require the detailed information that a set-builder would expect. It is bad practice, as well as inefficient, to muddle the objective of the drawing.

7 Be consistent with dimensions

A) Always ensure that dimensions are written in a standard form. **In the UK, use millimetres only – do not use centimetres or metres.** Do conform to this convention – '10 metres' is written as '10000 mm' or simply '10000'. You will often witness risible attempts at dimensioning in centimetres/millimetres, with wild guesses being taken as to where to place the full stop (or comma) that separates the two. But if millimetres alone are used, this error cannot occur.

B) When drawing for **overseas clients**, find out *their* local convention for dimensioning. Frequently, a comma is placed after the centimetre digit – just ahead of the millimetre digit – or a full stop is placed after the metre digit. (Once, while drawing in Madrid, I found that my local clients could not read my drawings because I had only used millimetres – and had no commas or dots. Obviously, I quickly changed and used their conventions – the drawings are a means to an end, so always adapt to suit that end.)

C) Feet and inches should not be used in Britain – be adamant about this! Just because someone in the team still thinks in **imperial**, that is no reason why everybody else should suffer. Everybody knows where he or she is with millimetres. We've all got calculators and know from experience that it is easier to calculate using one unit of measurement, one number: millimetres.

D) If asked to draw **American shows** (or work from American drawings), then feet and inches are inescapable. CAD drawings are easy to dimension in metric or imperial, or both. If drawing manually, good luck with the maths! An imperial scale rule is very useful, as are the scale rules that show imperial *and* metric.

E) When asked to draw a UK show from American drawings (often a show is first put on in the USA, then transfers), always convert everything to millimetres and – if necessary – place approximate imperial equivalents in brackets after the millimetre dimension. This will help the Americans to check your drawings.

F) Being consistent with dimensions also means retaining consistency in how those dimensions are written down. Overall dimensions may be stencilled, for example, and lesser dimensions hand-written; height dimensions may be preceded by a '+' sign and underlined or placed within an ellipse, whereas other dimensions remain unadorned; major dimensions may be written with a thick pen, others written with a thin pen. Whatever visual aids you employ to improve clarity, *be consistent* on that drawing, or set of drawings.

8 Drawing paper and copying

A) When **drawing with CAD**, no paper is involved until such time as a 'plot' (a print) is wanted. At that point the drawing can be plotted to any paper that the plotter will handle – most types imaginable, that is. I prefer to issue the drawings on white $90 g/m^2$ paper – lesser weights of paper are thinner and, in my view, too flimsy.

B) **When drawing manually**, it is usual to draw on **tracing paper**: this original drawing is known as 'the skin'. (Other types of paper may be used, but always ask about the properties of that paper – in relation to your pens, for example – and check that it is ideal for copying.) Tracing paper is semi-transparent, easy to work with, easy to erase and re-ink upon and easily copied. It is available in all the main sizes (metric: A4, A3, A2, A1 and A0) and in varying weights (thicknesses). I find that $90 g/m^2$ is too thin and insubstantial; try using $110 g/m^2$ only. Erase ink lines with a *Stanley* knife blade or scalpel, and over-rub with an ink rubber which has been injected with a solvent (as are the yellow *Rotring* ink rubbers). Damp weather conditions or damp hands on a warm day will cause the paper to shift and buckle upon your board: this is a nuisance, but keep on smoothing it out and re-taping it down, and consider wearing white cotton gloves (minus the fingers) during hot, clammy weather when drawing.

A drawing left on the board for several hours will gather dust and cause the pens to skid about or to clog up, so either rub down the drawing frequently with a clean cloth or protect it when not in use – in fact, do both. Humidity in the air will cause the paper to stretch or shrink at an alarming rate and, of course, likewise for copies (which is why one should never scale from a drawing). An A1 piece of paper, when folded in half along its shorter axis, becomes size A2; an A2, when similarly folded, becomes A3; and so on. Use masking tape to stick the drawing down to the board.

C) **Polyester drawing paper** (or draughting film) appears to be similar to tracing paper, but is easily recognisable by its waxy, silky feel, its high static electricity content, and its foul smell and higher cost. It has the advantage of being strong and virtually tear-proof, as well as being resistant to water (which tracing paper *certainly* is not!). Many venues have their ground-plans drawn on polyester because its natural durability will keep the skin pristine for far longer. However, when drawing on polyester, remember that special ink needs to be used (*Rotring* type 'F' for example) because ordinary ink will take much longer to dry and be non-permanent. Also, ordinary pen-nibs will wear out very quickly on polyester paper and so tungsten-tipped nibs are required (which are far more expensive, but are still better value over time).

D) **Dyeline copies** are cheap and attractive (but smell rather strongly of ammonia: I've seen trade-show producers, not always familiar with drawings, literally gag as the drawings are unrolled – not good for one's confidence). A dyeline copier is designed to copy drawings that are drawn on tracing paper – it needs the transparent nature of that medium in order to function. A square of white paper stuck on the original skin will print as solid black – the copier reads lines *through* the skin. The lightness and darkness of the copies can be controlled (dark copies do have a habit of revealing all the scratched-out lines). Dyeline copies are excellent at copying pencil shading or any other subtle toning methods. The copies do fade in sunlight.

E) **Plain paper copies** are more expensive, although rapidly becoming cheaper. The copiers are simply large photocopying machines. The copies replicate on to white paper (and it is very white, compared to dyeline paper), and will copy whatever is on the surface of the original – therefore you can stick bits of paper on to the skin and what is on those bits of paper will also be copied. The copier will also reduce or enlarge, which is its main advantage. Unfortunately, some shading will not copy as well as on dyeline paper; pencil shading will look very 'muddy'; and some people dislike the 'black or white' nature of these copies. Plain paper copiers can copy a skin on to another skin, but I have yet to see this done well enough to use with confidence.

F) Be prepared to use the advantages of **photocopiers** when producing drawings. What I mean here is that one can often reduce or enlarge something on a photocopier in order to trace over it on to an original skin. Company logos spring to mind: it can be very tiresome to have to draw logos of different sizes on a trade show drawing, so simply copy them on a photocopier at the size required and

trace through. (CAD users can easily 'import' the logo from the client.)

G) Paper copies or plots of drawings may have to be **faxed** to people in order to save time. If this involves cutting a copy of the drawing into strips of A4 width (210 mm) in order for it to pass through the fax machine, then *always* send a full, uncut copy by post as well. Fax machines and their operatives (us) can be unreliable and I have seen many mistakes occur because someone never had sight of a whole copy of a drawing. Obviously, if you are aware that a drawing will have to be faxed in this fashion, then draw it in such a way that suits being divided into strips 210 mm wide. Remember too that when faxing anything, the very edge of the paper (3–4 mm) does not print. Ideally, use A4 drawing paper – with title block and a border, say, 10 mm ($^3/_8$") in from the edge of the paper. Draw within that border and all should be well.

9 Use correct and consistent terminology

A) Using correct terminology or jargon is important in our industry. There are numerous conventions for **naming areas** of the stage or auditorium, some of which are indicated in **figure 2-02**. The theatre convention is quite an old system and is based on the idea that, when describing a position on stage, you are standing on the stage *facing out to the audience*: therefore, 'prompt side' (PS) is to your left and 'upstage' (US) is behind you. The American system has become very popular in recent years; this adheres to the same principle except that 'stage left' (SL) replaces prompt side, and 'stage right' (SR) is the term used instead of opposite prompt (OP) – a more logical system, in my opinion.

Just to confuse the issue, the convention used by **film and television** is different again: they use 'camera left' or 'audience left', and that is established from the viewpoint of the audience, not from the stage. Therefore, 'prompt side' (PS), 'stage left' (SL), 'camera right' and 'audience right' are all the same place!

You will not go far wrong if you adopt the American system (of SL and SR) when drawing for theatres, trade shows or conferences, etc., but adopt the 'audience left' convention for television work and museum work. As with all jargon, there will be some purists who may disagree with my summary, but few would misunderstand your meaning if you do as I suggest.

B) **Construction materials** have a terminology of their own – each according to its industry – and there is not enough space to cover this ever-shifting topic here. You will learn as you go along, and if you become a collector of brochures (*see* also page 38), all will be revealed. Manufacturers of materials tend to produce clear brochures which amply describe their product. Try to be placed on the mailing lists of the companies whose brochures you use regularly.

One tip worth remembering is the convention of **naming timber**, which does tend to cause confusion at first. Timber sizes are given as a cross-section of that timber – e.g. 100 x 50 (4" x 2") – and are based upon the notion that the timber is *still rough-sawn*. In other words, it is still coarse and not planed smooth; it is in its raw, cut, 'hairy' state. Normally, you will be nominating timber as being planed smooth, known as 'par' (planed all round). When

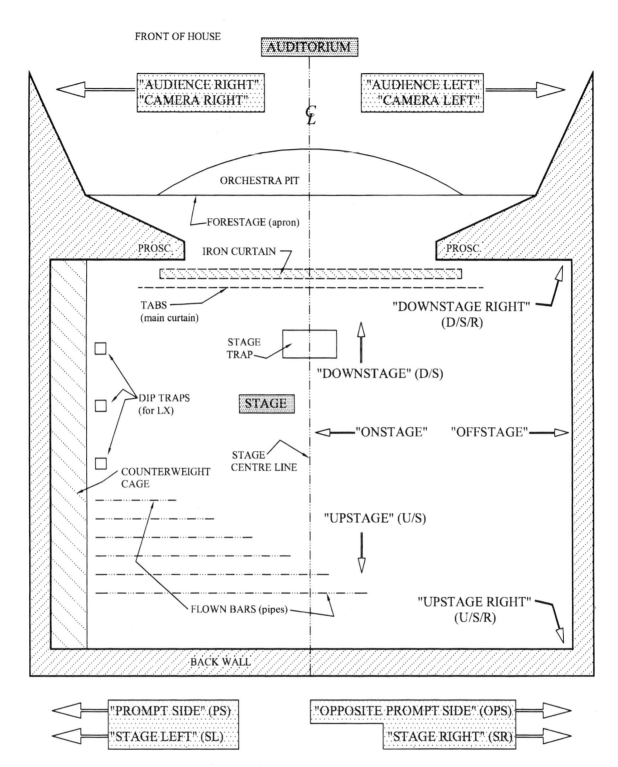

FRONT OF HOUSE

AUDITORIUM

"AUDIENCE RIGHT"
"CAMERA RIGHT"

"AUDIENCE LEFT"
"CAMERA LEFT"

C
L

ORCHESTRA PIT

FORESTAGE (apron)

PROSC.

IRON CURTAIN

PROSC.

TABS
(main curtain)

"DOWNSTAGE RIGHT"
(D/S/R)

STAGE
TRAP

"DOWNSTAGE" (D/S)

DIP TRAPS
(for LX)

STAGE

"ONSTAGE"   "OFFSTAGE"

STAGE
CENTRE LINE

COUNTERWEIGHT
CAGE

"UPSTAGE" (U/S)

FLOWN BARS (pipes)

"UPSTAGE RIGHT"
(U/S/R)

BACK WALL

"PROMPT SIDE" (PS)

"OPPOSITE PROMPT SIDE" (OPS)

"STAGE LEFT" (SL)

"STAGE RIGHT" (SR)

STYLISED PLAN VIEW ON A STAGE

> ### Note:
> *Bars/scenery are flown "IN" (down) or flown "OUT" (up.)*
> *This avoids confusion with 'upstage' and 'downstage'*
> *when calling to the 'flyman.'*

Figure 2-02 - <u>STAGE TERMINOLOGY</u>
A stylised plan view on a stage.

describing this on the drawing, you can either write '100 x 50 par' (4" x 2" par), which is the normal convention, or '95 x 45 fin' (3¾" x 1¾" fin) which is describing the *actual, finished* size of the timber to be used after it has been planed smooth by the mill. The carpenters would also understand '95 x 45 par'. **Tubular steel** is similarly described as a cross-section through the tube, with the addition of further information describing the *thickness* of the steel 'wall' and the type of steel tube described. Steel suppliers' brochures illustrate this rather well. Examples are:

- **50Ø x 1.5 erw** = 50 mm diameter *round* tube with a wall thickness of 1.5 mm (2"Ø x $^1/_{16}$"). The type of material is 'Electric Resistance Welded' – 'erw' – a cheaper type/grade of steel which is adequate for most light steelwork.
- **50 x 50 x 1.5 erw** = 50 mm x 50 mm *square* tube with a wall thickness of 1.5 mm (2" x 2" x $^1/_{16}$"). Again, it is erw, and one should note that the outer four corners of erw are slightly more rounded and less 'sharp' than are other types of square/rectangular steel.
- **50 x 50 x 3 shs*** = 50 mm x 50 mm *square* tube with a wall thickness of 3 mm (2" x 2" x 1⅛"). The type of material is 'Square Hollow Section' – 'shs'.
- **50 x 30 x 3 rhs*** = 50 mm x 30 mm *rectangular* tube with a wall thickness of 3 mm (2" x 1¼" x ⅛"). The type of material is 'Rectangular Hollow Section' – 'rhs'.
- **60.3Ø x 5 chs*** = 60.3 mm diameter (*round*) tube with a wall thickness of 5 mm (2³/₈"Ø x ¼"). The type of material is 'Circular Hollow Section' – 'chs'.

Note: the three types of steel marked above with an asterisk – shs, rhs and chs – are called 'Structural Hollow Sections' – a better class of steel than is erw and preferred by engineers when building structural steelwork. (I understand that their 'calcs' – structural calculations – are geared more towards using this, than erw.)

10 Maintain neatness when writing or dimensioning

A) **Handwriting** proficiency is a nightmare for many people and can cause much anxiety when first attempting to master the art of technical drawing. (Plainly, CAD drawing removes this problem – see 'C' below.) It is obvious that the writing on a drawing (including dimensioning) should be clear enough to be read by all and that to **stencil** every word and number manually would simply take too long to be efficient. There are jobs where this is requested, which is no problem as long as the client is told of the time implications. My personal solution to the problem of my own appalling handwriting has been to write only in **upper case** lettering on drawings: I, and others, have found this to be an easier route to take than to attempt to alter or improve handwriting that has evolved over the years into an indecipherable mess. Try working in upper case and you may find that it is easier to control than is your 'natural' handwriting. It can be useful to slip a piece of lined paper beneath the drawing paper when writing a paragraph – your hand feels less exposed on the bare paper having the reassurance of lines beneath it. But if you do have difficulties in this area ... practise.

B) *Letraset* and other types of sticky-backed, peel-off-and-apply lettering or shading are very attractive and can greatly add to the 'first impact appeal' of a drawing. However, these things are expensive and very time-consuming and so should be used with restraint. Use these only when they would be appropriate for the type of drawing that you are working upon – and remember that stencilled writing looks just as professional, but is quicker and cheaper.

Letraset shading (and other patterns) are stuck on to the drawing, and trimmed to shape with a new scalpel blade *on the drawing*. Be careful that you are not cutting through both the *Letraset* and the drawing. I prefer to add these things to the back of the drawing – it will still read when copied, but can be ripped off the back, avoiding causing damage to the face of the drawing. Just experiment.

C) **Computers** have come to the aid of us all in helping to produce attractive calligraphy. Obviously, if you draw on CAD then the letters and numbers are no longer a problem for you. However, you can still use the computer to help in this regard even if you do not draw on CAD. It is possible to write whatever you require on the computer, print off onto sticky-backed acetate or similar, and stick it on the drawing. You can also do this with *ClipArt* and other programmes to add scaled human figures to the drawing.

11 The scale of the drawing

A) There are no rules in our business regarding which scales to use for drawing. It is true that there are some general conventions, but they are not rules: the theatre world does favour 1:25 for ground-plans and elevations; the museum world seems to prefer 1:20. I believe that the sole criterion for choosing scale should be the question: '**Which scale(s) will fill the drawing in the most attractive/clear fashion?**' I tend to draw only on A1 paper and therefore choose a scale that will fill that drawing in the best manner.

B) Having stated the above, do try to establish a visual logic to a **series** of drawings, simply to make them more user friendly, e.g. ground-plan and elevations at 1:25, further detail at 1:10, detail at 1:5.

C) In the trade-show world I am frequently cursed for using 1:75 (not a common scale), but my defence is that I often *need* (not want) to have the ground-plan, long section and short section all on the same drawing (in order to establish the sight-lines in three dimensions). I then detail at more conventional scales. I mention this in order to stress that the drawings are practical, flexible tools used as a means to an end. The drawings themselves should not be restricted by rules and regulations that are merely cosmetic and owe more to etiquette than to practicality. For those who worry about such matters, the common scales used are: 1:200, 1:100, 1:50, 1:25, 1:20, 1:10, 1:5, 1:2, and 1:1. (I like 1:15, but few do.)

D) To save your own time, do give some thought to the scale you will use on a particular job. It is very annoying to begin elevations at, say, 1:25 scale, but later realise that you need more detail than that scale can give and so have to repeat yourself at another scale, say 1:15.

E) As previously stated (*see* also page 8), never draw with the intention that people will scale off the drawing –

but do draw in the knowledge that people will do it anyway! Therefore, be accurate.

F) CAD drawing eases the problem of scaling because one can plot drawings at any scale – the actual drawing in the computer being 'full size'. However, it is most irritating when companies issue CAD drawings at 'no' scale – they *are* to scale, but to a 'mad' one, such as 1:34.758. This happens when they have instructed the plotter to just 'scale to fit', i.e. reduce the drawing to fit a named size of paper. This is annoying when, for example, the drawing is being generally discussed at a meeting and people would like to be able to 'ball-park' a dimension by scaling from it, but realise that they are unable to do so.

12 Try to spell accurately

A) I am not 'holier than thou' in this matter: my own spelling leaves much to be desired (thank goodness for spell-check!), but I do feel that it is worth checking the dictionary before becoming a laughing stock. Put simply, why look an idiot? Your drawings become an extension of yourself sent forth into the world. Bad spelling puts you in a poor light. The commercial world can be less forgiving of this sin than the theatre world.

B) If **working abroad**, you may have to draw in a foreign language – that is, *label* in a foreign language. This is not as difficult as might be imagined, just ensure that you have a list to hand containing translations of all the relevant materials, etc. *and ask a friendly local to check it all for you.* This last point is crucial because you may be using a word in its wrong sense. On a Spanish drawing, I once wrote a word that I thought meant 'the ground' or 'the soil', but later found that it meant specifically *wet* earth – so I had written 'swamp'. (So what? you may think, but the drawing was describing a scene within an exhibition and soil is not swamp. A wrong word can cost money!)

13 Be consistent with line thickness and line type

A) Again, there are no strict conventions relating to the thickness of **drawn lines**. However, consistency is an obvious visual aid to those reading the drawings. Like most draughtsmen, I tend to draw with a .35 nib, but draw my dimension lines with a .25 nib. I use other pens to add effect. Dimensioning lines certainly need to be visually different from the rest of the drawing.

Again, CAD drawing eases this problem as one is given far more choice of line types. It is all the more irritating, therefore, to be presented with a CAD drawing where the lines have not been defined by a style – simply because it could be drawn so much more clearly. I tend to have the dimensioning lines as dotted, thereby accentuating the 'solid' lines of the item drawn.

14 Be aware of the budget

A) When drawing any production, the budget for that show must be kept uppermost in the draughtsman's mind: however unpalatable it may sound, **budget is king**. Clearly, the draughtsman must be aware of approximate material and labour costs and he must gain an understanding of which construction methods are quick (cheap) to use. A theatre show which is to undergo a gruelling tour must be built to withstand the rigours of touring, so mortise and tenon joints will be used in the construction of flattage, whereas a trade-show set which will stand up for three hours and then be 'trashed' only requires its flattage to be of 50 x 25 mm par (2" x 1" par), on edge, nailed together. The former is more expensive to build, but not in the long term; the latter is cheaper to build and is adequate for its purpose.

B) Remember to 'translate' a set design (when possible) into a form that suits available **material sizes**, in such a fashion as to avoid wastage. For example, if by trimming 80 mm (3¼") off the size of the show's floor, it can all be made of 2440 x 1220 mm (8' x 4') sheets of ply, then do this – check with the designer if you think that it may matter to him. Similarly, if a designer has drawn a flat which appears to be 2490 mm high by 1260 mm wide (8' 2" x 4' 1½"), discuss changing those dimensions to 2440 x 1220 mm (8' x 4') so that only one sheet of 4 mm (⅛" or ⁵/₃₂") facing ply is used. Otherwise, those extra few millimetres will waste another sheet.

C) Do not consider wastage in terms of timber/ply/steel only, because many flats will be **cloth-covered** and cloth can be expensive, especially if it has to be sewn-up into larger pieces. Therefore, when deciding how to break a set down into its component pieces of flattage, do find out the *width* of covering cloth to be used.

Having made the above point, remember that cloth can be a far cheaper material than timber/ply/steel and so it is more economic to have a 'wall' of cloth (sewn-up as one piece) than a 'wall' of flattage. Use your knowledge of materials and their prices to decide how best to tackle each problem.

D) Remember to discuss with the **production manager** how best to break a set down into its component parts. Sometimes, by leaving a piece of scenery as one large, unbroken unit, the truck space that it takes up may be greater – but it may save time on the fit-up to leave it as one piece. The PM is the one to decide.

E) Be aware of the fact that certain items are far more expensive than others – *this is not always obvious at first glance.* On many occasions the cost of **castors** can be the greatest single material expenditure of the whole set (and they are not even seen). Only specify castors that are adequate for the loads carried (heavy-duty castors are more expensive) or, even better, find out if there are any castors available from past shows (all theatres should keep castors). Lift-jack castors are expensive. Polycarbonate is expensive, PVC less so. Formica-type laminates are expensive, but some makes are far cheaper than others. Fibreglass is labour-intensive and therefore can prove to be expensive. Birch ply is expensive.

F) Finally, *you are expensive.* The drawings are expensive, so they must 'earn' their money by producing savings wherever possible.

15 Maintain consistency within a set of drawings

A) Visual consistency within a set of drawings (dimensioning conventions, scales, etc.) has been mentioned, but do ensure that drawings do not contradict one another in their *factual* content. Again, this sounds so obvious, but it is very easy to make such mistakes: by the time you are working upon drawing No. 15 you may well have forgotten an important point made on drawing No. 2. I always keep relevant drawings pinned on walls, so that a mere glance upwards can confirm what was drawn before. (This is when you occasionally discover that your early drawing was wrong! But better now than later.)

16 Place the set's break-points with care

All sets break down into component parts for travelling. Deciding where those break-points are is a key skill that must be acquired. When deciding, the following points must be considered:

A) **The design's aesthetic qualities** are prerequisite, so ensure that break-lines are disguised by the natural architecture/artwork of the design.

B) **Road haulage truck size** can vary from tour to tour and country to country. This information will often be a deciding factor in determining where the scenery has to break. Find out from the hauliers the internal dimensions of the truck type that will be used. The standard 40-foot articulated truck used for the transportation of scenery in the UK tends to have internal dimensions of approximately 2340 mm (7' 8") wide x 2650 mm (8' 8") high. It can be simple for the production manager to ask for higher-sided vehicles – up to approximately 3050 mm (10') high. Remember that an articulated truck has a 'kingpin' arrangement that forces up the floor level of the trailer at the front end, by the cab. This raised floor within the trailer is known as 'the dance floor' – it effectively reduces the height of the trailer by about 350 mm (1' 2") for about 3000–3600 mm (9' 10"–11' 10") at the front, not the door end. Of course, scenery can be transported 'at an angle' (leaning within the trailer), thereby utilising the diagonal size of the trailer's doors, but bear in mind that this does waste valuable truck space.

C) **Shipping containers**, rather than articulated trailers, are often used for 'long haul' tours. They have smaller internal dimensions! So ask if these are likely to be used for any show that you are drawing. One example of the internal dimensions of a 20-foot shipping container is 2337 (7' 8") wide x 2387 (7' 10") high x 5890 (19' 4") long (doors are 2337 (7' 8") wide x 2286 (7' 6") high). Various shipping companies use various containers, so some may differ from this example – 'jumbo' containers are taller, but rarer.

D) **Air cargo containers** can be bizarre shapes (largely ill-suited for set transportation), so always obtain a sketch of them from the freight handlers. In most cases, sets will not travel comfortably in these containers and so are flown 'loose', either in the hold of an aircraft or in a chartered cargo aeroplane. Theatre sets are usually complex and delicate items to transport and require skilled labour (stage crews). Therefore, when a set is flown and is handled by other types of crew, damage often occurs. I have known sets to be greatly damaged by being flown to their destination; in essence, the production manager can lose all control of the handling of the scenery at airports.

E) The **get-in size** tends to dictate the sizes of manageable lumps of set (along with truck sizes, *see* point 'B' above.) Theatres suffer fewer problems than most in this regard, whereas trade shows run the whole gamut of nightmare venues and their get-ins. Remember, when surveying the get-in, do not just measure the clearway into the building, but walk the *whole route* through to the stage – checking for the existence of low ceilings, ducts, pipes or stairs and, very importantly, *bends in a corridor*.

F) The **manageability of pieces** once the set has been broken down for travel must be considered. Do not expect the crew to have to manhandle awkward or dangerous pieces. Experience helps here, of course, and it can be gained by watching the stage crew handle a set that you have drawn – it soon becomes apparent as to what is an awkward piece (they let you know). A heavy item is not so much of a problem if many men can get around it and have places to lift from. Consider having 'dollies' made – 25 mm (1") birch ply, 1000 mm x 600 mm (3' 3" x 2') plus hand-holes + four bolted 75 mm (3") swivel castors. These can be pin-hinged or bolted to particularly awkward pieces of set for travelling (and are re-used many times). Consider secreting castors into the set at break-points, for use only while the set is being travelled. Consider too whether the use of flying bars or hoists can assist in a break down or build of a set – if so, add flying irons/attachments to the pieces in question. Consider the use of travelling battens/travelling braces/travelling frames – all of which serve the purpose of stiffening lumps of scenery that become awkward or ungainly upon being broken away from the rest of the set, i.e. they are used for travelling only, not for the show.

G) **Fragility of the set.** It is not sensible to break the set into pieces that have fragile edges exposed, as these will be damaged in transit. Breaking across vac-form is always a bad idea for this reason (also, when the set is put together, vac-form tends not to hold its shape and will produce ugly gaps). Heavy, large items with fragile edges are not desirable. Sometimes, there is no other obvious place to break the set *but* along a fragile edge: in these cases draw some sort of strong pin-hinged/bolted travelling protection. The set and the crew must be protected.

H) **Sheet sizes.** As discussed on page 16, promote economy by remembering the sizes of sheets of ply when deciding the placing of break-points. A wrongly placed break-point could result in having to waste a sheet of ply in order to obtain a thin sliver. (For ply, of course, read also cloth, laminate, polycarbonate, etc.)

I) **Structural integrity** is clearly of *vital importance* when deciding the positions of set breaks – yet this point has been left until last. The reason is that in so many cases, the break-points are a given, dictated by some of the reasons above (get-in, artistic/aesthetic reasons, etc.) and our job is to make it structurally sound. Most designers are aware of the fact that their sets will have to break down and have already considered and solved the problem, if necessary, by designing-in a suitable line or moulding that will disguise a join. Discuss all break joints with the designer and production manager and, if the impossible really is being requested, explain your structural doubts to them. After all, some things are impossible – or, more likely, too expensive – to achieve. But do not be too hasty: give the whole problem a lot of careful thought. We are asked to re-invent the wheel each week; after all, it is part of our job. Just look at all the 'impossible' shows we have seen in theatres! Therefore, in most cases, a satisfactory design is achievable, despite the technical problems.

17 Obtain correct logo references

A) When producing drawings for trade shows/conferences/exhibitions, you will need to include company logos. Companies can be rather precious about their logos, so never underestimate the care with which the logo will be studied. On the drawings, a reasonable interpretation is acceptable (trace them from copies made to size on a photocopier); but *on the actual set*, the logo must be perfect. Therefore always ask for a 'logo pack', or 'PMT', from which the actual logo can be produced. The majority of companies have specifically designed logo packs, including disks.

18 Be aware of Health & Safety issues

This important topic has already been raised (*see* page 5) and the draughtsman's responsibility has, I hope, been made clear. I have listed below some crucial points, but, in truth, this subject is too large to cover comprehensively. Each venue will have its own peculiar rules, so find these out, but also discuss your work with the appropriate fire officer and/or Health & Safety representative.

A) **Museum work** obviously involves sets sharing public space and is therefore very strictly controlled. It is usual to have Health & Safety and/or fire consultants representing the client's interests involved in the whole process. These consultants exist to advise upon all aspects of the production and will thoroughly discuss and check the drawings and the work. They have absolute authority, as they should do, and it can save time and money if you work with them and discuss issues before you draw. I have seen sets condemned, at the contractor's own cost, simply because the relevant consultants had not been consulted – this would be a draughtsman's fault as he could not have sought their opinion. (Note the verb 'sought'; the draughtsman has to be proactive, not reactive. Reactive, in this case, meant reacting by re-building the set!)

B) **Fire classification.** Establish whether materials are to be 'non-flameproof', Class 1, or Class 0. Some materials are 'inherently flameproof' – meaning that in their natural state they simply will not spread flame. Steel and concrete are good examples; wool is another, surprisingly – hence the occasional requirement for expensive, real woollen carpets. 'Non-flameproof' is simply untreated and carries no fire rating. 'Class 1' materials, if not inherently flameproof, have been treated with chemicals to conform to Class 1 classification of 'spread of flame' and is the usual UK standard required in theatres. 'Class 0' is a higher classification and can be insisted upon in public areas (e.g. in museum work), causing many problems to the contractor simply because so few materials can reach that standard. Always **obtain certification** from the manufacturer of materials that require classification – these will be requested by the client.

Remember that different countries adopt different fire/safety regulations. (France has a 'Class M' – similar, but not identical to the UK's Class 0. UK contractors working for *EuroDisney* had to import Class M plywood in order to build the sets because the correct certification was pre-requisite.)

In most types of work, a small percentage of non-flameproof material may be allowed – remember that it costs nothing to ask for dispensation.

The **iron curtain** in a theatre is a moving fire barrier, separating the auditorium from the stage. Upstage of the iron curtain is often a non-flameproof zone; downstage of the iron, Class 1. If a show's floor passes below the iron curtain, then the area of the floor immediately below it needs to be filled in solid to maintain the effect of the iron. The iron curtain must always have a clearway through which to pass – no fixed settings may be placed in its path. This occasionally necessitates the use of sprung traps, etc. within a large piece of scenery, which allow the iron to pass through unhindered. The fire officer will ask to see these ideas demonstrated onstage as a test.

Timber thicker than 25 mm (1") can usually be non-flameproof (untreated with fire-retardant chemicals). Hardwood can be non-flameproof (including balsa wood, surprisingly). Plywood floors that lay directly on the stage can often be non-flameproof.

Raised floors or rostra in public areas should have solid sides (no feet cut out of rostrum gates on the outside edge of the structure) to prevent lit cigarettes from rolling underneath. Open risers on stairs may be disallowed for the same reason – any fire compartment needs to be sealed off. These points rarely apply to theatre sets that sit on a stage and are separated from the audience.

Doors may have to be 'half-hour' or 'one hour' fire-rated. They may require intumescent strips – strips of material, housed into the edge of the door or door frame, that expand in heat and fill gaps between the door and the frame. Fire-rated doors need to be purchased, not built in a workshop. It is possible to buy 'door blanks' – these are simply very large flush doors that are cut down to the size required and, if necessary, have their edges re-lipped. Fire-rated doorframes require solid door stops that are at least 25 mm (1") thick and not 'planted on', but are inherent to the door frame – the section is machined from one piece of timber.

Structural steel may require fire protection in permanent structures – clad with mineral fibreboard, for example – to give time for egress before the steel would buckle and collapse in intense heat.

C) **Escape routes** must be maintained and the necessary clearway indicated on the drawings.

D) **Fire or safety equipment** within the venue must never be moved (without permission) or blocked in with other gear that might prevent its effective use. Extra fire or safety equipment specified for use on your particular show/project must be clearly labelled on the general arrangement drawings.

E) **Manageability of the set**, or pieces of the set, must be considered, as previously mentioned (*see* '16F' above). Make some considerable effort to solve the problems of handling the set. The safety of the crew, cast and public is paramount: unmanageable pieces of set will cause accidents. Our job is to consider these problems, solve them... and then be allowed to sleep at night! Nobody wants to carry the guilt of having caused an accident.

F) **No dangerous materials**, or potentially dangerous materials, are to be used. Never use glass on stage (use PVC, polycarbonate, sugar glass, etc.). Arris the edges of all timber-work to prevent splinters: i.e. have all corners slightly rounded. If water or other liquid is to be spilled during a show, test the flooring to establish how slippery it becomes. Ensure that all flame effects are passed by the fire officer (the production manager, pyrotechnics person, and/or stage electrics – LX – department usually have responsibility for this, but still be involved in the decisions taken – they may affect the set in other ways).

G) **Scenery that moves** needs care. Fit steel cable 'dead lines' to moving trucks that could possibly crash into the audience due to mechanical failure. Avoid finger traps and toe traps. Paint offstage edges with white lines for easy identification in the darkness of show conditions – use luminous tape where necessary. Add 'kicker' rails to platforms that are above the floor level in order to prevent items rolling off and falling onto anybody below. In essence, try to visualise in each case what could possibly go wrong and try to eradicate the problem.

H) **Flown scenery** should have no doors or windows that could fall open while being flown (fit locks or latches). Do not fit lift-off hinges to items on flown scenery, thus avoiding any danger of the item catching something while flying and simply lifting off and falling. Fit 'crash bars' to LX bars that may be brushed by passing scenery (to prevent 'barn doors' from falling from the lamps). Be aware of the problems of paging electrical cables. The main lifting cables should be steel with 'bottle-screws' ('turnbuckles' in the USA) fitted to each to allow for line length adjustment. Ensure that the piece can hang 'true' (level and perpendicular) by having adjustment in front elevation – the bottle-screws – as well as an adjustment in side section near the top (to move the cable up or down stage in order that it can hang perpendicularly, allowing for its centre of gravity). Fit deadlines or safety cables where possible to act as a back-up should the main cables fail. Ensure that the flown piece cannot 'turn turtle' and roll over while being flown.

Flying irons on timber scenery need to be bolted using M10 bolts and usually fitted to the bottom of timber flattage. Do not use knotty timber for flown scenery. Fit grommets (*see* fig. 16–16) with machine screws, not wood screws; likewise for crucial pin-hinges – the machine screws should be ³⁄₁₆" or 4 mm. Fit enough stiffeners to the back of flown scenery to prevent buckling and warping, and fit bolt-plates to flown timber flattage that bolts together, to prevent the M10 bolts pulling through the timber. Flown steel flattage/frames may be flown from the top. Consider also fitting bolt-plates to tubular steel to prevent bolts pulling through or buckling the wall of the tube (a simple square of steel, say 3 mm thick, welded where bolts pass through – acting as a stiffener to the wall of the tube). If worried, never be afraid to ask for the input of a genuine structural engineer who can 'prove' a design with calculations. Flown flats containing neon should have that neon encased, for example in clear PVC or polycarbonate, and a fireman's switch placed near stage management's desk.

I) **Handrails** in public spaces should be 1100 mm (3' 7½") high and meet the necessary local requirements of side loading, etc. Public balustrades must obey the '100 mm (4") ball rule': this dictates that a ball of diameter 100 mm must not be able to pass through, anywhere. Splinters and finger traps must be avoided. On a staircase that rises more than 600 mm (2'), handrails must be between 840 mm (2' 9") and 1000 mm (3' 3") high above the pitch-line

(measured vertically). If the stair is more than 1000 mm (3' 3") wide, it requires handrails both sides. Sets that do not involve the public having any access, such as an onstage theatre set, frequently break these rules to suit, say, an historic design – that is fine, provided that common sense prevails.

J) **Staircases** for public use must comply with the following rules: minimum headroom of 2000 mm (6' 7") measured vertically above the pitch-line, 1500 mm (4' 11") measured at 90 degrees to the pitch-line; tread length plus twice the riser height should be between 550 mm (1' 10") and 700 mm (2' 4"); maximum riser of 190 mm (7½"); minimum going of 230 mm (9"); maximum pitch of 38 degrees; no more than 16 risers per single flight; all risers to be equal and all goings to be equal, between consecutive floor levels. (Private stairs may have a rise of 220 mm or 8½".)

K) **Kick-boards** (raised edges to the sides of platforms – for example, 75 x 25 mm par or 3' x 1" par, on-edge) should be fitted to any raised area that may contain objects which could roll, or be kicked, and fall off the side. Also fit them to the back edge of rostra which contain loose chairs, to prevent someone shifting their chair back and toppling off.

L) **Headroom** should not drop below 2000 mm (6' 7"). As a visual aid, remember that a standard door is 1981 mm (6' 6") plus clearance, equals 1990 mm (6' 6½"). Ceilings below 2100 mm (6' 11") high are not recommended. If something is to be moving about just above headroom, then be extra-cautious – 2500 mm (8' 3") is a safe clearance for *most* applications.

However, be alert to all potential danger: on an Expo project some years ago, a visiting father placed his young daughter on his shoulders in order to secure a better view for her. The designers had not allowed for this possibility and she was killed by moving equipment that had been thought to be – and was, in a sense – above head-height. Try living with that on your conscience. This last sombre point is an apt place to end our glance at a topic which none of us can afford to ignore.

19 Accept responsibility

A) When drawing, one is taking decisions at every turn and accepting the responsibility for those decisions. It is just not possible to discuss every tiny query with the designer or production manager, it would drive them mad; you are being paid to make decisions and draw. The buck usually stops with the draughtsman, fairly or unfairly, and the confidence that is required to accept responsibility can only come with experience. Try to let it happen naturally (we all wake up in the night occasionally and suddenly think that huge errors have occurred in drawings done that day – that is just healthy paranoia!). Never stop asking questions, in that way you will gain the knowledge that allows confidence to grow.

B) Accept responsibility for telling whoever is paying you, **how long certain jobs may take to draw.** Only a draughtsman can know this and so it is your duty to inform others. Remember that it takes a similar amount of time to draw, say, a model of a shop-front at 1000 mm high, as it does to draw the same shop-front at 4000 mm high. Don't underestimate the number of clients who fail to realise that simple fact! A perspective set may contain a collection of buildings – a small village, say – constructed of 12 mm (½") ply and positioned upstage, that are actually only 1200 mm (4') high. If those small buildings are in 3D, then each can take nearly as long to draw as if the buildings were 'full size'. (The reason for this is that most of the work is in: a) absorbing the information from the design drawing or sketch; b) drawing the finished elevations and plan; and c) establishing and drawing the true views and any bevels, etc. of each part of the piece. Having done all that, it would then take very little longer to draw as flattage as opposed to the plywood used for smaller items.) Bear in mind also that sometimes it may be your responsibility to admit that it would be quicker to set something out at full size, on ply in the workshop, rather than draw it and then have someone else set it out from your drawing. Some prop items fall into this category. Occasionally, there are jobs that would result in horribly complex or messy drawings that few would understand or read, whereas the job could be quickly modelled (in ply or modelling polyboard) and labelled. Drawings can then be made of each labelled part. As long as all is clear to those who have to build what you draw, how you achieve it is immaterial.

20 Admit to your mistakes!

Having accepted responsibility, one must adopt an adult response to the inevitable fact that mistakes will occur. 'I *shall* be the cause of mistakes,' is a difficult sentence to utter with conviction, especially for those of us who could be described as 'control freaks'. Nevertheless, live with it.

Always own up to making errors: 'He who makes no mistakes, makes nothing' can be your defence here. We all make mistakes and have to deal with the consequences. *The sooner your mistake is spotted and broadcast to those who need to know, the less damage will have been done.* When an error is noticed, telephone those who need to know, alter the drawing(s) to suit, and reissue as a revision. Strangely, the quicker that an error is admitted, the quicker everyone forgets about it – but if you uselessly try to deny the error, everyone will remember the incident forever. (My personal favourite? I once spent four days unaware that my young son had changed the mode on my calculator. Cold sweat time! I spent two days retrieving and altering drawings.)

3 • The Types of Drawings Used

Knowing what *type* of drawing it is that you are producing will dictate the content of that drawing as well as its method of presentation – its 'look'. Each distinct type of drawing serves a different function and is targeted at a particular readership. By definition, then, it will contain separate, specific information. If you were to design a job and then take charge of the draughting or construction, you would probably have used all the types of drawings listed here during the process, because each type of drawing is specific to a particular show's development from design through to completion.

Remember to pay due respect to the work that has gone into drawings (and their subsequent cost) by carefully looking after original 'skins'. Store them in plan chests and only travel with them once they are carefully rolled – not too tightly – and safe within a proprietary drawing tube. Carefully preserve all old drawings, too – shows *do* return to haunt you.

When using CAD, I would advise that paper copies of all current, issued drawings be kept to hand. It is always preferable, when discussing drawings over the telephone, to have both parties looking at the same thing (looking at the screen is very different from looking at the actual plot). I further suggest storing a full, final set of plots when the show is complete. Obviously, store all CAD drawings electronically – to disc, CD, etc. (Check that drawings stored on floppy discs *can* be transferred back to your computer – sometimes one encounters faulty discs and the data they contain is not recoverable. It is a bore to have to redo a drawing you thought you had in storage!) CAD drawing also necessitates vigilance in naming files (drawings) and maintaining a sensible list of drawings in the show's folder. The ease with which drawings may be altered and revised can lead to the accumulation of differing versions of a drawing, and subsequent confusion as to which is the most current (or which was issued). If all current/issued drawings display a specific file name, it is obvious which drawings are final.

ROUGH LAY-OUT/PROPOSAL DRAWINGS

In the initial stages of a project, it is sometimes necessary to do a 'feasibility study' in order to establish whether or not the project can proceed. Similarly, a project certain to come to fruition may still require different versions to be proposed. Many designs involve a process of suggesting certain options which may, or may not, be finally selected – the budget may be the deciding factor (it usually is).

Proposal drawings, however, are not necessarily design drawings; frequently, a technical problem is only resolved by drawing a series of versions, calling a meeting of all concerned and thrashing out the exposed difficulties together. Such drawings may well be the only way of illustrating certain problems to the non-technical staff on the team. It is also common to have to draw a proposed technical drawing in order that the designer can really 'see' a problem arising from his design. **Figure 3–01** is a detail from a drawing that proposed a particular method of breaking down a set for removal from the stage. Once approved, the construction drawings could commence.

Audience seating lay-outs for shows involving the installation of their own seating invariably begin life as proposal drawings. The reason for this is that, primarily, someone has to indicate a reasonably accurate plan 'footprint' of the audience blocks in order that initial drawings may proceed. A seating contractor is then found (or the seats chosen), local authority regulations confirmed and the exact audience numbers finalised. (In trade shows, clients are forever tweaking with these numbers: empty seats give off the wrong signals, whereas insufficient seating is disastrous. They do worry.) It is only at this stage that the final drawing is achieved and issued.

Museum projects often involve proposal drawings being issued until such time as the actual exhibits are finalised. A particular exhibit may not be available and others, perhaps of a different size, have to be obtained from elsewhere.

Proposal drawings are therefore quite common, and their main **functions** are:

A) To provide a bare **framework of information** from which artistic decisions can be made. The producer/director will approve the design (or not) from these drawings.

B) To supply enough basic information for the production manager to be able to assemble an approximate **costing**, or 'ball-park figure', from each of the technical departments involved.

C) To facilitate the input of information *at an early stage* from all departments involved in the project, so that any glaring problems or omissions can be tackled before the project has been developed further. For no matter how experienced the designer may be, it is always imperative that he listen to up-to-date information supplied by technical departments: new developments in AV or rigging, for example, may neatly solve a current problem.

D) To show that a **problem exists** for which there is at present no answer. This is an important point: do not assume that drawings must always supply answers to problems. They are still fulfilling a vitally useful function if they also indicate problems for which an answer must be sought. A designer may wish to have a flat flown in a certain position, but have no idea whether or not this is feasible (for example, if the show were in the Royal Albert Hall, where flying positions are not obvious). It is perfectly adequate for them to indicate their wishes and to make a notation, such as 'TBC' or 'TBA' ('to be confirmed

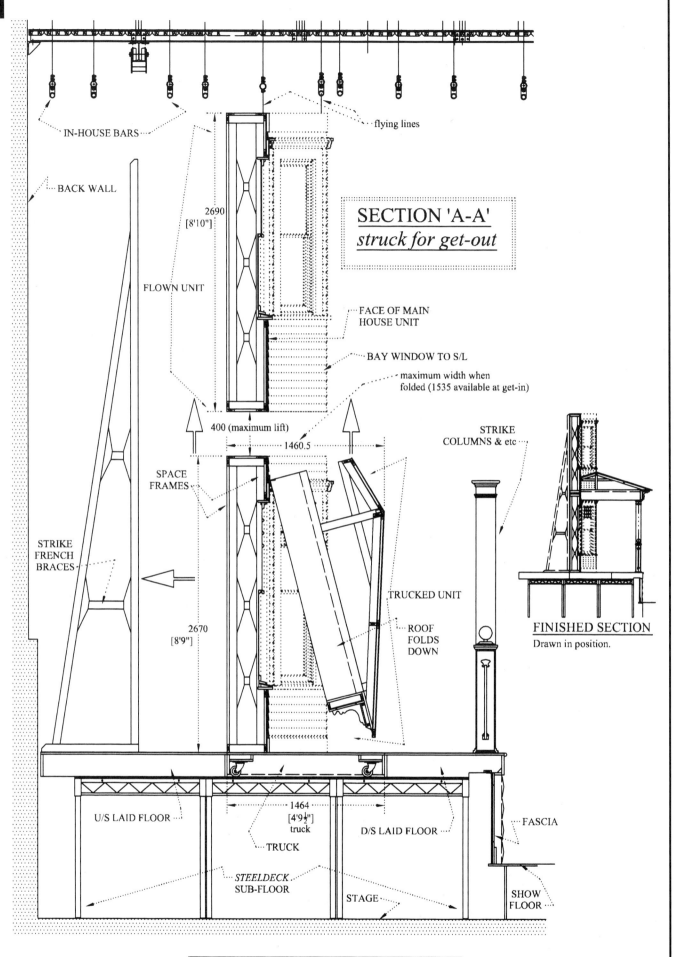

IN-HOUSE BARS

BACK WALL

flying lines

2690
[8'10"]

SECTION 'A-A'
struck for get-out

FLOWN UNIT

FACE OF MAIN
HOUSE UNIT

BAY WINDOW TO S/L

maximum width when
folded (1535 available at get-in)

400 (maximum lift)

1460.5

STRIKE
COLUMNS & etc

SPACE
FRAMES

STRIKE
FRENCH
BRACES

2670
[8'9"]

TRUCKED UNIT

ROOF
FOLDS
DOWN

FINISHED SECTION
Drawn in position.

U/S LAID FLOOR

1464
[4'9½"]
truck

TRUCK

D/S LAID FLOOR

FASCIA

STEELDECK
SUB-FLOOR

STAGE

SHOW
FLOOR

Figure 3-01 - A PROPOSAL DRAWING
Proposing the method of break-down for a set within a
theatre that has a narrow get-in.

or advised'), and then let the riggers evaluate what is possible. Frequently, a compromise is reached.

E) To give an early insight into the project to those who will be involved. In effect, this buys a little, precious 'thinking time' for all concerned. Forethought always leads to a more efficient production.

Given the above, it should be clear that proposal drawings (or rough lay-out drawings) are just that, and need not always be as fully comprehensive, mathematically correct or as neat as the drawings that will follow. However, they *must* be good enough to fulfil the above requirements – other contractors and technicians must be able to calculate rough costs from them. There is no urgent need to dimension everything on these drawings; this is the one occasion where **scaling**, *provided that it is done with some precision*, is adequate. At this stage in a job, few would need dimensions anyway. Obviously, do show particular dimensions relevant to any of the problems being identified.

It is important that these drawings – however loose and 'open to discussion' they may be – still indicate the whole of what will finally be placed within the area in question. This may seem to contradict what has gone before. To clarify, an attempt should still be made to position everything, even though the drawing may be admitting that many matters remain in question. The reason is obvious: if the purpose of the drawing is to obtain the input of other departments, those departments need to be aware of all the factors involved. For example, the carpenters may need to be informed of the existence of a speaker stack before they can help solve an apparent problem. Finally, ensure that all these drawings are clearly labelled: '*Proposal drawing, issued for discussion ONLY. NOT for construction.*'

DESIGN DRAWINGS

These should represent the design and positioning of the set. *All information required to construct the set and place it within the venue can, and should, be on these drawings.* Sadly, however, British custom dictates that in so many cases, design drawings are unclear, not dimensioned and bear little resemblance to the practical reality of the venue. 'Scale off it' is the usual cry! For some reason, in Britain we almost expect and accept these shortcomings from the designer. The client understandably knows no different: they often only expect a 'pretty' drawing from the designer and have no idea that these shortcomings will cost money.

When collecting a brief, it is advisable for the designer to take a check-list along to the introductory meetings in order that certain pertinent questions are not overlooked. This is of great use as a mental 'comforter' when embarking on the initial designs – it does help to have all information to hand – and safeguards against forgetting some of the crucial points listed below. I have reproduced my own check-list overleaf, entitled '**Project Data**': this is slanted towards trade shows, but the questions are self-evident and would be appropriate to most types of production.

Clients should expect professionalism from the designer, and that should include the provision of a final design package of drawings that fulfil the following principal **functions**:

A) To show the design from all viewpoints necessary for the understanding of that design. Every basic elevation and plan should be drawn, leaving no 'mysteries'. *All should be clearly dimensioned.*

B) To show each different scene or set. Each new scene will require its own drawings.

C) To prove audience sight-lines and maskings on stage.

D) To indicate all the areas of the venue that will be utilised for the project.

E) To clearly illustrate moving items. The drawings should show each position reached by moving trucks, etc. Clear flying plots must be included, showing the bars or hoists used for each scene.

F) To provide <u>all</u> **the information required by the set-builder** and others to commence construction drawings. This should include moulding references; what is 'hard' (ply faced) as opposed to 'soft' (cloth); fire ratings; cloth references; carpet references, etc. – *all information.* If the drawings allow for 'second guessing' then the designer can hardly complain that his design has been compromised (although, of course, he will).

G) To show all finishes, colours and added decor required and, if necessary, supply photographs or other references for the prop and artist departments (known as '*design refs*').

H) To allow final costings to be established. Everything that has a cost implication must be shown.

I) To indicate any preferred construction methods. An indication is adequate; fully drawn construction drawings are not expected (but would be nice).

J) To show cast entrances/exits. It is important to indicate how the cast (or the show crew) will enter and leave the set. This will often necessitate the use of secret, masked entrances and it is vital that all stage departments know of their existence (or Sound will place a speaker stack in the way).

K) To indicate lighting or projection. The design must allow for adequate lighting of the set, even though no real detail is necessary. The lighting designer will produce his lighting design drawings from the set design drawings – but cannot light an area if the designer has closed down all his options (it is not possible to light through a solid, unbroken ceiling, for example). Indisputably, all designs require good lighting for them to appear at their best; no designer can ever ignore the lighting requirements (but some try, once). Lighting slots must be considered, as well as any other method of secreting lamps about the set. Projection requires similar disciplines and thought-processes.

L) To highlight relevant Health & Safety issues.

The designer will either undertake the drawings or use a design assistant. Final design drawings should be marked clearly 'For Construction', which simply means that others may begin the construction process by producing construction drawings. (**Part Three** of this book includes a complete design drawing package of four drawings with accompanying text.)

John Blurton
& Margaret Easty Partnership.
Tel: XXXXX-XXXXXX **Fax:** XXXXX-XXXXXX **E-mail:** XXXXX@XXXXXXXXXX.XXX

PROJECT DATA   DATE:

OUR CLIENT: MAIN CLIENT: PROJECT TITLE: VENUE(S):
FIT-UP DATE/TIME: SHOW DATE(S)/TIME: GET-OUT DATE/TIME:
DATE THAT DESIGN DRAWINGS ARE TO BE DELIVERED/DISCUSSED:
SURVEY/RECCE DATE/TIME:
GOOD (DIMENSIONED) VENUE DRAWINGS SUPPLIED? *yes/no*
FIRE EXIT DETAILS SUPPLIED? *yes/no*
VENUE PHOTOGRAPHS SUPPLIED? *yes/no*   WILL VENUE BLACK-OUT? *yes/no*
LOGO REFERENCE SUPPLIED? *yes/no*   when?   send by post? (Hard copy).
LOGO COLOURS:

STAGING.
VENUE GET-IN: *good/bad details:*   ARE WE HAVING A RAISED STAGE? *yes/no*
FIRE RATING OF THE SET: EXISTING FIRE CURTAIN? *yes/no*
ON-STAGE ENTRANCES REQUIRED: *wings /backstage /other*
STAGE-TO-AUDIENCE ACCESS REQUIRED: *yes/no*
NUMBER OF LECTERNS: RENTED OR DESIGNED LECTERNS:
SPECIAL LECTERN REQUIREMENTS:
TYPE OF AUTOCUE: *lcd /within lectern /out-rigged   where?*
NUMBER OF SPEAKERS/GUESTS/ACTORS ON STAGE:
CONSOLE/DESK REQUIRED ON STAGE: LIVE CAMERAS USED? *yes/no   detail*
LIGHTING POSITIONS IN VENUE: *none /see drawings /discuss*
AUDIO SPEAKERS TO BE: *within the set /f.o.h. (masked?) /other*
IS SPACE REQUIRED BACKSTAGE: *road boxes /props /cast /other*
CONTROL AREA DETAILS/SIZE: PREFERRED SET-BUILDER, IF ANY:

SCREENS.
NUMBER OF SCREENS:
TYPE OF IMAGES: *video 4:3   /slide 3:2   /film   /other ratios*
F.P. OR B.P. ?   */no preference*   SCREEN MATERIAL: */no preference*
PROJECTORS: *existing booth/hanging point   /our choice*
PROJECTOR TYPE, IF KNOWN:

AUDIENCE.
NUMBER OF AUDIENCE: TYPE OF AUDIENCE: *mixed /business /VIPs /other*
USING EXISTING SEATING IN AUDITORIUM: *yes/no   all/or part.....detail*
WE DESIGN PROJECT-SPECIFIC SEATING: *yes/no*
STYLE OF SEATING: *theatre /schoolroom /rounds /raked /other*
SIZE OF SEATING/TABLES: MINIMUM AISLE WIDTHS IN VENUE:
LIVE CAMERA AMONGST AUDIENCE?   *yes/no   where?*
CAMERA PLATFORMS F.O.H.?   *yes/no   where?*
LX TOWERS/GEAR F.O.H.?   *yes/no   where?*
ANY F.O.H. DESIGN REQUIRED?   *yes/no   detail*
ANY OTHER RELEVANT AUDIENCE REQUIREMENTS? *yes/no   detail*

PROJECT PERSONNEL.
PRODUCER/DIRECTOR: PRODUCTION MANAGER:
LIGHTING DESIGNER: SOUND COMPANY/CONTACT:
A.V. SUPPLIER/CONTACT: RIGGING COMPANY/CONTACT:
STAGE MANAGER AND/OR SHOW CALLER:
VENUE CONTACT/TITLE: SET-BUILDER:

FEE AGREED: PAYMENT DATES (not invoice date):
PROJECT DETAILS / BRIEF / FEEL /& ETC.

A good design drawing package should include:

A)   Ground-plan(s). This is a plan view showing the set in relation to the venue. It should show the basic setting-out maths required to place items *exactly* in their correct position. It should label each piece – for reference on subsequent elevation or detail drawings – and should prove that the sight-lines are correct and that the masking of offstage areas is sufficient. It should also show the bar numbers of flown scenery. Complex shows may require more than one ground-plan; one for each set-change is common. Equal attention should be given to offstage areas or requirements as to onstage material.

A ground-plan should be drawn for each venue of a tour. **Figure 3-02** is an example of this, although here the venue has been stripped away for clarity. The set fits tightly upon a revolve (revolving stage), and on *one date* of the tour the in-house tabs (main curtain) land near the downstage point of the inner circle drawn. The stage-right unit was therefore made as a truck that pivots and folds inwards, ensuring that the set cleared the curtain line; the partial plan to the left shows the unit 'folded', the get-off treads being struck manually. (The revolve did not have to spin through 360°, only 180°; therefore, when spun *anti-clockwise*, only the bare floor of the revolve protruded downstage of the tabs.)

B)   Side section on centre-line. This is occasionally omitted – although why is a mystery. It is *vital*. It is a side section 'sliced through' the plan centre-line of the venue or the venue's stage. Again, it must mathematically place the set within the venue. The designer needs this in order to plot sight-lines from the stalls and circle; it is crucial to the lighting designer and serves to indicate the flying plot. It should prove that scenery flown out will rest out of view (grid height dictates this); it should prove the correct border heights (sometimes *after* the lighting designer has added his LX bars); and it should prove that any maskings work.

C)   Elevation. Again, this should be a drawing that places the set within the venue, signalling setting dimensions.

Note that the above three drawings serve the function of placing the design into the venue. They are often collectively known as the '**General Arrangement**' drawings, or the 'GA'. They *must* include the basic few dimensions necessary to physically place the set in position (far too many sets have had to be 'shoved around until they fit' because of the lack of this crucial information). Clarity is the main issue here, and it is perfectly adequate to show and label the basic outlines of the set – or shaded 'foot-prints' – on these drawings. The *details* of the design may be shown in following drawings. Remember that the 'fit-up' crew will use them most frequently. Do bear this in mind – the finer details of the set are of use when building the set and can be shown on separate drawings, but the 'fit-up' crew need to know where to place these items (now finished and existing).

If scale and paper size permit, have these three views on one drawing (the 'GA') because it is so much more convenient for the crew to read from a single sheet. Hence the earlier comment about the importance of clarity over detail for these views.

D)   Elevations and details. These must clearly show what the designer wants. Each piece should be labelled to match the labelling on the ground-plan. Colour references may be omitted at first issue of the drawings, but it is important to indicate finishes, if known, as the finish (paint, cloth, MDF, laminate, etc.) can often dictate the method of construction (think costs!). Dimensions should be included to prevent others scaling from the drawing. Timber mouldings, vac-form (or ABS) patterns and any 'bought' items must be chosen and indicated to prevent any future confusion. When creating design drawings, one should not be afraid of using more than one drawing. Although it is always easier for all concerned to have one drawing per piece of set, it is more important to have the whole piece detailed adequately.

Figure 3-03 has the front and side elevations of a set that represented an American clapboard house of the 19th century. For clarity, this drawing has been stripped of much detail, but the full (A0) version – coupled with a plan view, sections and details – gave all relevant information required to establish a firm budget.

E)   Specification/design references/samples/model. The final design package will not usually consist solely of drawings. A **model** is always supplied for theatre productions: it greatly assists those who are to produce the construction drawings to see the proposed design in 3D. Drawing lists, design references such as photographs or period pictures, and samples of fabric, finishes, etc. will be supplied.

Museum work tends to generate a different sort of design package – a *huge* one. The highly bureaucratic, contractual, structured (and dare I say litigious?) nature of how museum work is organised results in the designer having to produce far more paperwork than other sides of our business would expect.

Besides incorporating all of the above, the package will include a **specification** – a hefty document that describes *extensively* every aspect of the design, including graphics, exhibits, risk assessments, 'good practice' in workmanship, etc. The contractor must faithfully follow the instructions contained in the specification in order to comply with his own contract. Any variations must be approved *in writing*. This specification needs to be treated with respect – always study it carefully. Contractual obligations are inherent within the package and, if working for a contractor, your employer's profit and loss is inextricably linked to this document.

Finally, when supplying a design package, try to achieve the following goal: if the designer were to disappear tomorrow, the <u>whole</u> project would be able to reach a perfect conclusion from the information supplied within the package.

SURVEY DRAWINGS

An on-site survey should be undertaken for all productions, regardless of any trust held in a venue's own plans. Many venues have out-of-date drawings or drawings that are not dimensioned and/or have stretched to such a degree as to make them untrustworthy to scale from (which, as we know, is not a prudent thing to do anyway). For the sake of being able to sleep at night, why not check a few dimensions?

Survey drawings are drawn from a survey sketch – the paper(s) upon which dimensions were placed during the actual survey. Nobody will 'read' the survey sketch other than the surveyor(s). Chapter 6 on Surveying deals with the practical aspects of undertaking a survey, including comments on the survey sketch.

Some productions (particularly in museum work) really do require a full survey drawing to be produced. This will be a drawing that serves no other purpose than to show and dimension what exists in an 'empty' venue – and may be used by many others involved in the project. Other projects may simply require that an accurate representation of the existing venue be shown, within which the set is drawn. The drawing simply 'shows' the existence of the venue, having no need for its actual measurements. Theatre productions tend to use this method – the 'General Arrangement' drawings. *However*, even when this type of drawing is the one issued, it is always prudent for the draughtsman to keep a separate, full survey drawing – as described above – that is 'empty' of the set.

The function of a survey drawing is easily remembered: it is *to provide a mathematical representation of an existing venue (or part of a venue) in three dimensions*, from which – should the need ever occur – the venue could then be replicated at full size.

When producing survey drawings, consider the following:

A) A full survey drawing must be dimensioned in the simplest way possible, and the dimensions shown must be adequate for the maths to form a clear logic. This means translating the complex mass of information from your survey sketch into a straightforward set of maths: you must make it as simple as possible for others to be able to set out the shapes. This can involve much laborious work – it is easier to do when drawing with CAD.

B) Remember that the survey drawing may have to perform two functions. The first is obviously to supply the perimeters within which the construction drawings are bounded. The second may be to establish setting-lines for the crew who first install the set; for example, you may state that the setting-line is a string pulled from point A to point B, and that the set is placed 1000 mm upstage of that. Information of this sort is vital to the set-builder's draughtsmen. In short, the survey should include the relationship between the forthcoming production and the venue.

C) It is a good idea to draw the survey drawing at the same scale as the production's ground-plan. By doing this, it becomes easy to overlay one drawing upon the other, should the need arise (it also maintains the visual sense of continuity within the drawing pack).

D) Survey drawings tend to be re-used many times. Always store them and update the information they contain as and when future changes occur.

MATHS/GEOMETRY DRAWINGS

It is frequently desirable for the draughtsman to produce a drawing that only illustrates the maths/geometry of the shapes involved. This may be in reference to the whole set, or just one part of it. The drawing may, for example, allow the carpenters to set out the upper, 18 mm ply surface of

an odd-shaped floor or truck. However, the drawing may be issued for the sole practical use of the draughtsman: when producing the construction drawings he has only to glance at the maths/geometry drawing to confirm the critical angles or dimensions – to 'see the wood for the trees', as it were.

These drawings will often be produced after the survey and may therefore incorporate the maths of the venue along with the maths of the set. Once pinned on the wall above the drawing board, the draughtsman can now confidently proceed with the construction drawings, safe in the knowledge that the mathematical criteria have been set down and proved. All subsequent drawings will conform to the mathematical model constructed in this drawing. These drawings are the draughtsman's own 'comfort blanket', the rock upon which all else is secured.

Having stated that, frequently, it is only the draughtsman who will need and use drawings of this kind, include them nevertheless in the final 'package' of drawings. They may be of great use to the following: the production manager, if he is the type who truly understands the importance of the setting-out; the master carpenter if they are likewise interested; the foreman carpenter/set-builder, who may want this drawing as an aid to setting-out and checking his work; and contractors who are building pieces of the set, and will want their draughtsman to have this drawing.

Bear in mind that you may well be asked to produce this type of drawing *alone* – a project may only require your input to the maths and geometry. It is not unknown for one person to be asked to supply the survey drawing and to follow it with the basic geometric setting-out of the whole piece – others will then take on the rest of the drawing programme.

CONSTRUCTION DRAWINGS
('Bench Drawings')

These show exactly how the various trades will construct a piece of scenery. They will be used directly by those building the set, but indirectly studied by others involved in the production: the designer, for example – for him to approve the detail of what is being proposed. It is common for the construction drawings to have to be signed-off by the designer (or others) before being issued to the workshop.

The older term, 'Bench Drawings' describes more precisely what their **function is**: for use on the workbench. (Note that design drawings marked 'For Construction' usually require development into true construction drawings. The former need only indicate acceptable or preferred construction methods, and are really just an authorisation to build.)

It is quite usual (but certainly not prerequisite) for construction drawings to be drawn by a tradesman (carpenter or engineer) who, having gained experience of practical bench and/or stage work, moves into the drawing office. Obviously, the complete knowledge of a trade greatly helps in drawing something that will be built by that trade; however, it is quite possible for a layman to acquire enough knowledge to draw satisfactory construction drawings. In this business it is common for pieces to be constructed by

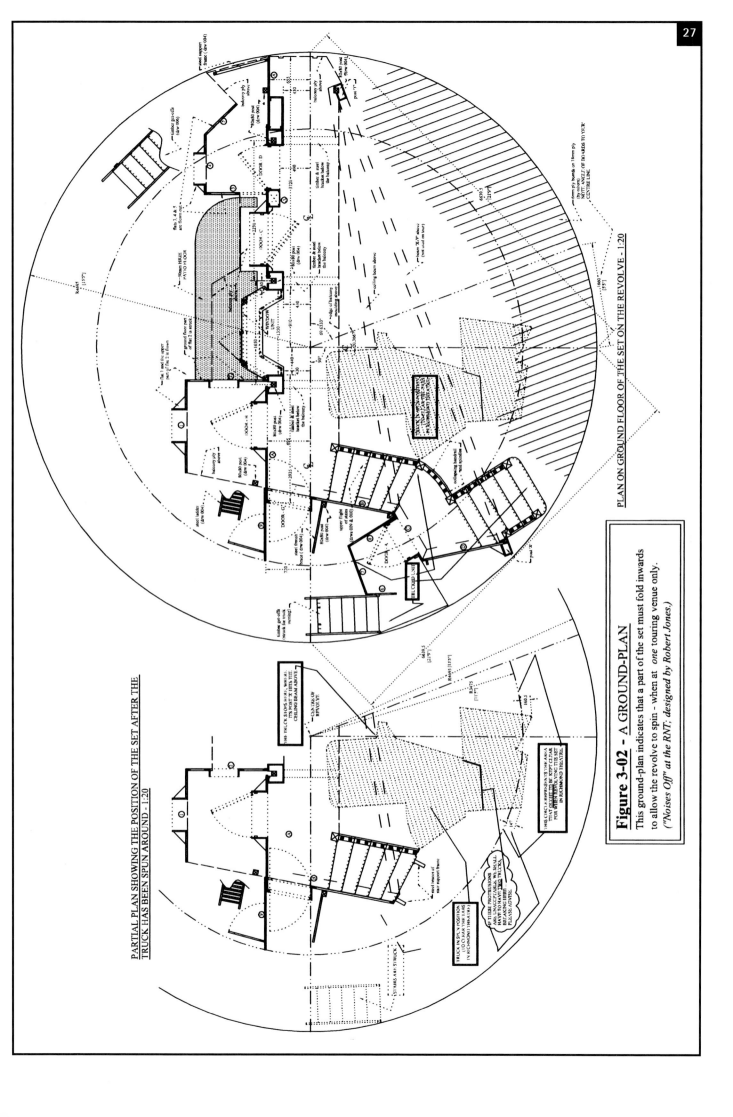

PARTIAL PLAN SHOWING THE POSITION OF THE SET AFTER THE TRUCK HAS BEEN SPUN AROUND - 1:20

PLAN ON GROUND FLOOR OF THE SET ON THE REVOLVE - 1:20

Figure 3-02 - A GROUND-PLAN

This ground-plan indicates that a part of the set must fold inwards to allow the revolve to spin - when at *one* touring venue only.
("Noises Off" at the RNT; designed by Robert Jones.)

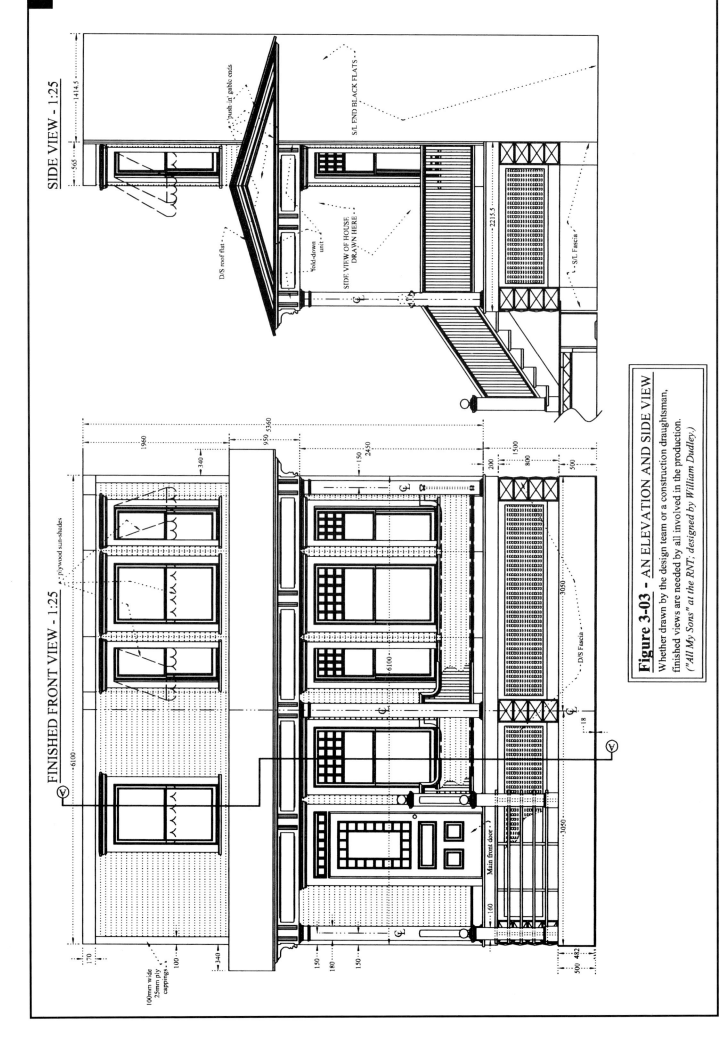

SIDE VIEW - 1:25

FINISHED FRONT VIEW - 1:25

Figure 3-03 – AN ELEVATION AND SIDE VIEW

Whether drawn by the design team or a construction draughtsman, finished views are needed by all involved in the production. (*"All My Sons" at the RNT: designed by William Dudley.*)

several trades, but of course, only one person (who is unlikely to have worked in all trades) will usually draw it. Experience is an esoteric attribute, impossible to teach; but don't spend time worrying about how to acquire experience. It is quite simple to attain: just give it time!

Paradoxically, although construction drawings involve a very wide range of knowledge (much of which is specialist knowledge), there is no need here for vast, wordy descriptions or explanations of how to produce them. The drawings need to be *understood* by tradesmen, it is as simple as that! It is not within the realms of this book to teach a trade (or trades – carpentry *and* engineering); however, 'Part Two – 'Scenic Construction' – does illustrate enough basic data to understand the main principles of construction.

Consider the following, common-sense issues when producing construction drawings:

A) **If in doubt, ask.** Whatever you draw will be built, or the attempt made (at cost), so be sure that it is practical. It is simple to telephone somebody who does have answers to your queries, so do it. Nobody will thank you for a pretty drawing that ultimately costs the show time and money.

B) **Do not attempt to draw something of which you are unsure:** *it could be dangerous.* Use common sense here: if an item is structural (i.e. load bearing) then be sure you know how to build it safely. If you are not confident, then do not draw it (or, attempt it, but clearly label the drawing 'Suggested Construction Only – Please Confirm').

C) Some jobs can only be drawn by a **qualified structural engineer.** If this is the case, then do not be too shy to say so. Frequently, it is the draughtsman who first becomes aware that a structural engineer needs to be involved. Be self-confident enough to refuse to attempt to draw what is beyond you. You will be thanked for this. In some cases – subject to the structural engineer's approval – the draughtsman may still produce the drawing from verbal information supplied by the engineer; the drawing is then presented to the structural engineer for him to check, 'prove' with calculations and sign off. The drawing can then be issued.

D) **Economy, durability and tradecraft** are the aims of the construction draughtsman. Construction drawings are the most difficult and exacting drawings to produce. All dimensions, materials, fixings, etc. must be shown in a clear fashion – that is the **minimum** requirement – but the successful construction drawing will also display the draughtsman's inherent knowledge of the most efficient way of building something.

E) The construction draughtsman will often have **more information about a project than anyone else involved.** As such, he or she is the centre of an information web. Get-in door sizes, truck or container sizes, crew numbers, scene changes, actors' movements, budget and programme will all affect how items are built. Therefore, always ensure that this knowledge is passed on through the medium of the drawings.

F) When drawing construction, **try to enter the mind of the tradesman** who will be using the drawing, and try to think of the chronological steps that must be taken from the beginning to the completion of that particular piece. On the **plan view**, give a number to each relevant piece of set, so that elevations can be matched to the plan. Always supply a **finished elevation** to show the completed piece – the

craftsmen need to see the end result of what they are about to build. **Figure 3-04** shows four elevations on a large exhibition stand; when read with the plan (not shown here), parts can be named or numbered, and the general 'geography' be understood. **Figure 3-05** has a simple elevation and section of a large theatre flat. Again, parts can be identified, numbered or commented upon. A glance at the section shows that the flat is 'leaning back' to the audience and sits upon (and around) a steel truck that has a raking top.

Draw each piece in stages if necessary: the basic skeletal framework first, then any additions that are applied to that frame, and so on, culminating with any final decorative 'decor' applicable. **Figure 3-06** includes three general construction views (of *many*) of a complicated piece of set – a collapsing church tower with an 'exploding' spire. The front elevation is split vertically, one side showing timber cladding, the other the steel core. The side section and side view show timber and steel, and they indicate where the next, lower piece of set is placed. These straightforward drawings were necessary for the later, more detailed drawings to be understood.

It is a universal human characteristic to understand drawings by **progression**: start with the finished view, then the support 'skeleton', then the details.

G) **Draw detail at a good large scale** that is easy to read – tradesmen hate having to squint and study a drawing amidst the chaos of a workshop.

H) **When drawing steel-work which is to be clad by carpenters**, it may be suitable to draw the steel-work separately from the wood-work, but it is always advisable to indicate both the timber cladding on the steel drawings and the steel on the timber drawings. Each trade is better off being made aware of the other trade's requirements.

I) Keep informed of new developments in tradecraft, and be well-stocked with up-to-date **brochures** of goods and materials used. The appearance of new materials or new fads in using certain established materials necessitates having to be aware of many types of goods – brochures are perfect for containing all relevant information. It's also important to know current costs.

'AS-BUILT' DRAWINGS

When drawing productions that are permanent or semi-permanent installations (having a specified 'lifetime' agreed in the contract, such as museum projects), the client may often want 'as-built' drawings. These are a full set of drawings that accurately describe the work *as it was finally built* – not as it was *intended* to be built – and are required for future maintenance work as well as for the execution of a safe 'strip-out' when the job is eventually removed.

There is little to say about this type of drawing, except to point out the obvious fact that it can save the draughtsman an awful amount of work if he knows *in advance* that these drawings will be needed. If known, it is a relatively simple matter to have a pack of copies of the original drawings upon which any workshop or on-site alterations can be annotated, say in red ballpoint pen. Then, when the job is complete, all drawings can be updated and re-issued. Close liaison is required between the draughtsman and the on-site foreman to ensure that all changes are recorded.

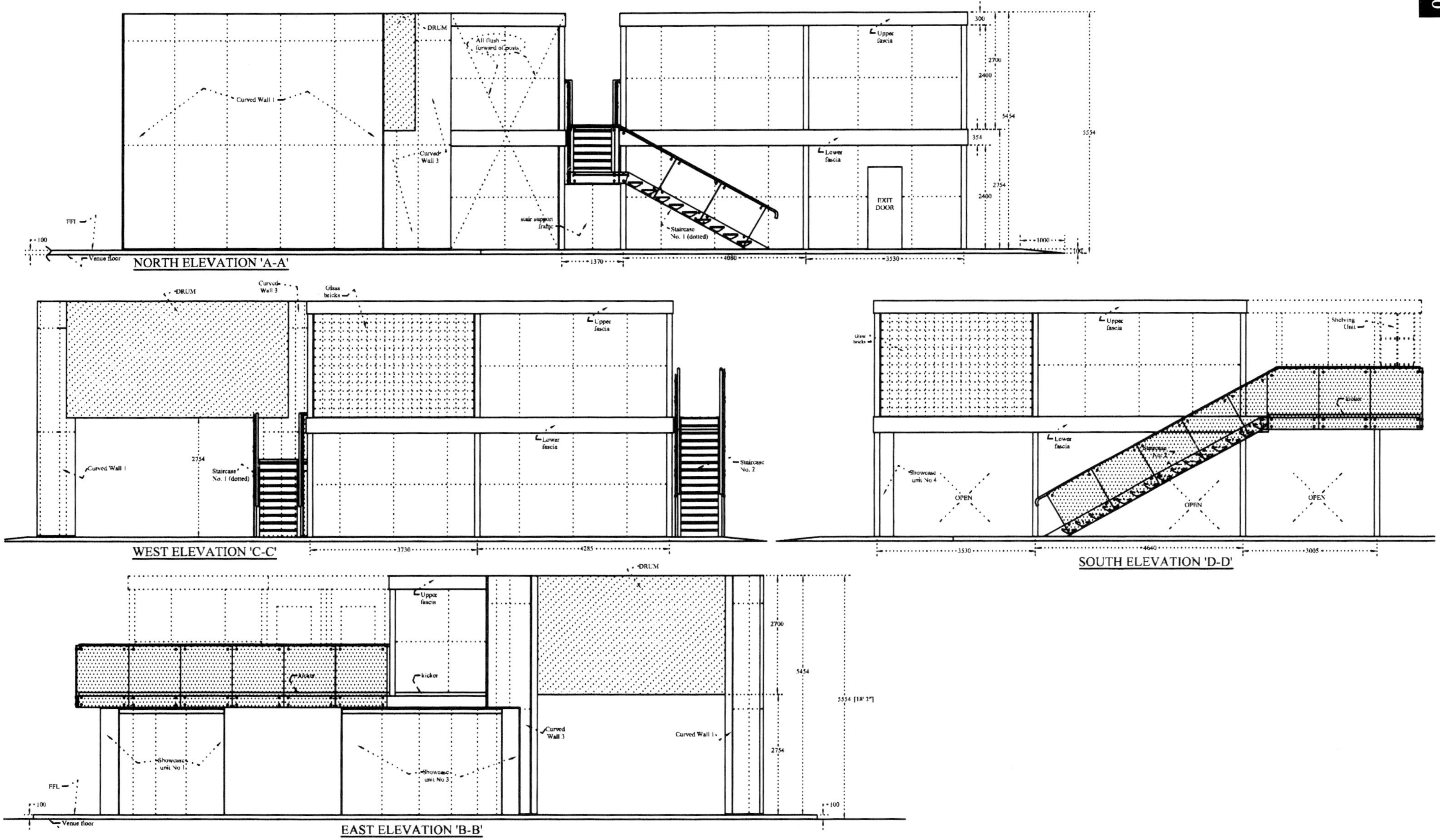

Figure 3-04 – ELEVATIONS ON A 'DOUBLE-DECKER' STAND
All four elevations, stripped of detail, of an exhibition stand. *(designed by Imagination.)*

FINISHED ELEVATION

SECTION

Figure 3-05 - A FINISHED VIEW ON A MAIN FLAT

The finished view is the basis upon which the construction drawings are founded. Coupled with the section, this view allows the whole scheme to be understood. *("Private Lives" at the RNT; designed by Stephen Brimson-Lewis.)*

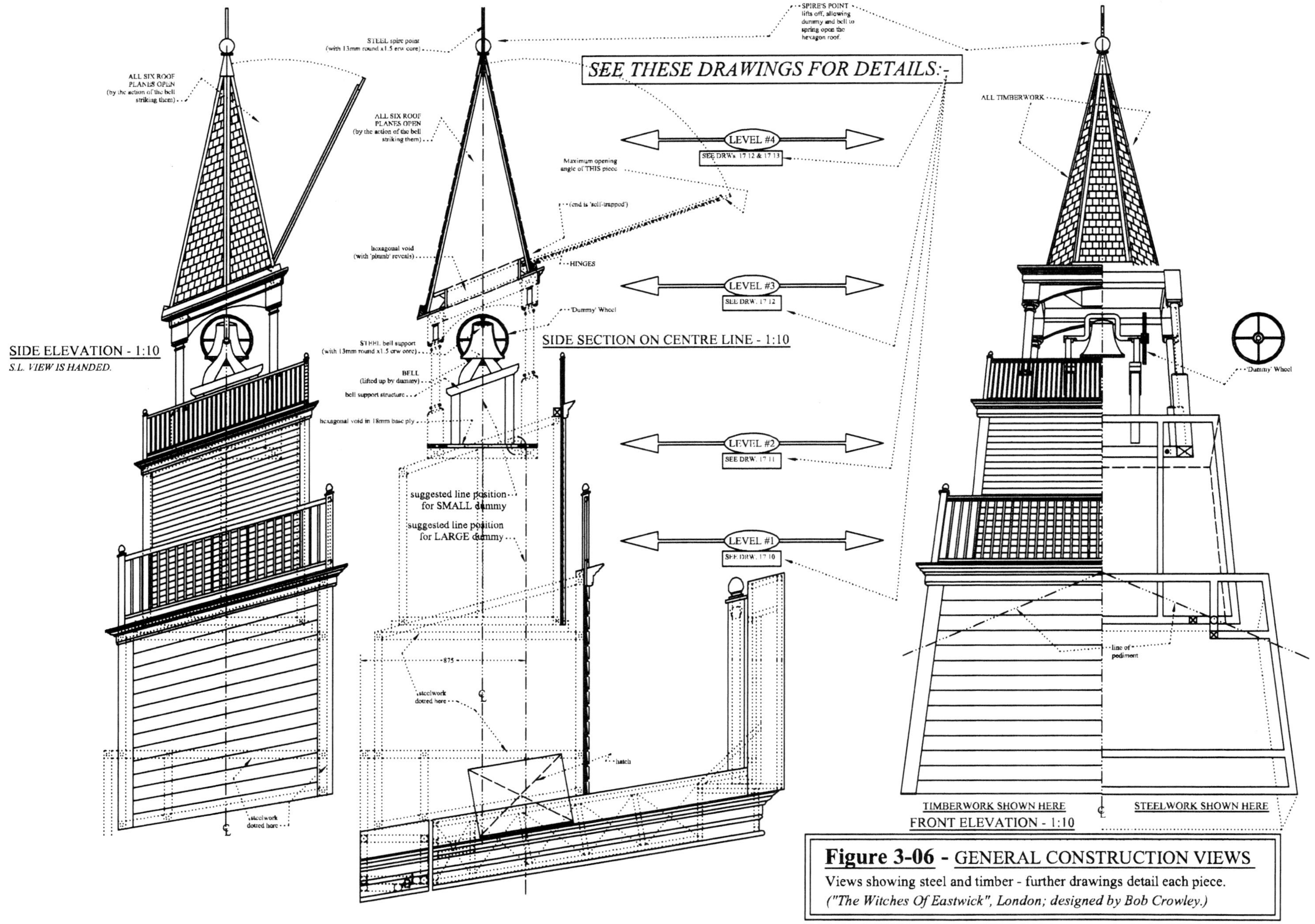

Figure 3-06 - GENERAL CONSTRUCTION VIEWS

Views showing steel and timber – further drawings detail each piece.

("The Witches Of Eastwick", London; designed by Bob Crowley.)

FRONT ELEVATION - 1:10

STEELWORK SHOWN HERE

TIMBERWORK SHOWN HERE

ALL TIMBERWORK

Dummy Wheel

line of pediment

SEE THESE DRAWINGS FOR DETAILS:-

SPIRE'S POINT
lifts off, allowing
dummy and bell to
spring upon the
hexagon roof.

Maximum opening
angle of THIS piece.

(end is 'bell-shaped')

HINGES

Dummy Wheel

LEVEL #4
SEE DRW. 17.12 & 17.13

LEVEL #3
SEE DRW. 17.12

LEVEL #2
SEE DRW. 17.11

LEVEL #1
SEE DRW. 17.10

SIDE SECTION ON CENTRE LINE - 1:10

STEEL spire pour
(with 13mm round x 1.5 core core)

ALL SIX ROOF
PLANES OPEN
(by the action of the bell
striking them)

hexagonal void
(with 'plumb' reveals)

STEEL bell support
(with 13mm round x 1.5 core core)

BELL
(lifted up by dummy)

bell support structure

hexagonal void in 18mm birch ply

suggested line position
for SMALL dummy

suggested line position
for LARGE dummy

latch

steelwork
dotted here

875

SIDE ELEVATION - 1:10

S.L. VIEW IS HANDED.

ALL SIX ROOF
PLANES OPEN
(by the action of the bell
striking them)

steelwork
dotted here

4 • Drawing Equipment

As with any profession involving the use of specialist equipment, it soon becomes apparent that it is always worth buying the best-quality equipment available. Drawing equipment is expensive, but the better the quality, the longer it will last (and retain its precision). It can be worth dealing with one supplier for your needs; make it clear to a supplier that you are professional and intend to use their services, and you should obtain a decent 'trade' discount. Consider doing likewise with a print or copy shop.

The following points are not meant to be exhaustive, and there is bound to be equipment that has been omitted here – different countries naturally display different preferences. Just ensure that the tools you use most are of the best quality and that you are comfortable with them.

1   Drawing manually and with CAD

In recent years, technology has enabled the draughtsman to choose between drawing manually and drawing by computer – CAD (*Computer Aided Drawing*). Most have chosen the CAD option, and more will certainly do so. It is still common to use both methods, although once CAD has been embarked upon, manual drawing loses its appeal somewhat. Remember, though, that CAD is only a tool. It is a very clever pen, but it does not draw for you and may not make you a more adept draughtsman – just more adept at CAD. Its accuracy depends solely upon what you, the operator, tell it ... and so mistakes made in CAD are *your* mistakes. The machine only reacts to your input. Having said this, CAD *is* a very efficient means to an end – the end being the drawings.

In our industry, a CAD drawing is not necessarily a *quicker* drawing to produce – this is important to realise, because it is rarely mentioned. Our work tends not to be repetitive; we continually draw 'from scratch' and a new, original drawing can take as long to produce in CAD as it does manually. An example of this may be when drawing your own finished view of, say, a house exterior, from a copy of the designer's undimensioned drawing. Each line has to be scaled from the design drawing and transferred to your own drawing – and changed, if necessary, to suit your needs. This process usually takes as long in CAD as it would manually.

Drawing 'wavy' or 'artistic' lines on the computer can be time-consuming. For example, a large, fretted or cut-out scenic tree will require an accurate drawing of the designer's vision of the finished tree: manually, one might simply trace his drawing – the pen being so simple to use when tracing irregular shapes. To *draw* all the differing leaves and branches using CAD would take an unthinkably long time. (Of course, it may not need drawing at all, if the designer can have the image 'scanned' into computer format – *see* below.)

When first learning CAD, I would recommend attending a short course in order to become comfortable with general concepts and procedures. (I did not do this and, frankly, I regret it – any self-taught skill tends to induce 'bad habits' that are then difficult to eradicate.)

Some advantages of CAD are:

A) It becomes so much simpler and quicker to alter a drawing in CAD – and to transfer some or all of it to another drawing. When drawing manually, it is heartbreaking to have to destroy a 'skin' and re-draw it in order to incorporate an alteration. Even to make a minor change involves scratching and re-drawing, each time causing further damage to the skin and resulting in copies of poorer quality. In CAD, alterations are made to the drawing on-screen, then printed (duly revised) – and re-drawing has been avoided. When manually transferring drawing information to another drawing, tracing or re-drawing is necessary. In CAD, it is simple to transfer all or part of a drawing to another, regardless of scale.

B) The ability to '**copy and paste**' any part, or all, of one drawing to another or to a different part of the same drawing is one of CAD's major advantages. Nothing needs to be drawn twice. Any object on a drawing, or the whole drawing, can be moved, re-scaled, copied, arrayed in chosen patterns, rotated, erased, etc. with comparative ease.

C) '**Blocks**' are extremely useful when using CAD: you simply decide to create a separate file (drawing) of any object that has been drawn or imported into the computer. This means, in effect, that once you have drawn an M10 bolt and nut (or imported a drawing of one from elsewhere), it can be saved as a 'block' – named 'M10 nut and bolt' – and used again and again in future drawings. Temporary blocks can be created to ease the process of copying/moving/rotating large, complex objects about the drawing.

D) '**Layers**' are another fundamentally important tool that the CAD provides. Imagine drawing on two layers of glass: one layer is called 'timber' and is drawn in red ink; the other, 'steel', is drawn in blue. If these were placed over one another, you would see the steel and the timber in relation to each other. Layers in CAD use this simple principle – but there are limitless layers available for you to name and colour as you see fit, all within the same drawing. You may then simply turn these layers on or off: if layer 'timber' is turned off, only the 'steel' layer is revealed for working on or printing. Layers can be given distinctive line types (dots, dashes, etc.) and colours.

E) **Dimensions** are easier to draw in CAD. The text is always clearer – a vast choice of fonts is available. More importantly, you 'ask' the CAD the length or angle of something, and it 'prints' the answer. Always read this answer; if you know it to be incorrect then either the drawing is wrong, or the length between wrong points has been requested (the latter being surprisingly easy to do!).

CAD also has measuring tools that allow the user to ask for all information concerning the geometry of drawn circles, lines, ellipses, etc. without that information being 'placed on the drawing' – i.e. it is only shown on the screen. Therefore, it is very easy, and prudent, to ask for information in order to confirm the accuracy of what is being drawn.

F) **Labelling and title blocks** are again easier and clearer in CAD. Title blocks and borders are simply copied from drawing to drawing, or templates are made which ensure that all drawings maintain the same identity. It is simple to change the title block to suit the project (import a client's logo, etc.). When labelling – adding notes and arrows to items on a drawing – there is a great choice as to how the note looks, giving control of emphasis over which notes are to be most highly visible.

G) **Shading and hatching** is, again, far simpler in CAD and the choices offered are vast.

H) **Information flow and drawing distribution** are two of CAD's main advantages. Drawings can be e-mailed anywhere in the world within minutes, or can be passed on via floppy disc or CD. External information can be 'scanned' into drawings. This can be most useful to contractors working upon the same set: for example, a steelwork contractor can e-mail drawings of a steel skeleton to the carpentry contractor who – once the drawing has been checked – can simply import it and begin drawing the timber cladding directly onto the steel. He no longer has to physically draw that steel.

I) **Geometry** – or rather, the use of geometry – alters somewhat when changing from manual drawing to CAD: a subtle change of 'mind-set' as to the use of geometry occurs. It does change the way you think about and then draw objects. Three points leap to mind:

(i) The drawing of most geometric shapes becomes far simpler. For example, when drawing a hexagon one simply 'asks' for a polygon of six sides plotted around, or within, a circle of a given radius, and it 'draws itself'.

(ii) Information can be placed into the computer without first having to work out figures with the calculator. For example, when drawing by hand, survey information has to be converted into mathematical information (sides of triangles, etc.) before lines can be drawn and dimensioned, whereas in CAD the actual survey dimensions are entered and drawn. Any dimensions can then be 'asked for'. To clarify that point: surveys are a series of triangles that are drawn from fixed points within the venue. By hand, one has to calculate the positions and angles of points on the drawing before they can be drawn and dimensioned. In CAD, if you know that a point is 5000 mm from fixed point 'A' and 7000 mm from fixed point 'B', you simply draw a circle of radius 5000 mm centred on point 'A', a circle of 7000 mm from point 'B', and where the circles cross will be the point desired (a third fixed point, 'C', is always advisable for use as a 'check dim'). In CAD you draw accurately, then ask for the dimension text. Calculators are used far less regularly, the benefit being that human error is minimised.

(iii) The almost frightening accuracy of the computer tends to make you draw a shape using simple geometry (because geometry cannot be wrong), rather than – as when producing manual work – drawing a reasonable fac-

simile of the shape and then dimensioning it correctly, using the calculator. In other words, you have to draw very accurately in CAD by using geometry in order that the computer can be confidently asked for any dimension. Remember that when drawing in CAD, you are drawing the objects at full size, so accuracy is prerequisite (for printing, the drawing is 'reduced' to, say, 1:25). A line drawn by hand at 1:25 is never meant to be 100% true – the dimension it is given is accurate; but a line drawn in CAD has to be true, or the written dimension size will be wrong. Simple geometry produces highly accurate drawings, so when drawing in CAD, always use it as often as possible.

2 Equipment for CAD drawing

The basic equipment required to draw in CAD makes a mercifully short list. The speed at which technology changes has meant that most of this equipment needs replacing or updating every three to four years, depending on how necessary it is for you to be kept at the lively front line of technology. If you need to update, then do so – it tends to be clients who force the pace of change, often unwittingly, by suddenly sending you a drawing that your (ancient, cobwebb'd) computer cannot deal with. In truth, each update (or upgrade) *does* improve the efficiency of the tools and so should be carefully considered.

Because of the current speed of change, the following list is deliberately free of many technical specifications and recommendations – such things as computer memory increase by unimaginable amounts over a few years. To find out 'the latest', contact a couple of large computer suppliers and obtain brochures or prices, or look at their websites. There are countless fat books out there that satisfy the more passionate computer enthusiast – go for it, *when you are ready to buy*.

Most of the CAD users that I know have ordered their equipment from large computer suppliers for the simple reason that technical support (after-sales service) can be more reliable from the bigger companies. Always find out the details of technical support before buying.

A) **The computer** is obviously the nerve centre of all CAD equipment. It holds the **hard drive** which is controlled by computer chips and dictates the amount of information that can be handled or stored (e.g. 10GB). Go as high as you can afford: you will want to store a lot of drawings. Software is added (*see* 'G' below) which allows the use of the programmes chosen. The computer will hold a CD drive and a floppy disc drive (to import and export programmes, data, information, drawings, etc.). It has various 'ports' at the back into which 'cards' can be placed (video card, sound card, modem, etc.) as well as sockets connecting it to the monitor, keyboard, mouse, printer/plotter, etc. CAD programmes tend to use quite a lot of memory (more than, say, word processing) so ensure that the supplier is made aware of your intended CAD use before you purchase.

The processor ('chip') affects the speed that data is processed within the computer (e.g. 700MHz). Go as high as you can afford – in three years it will seem slow.

Memory or RAM – Random Access Memory – dictates the amount, and speed, of data than can be accessed. Again, go as high as you can afford: at the time of writing, 32MB RAM is the recommended minimum for many CAD programmes.

B) **The keyboard** is self-explanatory – a few standard types are available.

C) **The mouse** is used to direct actions on-screen. I would recommend that, for CAD, a mouse with a 'third wheel' be used, enabling you to zoom in and out of CAD drawings on-screen. (This sort of mouse has a left button, a right button and a small rubber wheel between the two: the wheel can be spun – to zoom in or out of the drawing – and can be clicked and held to 'drag' the drawing about on-screen.) Keep the mouse clean. The ball can be removed for cleaning and the inner wheels accessed (I pick off any fluff with something plastic, e.g. a ballpoint pen top). **Mouse mats** are required (a smooth pad of material allowing free passage of the mouse).

D) **The monitor** (television screen) offers greater benefits to the CAD user when its size is increased, it being the sole 'peep-hole' into the drawings. Monitor size is measured across the diagonal of the screen and 'screen resolution' defines how many 'pixels' are viewed (pixels are the points of 'light' – electronic information – that make up the whole image). Monitors allow for different screen resolutions to be chosen by the user; most CAD programmes demand a minimum resolution of 800 x 600 pixels; if one chooses a resolution of, say, 1152 x 864 pixels, a larger, sharper image is seen on the screen. More image is compressed into the screen – having the effect of reducing the size of the 'buttons' used by the software and providing a larger, clear 'drawing area'. Consequently, a large screen has a double benefit: the screen is physically larger and it can show an image of a higher resolution.

Unfortunately, the monitor represents a hefty proprotion of the cost of the entire CAD equipment, its price rising dramatically as screen size increases. If you cannot afford a 21" monitor, don't despair; I used a 17" monitor for a couple of years with no problems. You do get used to your monitor, and only get restless when you see how the world looks using a larger one. As in life.

E) **The modem** is a 'clever little black box' that connects the computer to the Internet – it can be situated inside the computer, of course. Again, it has a speed (e.g. 28,800 bps), and the faster the better – large CAD drawings, even when 'zipped' (*see* 'G' below) can be irritably time-consuming to e-mail. However, this problem may be short-lived: at the time of writing, Internet Service Providers (ISPs) are about to launch better/faster systems.

F) **A scanner** is a useful and cheap tool. Images on paper are 'read' by the scanner and fed into the computer in a format that allows the image to be brought up on screen, altered, re-coloured, re-sized, cropped, stored, e-mailed, printed and so on. It has great use in our business because it can hold various file formats (the formats of individual programmes) – thereby allowing for images to be imported in one format and converted to the format of the programme that you use (if you're lucky).

G) **Software** is the term given to the programmes that are added to the computer. The main software is the 'operating system' (e.g. Windows '98) which controls the way all programmes are to be run. Other software is added to the computer, as required. **CAD software** is usually bought in the form of a CD and placed into the computer. The choice of CAD software is considerable and it can be problematic deciding upon which one to use. Obviously, choose one that allows you free flow of electronic information with those individuals or companies with whom you communicate most frequently – in other words, ensure that the CADs can 'talk' to one another. Not all CAD programmes can easily share information with others, although, in most cases, a way can be found to save a format so that another CAD can read it. Individual software companies do ensure that all their products can 'talk' to one another, regardless of how old or new they are.

I chose to use *AutoCAD LT* ® software simply because I was advised that, in our business, *AutoCAD* ® is widely used across the world and I wanted to ensure that my software would accommodate as varied a client base as possible. (The 'LT' stands for 'light' – a reduced, cheaper version of full *AutoCAD* that omits certain 3D capabilities. This is a matter of personal choice.) After two years of use, I can only confirm the accuracy of this point of view – at the risk of being accused of 'product placement', this has been my experience, so it may be worth reporting. I have been able to exchange drawings freely by e-mail with Europe, the USA and the Far East. Once the initial software package has been purchased, future upgrades to newer versions are obtainable at cheaper rates. Upgrades seem to be arriving every two or three years. (*Autodesk*, the *Autodesk* logo, *AutoCAD* and *AutoCAD LT* are registered trademarks of *Autodesk, Inc.* in the USA and/or other countries.)

Zip software is highly recommended. It is a very cheap software package (easily downloaded via the Internet) that takes computer files and compresses ('zips') them for ease of e-mailing and/or storage. It somehow manages to compress large files that, when e-mailed, are 'unzipped' by the recipient (who also requires the necessary software, of course). This saves a lot of time when sending drawings by e-mail.

H) **A plotter** – a large printer – is required to print the CAD drawings. A1 plotters are available, as well as A0. Black-and-white plotters are cheaper than colour versions; plug-in cartridges add ink to the plotter. Paper can either be 'sheet fed' or 'roll fed': the former requires that each sheet of blank paper is manually fed into the machine; the latter takes its paper automatically from a large roll of paper, cutting off from the roll once plotted. I would definitely recommend opting for a roll-feed plotter – you simply add a 50 m roll of paper and let the machine do the rest.

I) Many types of **paper** can be plotted upon, and choosing which one is a matter of personal preference. Paper is graded by weight – the weight of one square metre of paper – and the higher the weight, the thicker it is. Many companies plot on thin white paper for bench work and maybe use a thicker type for drawings being sent to clients. I use only white 90 g/m^2 because I think that the extra thickness makes the drawings more robust and makes them appear cleaner. Below is a table showing standard (European) paper sizes. Remember that if A0 were to be cut in half along its longer side, the size of paper would now be A1; if that were cut in half along its longer side, A2 would remain, and so on. (See more about paper in the following section, 3 'R'.)

Table 4.1 *Standard (European) paper sizes*

Designation	Dimensions in mm	Surface area
A0	841 x 1189	1 square metre
A1	594 x 841	5000 sq. cm
A2	420 x 594	2500 sq. cm
A3	297 x 420	1250 sq. cm
A4	210 x 297	625 sq. cm

3 Equipment for manual drawing

A) Drawing boards vary from the home-made variety to professional machines that have an adjustable-height pedestal, adjustable-angled board, full drawing machine, lamp and equipment holder. The latter is ideal, if it can be afforded. It is certainly worth the investment, and remember that second-hand equipment is readily available at reasonable prices. Ensure that your board is faced with *Papyrobord* or similar facing material. This is an easy-clean surface that forms an ideal substrate for drawing. It is bought in sheet form, trimmed and stuck to the board with double-sided tape. When kept clean, it allows for a perfect surface on which to tape the paper and gives the correct amount of 'spring' beneath the paper when using pens or pencils. Ensure too that your board is comfortable to use and well lit. Use 'daylight' fluorescent tubes in the drawing lamp. Have a comfortable chair: adjustable gas-jet chairs are ideal.

B) T-squares are the old method of obtaining horizontal, parallel lines across the paper. The T-square is moved up and down manually. Set-squares (see 'F' below) are used to obtain vertical lines by sliding them along the arm of the T-square. Some dexterity is required to use these tools accurately, but as with most things, practice makes perfect.

C) Parallel motion boards are still in common use. They have a horizontal blade, attached to the board at each end, that slides up and down (again, set-squares are used to obtain vertical lines). Care is needed to ensure that the blade remains clean: try to remember, when erasing, to lift the blade above the point where you will be erasing, otherwise the rubber particles will fall between the paper and the blade, creating dirty smudges. Personally, I dislike this type of board – it is clumsy, grubby and makes it difficult to maintain accuracy when drawing. However, it is worth trying to master the technique as you may be asked to do some drawing abroad, and this type may be all that is on offer.

D) Drawing machines are the most practical type of manual drawing equipment in use. They have fully adjustable rulers that can sweep horizontally and vertically across the board, and incorporate 'click stop' angle settings every 15 degrees (as well as any manually set angle in between). Since this is the best type of manual drawing-aid it is also the most expensive – again, try to obtain a good-quality machine.

E) Portable boards can be very useful gadgets to own. I have a small (A3 size) *Rotring* board which has its own sliding rulers, etc. and have found it to be most useful for certain jobs. It can be used for making quick but clear drawings (details, etc.) when on-site or from one's hotel room. It takes up little space in a suitcase.

F) Set-squares are triangular-shaped pieces of plastic (usually) with a 90-degree corner and either two 45-degree corners, or a 30-degree and a 60-degree corner. They are handy for general use, but are essential if using parallel motion or T-square boards (see above). They come in various sizes. Keep them clean. Ensure that one face is suitable for use with pens (it will have a rebated edge that prevents ink from running underneath the set-square). An adjustable set-square is a very useful tool to have and is quite inexpensive.

G) Protractors are circular or semi-circular pieces of plastic that enable degrees to be marked on a drawing. I use these rarely, preferring to use the drawing machine or maths to establish an angle. The large type (aproximately 300 mm diameter) is quite handy.

H) French curves are bought as a set of three plastic curves that are of great use when drawing odd shapes. Ensure that one face is suited to pens. Keep them clean.

I) Compasses. The preferred size is a matter of personal choice: buy what feels most comfortable – a good average size would be ±170 mm long. Ensure that they have a pen attachment, spare points, and an extension arm. Try them out for comfort in the shop and check that they feel firm and secure during and after adjustment.

J) Beam compasses are essential, though quite expensive. They consist of a 'beam' of aluminium, 1000 mm long, with a pen or pencil holder at one end; along this beam slides a point, which becomes the centre of the circle that is to be drawn. Some pull apart into four sections for ease of use and carrying.

K) Pencils are largely a matter of personal choice. It does not matter whether you use wooden pencils, clutch pencils or propelling pencils (I favour a *Staedtler* clutch pencil with 2 mm, 3H leads and a *Staedtler* rotating sharpener). The type of lead preferred can vary according to the type of paper that is being drawn upon, and depend too on whether the drawing is to be finished in pencil or pen. As I produce ink drawings, my pencil lead is always 3H – this reads well enough and is easily erased after inking. It is common to use 5H for working lines and 2H for finishing when producing pencil drawings, but this is a guide only. Special pencils are made for use on polyester paper, for shading on tracing paper and for many other specific tasks. Keep them sharp is the only, rather obvious, point to make here.

L) Pens are the preferred way of producing clear drawings and it is worth buying the best affordable. Some pens are refillable while others use cartridges. The most commonly used sizes of nibs are 0.25 mm, 0.35 mm, 0.5 mm and 0.7 mm (these can be bought in sets of four); it is also prudent to have a 0.10 mm for very fine work, and a 2 mm for thick lines. It is important to clean your pens thoroughly and regularly; do this with running water at a sink, taking the pen apart and cleaning each piece. Soak the pens occasionally in a proprietary pen-cleaning fluid. Ordinary nibs work well on tracing paper, but you will need tungsten-tipped nibs for work on polyester paper, as this material will wear out ordinary nibs very quickly. Spare nibs are easily obtained. In truth, it is well worth having tungsten-tipped pens for all use because of their longevity: I used the same four *Rotring* pens and nibs for seven years without a single problem.

Ordinary **ink** is fine for tracing paper, but etching ink is required for polyester. Black is the clearest colour, both for visibility on the 'skin' and for subsequent paper copies.

There are various gadgets for holding the pens and preventing them from drying out. I favour a simple plastic container that has four holes into which the pens are placed, and a tray below for holding a few drops of water within a sponge (this straightforward gadget is often sold as part of a set of four pens). Some pen storage units require no water.

M) Erasers need little explanation. Two types are required: white pencil erasers (*Staedtler Mars Plastic Soft* is a good example) and ink erasers. Both need to be kept clean – a rub on the carpet does this efficiently. Use an ink eraser that incorporates a cleaning fluid within the eraser material itself, such as the yellow *Rotring T30*. When erasing ink from a drawing, scratch the line off with a blade, then carefully rub over the area with an ink eraser; this will repair the paper's surface so that the next line that is drawn over that area does not appear fuzzy. When scratching-off ink, hold the blade at a very shallow angle to the paper; failure to do this will result in deeply scored scratches that may appear on copies of the drawing. Many use a razor blade for scratching; I prefer a *Stanley* **knife blade** with one end wrapped in masking tape (for safety). Do ensure that you remove the blade's protective film of oil before use. Bitter experience will teach you that heavy scratching on tracing paper will often be plainly visible when the drawing is copied using dye-line machines.

N) Scale rules come in various shapes and sizes. I prefer the triangular-shaped type rather than the flattened ones. Again, get the best that you can buy – this tool will dictate how accurately your drawing will be drawn! Each manufacturer has scale rules that accommodate various scales on the same rule. The one that I use most is a *Rotring* No. 802024 incorporating the scales: 1:10/100, 1:15/150, 1:25/250, 1:20/200, 1:50/500, and 1:33⅓. (I find *Rotring* scale rules to be clearer and easier on the eye than other makes.) I use other scale rules for 1:75, etc. **Imperial scale rules** may also need to be purchased (for drawing American work – *see* also page 12); they adopt a slightly more confusing convention and require great care when first using them. For example, 1" to 1' may be read across the rule in one direction, while ½" to 1' may be read in the opposite direction (causing some confusion in the middle!). It is possible to obtain various versions of scale rules that convert metric/imperial scales.

O) Straight edges are invaluable, but expensive. Try to have a 1000 mm clear plastic straight edge that has a steel insert along one edge (for knifing) and non-slip pads on the back face. Keep the edges protected! Ensure that it is pen-friendly.

P) Masking tape is used to hold drawing paper on to the board. There are specialist masking tapes made for draughting but, in truth, I have always found that the cheapest masking tape usually works best. It is the bane of a draughtsman's life to be forever re-sticking down the drawing paper (this is because of the unavoidable fact that tracing paper stretches and shrinks according to humidity). Be patient and keep on smoothing it out and re-sticking until it settles down a little.

Q) Buy the **calculator** that you are most comfortable with. It should be a 'scientific' one – one that includes scientific or engineering functions, and I recommend that it have more than one memory and a clear face, and be battery-powered rather than solar-powered. Get into the habit of checking that it is set in the correct mode.

R) Tracing paper (*see* also page 12) will probably be the main type of paper that you will use. It is sold in different sizes and in grades of thickness, expressed as 'grams per square metre': 60 g/m^2 is very thin, 110 g/m^2 is thick. For your main drawings use 110 g/m^2, as its thickness makes it behave better and allows for more scratching-out than the thinner types. **Polyester paper** is very much stronger, but more expensive and requires etching ink and tungsten nibs.

S) Travelling. If you are asked to work abroad, or anywhere other than your normal place of work, you may be unsure of the drawing facilities available. This can be worrying if you have become used to a good-quality drawing machine, for example, and you will naturally be concerned that if you now have to draw on a parallel motion board (of dubious quality) you will be slower and less efficient. Well, you will be – but by no means as slow as you might imagine: within a day or two your dexterity will overcome the shortcomings quite effectively. However, be prepared for the worst and take every possible drawing aid with you. By this I mean take set-squares, protractors and all the basic equipment that you would need if the drawing board were to be truly awful. Finally, when transporting equipment, ensure that you place each item in its original case: it is imperative that scale rules do not become chipped at the edges or set-squares dented, etc. Drawing equipment is expensive, designed for precision work and can be damaged through carelessness. Take care of the tools of your livelihood.

5 • Materials Commonly Specified

It is imperative that the draughtsman be familiar with the materials that he specifies for use through the medium of his drawings. Maintaining awareness of new developments is equally important. Obviously, in our business, this is a mammoth task: in a sense, each production 're-invents the wheel' and so the array of materials that may be used is vast. The safest way of attempting to keep abreast of this subject is to wholeheartedly enter the brochure culture – in other words, become an avid collector of brochures. This can be addictive. Good! Just say yes! Get into the habit of noting the telephone numbers of companies that you spot who supply goods that you may, one day, find a use for. Certain suppliers will produce brochures to which you find yourself referring on a weekly basis (brochures for steel and plywood/MDF leap to mind). In such cases ensure that you are kept up to date with the most recent of those brochures.

The following pages contain only very basic information on materials that you would expect to be specifying regularly. It would be impractical (and painfully boring) to attempt to take this any further because, firstly, the subject is too vast; secondly, the information would soon be out of date; and thirdly, the best, most up-to-date information will come from the brochures that you *must* collect from suppliers local to yourself. A few of the more unusual items that may be of some use have been included.

When specifying a material, ensure that it meets with the Fire Classification of the project on which you are working and check that its cost is not prohibitive. Ensure that it is structurally suitable for the task in hand. Add the supplier's name and telephone number to the drawing if it is an unusual material or you want a specific item from a specific manufacturer. If necessary, obtain samples from the supplier.

If in doubt as to what materials to specify, either express that doubt on the drawing in a clear, unembarrassed fashion, or ask for advice from the individual trade foreman involved. Remember that the foreman carpenter, or engineer, or prop maker is only a telephone call away, and is frequently the person who orders the materials.

1 Timber

Timber can be **softwood** (coniferous) or **hardwood** (deciduous). Softwood is the most common timber used in construction; hardwood, we all recognise as being used for furniture and high-class second fixing (the visible finishes in a building, such as skirting, architrave, doors, panelling, etc.). Softwood is cheaper than hardwood and some hardwoods are becoming rare enough to have restrictions placed upon their availability. Softwood is not classed as having inherent flameproof qualities, although many fire authorities allow untreated softwood to be used *over 25 mm (1") thick*. Hardwood is considered to be inherently flameproof for most projects (a slight anomaly here: balsa wood is classed as being a hardwood, yet it does not 'feel' as if it is flameproof). Timber can be treated with flameproof material at the timber plant.

Most of the timber that you draw will be softwood. Use hardwood sparingly: for furniture, if necessary, for the 'lipping' of edges prone to wear, for use as skids or runners and for tasks that would cause softwood to wear or fail.

Timber is ordered either **rough sawn** (coarse, splintery, not planed), or **par** ('planed all round', i.e. smooth and finished). Remember that timber is always sawn first, then planed if required; therefore a piece of 50 x 50 R/S (2" x 2"), when planed, becomes 45 x 45 par (1¾" x 1¾"). If you wish to specify a particular **finished size**, say 45 x 25, then write it as '45 x 25 finish'.

Overleaf is a table of commonly available timber sizes. In truth, you can order virtually any timber size, but those shown are the sections that you will be specifying most often. Note that you may have to specify timber sizes other than those listed (for example, tall flats require the timber to be '70 x 25 finish' or '2¾" x 1" finish') and so the 'lead time' – delivery time – may be extended.

2 Plywood and MDF

Plywood is a strong sheet material that can be manufactured in various ways to suit specific tasks. The more laminations, the stronger the plywood – birch plywood is the strongest, but is expensive. Plywood can be flameproof to Class 1 and to Class 0 – (check with the supplier), and it can be interior grade, or exterior, waterproof, boil-proof, etc. For ease of expression the imperial size is still used colloquially, as in 'eight by four' (8' x 4', or 2440 mm x 1220 mm). However, note that if a plywood is referred to as being 'four by eight' (4' x 8', or 1220 mm x 2440 mm), it means that the grain is running across the *narrow* width of the board ('short grain' ply) as opposed to the more usual *long* side of the board ('long grain ply'). The direction of grain will affect the plywood's strength and its ability to form a smooth curve, if that is what is required. (Looking in plan view upon a curved piece of plywood – looking at its edge/thickness – it bends easier if one is looking down at the end grain.)

MDF (medium density fibreboard) has become popular in recent years, although less so in the theatre world. It is cheap, easy to work and facilitates a very good finish. It can be a little heavy and does not repair easily; it is also susceptible to damp, and reacts by swelling and buckling. Class 1 and Class 0 grades are available.

Details of **blockboard, softboard, chipboard, mineral board** and many other sheet materials have not been detailed here because they are used less often in our industry. When you do need to use them, or want to know more about them,

Table 5.01 *Commonly available timber sizes*

Rough Sawn Imperial (in)	Par Imperial (in)	Rough Sawn Metric (mm)	Par Metric (mm – +/-)
1 x 1	$^7/_8$ x $^7/_8$	25 x 25	21 x 21
2 x 1	$1^3/_4$ x $^7/_8$	50 x 25	45 x 21
3 x 1	$2^3/_4$ x $^7/_8$	75 x 25	70 x 21
4 x 1	$3^3/_4$ x $^7/_8$	100 x 25	95 x 21
6 x 1	$5^3/_4$ x $^7/_8$	150 x 25	145 x 21
2 x 2	$1^3/_4$ x $1^3/_4$	50 x 50	45 x 45
3 x 2	$2^3/_4$ x $1^3/_4$	75 x 50	70 x 45
4 x 2	$3^3/_4$ x $1^3/_4$	100 x 50	95 x 45
6 x 2	$5^3/_4$ x $1^3/_4$	150 x 50	145 x 45
8 x 2	$7^3/_4$ x $1^3/_4$	200 x 50	195 x 45
9 x 2	$8^3/_4$ x $1^3/_4$	230 x 50	225 x 45
3 x 3	$2^3/_4$ x $2^3/_4$	75 x 75	70 x 70
4 x 3	$3^3/_4$ x $2^3/_4$	100 x 75	95 x 70
6 x 3	$5^3/_4$ x $2^3/_4$	150 x 75	145 x 70
9 x 3	$8^3/_4$ x $2^3/_4$	230 x 75	225 x 70
4 x 4	$3^3/_4$ x $3^3/_4$	100 x 100	95 x 95
6 x 4	$5^3/_4$ x $3^3/_4$	150 x 100	145 x 95

study the brochures and call the sales office for help. Many companies have a technical department that is best placed to advise you of their product. Always ask around for information – the tradesmen are happy to supply this.

Below are two tables giving the various sizes of plywood and MDF that are readily available in the UK; materials commonly used in our industry are shaded.

3   Steel

Obviously, steel is manufactured in all shapes and sizes. In our industry we tend to specify fairly lightweight steel members, and so those types are listed below. If in *any* doubt, always have an engineer confirm the type of steel specified on your drawings. Steel drawings of structural items must not be issued by anyone other than a structural engineer – if the engineer has not actually produced the drawing himself, it

must be approved and 'signed-off' by him. As to what is a structural item ... it can only be defined as being something that, if it failed, could cause injury or damage. Logic and common sense must be applied. I have drawn hundreds of steel items, but I am not an engineer and am *very* aware of that fact – and so if I entertain *any* doubts, I always seek help.

Erw ('electric resistance welded') tubular members are cheap to buy, so try to specify these where possible – provided that structural integrity has been taken into consideration. Do remember that, in terms of strength, erw is limited by having a fairly thin wall thickness (maximum of 3 mm – and that only for certain tubes). It is very commonly used in theatre and trade show projects; its lightness is an advantage and, despite its thin walls, it can still be configured into very strong shapes – truss members are an example. Good bracing in all three dimensions is

Table 5.02 *Plywood sizes in the UK*

Plywood	5 x 5 feet	8 x 4 feet	9 x 4 feet	10 x 4 feet	10 x 5 feet
Thickness	1525 x 1525	2440 x 1220	2745 x 1220	3050 x 1220	3050 x 1525
0.8 mm or $^1/_{32}$"	✔				
1.5 mm or $^1/_{16}$"	✔				
4 mm or $^5/_{32}$"		✔	✔		✔
6 mm or $^1/_4$"	✔	✔			✔
9 mm or $^3/_8$"	✔	✔			✔
12 mm or $^1/_2$"		✔			✔
15 mm or $^5/_8$"		✔			✔
18 mm or $^3/_4$"	✔	✔		✔	✔
21 mm or $^7/_8$"		✔			
24 mm or $^{15}/_{16}$"		✔			✔
25 mm or 1"		✔			✔

Table 5.03 *MDF sizes in the UK*

MDF	8 x 4 feet	8 x 5 feet	8 x 6 feet	10 x 4 feet	10 x 5 feet
Thickness	2440 x 1220	2440 x 1525	2440 x 1830	3050 x 1220	3050 x 1525
2 mm or $5/64$"	✔				
3 mm or $1/8$"	✔				
4 mm or $5/32$"	✔				
6 mm or $1/4$"	✔		✔	✔	
9 mm or $3/8$"	✔		✔	✔	
12 mm or $1/2$"	✔	✔		✔	✔
15 mm or $5/8$"	✔			✔	
18 mm or $3/4$"	✔	✔		✔	✔
25 mm or 1"	✔	✔		✔	✔
30 mm or $1^3/16$"	✔		✔	✔	
32 mm or $1^1/4$"	✔				
36 mm or $1^7/16$"	✔				
38 mm or $1^1/2$"	✔			✔	

the key to constructing strong units. Erw is probably the most commonly used steel in our business.

However, when drawing anything structural, remember that it can ease the task of the structural engineer (who may be asked to provide calculations to 'prove' your proposed structure) to specify **shs** ('square hollow section'), **rhs** ('rectangular hollow section'), or **chs** ('circular hollow section'). This type of steel has a variety of wall thickness from which to choose – considerably thicker walls are available than in erw.

Tubular steel has to be specified to include the **wall thickness** – e.g. '50 x 50 x 3' (2" x 2" x ⅛"), 50 mm square tube with 3 mm thick walls; or '50 OD x 3' (50 mm outside diameter with 3 mm wall thickness).

Steel will not weld to aluminium. In outdoor conditions or damp conditions, steel must not directly touch aluminium as some sort of electrolysis can occur, causing corrosion. Always separate with a membrane (PVC tape will often suffice).

Steel (and aluminium) can be **powder coated** to virtually any colour to provide a good, hard-finished coat. Enquire as to the size of the oven in order that you can break down a unit into pieces suitable to pass through the oven. Some companies have large ovens, others do not.

Steel sizes commonly available in the UK are listed below. However, *obtain your own brochures* in order to stay abreast of the situation and to ascertain details of the various steel types available in your local area. In America, equivalent steel sizes are given in imperial measures.

4 Aluminium and stainless steel

Both of these products are more expensive than mild steel, and so their use in our industry is limited to specific tasks. The labour costs involved in construction also rise when these materials are used.

Aluminium is generally used in circumstances where weight is of an issue. But be careful here: bear in mind that the natural lightness of aluminium *can* be offset by the fact that it is less strong than steel, therefore a box section in aluminium may require a far greater wall thickness than would

its structural equivalent in steel, thereby making it heavier than first imagined. Frequently, with 'one-off' structural items, the weight saved by using aluminium is so negligible that the idea can be abandoned and steel is used. Remember too that aluminium requires a bulkier weld (as well as special welding equipment – 'Argon Welding') and that the number of welds on a flat can increase its weight considerably.

Stainless steel is generally used for its aesthetic qualities. It requires considerable skill from the engineers to ensure that its finished state is neat and unmarked (so labour costs rise).

Both materials tend (still) to be sold in imperial sizes in the UK, although this is slowly changing.

5 Airex type foam

Airex is rigid foam material sold in sheet form. (I believe that *Airex* is the trade name of a particular type of rigid foam – other names exist for other, seemingly similar, foam sheets. For details, if in the UK, contact: *Impag (GB) Ltd*, tel: 01453 890077.)

This material will meet most of the fire regulations you will encounter. It has a good, 'tight' grain and so it cuts cleanly and easily. It is not for surfaces that are to be walked upon – unless props treat the surface with fibreglass, or similar. It is ideal as a lightweight covering material, say to represent roof tiles or clapboard (again, props and artists can 'dress' it to suit the design). It is fairly expensive when compared to many of the more basic materials used in our business, but its versatility often demands its use. Some available metric sheet sizes are as follows: 1300 x 2900, 1400 x 3100, and 1450 x 3250. Thicknesses: 5, 8, 10, 12, 15, 20, 25, 30, 35, 40, and 50.

6 Polystyrene foam

Props will often use blocks of polystyrene – or many blocks, glued together – to carve shapes such as statues and rocks. The resulting form can then be covered with another material to provide stability. A moment's thought will confirm a myriad of possible uses for polystyrene in our industry ... however, please be aware of its main draw-

Table 5.04 *Erw tubing*

Rounds		Squares		Rectangles	
Size (mm)	Weight (kilos/metre)	Size (mm)	Weight (kilos/metre)	Size (mm)	Weight (kilos/metre)
13 x 1.5	0.445	12 x 12 x 1.5	0.541	25.4 x 12.7 x 1.5	0.888
16 x 1.5	0.573	15 x 15 x 2	0.76	35 x 15 x 1.5	1.08
19 x 1.5	0.65	16 x 16 x 1.2	0.531	40 x 20 x 1.5	1.356
22 x 1.5	0.758	20 x 20 x 1.25	0.726	50 x 25 x 1.5	1.71
25 x 1.5	0.91	20 x 20 x 1.5	0.857	60 x 30 x 1.5	1.988
25 x 2	1.13	22 x 22 x 1.2	0.766		
32 x 1.5	1.128	22 x 22 x 1.5	0.966		
38 x 1.5	1.35	25 x 25 x 1.25	0.922		
50 x 1.5	1.976	25 x 25 x 1.5	1.09		
		25 x 25 x 2	1.42		
		32 x 32 x 1.2	1.17		
		32 x 32 x 1.5	1.592		
		32 x 32 x 2	1.911		
		40 x 40 x 1.5	1.828		
		50 x 50 x 1.5	2.455		

Table 5.05 *Shs tubing (square)*

Size (mm)	Wall 2.0	Wall 2.5	Wall 3.0/3.2	Wall 3.5	Wall 4.0	Wall 5.0	Wall 6.3	Wall 8.0
20 x 20	✔	✔						
25 x 25	✔	✔	✔					
30 x 30		✔	✔					
40 x 40		✔	✔		✔			
50 x 50		✔	✔		✔	✔		
60 x 60			✔		✔	✔		
70 x 70			✔	✔		✔		
80 x 80			✔	✔		✔	✔	
90 x 90				✔		✔	✔	
100 x 100					✔	✔	✔	✔
120 x 120						✔	✔	✔
150 x 150						✔	✔	✔
180 x 180							✔	
200 x 200							✔	✔
250 x 250							✔	✔

back: it is *not* accepted by most fire authorities as being suitable for use in theatres, museums and public places. A certain, small amount *may* be allowed if it is trapped within a flameproof skin for example, but *always enquire as to how much, if any, is allowed*. The 'blue' foam – yes, it is blue – is more favourably looked upon, but its use may be restricted to a nominal amount (I believe that blue foam performs better under 'spread of flame' tests, but, nevertheless, still produces smoke).

Regardless of the fire regulations governing a particular production, polystyrene is used to form shapes that are coated with, say, fibreglass; the polystyrene core is then removed.

Props do, of course, find other types of foam for use in carving shapes that are acceptable to the fire authorities. I have seen *Oasis* used – the green foam that plants are grown in. The point is, always discuss how sculpted parts of the set will be constructed and confirm that all is acceptable to the relevant fire authority.

7 Aerolam

This is a rigid, super-lightweight board material that is stronger than plywood. It was developed for the aeronautical industry, but its lightness occasionally makes it an ideal material for use in our business: only occasionally, because of its expense! There are two types of *Aerolam* sold:

(i) 'F' board has fibreglass outer skins, within which is a layer of 'egg-box' shaped, thin alloy foil. Board size is

Table 5.06 *Rhs tubing (rectangular)*

Size (mm)	Wall 2.5	Wall 3.0/3.2	Wall 3.5/3.6	Wall 4.0	Wall 5.0	Wall 6.3	Wall 8.0	Wall 10.0
50 x 25	✔	✔						
50 x 30	✔	✔						
60 x 30		✔						
60 x 40		✔		✔				
70 x 40				✔				
75 x 50		✔						
76.2 x 50.8		✔						
80 x 40		✔		✔				
90 x 50			✔		✔			
100 x 50		✔		✔	✔			
100 x 60			✔		✔			
120 x 60			✔		✔	✔		
120 x 80					✔	✔		
150 x 100					✔	✔	✔	✔
160 x 80					✔	✔		✔
200 x 100					✔	✔	✔	✔
250 x 150						✔	✔	✔

Table 5.07 *Chs tubing (circular)*

Diameter (mm)	Wall 3.0/3.2	Wall 3.5/3.6	Wall 4.0	Wall 5.0	Wall 6.3	Wall 8.0	Wall 10.0
21.3	✔						
26.9	✔						
33.7	✔		✔				
42.4	✔						
48.3	✔		✔	✔			
60.3	✔		✔	✔			
76.1	✔			✔			
88.9	✔		✔	✔			
114.3		✔			✔		
139.7					✔	✔	
168.3							✔
193.7							✔
219.1					✔		✔

2440 x 1220 (8' x 4') and the three thicknesses sold are 13.8 mm, 26.5 mm and 52.3 mm (½", 1" and 2").

(ii) 'M' board is of similar construction but is faced with thin aluminium instead of fibreglass sheet. Board size is 2440 x 1220 (8' x 4') and the thicknesses are 13.9 mm, 26.6 mm and 52 mm (½", 1" and 2").

Brochure/samples from: *Ciba-Geigy Ltd*, tel: 01223 833141 (in the UK).

8 Vac-form/ABS

Vac-form is a thin plastic sheet (about 0.5 mm thick) which is vacuum-formed into virtually any possible shape – sheets of 'brick' patterns, sheets of 'roof tile' patterns, armour,

cornices, statues, etc. It is cheap, light and passes most fire authority requirements. Specials can be made to order: a mould has to be made that is drilled with small holes to allow the vacuum to 'suck' the thin plastic into shape.

ABS is a more rigid form of vac-form. It is 1.2 mm to 3 mm thick (¹⁄₁₆" to ⅛"). It is surprisingly strong and can often negate the necessity for internal timber or ply formers.

Brochures/samples from: *Peter Evans Studios*, tel: 01582 25730; *Pinewood Studios*, tel: 01753 656277 and *Camouflage*, tel: 0208 742 9292 (all in the UK).

Table 5.08 *Mild steel equal angles (not heavy angles)*

13 x 13 x 3	30 x 30 x 3	40 x 40 x 5	50 x 50 x 5	60 x 60 x 10	75 x 75 x 8
20 x 20 x 3	30 x 30 x 5	40 x 40 x 6	50 x 50 x 6	70 x 70 x 6	75 x 75 x 10
25 x 25 x 3	30 x 30 x 6	45 x 45 x 5	50 x 50 x 8	70 x 70 x 8	80 x 80 x 6
25 x 25 x 5	40 x 40 x 3	45 x 45 x 6	60 x 60 x 6	70 x 70 x 10	80 x 80 x 8
25 x 25 x 6	40 x 40 x 4	50 x 50 x 3	60 x 60 x 8	75 x 75 x 6	80 x 80 x 10

Table 5.09 *Mild steel unequal angles (not heavy angles)*

40 x 25 x 4	50 x 40 x 6	65 x 50 x 5	65 x 50 x 8	75 x 50 x 8	80 x 60 x 6
50 x 40 x 5	60 x 30 x 6	65 x 50 x 6	75 x 50 x 6	75 x 50 x 10	80 x 60 x 8

Table 5.10 *Mild steel flat bar*

Width (mm)	Thickness (mm)											
	3	5	6	8	10	12	15	20	25	30	40	50
10	✔											
13	✔	✔	✔									
16	✔	✔	✔									
20	✔	✔	✔	✔	✔	✔						
22	✔											
25	✔	✔	✔	✔	✔	✔		✔				
30	✔	✔	✔	✔	✔	✔						
40	✔	✔	✔	✔	✔	✔	✔	✔	✔			
45	✔	✔	✔		✔	✔	✔	✔				
50	✔	✔	✔	✔	✔	✔	✔	✔	✔		✔	
60	✔	✔	✔	✔	✔	✔	✔		✔	✔		
65	✔	✔	✔	✔	✔	✔	✔	✔	✔		✔	
70			✔		✔	✔						
75			✔	✔	✔	✔	✔	✔	✔			✔
80	✔	✔	✔	✔	✔	✔	✔	✔	✔	✔	✔	
90		✔	✔		✔	✔	✔	✔	✔			
100	✔	✔	✔	✔	✔	✔	✔	✔	✔	✔	✔	✔
110			✔		✔	✔		✔	✔			
130	✔	✔	✔		✔	✔	✔	✔	✔		✔	
150	✔	✔	✔	✔	✔	✔	✔	✔	✔		✔	✔
180			✔		✔	✔		✔				
200			✔	✔	✔	✔	✔	✔	✔			
220			✔		✔	✔		✔	✔			
250			✔		✔	✔	✔	✔	✔			
300			✔		✔	✔	✔	✔	✔			
350						✔						

9 Plastic extrusions

These are under-used in my opinion, as plastic extrusion is cheap, supplied in various colours, self-coloured throughout and easy to fix. White plastic angle is ideal to add as nosing to stage treads/get-offs. Plastic angle can be used as a nosing to hide the join between a vertical fascia and a carpeted floor. It is non-flameproof, but small quantities are *normally* allowed.

Brochure: *SKV Extrusions*, tel: 0208 653 4941 (in the UK).

10 Superseal brush systems

These are black nylon brushes trapped within an aluminium extrusion that are frequently fitted to the edge of patio doors/revolving doors as draught excluders. They can be obtained in surprisingly large sizes and so can be useful as light-leak fillers on moving scenery – they only 'read' to the eye as a black strip and slip neatly and noiselessly over any tracks or obstructions that may occur on the stage floor.

Brochure: *Kleeneze Ltd*, tel: 01179 604275 (in the UK).

Table 5.11 *Mild steel rounds (solid)*

All diameters given in mm					70	90	115	150
6	12	22	40	55	75	95	120	165
8	16	25	45	60	80	100	125	180
10	20	32	50	65	85	110	140	200

Table 5.12 *Mild steel squares (solid)*

All mm			16	22	30	45	60	75
8	10	12	20	25	40	50	65	100

Table 5.13 *Cloth widths available in the UK*

Cloth type	Width (mm)	Cloth type	Width (mm)
Bleached flax scene canvas	1830/2440	Brown flax	1830
Unbleached flax scene canvas	1830	Cotton duck	1830/2740
Proban flax scene canvas	1830	Underfelt	1370
Super bleached flax scene canvas	1830/2440	Polypropylene carpet	2000
Deluxe bleached flax scene canvas	1830	Molton	1500/1980/3000
Bleached cotton scene canvas	1830/2440	Wool serge/Melton	1500
Unbleached cotton scene canvas	1830/2440	Satin	1600
White sheeting (cotton)	2740/6000/10,000	Voile	3000/3300/1500
Calico	1830/2740/6000/ 10,000	Muslin	1220
		Unbleached muslin	6000/10,000
Matting duck (cotton)	2740	Bleached muslin	6000/10,000
Hessian (jute)	1830/1780	Casement	1220
Scrim	840/1830	Polyline (polyester display fabric)	1500/3000
Fine gauze (cotton)	3660/7320	Curtain lining	1220/1400/1420/ 1500
Scenic gauze (cotton)	9140		
Bobbin net	9500	Jap silk	910/1400
Reflective gauze	8500	Bolton twill	1220
Square gauze	10,970	Velour	1220
Sharkstooth gauze	8890/10,970	Heavy velour	1220
Scenery netting	9140	Tweed	1370
Tiger net	5500	Baize	1830
Filled cloth	9140	Stage felt	1830
Unbleached cotton canvas	4200/7500/9500	Tricord	1300
Bleached cotton canvas	4200/7500/9500	Display suede	1420
Clevyl canvas	4980/10,000	Loop nylon	1320

11 Cloth

The width of available cloth will often dictate how wide flattage can be. It is not always practical or desirable to have the cloth sewn-up into larger pieces. Always check the cloth's flame retardant qualities. Above is a list of various cloth widths available in the UK (for cloth in imperial widths, please consult your local supplier).

Brochures/samples: *J D McDougall Ltd*, tel: 0208 534 2921; *Gerriets*, tel: 0207 232 2262; and *B Brown Ltd*, tel: 0207 696 0007 (all in the UK).

6 • Surveying

Brief mention has already been made of survey drawings in Chapter 3, page 25; the points raised referred to the completed survey drawing, the final issue. The function of this drawing is worth repeating: it is to provide a *mathematical representation of an existing venue (or part of a venue) in three dimensions*, from which, should the need ever occur, the venue could be replicated at full size. This chapter illustrates the various steps that should be taken to achieve a successful survey drawing.

Surveying is a vitally important part of producing a complete drawing package for any given production due to inhabit a venue 'unknown' to the draughtsman. If the survey is wrong and the set does not fit into the venue as a consequence, then the buck firmly stops with whoever attempted the survey.

The sketches taken on-site during the survey are later used to produce the completed survey drawing: if these sketches are wrong or indecipherable, the survey drawing will be wrong – and untold costs incurred.

Given that the preceding two paragraphs seem to state the obvious, it is amazing that the survey can often be treated with so much disdain by production managers. It is common for some production managers to fly off somewhere to do their 'recce' (reconnoitre), full of assurances that the survey can be left in their hands, only to return with the vaguest of surreal scribbles and a photograph. Obviously, experience soon teaches production managers that it is not only prudent to include the draughtsman in the recce, it is *vital* when the production warrants it (and it usually does – an airfare paid at the beginning of a project can subsequently save huge costs, or even the whole show, later).

NOTES ON SURVEYING

A) Always consider preparing a **check-list** *before* visiting the venue; some of the following points may well be included in it. Bear in mind that the venue may not be quiet and empty – indeed, it may be noisy, busy and under-lit – so it does help to steady one's thoughts to have such a check-list to refer to. It can be frighteningly easy to leave the venue, dash for a cab and completely forget to survey the get-in, or some other vital area.

B) Always try to have **two people** to survey – one alone simply cannot manage it in any sizeable venue, unless a laser measurer (*see* page 48) is utilised – and try to *involve* both people, for the simple reason that two heads are better than one. If a partner is merely holding the end of the measuring tape and staring out of the window then a great opportunity is being squandered: the second surveyor should be aware of what dimensions are being taken so that any omissions may be spotted.

C) Surveys for permanent installation work, such as museum jobs, need to be taken with great precision and **all potential obstructions** carefully noted and fully dimensioned (such as air conditioning ducts, electrical conduits, pipes, etc.). You may be surveying ahead of any proposed building works that are to be installed prior to the production's get-in. If so, try to obtain drawings of the proposed works and return to check that those items have been installed correctly (or at least, in a manner that does not impinge upon the production).

D) **Photographs** do help in providing visual reassurance when translating the survey sketches into the survey drawing. They are useful to have when attending meetings – to show others who have not seen the venue, for example. Keep them secure for future reference and label them with some care (it is annoying to be unsure of 'what wall' one is looking at in a photograph of a venue that shares similar architecture throughout).

Digital photographs (pictures in computer format) are increasingly being used for surveys/recces; their advantage is that they can be sent instantaneously, via e-mail, to whoever wants them, avoiding the time taken to develop and print conventional photographs. Again, label these carefully (a good tip is to change each picture's file name so that it 'describes' the picture's view – as in 'NEC Hall 4 West View').

E) **Pay due respect to the venue** when surveying by not leaving ink marks about the place. Ensure that the marks you need to place are temporary and are quickly removed after use. The only exception to this is if you are placing permanent setting-out marks on a site for future use by the contractors – ensure you have the necessary permission to do so.

F) **The method of surveying** is, in principle, very straightforward: *in order to faithfully mimic the shape of a room, the overall pattern needs to be broken down into a series of triangles that have a relationship to one another.*

Triangles are fixed objects in a way that four-sided shapes are not: given three sides of a triangle, it can be faithfully replicated at any scale – its internal angles become 'fixed'. On the other hand, given the four sides of a quadrilateral, this does not then allow the accurate replication of that shape, because its angles need to be known also. However, taking a diagonal measurement of the quadrilateral will 'fix its shape' mathematically – because it has been broken into two triangles (in reality, take both diagonals, just to be sure). That is why triangles are used to gather survey information.

Take as many 'check' dimensions as you please, the more the merrier, but your main dimensions will be based upon triangles. With triangles, one can know the angle that two walls make when they meet. Certain key dimensions, such as overall widths and lengths at specific, fixed points, usually become the points within which the main triangles are based – smaller triangles can be added within these as necessary.

Do remember to ensure that the numerous triangles sketched at the time of survey are linked geometrically to one another. Otherwise, when attempting to draw the 'proper' survey drawing back at the office, you may find that two areas of a venue are detailed perfectly, but there is no geometric/mathematical way of placing those areas in relation to one another. And never assume that rooms have 90-degree corners just because you suspect that the builder had that intention in mind.

G) '3–4–5 triangles' are worth a mention here: they are an invaluable aid to setting-out on-site or onstage. While surveying, it may be necessary to physically set out a line – say a chalk line on the floor – that is at 90 degrees to another line or a wall. A simple method of setting-out a right-angle (90°) is to use a '3–4–5 triangle'.

Any triangle that has sides of 3, 4 and 5 units in length will be a right-angled triangle – i.e. it will contain a 90-degree angle. The units can be inches, metres or miles; the result is the same. Pythagoras' Theorem expresses the proof of this fact: the square of the hypotenuse of right-angled triangles is equal to the sum of the squares of the other two sides. Therefore, in a 3–4–5 triangle, $3^2 + 4^2 = 5^2$ (9 + 16 = 25), proving that it is a right-angled triangle. Knowing the above, it is simple to measure 3 metres along a wall, strike an arc of radius 4 metres from the origin of that line, and an arc of radius 5 metres from the other end of the line. At the point where the two arcs cross, strike a line back to the origin of the 3-metre line: this new line will be 4 metres long and will be at 90 degrees to the wall.

H) Try to obtain any drawing that exists of the venue before going on-site. This can be of great use: sit down quietly with a paper copy of the drawing and imagine that you had to draw the venue now. Ask yourself what information you would need in order to do that – knowing that you cannot assume to know the angles that exist in the room. Then mark that drawing with all the dimension lines (leaving the dimension spaces blank) that you would require in order to draw it faithfully. Add 'check' dimensions also. (I subsequently highlight all the empty dimension spaces in yellow.) When on-site, simply fill in all the blank dimension spaces (I don't leave until I have no more 'empty' highlighted blobs on the drawing). By operating in this fashion you will have ascertained *before you visit the venue* which dimensions you need to obtain. You will also be confident in your knowledge of how to break the shape down into triangles that make a mathematical logic of the entire pattern.

This is a very safe method of approaching a survey because often, when you first visit a room, it may be half-full of equipment or workmen and you cannot calmly visualise the mathematical logic that lies behind its shape. It also helps to prevent the oh-so-familiar problem of missing out a dimension on the survey and having to re-visit the venue sporting an embarrassed leer. (Don't feel too bad about this, everybody has done it. The most important thing is to confess.)

I) If you cannot obtain a drawing of the room beforehand, upon arrival and after having familiarised yourself with the lay-out, just sit down quietly and sketch the outline of the room using a pen of one colour. Then mark the dimensions required (as in point 'H' above), preferably using different coloured pens.

J) Use '+' or '−' dimensions to note heights of doorways, etc. and sketch any relevant elevations. (It is easy to become so engrossed by the maths problems involved in the plan view, that the height of objects is overlooked.)

K) Heights can be awkward to obtain in venues where no access equipment is available. A laser measure will solve this problem. Failing that, use lateral thought to try to obtain the desired dimension. Try to find a long batten (not difficult to locate backstage in most theatres) and measure it; if that batten is then pushed up so that it is touching the point required, one only need measure from the bottom of the batten down to the floor or stage in order to establish the total height.

Remember that by utilising any existing architectural features, such as brickwork or stone cladding, one can arrive at *approximate* heights. For example, carefully measure the distance between brick 'courses' (measure ten courses, say, and divide by ten to get a more accurate average), stand back and count courses going up to the point you cannot reach. This sounds a somewhat amateurish approach, but in some situations it may be the best you can do. Another (again rather inaccurate) method of establishing a visual aid in order to judge certain unattainable heights in a theatre is to use a measuring tape fixed to an empty flying bar (using adhesive tape). The bar is flown out to an exact height by reading-off the tape, which then allows one to stand back – or stand in the auditorium or the circle and 'eye-up' the rest of the theatre in relation to the bar.

L) Datum lines can be used for referring a series of dimensions back to a known line/plane. A datum line is any convenient straight line that is used as a 'base' line from which other dimensions are set. It can be a plan-view line – the centre-line of a stage, for example – or a vertical or horizontal line.

Most building sites have a horizontal datum line drawn around the (unfinished) walls or columns at '+1000 mm above FFL', meaning that the site engineers have plotted a truly horizontal, 'level' line, or marks, at 1000 mm above what *will be* the finished floor level. The height of objects, such as ceilings, picture rails, etc. are then shown as being '+2000 mm above datum', or something lower down as '−600 mm below datum'. Bear in mind that the intended finished floor may be *well above* the structural floor existing at the time of the survey. Where an 'official' datum line exists, ensure that subsequent drawings refer to it – link main dimensions back to the datum line.

Obviously, where no specific datum line exists, one can use any convenient line or draw a line solely for this use; chalk-lines are useful here. Frequently, the datum line is used by the draughtsman only, whose resultant survey drawing will probably 'convert' a clear existing line – or points – into the setting-line used by the rest of the production team on-site.

When surveying stages and venues, as opposed to building sites, obtaining a good horizontal datum line can be a problem as it is unlikely that you will possess all the extravagant equipment needed to recreate a true horizontal line. Common sense has to prevail: usually the stage itself is as level as can be reasonably expected. If it is a raked stage, ask what that rake is and try to check it with a spirit level placed upon a long 'straight edge' (any straight and true batten). Alternatively, look for a horizontal architectural feature that appears to be truly level. Remember that the lines formed by brick courses are pretty good at maintaining level, because bricklayers lay their bricks to string lines that are generally fairly accurately placed.

M) Try to identify three immovable points in the room that become the basis for the trigonometry you will employ. External corners of walls or columns are perfect. Two points *can* be barely adequate, but three allow for 'check dimensions' and greater accuracy. In truth, it is possible to survey a room by just hammering two nails into the floor, a decent distance apart, and making them the basis for the maths of the room.

N) In rooms that have curved structures requiring a survey, try to establish a chord length and the *maximum distance* from that chord to the circle (if the structure is truly circular, this will be half-way along that chord). Then later, you can establish the radius by using maths. However, never assume that a curve is truly circular – place marks at chosen distances around the curve and measure these points back to your three main points. Alternatively, using a chalk-line, 'ping' a line on the floor (if you can make it a chord, all the better), divide the line into any number of equal parts and measure the distance to the curve at 90 degrees to the line (remembering to plot where the *line is* in space). With internal, or concave, curves you can try to find the radius and the radius point by using geometry chalked onto the floor (bisect two chords); then go on to test it with string or a piece of batten. Again, having done all that, *do not forget* to plot where that radius point *is* in space (and the ends of the curve, of course).

O) Note the existence of any of the following: fire hose reels; permanently installed fire fighting equipment; fire exits; fire exit clearways; the get-in route; power supply (if the production manager wishes); safe hanging points; changes in floor levels that are relevant; clear ceiling heights, if relevant. Note down the construction method of any existing walls that fixings will have to be applied to. Take note of chandeliers, and whether they move up or down; routes to public toilets; the venue's setting-line; any adjustable proscenium arch details; the SWL (Safe Working Load) of flying equipment (and maximum speed, if needed); where the prompt corner is positioned; stage traps/orchestra pit details; in-house iron curtain and details of main tabs; parking for articulated trucks (the local police may need to be informed); any local workshop facilities/goods suppliers; show staff accommodation facilities; and catering facilities.

P) Always talk to the venue's manager to discuss in-house Health & Safety issues, such as fire ratings for materials (*see* above pp. 5 and 18).

SURVEYING EQUIPMENT

It would be fair to say that most surveys taken in our business involve no more equipment than a measuring tape and a pen and pad. However, a professional draughtsman will be required to survey on a regular basis, and the various experiences that he or she encounters will inevitably ensure that more and more bits and pieces are seen as being necessary. The basic equipment to consider is listed below.

A) A **steel measuring tape**, roll-up type. I prefer the wider variety (25 mm or 1"), eight metres long (8000 mm or 26'). A shorter one – say, five metres long (16' 6"), is adequate, but know that you will at some point wish it were longer.

B) A **long measuring tape**, about 30 metres (30000 mm) or 100' in length. Steel tapes at this length can be clumsy, have sharp edges and tend to snap and/or corrode after much usage. There are good, soft, 'non-stretch' types available in man-made fibre which are easy to clean and are more 'forgiving' when caught, bent or trapped by on-site rubble than are the steel versions.

C) A **chalk-line** with white chalk: white seems to cause less staining and is usually very easy to read. A chalk-line is a simple tool that strikes straight lines upon a floor using string saturated with powdered chalk. It does take two people to operate (ideally three for lines longer than about 10 metres). Do remember to have a spare chalk carton.

D) Chalk sticks, and something to sharpen them. Even in an elegant venue, few could complain if your survey marks were drawn in chalk – wipe them away after use.

E) Pens, pads, calculator, etc. Take a ready supply of pads and pens or pencils; it is infuriating to have to leave site to find a stationers – abroad, miles from anywhere, can't speak the language, no cabs, it's hot ...

F) A **set-square** is handy when striking small, straight lines at 90 degrees to another line, as when plotting curves from a straight line (*see* page 56). A large, clear plastic set-square is advisable.

G) A **ball of string** (hammer and nails you can usually scrounge). Stretched string gives a good straight line from which one can measure. Fine nylon-type string is good and, if orange, even better – it does need to be visible (everybody in the venue that day will appear to make a determined effort to trip over your line, often twice).

H) A roll of white 'gaffer' tape and a 'permanent' marker pen. These are ideal for placing survey marks on carpet: tear off a piece of tape and place it on the carpet near where your point is to be, then mark the exact point with the marker pen. After your survey, remove the tape. Clearly, this works not only for carpet but for most surfaces, horizontal or vertical; however, do take care that the act of removing gaffer tape does not also strip away the surface below! In order to avoid this, also carry a roll of masking tape for use in more sensitive areas: it is less adhesive, causing no trauma to the surface below it.

I) I take **trammels**, just in case, although I have rarely needed them. Trammels are two clamps, one with a downward-pointing steel spike that acts as a compass point and the other with a downward-pointing slot that receives and holds your pen or pencil. Obtain a batten – say of 50 x 25 par ('two–by–one') – of any length to suit the task in hand, and clamp these on. One is the compass point; the other draws a circle, the distance apart being the radius.

J) A **spirit level** is obviously very handy. Try to have one that is a good make and at least 600 mm (2') long –

the voided alloy 'I' beam type is very strong and easy to handle. Adjustable 'bubbles' can be useful, although the best makes guarantee that the bubbles cannot be knocked out of alignment. Despite the manufacturer's claims, do treat this expensive tool with respect.

Check your spirit level for accuracy on a regular basis! This is a very simple task, although it does make a good brain teaser: 'How do you check that your spirit level is accurate without knowing of any adjacent, level surface against which to check it?' Place the spirit level horizontally against a flat wall, move it until the upper centre bubble is reading 'level' and draw a fine line on the wall along the top edge of the spirit level. Next, take the spirit level and turn it around end-to-end, without rotating it – i.e. the right-hand end of the spirit level is now on the left-hand side, but the same, upper centre bubble is being used. Now draw a line as before, starting at one end of the previous line and overlaying it: if the lines are identical, then the spirit level is true. If the lines are diverging then the bubbles need adjustment. 'True level' would be exactly between the two lines (usually, this adjustment is achieved by the use of an adjusting screw that is built into the body of the spirit level). This simple check can then be repeated for the other horizontal bubble – the lower one – as well as for both of the vertical ones.

K) Laser range-meters (laser measurers) are extremely useful tools for obtaining dimensions in a large venue. They are now becoming affordable, but can also be hired for a small daily rental fee. Do not confuse this tool with an 'estimator', which is a measuring device that approximates dimensions (the sort of gadget used by estate agents to measure rooms). The more recent laser measurers are accurate to ±3 mm over 100 metres. The instrument is held or placed at a relevant position and turned until the red laser beam is seen to alight upon the requisite spot; a button is then pressed which generates a digital read-out of the distance to that spot. It is cleverly configured so that it can measure from external and internal corners of rooms, as well as edges of columns, etc. It will attach to a tripod, if desired. It is at its most useful if overhead heights are needed, but no access is available – simply lay it on the stage and point to any object above.

The laser beam does seem to 'prefer' certain surfaces and will not give a measurement if the reflective nature of a surface is inadequate. It is for this reason that one should always carry '**targets**': these can be purchased as sticky-backed reflective paper, or alternatively, use a handful of orange squares of thin cardboard (100 x 100 mm) and some *Blu-Tack*. The targets are attached to the various points that are to be measured, and the laser is then used to measure the distance to those points from two, or preferably three, fixed points within the venue (remembering to also measure between the three fixed points!). Be aware that eye damage can result from careless use of lasers. Safety goggles are available.

L) Laser levels fall into the category of 'professional' surveying equipment, along with 'dumpy' levels and theodolites. These tools allow for full 3D measuring. It is not uncommon to come across laser levels in our business and they are often used by engineers to survey the stage and auditorium of theatres. The unit consists of a free-spinning laser beam mounted on a self-levelling base set upon a tripod – thus giving a visible 'level' (horizontal) datum line upon the walls of the venue (it can be rotated to the vertical plane also). This tool is invaluable for providing highly accurate measurements of the relative heights of objects in the venue.

In normal operation, the laser is placed at a point where it can reach the areas required and the operator aims the beam at a vertical stick held by an assistant. By measuring from the bottom of the stick (i.e. the floor, or any horizontal surface) up to the red laser beam, the relative heights of surfaces are obtained (because the laser beam represents a horizontal plane datum). The beam can also be spun by a motor, giving a clear, if slightly flickering line, about 5 mm wide, all around the walls of the venue – measurements can then be taken from this line.

M) Water levels are worth a mention, even though they are very rarely used in the entertainment business. They are worth a mention because the material required to make one is easily available, and that is what you may have to do if heights and levels are important to your survey (anything that can get you out of trouble and back into the departing cab is well worth mentioning). Although these can be bought as manufactured items of brass and rubber, a simpler version is to obtain a piece of long, clear plastic tube, say, 6000 mm long x 15 mm diameter. Push a piece of stout wire through the tube, about 50 mm from the end – at each end – and twist the wire to form simple hooks from which both ends can be hung. Partly fill the tube with water, hanging up both ends to a convenient point to allow any bubbles in the water to percolate out through the open ends. Ensure that no large bubbles or air pockets are in the tube (which is why clear tube is used) and have the top of the water about 400–500 mm below the tube's ends. Obviously, if either end of the tube is allowed to fall below any other part of the tube, the water will spill out.

When using a water level have two people – say, Jack and Jill – each take an end of the tube. Jill will hold her end of the tube vertically against a wall and move the tube up or down until the level of the water within it is exactly level with a line or mark she has drawn on the wall – call her mark a datum line. Meanwhile, Jack has placed his end of the tube vertically against a wall that requires the datum – he must ensure, visually, that his tube is about the same height as Jill's (or the water will pour out over him). He then holds his end of the tube absolutely still, leaving Jill to move her end of it until she can see that the water is level with her datum mark. When Jill has done this, Jack places a mark on the wall exactly level with the water level at his end of the tube. He now has a datum that is known to be level with the one on Jill's wall. This works because water always finds its own level. (Remember to be aware of the few seconds it takes for the water level to 'settle' after each time the tube is moved.) Using this system – which is far easier to accomplish than to describe – datum marks are transferred around the room, and if you return to the original starting point you will be surprised by its accuracy.

(A tiny, nerdy note: water tension gives the water in the tube a curved surface – it curves down to the centre by a few millimetres – so, Jack and Jill need to agree on whether the centre of the water line is being used, or the edges. If they fail to establish an agreement, those few millimetres will begin to add up as they work around the room – resulting in a broken crown for him, I imagine.)

SURVEYING: AN EXAMPLE

For the purposes of this exercise a fictional venue has been created; the empty rooms are shown in **Figure 6.01**. Quite deliberately, this venue is not a theatre – it is just a couple of rooms within which one may be asked to place a trade show set or a museum set. The method of surveying does not change, regardless of the venue's function.

The following six drawings have metric dimensions shown, but the sizes or units are irrelevant: it is the *method* employed that is being illustrated. The drawings would have been muddied by the addition of unnecessary imperial equivalents – and to stress the point, the metric dimensions shown are printed in very small type!

As mentioned in the Preface to this book, dimensions that are not important have been treated in this fashion (i.e. in small print throughout); it is enough to be aware that a dimension of some type *would be required* where shown, when drawing the real thing. Important dimensions, or dimensions relevant to the text, are shown clearly, and imperial equivalents included [shown within square brackets] where necessary.

These notes describe the methods involved in completing the survey sketch, or sketches, from which the final 'proper' survey drawing will be developed and issued.

Figure 6.01 – the 'empty' venue

A) This is a small venue that contains a main room, a back room, ceilings, openings, a doorway, piers (or nib walls), overhead beams, vertical pipes, a concave curve and a convex curved wall.

B) Think laterally! *Do not make any assumptions about the room!* Do not assume that any angles are right-angles (90°), or that curves are true arcs – the *intention* may have been to build the room geometrically, but the reality may well be different.

C) Having said that, we shall assume that the floor is level – 'it looks level' is often good enough for our industry (if it is critical, use a laser level or a water level). For height dimensions, we shall assume that the floor is '±0', and that objects are measured at being '+' above that floor.

D) Either sketch the room or obtain a previous drawing of the room and mark on it all the dimensions that you know you will need. I find it easier to do this before measuring begins as it focuses the mind on what will be required to draw the final survey drawing/ground-plan. When deciding what to measure, keep thinking, *'When I have a blank sheet of paper on my drawing board, what will I need to be able to replicate this shape?'* Imagine trying to plot the shape using compasses – i.e. imagine the *triangles* that you need to plot.

E) Use any coloured pens, highlighters, etc. in order to ensure that this survey sketch will be legible to yourself at a later date. This sounds blatantly obvious, but it is very easy to scribble away on-site, where everything is in front of you – and therefore seemingly very obvious (plus, it may be dark, dusty and hot, making the exit door seem very appealing) – only to get back to the office and struggle to comprehend your own jottings.

Figure 6.02 – dimensions of the back room

A) The back room's dimensions have been entered here. It is quite simple in shape and so the only plan-view dimensions required are the lengths of each wall's face and the corner-to-corner diagonal dimensions. Triangles have been established.

B) It can be seen that from these dimensions, the angles that the walls make to one another can be calculated, if required, at a later date.

C) Obtain ceiling, doorway and opening heights to suit, as well as detailing any pertinent objects (e.g. around the door-frame's jambs).

D) Remember to note any skirting boards, shelves, radiators, etc. that may impact upon the production – measure all, however boring the process.

Figure 6.03 – the 'upstage' section of the main room

A) The smaller, 'upstage' section of the main room has been dimensioned on this sketch and it can be seen that diagonal dimensions are not practical to obtain due to the presence of pipes near two internal corners. A different method of surveying has been used.

B) The dimension of each wall's face has been taken, obviously, but then two fixed points are chosen (A and B) and from those points all relevant points or corners are measured. It can be seen that there is no need to cover your drawing with these dimensions, merely list them (listing them also gives you a visual reassurance that every point is being measured from both A and B).

C) Point 'F' is an 'artificial' point (i.e. it is not a physical object – just a mark made on the wall), and its function here is to resolve the problem of not being able to take diagonal measurements into the corners. Artificial points, combined with good lateral thinking, can be utilised to resolve practical geometric problems. These points will not be shown upon the completed survey drawing – they are of no use to others – but they are essential to the operation of plotting the exact geometry of the space.

D) The diameter of pipes may be measured with the use of two sticks (or rulers, or whatever) held parallel, gripping the pipe, as sketched. Clearly, callipers would also work rather well! It is extraordinarily difficult to *accurately* measure a pipe 'by eye' (by holding a tape measure across the pipe and trying to 'eye-up' its diameter against the tape), so don't bother. If the exact diameter is required, remember that it is simple to wrap a piece of paper around the pipe, mark the circumference upon it and deduce its diameter by maths.

E) **Elevation 'X–X'** is sketched in order that the configuration of the pipe be recorded. Most surveys will require elevations of some kind.

Figures 6.04 and 6.04a – the 'downstage' section of the main room

A) This section of the venue is somewhat irregular in shape but it soon becomes apparent that points G to P need marking and plotting – leaving the curved sections until later (*see* figure 6.05). All the straight walls need to be measured. Use a straight edge of some description to establish where walls cease to become straight and begin to curve, as at points I, J, M and N (mark those points with chalk).

Two methods of surveying could be employed here:

B) **Figure 6.04** illustrates the more obvious way of surveying this room. Points P, G and I are used as three fixed points from which all other points are measured. It can be seen that point P does not have a clear view of point M, so that dimension P–M cannot be taken directly; this problem is overcome by the liberal use of dimensions around that area. (The following dimensions will 'fix' point M: M–G, M–I, G–I, P–G, P–I, P–L, L–M, L–G and L–I.) Alternatively, point P could be moved over to become an 'artificial' point (shown as Pa on the sketch).

C) **Figure 6.04a** shows another method of surveying the same area. Artificial points in the form of nails are used (although, of course, these 'nails' could be marks upon gaffer tape). Two nails are placed in the floor and all relevant points are measured from them. The nails can be placed anywhere, but plainly they need to have a clear view of the points to be measured. Generally, the further away from each other, the better. Always remember to measure the distance between the two nails: it is horribly easy to forget this during the frenzy of measuring that follows. As previously mentioned, *three* nails make the perfect set of main points from which to measure – and many venues will require the use of all three. However, this particular room has other clear points, such as P, G, K and L, and so two nails are sufficient.

Figure 6.05 – the curved areas

A) The preceding sketches have established the geometry of the room while omitting the details of the two curved walls. The *ends* of each curve, the two chords, have been plotted – and that is important: it places the curves in relation to the rest of the room. Remember that a rounded wall may not necessarily be part of a perfect circle, or arc, and so needs careful surveying; if it *is* a perfect arc, you *cannot be certain* of that until you measure and plot it.

The shapes of the curves have to be established, and this can be done in various ways:

B) **Plotting curves from fixed points** is a safe method to adopt. The nails used previously in **figure 6.04a** are ideal for use as fixed points from which to plot the positions of marks placed upon the curved walls. The more marks added, the more accurate becomes the final plot. These marks can be randomly placed; however, I prefer to have the marks equidistant from one end of the curve because it establishes a further set of check dimensions.

i) *To place marks around a convex curve:* starting at one end, bend a tape around the curve and place a mark every 300 mm (or 1'). Then measure the final arc's dimension (the arc remaining between the last 300 mm mark and the end of the curve). Measure the *overall* visible circumference also.

ii) *To place marks around a concave curve:* starting from one end, mark chords on the curve with a straight ruler or stick and then measure the final chord. Ensure that the *overall* chord is known.

C) **Plotting curves from straight lines** is a reasonable option to utilise. The straight line itself can be a chalk-line struck upon the floor, or a timber batten used as a straight edge. Two methods are shown in **figure 6.05**:

i) *On a convex curve*, strike a tangential line that touches the curved wall and extends out to any other convenient points. At suitable points along that line use a set-square to strike further lines at 90 degrees to the original, each of which ends by touching the curve. A copy of the curve is obtained in this fashion. (The tangential line need not actually *be* tangential, of course; in fact it need not touch the curve at all. Any known line can be used: it is just much simpler to use a line that is immediately adjacent to the curve.)

ii) *On a concave curve*, draw an overall chord-line and, again, strike lines at 90 degrees to that chord, each line ending when it touches the curve. When doing this, it is always prudent to have one of these 90-degree lines *exactly on centre* of the chord – it may be that the curve is a perfect arc, in which case knowing the chord and the length of the centre-line will provide the correct radius. The maths behind this is: if *half* the chord is x, and the length of the centre-line is y, the radius can be found by the use of the following formula:

$$radius = [(x^2 \div y) + y] \div 2$$

Clearly, if the curve is *not* a perfect arc, the other lines plotted (not the centre-line) will soon begin to demonstrate this fact.

D) Establishing a radius point on-site may prove useful, particularly where there is reason to believe that the curved structure in question is perfectly round, or is a perfect arc. Any two chords are bisected, the radius point established and the arc struck in order to 'test' the structure's accuracy.

E) Remember – *with all methods* – to plot the endpoints of the arc, chord or straight line **in relation to the rest of the room** (or nails). For some reason it is very easy to forget to do this, resulting in a situation whereby, having plotted a perfect replica of the curve, you are unable to place it within the room.

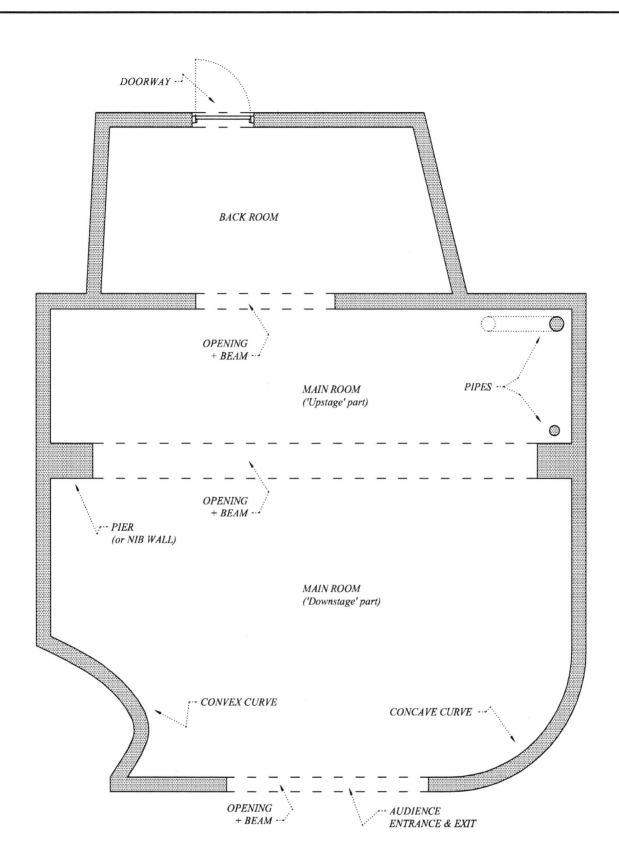

Figure 6-01 - AN EMPTY VENUE

A survey *sketch* of the venue, awaiting dimensions.

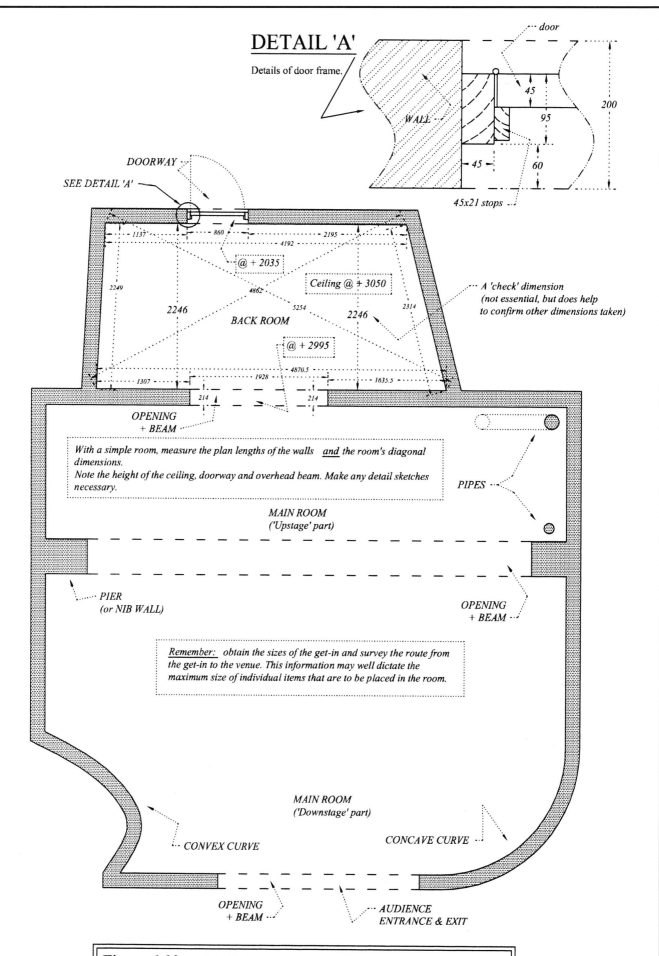

DETAIL 'A'

Details of door frame.

door

WALL

45

95

200

45

60

45x21 stops

DOORWAY

SEE DETAIL 'A'

1137   860   2195

4192

@ + 2035

Ceiling @ + 3050

2249

4862

2246   5254   2246   2314

BACK ROOM

A 'check' dimension
(not essential, but does help
to confirm other dimensions taken)

@ + 2995

4870.5

1307   1928   1635.5

214   214

OPENING
+ BEAM

With a simple room, measure the plan lengths of the walls *and* the room's diagonal
dimensions.
Note the height of the ceiling, doorway and overhead beam. Make any detail sketches
necessary.

PIPES

MAIN ROOM
('Upstage' part)

PIER
(or NIB WALL)

OPENING
+ BEAM

Remember: obtain the sizes of the get-in and survey the route from
the get-in to the venue. This information may well dictate the
maximum size of individual items that are to be placed in the room.

MAIN ROOM
('Downstage' part)

CONVEX CURVE

CONCAVE CURVE

OPENING
+ BEAM

AUDIENCE
ENTRANCE & EXIT

Figure 6-02 - THE BACK ROOM

A simple room to survey.
Please note that metric sizes have been used - and to have included Imperial would have made
the drawing illegible. *The sizes do not matter!* The *method* is more relevant.

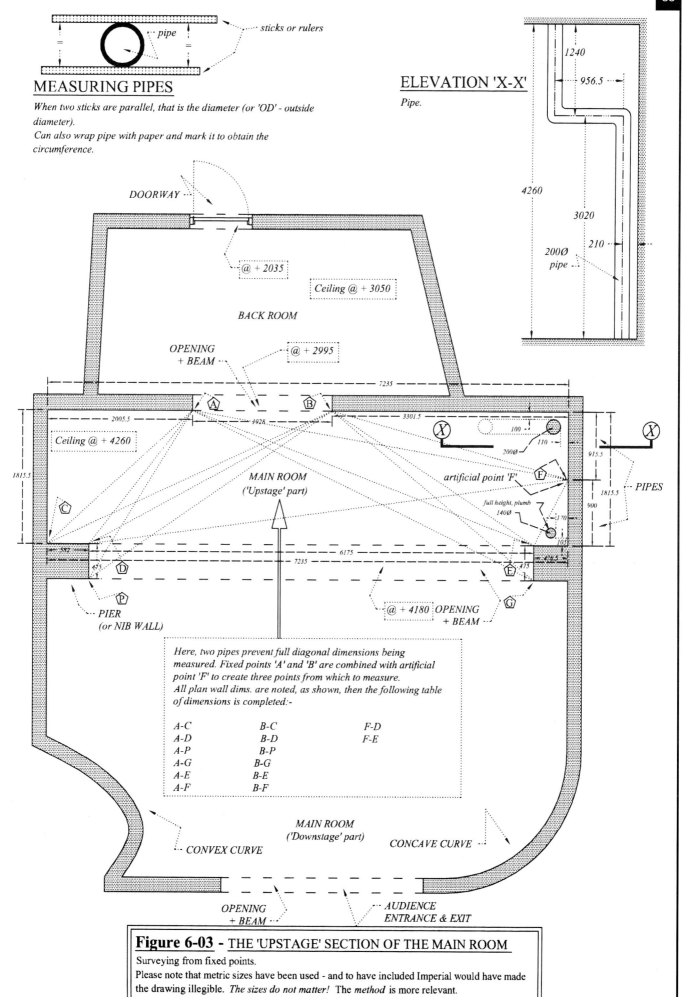

MEASURING PIPES

When two sticks are parallel, that is the diameter (or 'OD' - outside diameter).
Can also wrap pipe with paper and mark it to obtain the circumference.

— sticks or rulers
— pipe

ELEVATION 'X-X'
Pipe.

1240
956.5
4260
3020
200Ø pipe
210

DOORWAY

@ + 2035

Ceiling @ + 3050

BACK ROOM

OPENING + BEAM
@ + 2995

7235

A   B

2005.5   4928   3301.5   100   (X)   (X)
200Ø   110

Ceiling @ + 4260

1815.5   MAIN ROOM ('Upstage' part)   artificial point 'F'   F   915.5
PIPES
1815.5
C   full height, plumb   900
140Ø   170
105

585   6175   435
475   7235   475
D   E

P   @ + 4180   OPENING + BEAM   G

PIER (or NIB WALL)

Here, two pipes prevent full diagonal dimensions being
measured. Fixed points 'A' and 'B' are combined with artificial
point 'F' to create three points from which to measure.
All plan wall dims. are noted, as shown, then the following table
of dimensions is completed:-

A-C	B-C	F-D
A-D	B-D	F-E
A-P	B-P	
A-G	B-G	
A-E	B-E	
A-F	B-F	

MAIN ROOM ('Downstage' part)

CONVEX CURVE   CONCAVE CURVE

OPENING + BEAM   AUDIENCE ENTRANCE & EXIT

Figure 6-03 - THE 'UPSTAGE' SECTION OF THE MAIN ROOM
Surveying from fixed points.
Please note that metric sizes have been used - and to have included Imperial would have made
the drawing illegible. *The sizes do not matter!* The *method* is more relevant.

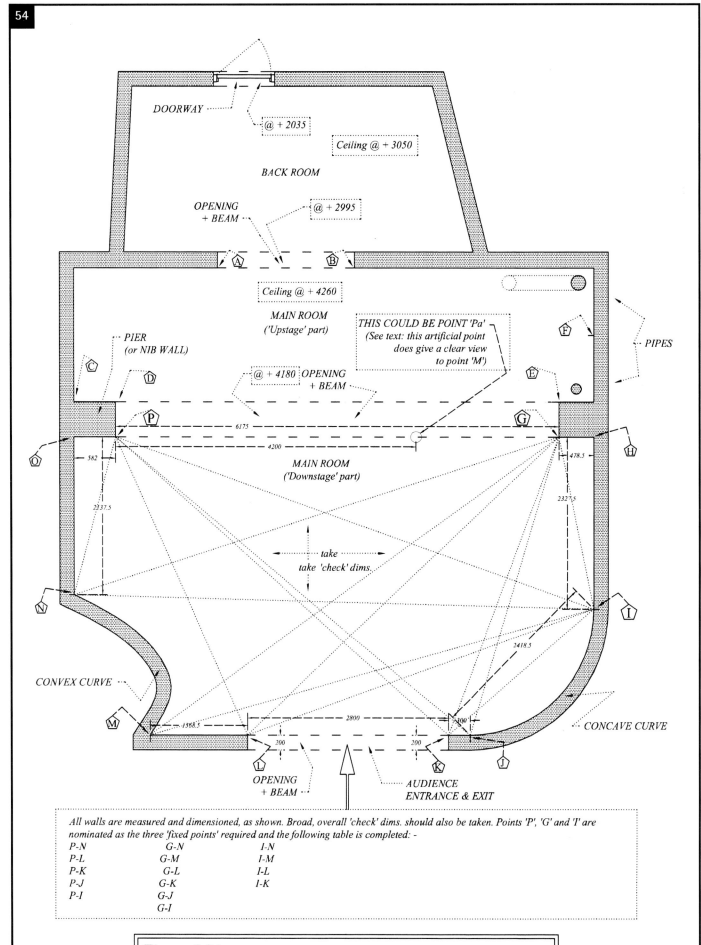

DOORWAY

@ + 2035

Ceiling @ + 3050

BACK ROOM

OPENING
+ BEAM

@ + 2995

A   B

Ceiling @ + 4260

MAIN ROOM
('Upstage' part)

THIS COULD BE POINT 'Pa'
(See text: this artificial point
does give a clear view
to point 'M')

F

PIER
(or NIB WALL)

PIPES

C

D

E

@ + 4180   OPENING
+ BEAM

P   6175   G

O

582   4200   478.5

H

2337.5

MAIN ROOM
('Downstage' part)

2327.5

take
take 'check' dims.

N

I

2418.5

CONVEX CURVE

CONCAVE CURVE

M   1368.5   2800   300

L   200   200   K   J

OPENING
+ BEAM

AUDIENCE
ENTRANCE & EXIT

All walls are measured and dimensioned, as shown. Broad, overall 'check' dims. should also be taken. Points 'P', 'G' and 'I' are
nominated as the three 'fixed points' required and the following table is completed: -

P-N	G-N	I-N
P-L	G-M	I-M
P-K	G-L	I-L
P-J	G-K	I-K
P-I	G-J	
	G-I	

Figure 6-04 - THE 'DOWN-STAGE' SECTION OF THE MAIN ROOM

Surveying from fixed points, as fig 603. The endpoints of curves must be plotted.
Please note that metric sizes have been used - and to have included Imperial would have made
the drawing illegible. *The sizes do not matter!* The *method* is more relevant.

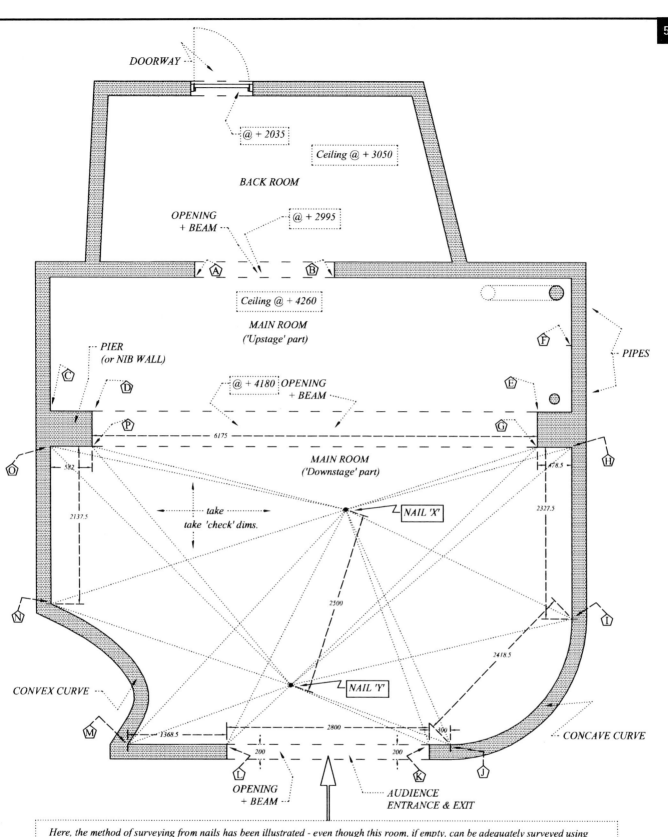

DOORWAY

@ + 2035

Ceiling @ + 3050

BACK ROOM

OPENING + BEAM

@ + 2995

Ⓐ   Ⓑ

Ceiling @ + 4260

MAIN ROOM ('Upstage' part)

PIER (or NIB WALL)

PIPES

Ⓒ

Ⓓ   Ⓕ

@ + 4180 OPENING + BEAM   Ⓔ

Ⓟ   Ⓖ

6175

MAIN ROOM ('Downstage' part)

Ⓞ   582   478.5   Ⓗ

2137.5   2327.5

take   take 'check' dims.   NAIL 'X'

2500

2418.5

Ⓝ   Ⓘ

CONVEX CURVE   NAIL 'Y'   CONCAVE CURVE

Ⓜ   1368.5   2800   300   Ⓘ

200   200

Ⓛ   Ⓚ   Ⓙ

OPENING + BEAM   AUDIENCE ENTRANCE & EXIT

Here, the method of surveying from nails has been illustrated - even though this room, if empty, can be adequately surveyed using the existing fixed points (see fig 6-04).
All walls are measured and dimensioned, as shown.
From nail 'X' measure to points 'G - to -P'.
From nail 'Y' measure to points 'G - to -P'.
Take check dims.
Note that in some circumstances three nails would be ideal. (Here, the check dims. available render the third nail unnecessary.)

Figure 6-04a - THE 'DOWN-STAGE' SECTION OF THE MAIN ROOM

Surveying from two nails, adding 'check' dims. to suit. The endpoints of curves must be plotted.
Please note that metric sizes have been used - and to have included Imperial would have made the drawing illegible. *The sizes do not matter!* The *method* is more relevant.

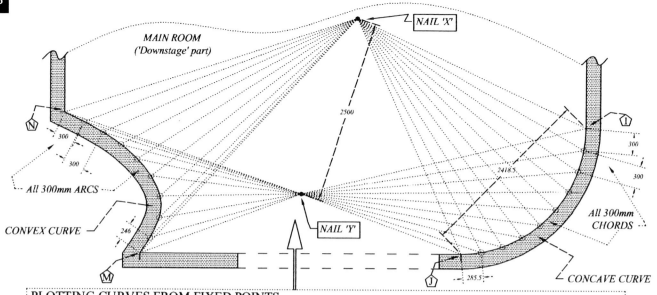

PLOTTING CURVES FROM FIXED POINTS

The two nails used in fig 6-04a have been utilised as two fixed points from which measurements are taken to marks placed upon the curved surfaces. The marks placed upon the walls are equal distances taken from one end of of the curve - see text.

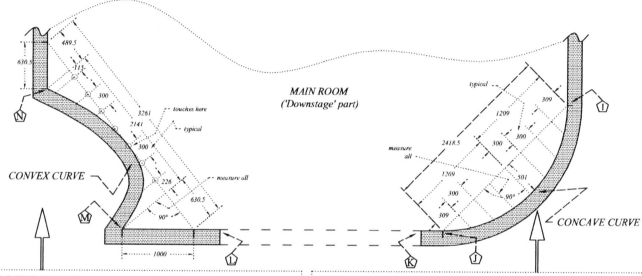

PLOTTING CURVES FROM STRAIGHT LINES

A line is struck (here, it touches the curve) and its position fixed in relation to the room. Lines are drawn at 90° from this line to the curve, it is preferable to have these lines equally spaced. Add one of these lines to each end of the curve. Measure all.

PLOTTING CURVES FROM STRAIGHT LINES

A chord line is struck, its centre point established and its position fixed in relation to the room. Lines are drawn at 90° from this line to the curve. It is preferable to have these lines equally spaced, but it is often good to have more lines, say half-spaced, near the chord's end. Measure all.

'3-4-5' TRIANGLE

*To obtain an accurate 90° angle: -
set-out a triangle whose sides are 3, 4 and 5
units in length. Here, the unit used is 400mm
(3 x 400 = 1200; 4 x 400 = 1600; 5 x 400 = 2000)*

ESTABLISHING A RADIUS POINT ON-SITE

*If the curved wall is felt to be a true arc, it can be 'tested' on-site.
Any two chords are marked, bisected by lines at 90° to them, and the radius point will be where these lines intersect. It is simple to use arcs (here shown at 2500mm) to establish these two radial lines.*

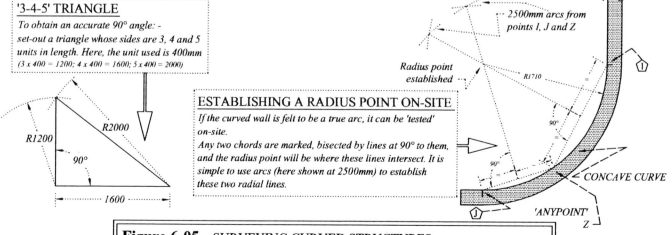

Figure 6-05 - SURVEYING CURVED STRUCTURES

Concave and convex curves. They *may* be perfect arcs, but that cannot be known without surveying.
Please note that metric sizes have been used - and to have included Imperial would have made
the drawing illegible. *The sizes do not matter!* The *method* is more relevant.

Part Two:
SCENIC
CONSTRUCTION

Introduction

Scenery is built in a unique way: our business usually dictates that items of set be reasonably lightweight yet strong, and include the potential to be broken down, transported and re-built while avoiding damage to the design. The skills needed to produce scenery have accumulated over a period in excess of 300 years, and scenery-building is a fine example of a labour-intensive, specialist trade. A skilled carpenter who has trained and worked in the building trade, for example, has to learn entirely new skills in order to work comfortably within the scenery industry – and this process of learning afresh can take a year or so (I know, I *was* that carpenter!).

The very basics of some trades have evolved and become distorted over time to suit our business; in the case of the carpenter, some traditional joints are made differently – designed, for example, to facilitate repair work. Engineers have become adept at using light steel sections to create strong units, whereas on a building-site project they are more free to specify heavy steels and a simpler design. Furthermore, the two main trades, engineering and carpentry, have grown to understand each other's trade more fully in stage work than perhaps they do on a building site. Fit-ups often involve both trades working side-by-side on one piece of set – they are forced into a symbiotic (if not always sympathetic) relationship. The early meetings called to discuss a show usually include representatives from both trades, and their understanding of one another's needs is evident from the way that they each propose solutions to problems that will suit *both* trades.

During the past few decades steel has become more commonplace. Older, traditional scenic workshops tended to be entirely carpentry-based, whereas almost all workshops now have a steel department. Steel is generally cheaper than timber and welding is an easy, quick and safe method of joining members.

The following chapters illustrate how standard scenic items can be constructed and it will be noted that, in many cases, a timber version is included alongside a steel, or steel and timber, version of the same thing. When drawing a part of a set, the choice of whether to use all timber or a mixture of steel and timber is usually dictated by the following circumstances:

- A stiff steel or aluminium skeleton may be the ideal structural framework onto which timber flattage or plywood is attached.
- It may be the case that a steel structure is lighter than a timber one. Timbers that have a large sectional area are heavy, whereas most steel used in our business is of box section (i.e. hollow). Lightweight steel members can be used to create very strong truss units.
- Frames of certain awkward shapes may create problems for the carpenters if they cannot obtain enough strength from the corner joints – if mortise and tenons would be too thin, or if half-laps would have inadequate glue/screwing surfaces, etc. You cannot weld timber! A steel frame often seems to involve fewer requirements necessary to make it 'work' structurally – joints are simply welded.
- Frequently, it does not matter whether steel or timber is favoured, but the choice of set-builder will dictate the style of construction adopted by the draughtsman.

The next eight chapters are intended as a quick-reference guide. They contain drawings accompanied by a minimum amount of text. Some of the drawings have been created for use here; others have been harvested from many and varied projects, the intention being to exhibit a broad range of acceptable construction methods. Some of these methods are of the 'conventional' type, but many are not. There will always be other, and perhaps better, methods of drawing and building the items illustrated, have no doubt about that. Considering that lateral thought is the draughtsman's greatest asset, it would be amazing if others would have drawn these structures in the same manner.

7 • Stage Flooring

Stage flooring can consist of a multitude of various construction methods. Large, outdoor 'rock and roll' stages, for example, can be of scaffolding decked with timber and plywood, or of rented 2000 x 2000 mm (say) unitised steel bays. Trade shows tend to use rented proprietary 'deck' systems – with some 'specials' made to suit (in-fill units made especially for that show). Theatre generally prefers purpose-built flooring for each show, using stock rostra where possible. These are huge generalisations of course, but still largely true. A factor common to all types is that the flooring must be able to be broken down for transportation to and from venues. Even 'permanent' installations, such as museum projects, still tend to have flooring based upon this premise.

NOTES ON FLOORING/ROSTRA

1 The finished, visible surface

A) The **thickness** of the final covering – the finished surface – must be deducted from the overall height wanted, in order to establish the height to the top of the 18 mm ply (¾") or 25 mm ply (1") surface of the rostra.

B) The **finished surface** can, of course, be of various materials, including: paint; carpet; laminate (such as *Formica*); 'ballet floor' (rolls of vinyl, suitable as a good dancing surface, laid out and taped at each venue); 4 mm (⅛") or 6 mm (¼") ply/MDF tiles; plywood or timber boards; a stage cloth (a large piece of painted canvas that is stretched out over the whole floor and tacked down at each venue); canvas-on-underfelt (each individual rostrum has an edging strip, all around, of 50 x 6 mm (2" x ¼") ply, within which is glued underfelt. Canvas is stretched and glued or tacked over all of this to form a soft surface with a clean, hard edge).

C) The **break-down** of the floor (the decision as to where the individual flooring units or rostra break apart) will be influenced by the pattern designed into the finished layer. This issue may mean a discussion with the designer, who will not want to see 'unnatural' break-lines across the floor (or 'undesigned' breaks, if such a word existed).

D) **Protection** during transit should be considered if the surface is susceptible to damage. 'Bubble-wrap', hardboard, polythene, and stiff cardboard corner-protectors are all in common use. Protection is often given scant attention, yet time and time again, expensive, under-protected items are found to be damaged on arrival. This causes further expense and, more importantly, delay. (I once opened a container in the Far East to be greeted with the sight of smashed laminated wall panels, all gloriously unprotected. That laminate was not available in Taiwan.)

2 Strength

A) Obviously, all rostra must be strong enough to withstand the loads that are to be imposed upon them. For general staging purposes a **top surface** of 18 mm (¾") ply, supported every 610 mm (2') across its narrow width, is adequate. To increase strength, supports may be spaced every 406 mm instead – joists in houses are spaced at this size, 16". It is common, however, to simply double-skin the top surface (2 x 18 mm ply), or to use 25 mm (1") ply, to increase surface strength.

B) Be alert for potential **'point loads'** – objects with a high loading on a small point or points. A heavy object on four small castors may produce point loads high enough for the castors to punch through a single skin of 18 mm ply. In extreme cases, either increase the plywood thickness or consider using thin steel plate laid where the castors are to run (if artistic considerations allow). In areas of concern, increase the number of support gates or joists.

C) Shows that include **cars or other vehicles** need strong flooring – it is wise to double-skin the top 18 mm ply, even when using *Steeldeck®* (which has a 5-ton spread load capacity). If cars are to be driven up or down ramps, then consider adding a third skin of alloy or steel treadplate to increase grip and to withstand the high impact loads imposed at the lower ends of the ramps.

D) If the public is to use the stage, seek advice from the local authority's representative and consult the venue's technical manager because the floor's specifications may be decided locally.

3 Noise reduction

A) Rostra can sometimes act like a giant drum, magnifying the sound of footsteps. Microphones will pick this up and exaggerate the problem. Always specify that **underfelt** (or similar) be stapled to the underside of the top surface to insulate against sound.

B) Loose, wobbly or ill-fitting tops will increase noise pollution problems. Removable tops may be fixed down to the rostra with pin-hinges and the simple act of rubbing **candle-grease** along the edges of all tops will dramatically cut down unwanted noise.

C) Some removable tops have thin rubber or **neoprene strips** glued to their undersurface; these strips are placed where the top rests upon a gate or joist and they help to muffle unwanted sounds.

4 Stability and the use of 'feet'

A) Always ensure that flooring structures have **'feet'** rather than long edges that sit directly upon the stage proper. Long edges will rock-about on any unevenness in the main stage, causing instability and increasing noise pollution. Feet are simply pads that keep the body of the structure off the main stage. '**Legs**' are the members that go down to the stage; feet are added between legs, if needed.

Feet should be of timber or plywood, allowing the carpenters to plane them down and scribe them to the sub-surface. Plywood rostra can simply have feet cut into the plywood gates; traditional folding-gate rostra have 'blind toggles' fitted between the legs – these act as feet, and are easily planed down.

B) When building **low floors** – floors that consist of 18 mm (¾") ply laid on 70 x 21 (3" x 1") frames, or ply on individual joists – allow for the application of 12 mm (½") ply pads (feet) below the frame or joist. These 12 mm ply feet are normally about 100–150 mm (4–6") long, spaced at approximately 610 mm (2') centres. They are the width of the material to which they are glued and screwed, and it is good practice to bevel their edges. This helps to prevent them being torn off and/or splitting while the floor is being manhandled.

5   Fit plastic caps to steel legs

A) Always specify that proprietary **plastic caps** be fitted to the bottom of any steel support legs used. These protect the venue's stage from being scored by the raw, cut edges of the steel legs.

B) These caps, when fitted to a steel decking-unit or rostrum, can greatly assist the crew in moving the unit around the stage. On a good hardwood stage, the caps allow the unit to be slid with comparative ease.

6   Connections

A) Ensure that rostra can be **bolted together** in order that the whole floor becomes one rigid unit, thereby increasing its total strength and safety. Think about *how* the crew can bolt it together – this may be tricky on a low floor, where access from below is not possible (consider having removable tops, or hand-access traps). Normally, M10 bolts are used – timber rostra should have bolt-plates pinned to them.

B) 'Drop-cleats' can be used on low flooring. These are usually cut from a piece of 70 x 21 (3" x 1" par). On tour, or during a long run in a repertoire, these may dry out and split, causing units to jam and not fit correctly. In order to help prevent this, cut the split batten at 30°, *not* 45°, and arris the exposed edges (give them a slight 'round').

7   Bracing

A) As rostra gain in height, the importance of **side bracing** increases. *Bracing needs to be in all three planes* – although the plywood tops are often sufficient to solve the plan-bracing problem. Timber-gate rostra can have braces built into the frames (or 'gates'). Gates of 18 mm plywood need no bracing, like the tops, the plywood sheet is itself a brace, even when voided.

B) A *Steeldeck*® floor will need diagonal scaffold-tube bracing if its height is over ±1550 mm (±5'). A very high floor will require horizontal scaffold-tubes every 1830 mm (6') high, plus diagonal bracing. Remember to consider whether the structure has adequate bracing to *each* of its three dimensional faces – plan, front and side.

C) **Bracing in general:** remember, when drawing braces, that **timber** is stronger *in compression than it is in tension*, whereas **steel** is stronger *in tension than it is in compression*. **Figure 7.01** provides a visual 'memory-jogger' of this fact – it bears no relation to flooring specifically, but gives a general rule of thumb for bracing.

Bracing is such an important factor that it *must* be borne in mind when first glancing at how to build any structure – when first seeing the model of a theatre set, for example. All structures have forces imposed upon them that attempt to distort the shape of the structure: braces resist these forces.

8   Fascias

A) Any vertical change of height will normally require a fascia if it is 'in view' (of the audience). The fascia may be formed by the flooring structure itself – a traditional timber gate, clad with painted 4 mm ply, for example – or it may be a separate item that fits to the flooring units. Some venues will insist on having fascias throughout, especially if the public is using the rostra – this is a fire precaution, helping to avoid having lit cigarettes roll under the floor.

B) Obviously, fascias have a **thickness in plan view:** so do remember to include this in the ground-plan and flooring drawings. It is a common error for an inexperienced draughtsman to draw the floor without considering fascias, thinking, perhaps, that fascias are 'something that can be added later'. Wrong!

C) Where possible, allow the **18 mm ply top** of the flooring to overhang the fascia, protecting it. If the aesthetics of the job prevent this, then consider having the top overhanging enough for it to sit in a rebate in the top of the fascia. Clearly, the fascia needs to be sufficiently thick to allow this – if it has a large timber moulding at the top, for example. The idea is to avoid a complete separation line between fascia and top, as one may drop in relation to the other and look a mess.

D) Most flooring requires fascias somewhere; they are usually simple to draw, but always **consider how they will be fitted**. If the floor is high enough, then back access is possible and fascias can be bolted or pin-hinged with ease. On low floors, consider using drop-cleats, secret screws or even *Velcro* (if the fascia is overhung by the top).

E) Ensure that someone exiting the stage cannot accidentally 'kick off' a fascia. If the fascia has some substance to it, then use stud plates/step hooks/pin hinges or the like. **Trade show work** frequently involves using 4 mm or 6 mm ply fascias that are wrapped with felt and pinned onto the floor and staircase risers. *Always* ensure that the top edge is bevelled and fitted slightly down from the floor or tread above. It does ruin a trade show if the guest speaker walks offstage to thunderous applause and trips, kicking off fascias as he goes.

9   Tracks

A) Scenery that moves across the floor in view of the audience will often require **tracks** to guide it. The floor adjacent to the track may also conceal the secret method used to drive the moving piece of set – cables, etc. There are many different types of tracks, and often, 'one-off' inventions are designed specifically for the job in hand. **Figure 7.02** illustrates two common types.

B) Some high-tech shows incorporate moving trucks with a drive unit that 'reads' the location of a copper wire let into the flooring below – the truck then follows the path of that wire. This method looks wonderful because the

GRAVITY dictates that doors want to drop down at this point - in time, they often do. Any boards or cladding on the other face help to prevent this, but they also add to the weight, *so the brace is necessary.*

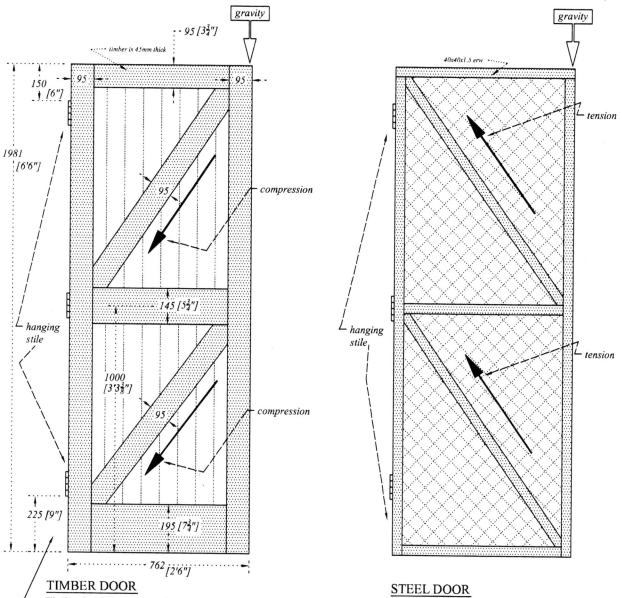

TIMBER DOOR

The bracing follows a logical pattern: the braces can be seen to be taking the top, right corner load directly along their length, back to the hanging stile - *in compression*. This method is adopted because **timber is stronger in *compression* than in tension.**

STEEL DOOR

The bracing direction is reversed, seemingly against logic. The braces are 'holding-up' the middle and bottom rails, supporting them from the hanging stile. This method is adopted because **steel is stronger in *tension* than in compression.**

Please note: - *This is all a bit theoretical when considering most steel doors - if the steel door were to be made with its bracing reversed, with its bracing being in compression, then very little difference would be detectable. However, remember this example as an illustration of a profound principle that gains more importance when dealing with larger, load-bearing items.*

NOTE ON TIMBER DOORS: -
A 'framed, ledge and braced' door is drawn here - it is clad on the opposite face with 10mm tongue and grooved boards. **Flush** *doors are clad with 4mm ply to both faces and this plywood acts as its own brace - structural bracing timbers are not required.*

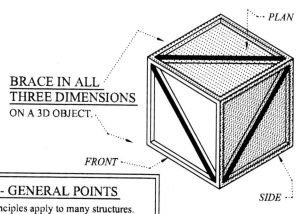

BRACE IN ALL THREE DIMENSIONS ON A 3D OBJECT.

Figure 7-01 - BRACING - GENERAL POINTS
Doors are illustrated here, but the principles apply to many structures.

62

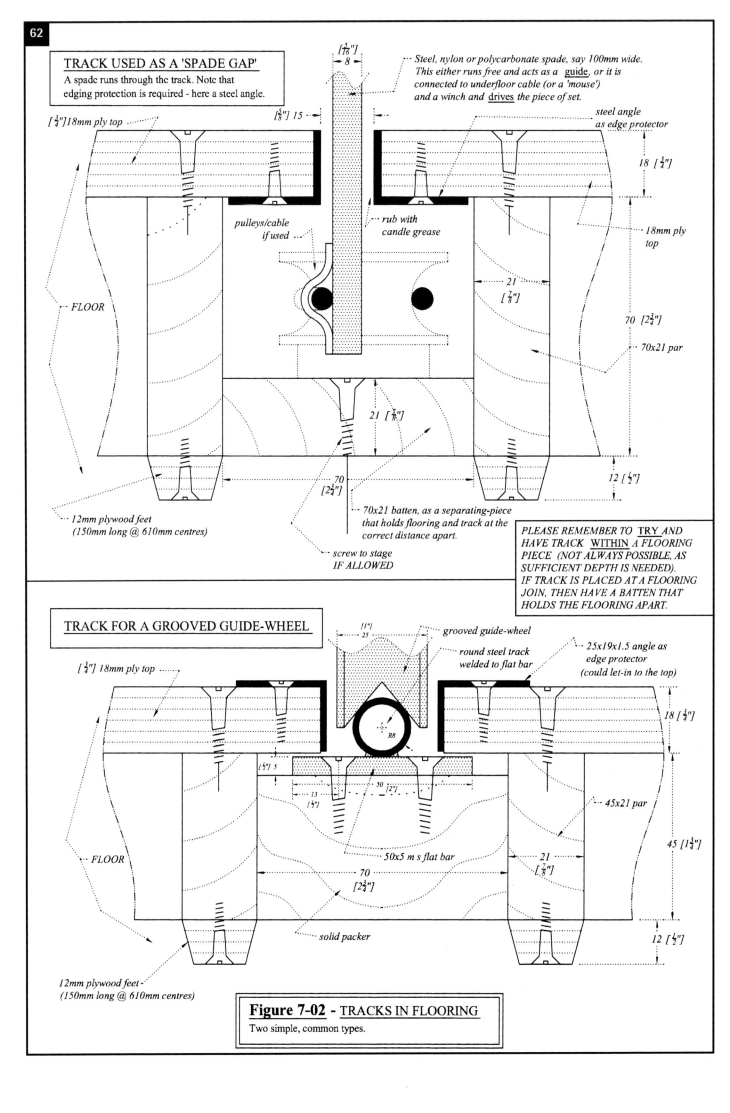

Figure 7-02 - TRACKS IN FLOORING
Two simple, common types.

trucks seem to move around the stage of their own volition, without any visible tracks. To date, my experience of this technology is limited, but I do know that signal interference can be a huge problem with systems of this type and can require the use of metal sheathing to be laid on or under the floor. My only point here is that, when using industrial systems of *any* type, ensure that the manufacturers are completely aware of all potential problems. Insist upon a test of some kind being performed.

C)   **Track protection** is usually required to prevent the edges of the track being gnawed and worn by the action of the spade or guide wheel. The examples drawn have thin angle fitted to the exposed edges of the 18 mm ply top; however, flat-bar may be used, or a laminate (a *Formica* strip). Candle-grease acts as a lubricant that does not damage the painted surface of the floor.

D)   Bear in mind that the track literally splits the top flooring plywood in two, but it is preferable *not* to make this a flooring break. It is better, if possible to have the track contained *within* a piece – or pieces – of flooring. This will ensure that the track remains a constant width, because it is 'held' within a section of floor. If this is not possible (there may not be enough depth to the floor, for example – as sketched here, in fact), then ensure that some sort of batten is introduced that allows each section of floor to butt against something solid as it is being positioned by the crew. This batten is intended to help maintain a constant width of track.

SOME TYPES OF FLOORING

1 Traditional 3" x 1" folding-gate rostra – figure 7.03

A)   This type of rostrum has long been the traditional type used in theatre. It is lightweight, long-lasting, easy to lay and folds for travel (saving truck space). It is normal to have sash-cord knotted through the bottom rail; this is used to tie the folded gates together. (The 3" x 1" refers to the fact that the rostrum is composed of frames made from 3" x 1" par timber – now known as 70 x 21 mm.)

B)   The materials used (70 x 21 mm) are quite cheap but the labour costs are high, since it is labour-intensive for the carpenters to create so many mortise and tenon joints. Specify this type of rostrum when durability and lightness are important factors. (Bear in mind that although plywood gate rostra are quicker to build, the material costs more, is heavier and is limited in size.)

C)   Note that the 18 mm plywood tops are removable. It is usual to have six plywood corner blocks, as shown, which locate the top and prevent the rostrum's gates from folding when in use. Pin-hinges may also be added, provided that access is feasible.

D)   The tops should have underfelt (or similar) applied to their undersurface as a sound insulator.

E)   The braces used in the gates may be 45 x 21 mm (2" x 1"), screwed, or 70 x 21 mm (3" x 1").

F)   If the rostrum is to form part of a large floor, and not be a stand-alone unit, then it is bolted to its neighbours with M10 bolts. Thin steel bolt plates are pinned to the 70 x 21 mm gates in order that the bolts do not damage the gates after continuous use.

G)   Note the plan-view positions of the hinges, allowing the unit to fold. Two of the hinges are reversed and countersunk on their back faces. *Each* hinge must be 'stove-bolted' – i.e. a thin machine screw ('three-sixteenth' – 4.7 mm) is used to bolt through one of the hinge's holes *nearest the knuckle*. Flat, square nuts are used that are let-in flush to the timber and any protruding, threaded part of the machine screw is cut off.

H)   The overall dimensions of the folding gates can be larger than the size of a plywood sheet – the top would be 'plated' together to form the size desired. To 'plate' a top is to join the pieces with a piece of plywood (a plate) on their undersurface; the plate is well screwed and glued and is trimmed to miss any gates. It is is approximately 200 mm (8") wide.

I)   Odd-shaped rostra (not rectangular) can still be made to 'fold' if care is taken. The bulk of the shape is made up of a rectangular formation of gates, while having the 'odd' shape supported by gates that pin-hinge: these gates are removed before folding the rest.

J)   Folding-gate rostra can, of course, be raked.

K)   This style of rostra can be built in steel or plywood.

L)   **Figure 7.03**, like those that follow, illustrates a standard 'stock' rostrum – an 8' x4' (2440 x 1220 mm). Clearly, the rostrum can be far bigger if necessary.

2 Plywood-gate rostra – figure 7.04

A)   As mentioned above, plywood rostra may be folding-gate rostra – they are heavier and more expensive in materials, but cheaper in labour terms. Hinges *must* be bolted (*see* 'G' above).

B)   **Figure 7.04** shows a rigid, non-folding rostrum (a rostrum 'block'). This type of rostrum is simply screwed together as a single unit, including the top – this can help to protect the edges of the tops if the artwork above is fragile. Each unit is drop-cleated together, using drop-cleats (sometimes called split-battens) as shown.

C)   Drop-cleated flooring must be laid in a certain order, so always number the rostra in order of laying to simplify the crew's task.

D)   Note that the gates are 21 mm back from the top, along the edges that are to 'hook' over the previously laid rostra; this is to allow for the thickness of the split-battens. A study of Section 'A-A' will clarify this important point.

E)   Always cut feet into the bottom of the gates as shown (to prevent the unit rocking upon an uneven floor or stage). The only exception to this is if the gate is to be visible to the audience and has no fascia (*see* page 60).

F)   Note that the gates/frames are 'voided out' in order to save weight (unless seen by the audience!). It is normal to leave about 100 mm (4") of plywood all around, as sufficient support.

3 Bridging-pieces and rostra – figure 7.05

A)   Bridging-pieces can save considerable labour and materials costs because, in effect, every other rostrum can be replaced with one.

B)   Each bridge-piece usually consists of an 18 mm ply top screwed to 145 x 21 mm (6" x 1") timber framing. It locates onto a 145 x 21 mm batten that is bolted to the adjoining rostrum. This batten should have legs down to the floor or stage as support. Flushing plates hold the units in place but bolts may be used instead, or additionally.

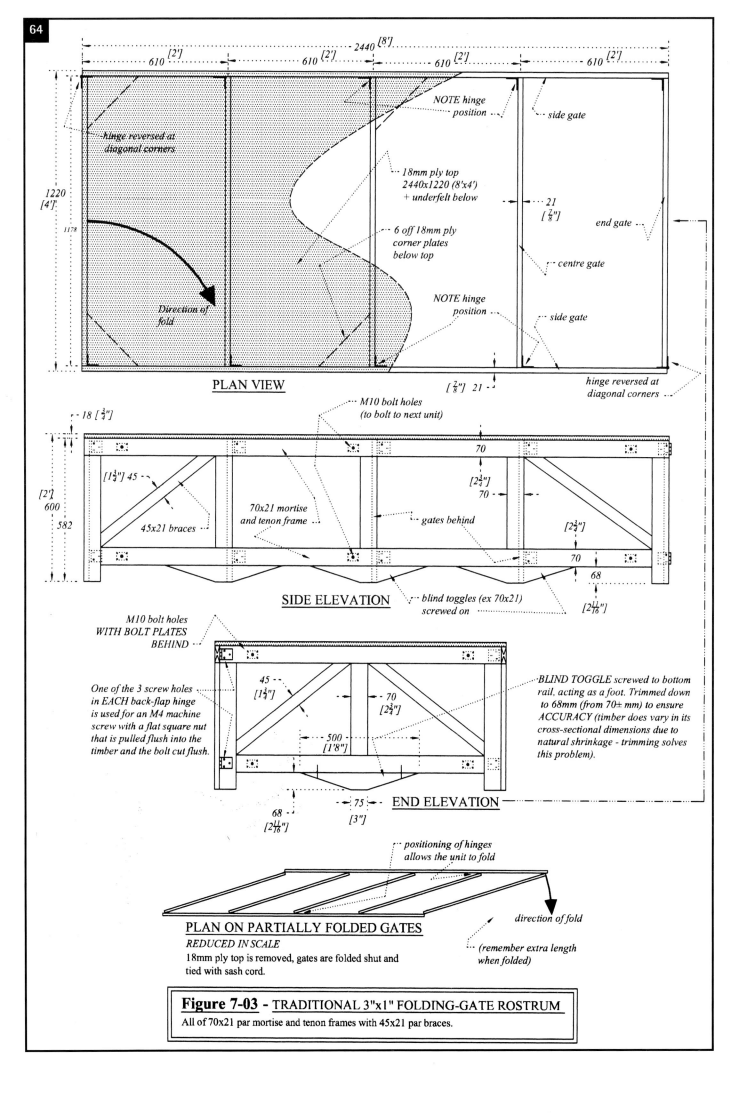

64

2440 [8']

610 [2']   610 [2']   610 [2']   610 [2']

hinge reversed at diagonal corners

1220 [4']

1178

Direction of fold

NOTE hinge position

side gate

18mm ply top 2440x1220 (8'x4') + underfelt below

21 [⁷⁄₈"]

end gate

6 off 18mm ply corner plates below top

centre gate

NOTE hinge position

side gate

[⁷⁄₈"] 21

hinge reversed at diagonal corners

PLAN VIEW

18 [³⁄₄"]

M10 bolt holes (to bolt to next unit)

70

[2'] 600

582

[1¾"] 45

[2¼"] 70

70

45x21 braces

70x21 mortise and tenon frame

gates behind

[2¾"]

70

68

[2¹¹⁄₁₆"]

blind toggles (ex 70x21) screwed on

SIDE ELEVATION

M10 bolt holes WITH BOLT PLATES BEHIND

One of the 3 screw holes in EACH back-flap hinge is used for an M4 machine screw with a flat square nut that is pulled flush into the timber and the bolt cut flush.

45 [1¾"]

70 [2¾"]

500 [1'8"]

BLIND TOGGLE screwed to bottom rail, acting as a foot. Trimmed down to 68mm (from 70± mm) to ensure ACCURACY (timber does vary in its cross-sectional dimensions due to natural shrinkage - trimming solves this problem).

68 [2¹¹⁄₁₆"]

75 [3"]

END ELEVATION

positioning of hinges allows the unit to fold

direction of fold

PLAN ON PARTIALLY FOLDED GATES

REDUCED IN SCALE

18mm ply top is removed, gates are folded shut and tied with sash cord.

(remember extra length when folded)

Figure 7-03 - TRADITIONAL 3"x1" FOLDING-GATE ROSTRUM

All of 70x21 par mortise and tenon frames with 45x21 par braces.

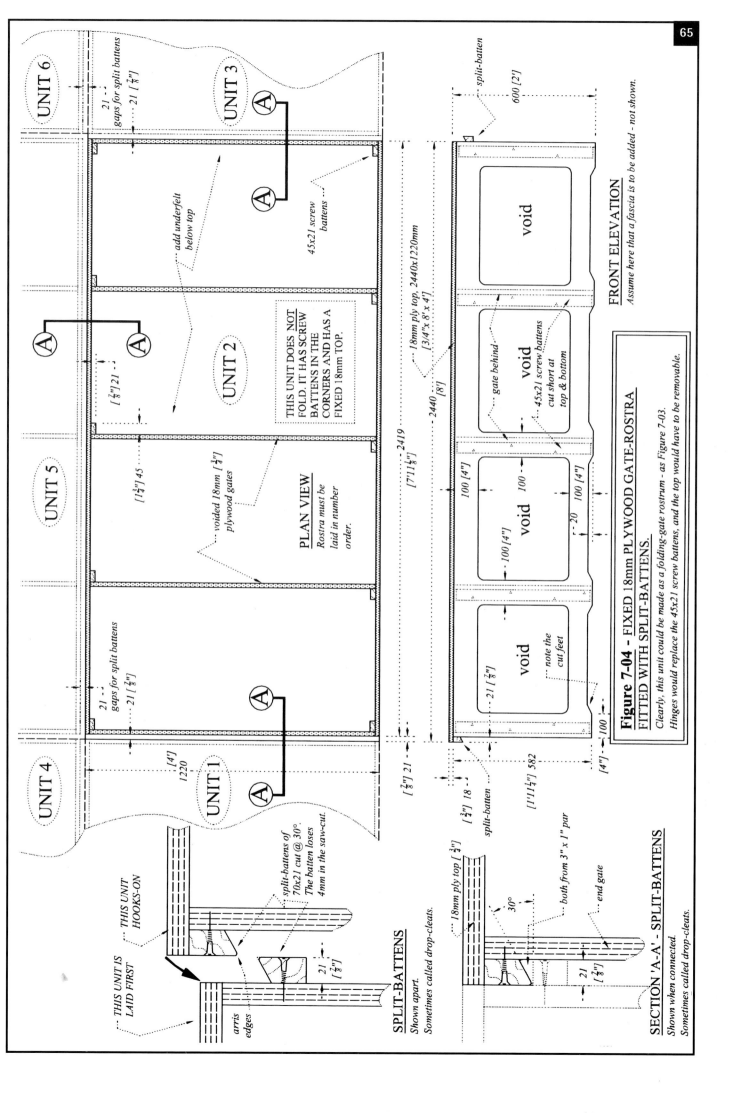

UNIT 6

21 - -
gaps for split battens
21 [⅞"]

UNIT 3

Ⓐ Ⓐ

Ⓐ Ⓐ

UNIT 5

[⅞"] 21 - -

add underfelt
below top

45x21 screw
battens ·····

[1¾"] 45

voided 18mm [¾"]
plywood gates

UNIT 2

THIS UNIT DOES NOT
FOLD. IT HAS SCREW
BATTENS IN THE
CORNERS AND HAS A
FIXED 18mm TOP.

PLAN VIEW
Rostra must be
laid in number
order.

UNIT 4

[4"]
1220

UNIT 1

Ⓐ

21 - -
gaps for split battens
21 [⅞"]

THIS UNIT IS
LAID FIRST

THIS UNIT
HOOKS-ON

split-battens of
70x21 cut @ 30°.
The batten loses
4mm in the saw-cut.

21
[⅞"]

arris
edges

SPLIT-BATTENS
Shown apart.
Sometimes called drop-cleats.

2419
[7'11⅛"]

18mm ply top, 2440x1220mm
[¾"x 8' x 4']

2440 [8']

[⅞"] 21 - -

[¾"] 18 - -

split-batten

[1'1½"] 582

100 [4"]

100 [4"]

split-batten

600 [2']

void

gate behind

void

45x21 screw battens
cut short at
top & bottom

void

- 100 [4"]

20

100 [4"]

void

21 [⅞"]

note the
cut feet

[4"] - 100 -

[4"]

FRONT ELEVATION
Assume here that a fascia is to be added - not shown.

18mm ply top [¾"]

30°

both from 3" x 1" par

end gate

21
[⅞"]

SECTION 'A-A' - SPLIT-BATTENS
Shown when connected.
Sometimes called drop-cleats.

Figure 7-04 - FIXED 18mm PLYWOOD GATE-ROSTRA
FITTED WITH SPLIT-BATTENS.

Clearly, this unit could be made as a folding-gate rostrum - as Figure 7-03.
Hinges would replace the 45x21 screw battens, and the top would have to be removable.

C) *Always* use a bolted support batten – *never* have the bridge-piece just bolted through to the rostra.

D) Clearly, steel versions of the same principle can be utilised.

E) Remember to consider this system when a clear-way is wanted beneath the rostra (for cables/pulleys/walkways, etc.).

4 Laid flooring 3" x 1" – figure 7.06

A) This tough, light staging is used when a low floor is required. The 18 mm plywood top (plus underfelt) is screwed to a frame of 70 x 21 mm (3" x 1") on edge, forming one unit. Obviously, this frame may be of 145 x 21 mm (6" x 1") – the extra depth may be required in order to conceal a special track, for example. Plywood sheet sizes of 3050 x 1525 mm (10' x 5') are frequently used, reducing the number of units and the number of visible joins.

B) Split-battens (drop-cleats) are invariably used for floors of this type, so number each unit in order of lay!

C) Two types of feet may be introduced: either have the 70 x 21 mm scooped out 6 mm in between cross-members, or have 6 mm (¼") birch ply feet pinned and glued to the underside (adding feet can be a convenient way of obtaining a specific overall height, if that is important).

5 Steel rostra – figure 7.07

A) Clearly, any of the previously mentioned types of flooring can be constructed using steel instead of timber. High rostra can often be cheaper, lighter and stronger if made of steel rather than timber. The decision to 'go with steel' is often made on the basis of evaluating the services offered by the contractor employed to do the work.

B) Until enough experience is gained, always consult with a qualified structural engineer before deciding on the steel tube sizes that are to be used – usually, a chat with the intended contractor will clarify this issue.

C) Try to specify erw (electric resistance welded) steel where possible, as it is cheap and readily available. It does have a thin wall, so it may be insufficient for structural work. Do obtain a steel brochure from a supplier!

D) Figure 7.07 shows two versions of a rigid, non-folding rostrum and one version of a folding-gate rostrum. The drawings are self-explanatory, but note that a fixed, non-folding steel rostrum may not require middle gates/frames – a top member of steel is adequate.

E) Note that there are as many types of steel rostra as there is the imagination to dream them up! The only 'rules' are that the units are *strong* enough and *convenient* enough to do the job in hand. If you have to invent a new version, or adapt an old version, and are unsure of its structural capabilities, then consult an engineer and/or indicate upon your drawing that you would like a qualified engineer to check your proposals *before* construction commences.

6 Steel 'drop-in bar' flooring – figure 7.08

A) This type of flooring system is ideal for producing a large area of staging that can be struck and rebuilt while keeping the number of frames used down to a minimum. There are many varieties of drop-in bar flooring, but in essence, it consists of having two long side-frames, a braced end-frame at *each* end and drop-in bars in between.

B) The length of these units need not be dictated by plywood sheet sizes, as long as the edges of the removable tops are supported by steel. The ply tops should be fitted with corner blocks to help locate them. Underfelt and neoprene strips should always be fitted to the tops.

C) A floor of this type breaks down into convenient parts for travelling. Once struck, you are left with a pile of drop-in bars, some end-frames and a few long side-frames. Consider building a strong plywood box on castors that will be used to store the drop-in bars – this is essential if the show is to tour.

D) The end-frames may be bolted to the side frames, using lugs. Strong pin-hinges may also be used; these are quicker and simpler to use than bolts.

E) Note that the frames are made of erw steel, with a 1.5 mm (¹/₁₆") wall thickness as is standard. However, the drop-in bars are of 50 x 25 x 3 mm rhs (2" x 1" x ⅛") – the thicker wall steel being stronger and more rigid. These bars are taking a direct load, whereas the framing steel has its load spread across all its members.

7 Proprietary flooring systems – figure 7.09

A) Numerous flooring systems are available for hire or to buy; always consult the brochure and the manufacturer for relevant details. Some types are in the form of individual rostra, such as *Steeldeck®*, while others form bays of steel members that bolt together (each bay being, say, 2400 x 2400 mm in plan view). Most are of steel construction, but some are aluminium. Timber or plywood rostra can be hired from most contractors – these are usually in stock sizes, 2440 x 1220 mm (8' x 4') being common. European systems are frequently made to sizes that are purely metric, such as 2000 x 1000 mm.

B) Figure 7.09 shows a *Steeldeck®* rostrum. This has long been the industry leader, as familiar in California as it is in London – hence the details illustrated here. These ubiquitous decks utilise scaffold tube as their legs; this is very convenient because scaffold tube is readily available throughout the world, so replacement or new legs are easy to obtain. The legs slip into a corner socket and are held by tightening a captive bolt. They have plastic feet fitted to the legs. Each deck can sustain a spread load of 5 tons. The decks bolt together from below – they have to, given that the decks have fixed tops. Raked flooring simply requires the use of welded angled legs, as drawn. These are usually ordered from *Steeldeck*.

As shown in the drawing, *Steeldeck®* floor will need diagonal scaffold-tube bracing if its height is over ±1550 mm (±5'). A very high floor will require horizontal scaffold-tubes every 1830 mm (6') high, plus diagonal bracing. Remember to consider whether the structure has adequate bracing to *each* of its three dimensional faces – plan, front and side.

C) Never *attempt to replicate a proprietary system!* Patent laws rightly protect these systems and court action *will* follow any attempt to manufacture copies. You, as draughtsman, could be implicated in that court process – so 'just say NO' to your boss if you are asked to draw a replica for manufacture by anyone other than the *bona fide* manufacturer.

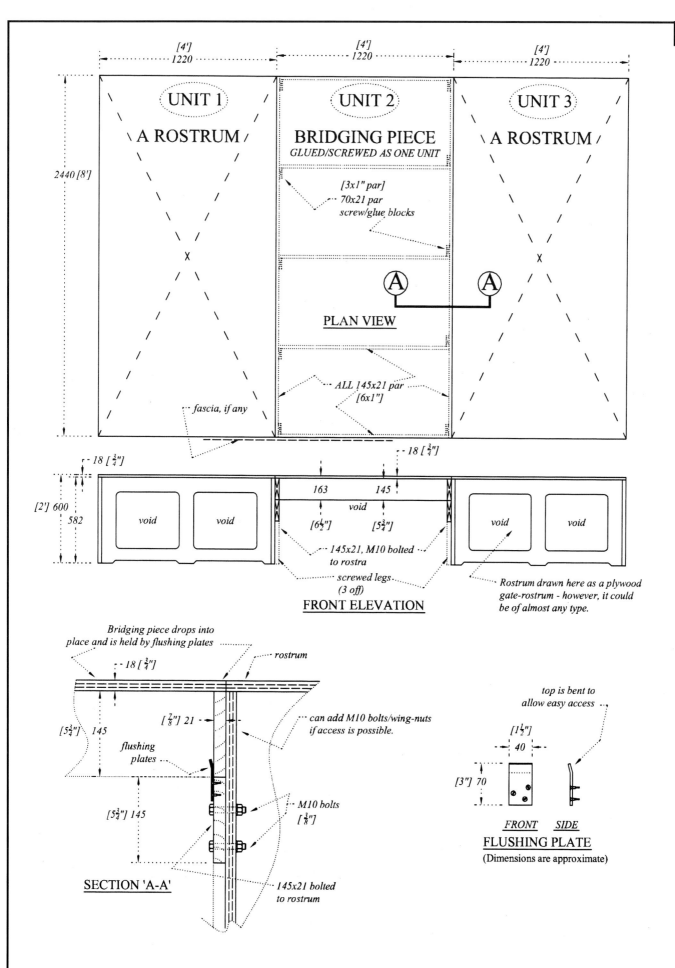

Figure 7-05 - BRIDGING PIECES

Used to save materials. Lightweight and cheap.

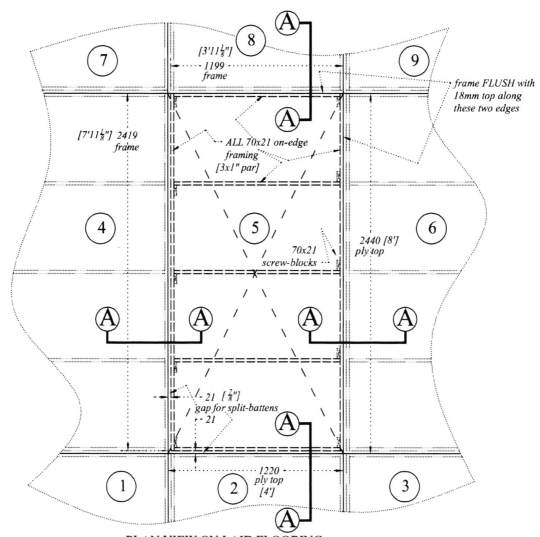

⑦ ⑧ ⑨

[3'11⅛"]
1199
frame

frame FLUSH with
18mm top along
these two edges

[7'11⅛"] 2419
frame

ALL 70x21 on-edge
framing
[3x1" par]

④ ⑤ ⑥

70x21
screw-blocks

2440 [8']
ply top

Ⓐ Ⓐ Ⓐ Ⓐ

- 21 [⅞"]
gap for split-battens
- 21

Ⓐ

① ② ③

1220
ply top
[4']

Ⓐ

PLAN VIEW ON LAID FLOORING

Laid in NUMBER ORDER - they join by the use of split-battens.
Each piece is made of an 18mm ply top (2440x1220, for example) screwed to
a frame of 70x21 par on-edge (frame size here is 2419x1199).
Add underfelt below all tops.

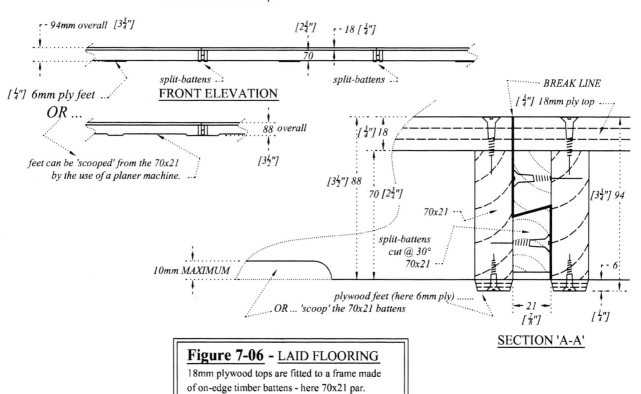

- 94mm overall [3¾"]

[2¾"] - 18 [¾"]

70

split-battens split-battens

[¼"] 6mm ply feet

FRONT ELEVATION

BREAK LINE
[¾"] 18mm ply top

OR ...

88 overall

[3½"]

feet can be 'scooped' from the 70x21
by the use of a planer machine.

[¾"] 18

[3½"] 88

70 [2¾"]

[3¾"] 94

70x21

split-battens
cut @ 30°
70x21

10mm MAXIMUM

- 6

plywood feet (here 6mm ply)
... OR ... 'scoop' the 70x21 battens

21
[⅞"]

[¼"]

SECTION 'A-A'

Figure 7-06 - LAID FLOORING

18mm plywood tops are fitted to a frame made
of on-edge timber battens - here 70x21 par.

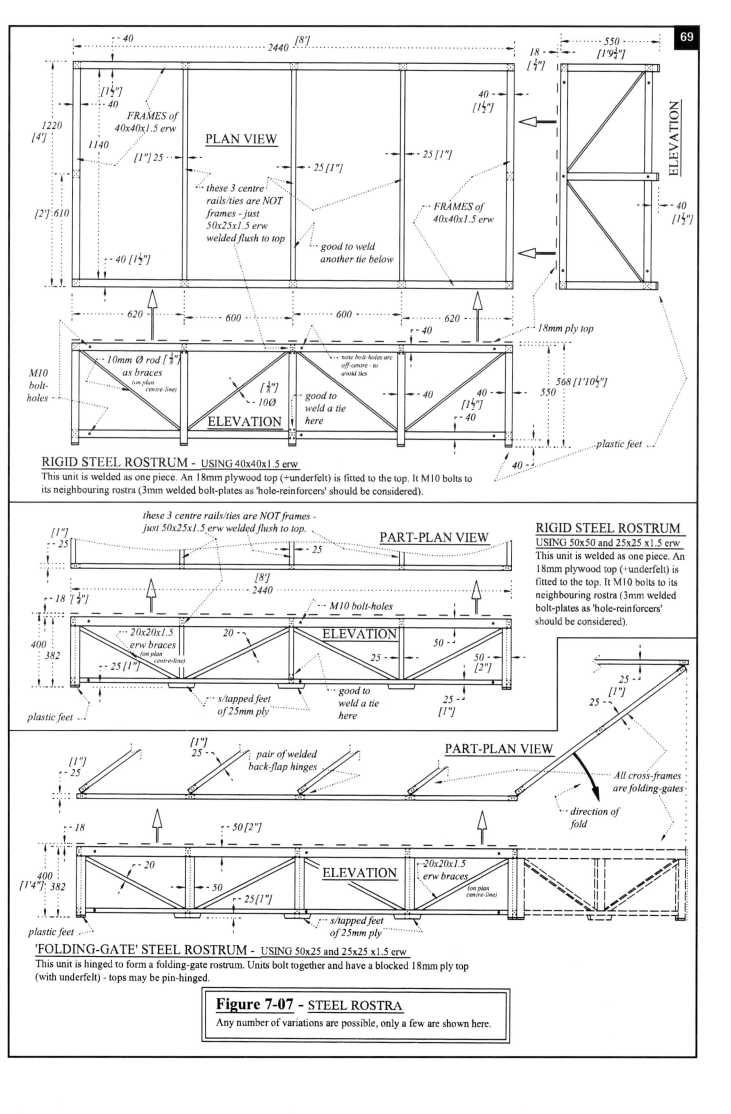

RIGID STEEL ROSTRUM - USING 40x40x1.5 erw
This unit is welded as one piece. An 18mm plywood top (+underfelt) is fitted to the top. It M10 bolts to its neighbouring rostra (3mm welded bolt-plates as 'hole-reinforcers' should be considered).

RIGID STEEL ROSTRUM
USING 50x50 and 25x25 x1.5 erw
This unit is welded as one piece. An 18mm plywood top (+underfelt) is fitted to the top. It M10 bolts to its neighbouring rostra (3mm welded bolt-plates as 'hole-reinforcers' should be considered).

'FOLDING-GATE' STEEL ROSTRUM - USING 50x25 and 25x25 x1.5 erw
This unit is hinged to form a folding-gate rostrum. Units bolt together and have a blocked 18mm ply top (with underfelt) - tops may be pin-hinged.

Figure 7-07 - STEEL ROSTRA
Any number of variations are possible, only a few are shown here.

8 Profiled flooring – floors that do not have a flat surface – figure 7.10

A) It is common for shows to have an undulating floor – for example, the design may require the floor to resemble a grassy bank. The most usual method of forming these shapes is to use 'formers' of 18 mm (¾") ply, placed about 610 mm (2') apart and having their upper surface profiled to the desired shape. These formers may include profiled cross-members of either plywood or timber, creating an undulating shape to the show floor in both side-section and elevation.

B) The surface cladding to undulating floors may be:

(i) **Interwoven plywood strips**, say 50 x 4 mm (2" x ⅛") birch ply (birch is stronger – and dearer). These are soaked to give them more elasticity, and pinned and glued to the formers. Each strip passes over, then under, the strips going across it. Canvas 'handkerchiefs' are soaked in glue and laid in overlapping layers over the plywood strips. Underfelt can then be stuck down, then carpet, shaved and painted to suit the design. This method gives a very strong but still 'sprung' surface. Sadly, however, this is a very expensive method of flooring, it being a highly labour-intensive process to weave and pin all the ply strips.

(ii) **EML** (expanded metal lathe) can be used instead of interlocking ply. It is cheap and readily available. Nail it to the formers using flat-head, cement-coated nails. The canvas handkerchiefs can still be made to adhere to this material – add some from below, to form a glued sandwich.

(iii) **6 mm plywood** – if a smooth, harder surface is required and the undulations are gentle enough, three layers of 6 mm ply may be pinned and glued to the formers. Each sheet may need soaking to soften it. Ensure that the sheet-joins of each layer are staggered.

C) **Figure 7.10** illustrates a profiled plywood flooring unit, 2440 x 1220 mm (8' x 4'). The construction is very similar to a standard plywood-gate rostrum (*see* **figure 7.04**), the main difference being that the upper edges of the gates/frames are profiled. A cross-member of 145 x 21 par (6" x 1") has been introduced to stiffen the structure and to reduce the area of unsupported surface; this cross-member could be of 18 mm ply. Either type should be half-lapped and blocked and screwed to the main formers.

Note that in Section 'A-A', a simple method of giving dimensions to undulating surfaces is shown. Perpendicular lines are 'dropped' at regular intervals down to the surface; each one is dimensioned, and the carpenters merely join the dots and cut the shape drawn. The designer sometimes prefers the carpenters to make the units over-sized, in which case the artists draw the shapes and the carpenters then cut the formers and complete the unit.

Each frame or gate will need an elevation drawing. This is the only safe way of ensuring that the overall shape is achieved.

D) If the show floor is very high, units such as the one drawn can sit upon a sub-floor. The sub-floor may be a simple deck system, allowing access below.

E) Floors of this type can be made in steel. Plywood formers can be bolted to the top of 'normal' steel rostra, creating the same upper surface as the timber version. The formers themselves can be steel tube, bent to shape and clad with mesh, spot-welded to the tubes.

9 Flooring that is curved in plan view – figure 7.11

A) Floors that have an irregular plan-view shape may require their edges to be 'finished' – made presentable – if they are in view of the audience. The simplest method of doing this is shown in **figure 7.11**. A plywood 'rib', or 'sweep', is fitted to the underside of the unit and thin plywood – 4 mm (⅛") or 6 mm (¼") – is pinned and glued around this. The sweep should be at least 70 mm (3") wide and screwed to support timbers. The floor shown is a low floor, 120 mm high (4¾"), but the principle used to furnish it with a clean edge can be used for higher flooring: extra, intermediate ply ribs may be added between the bottom sweep and the plywood top.

B) Section 'B-B' shows the use of screw-battens to join flooring pieces. These allow each section of floor to screw to its neighbour – each being laid in number order. This method is only used where the top surface is to be covered (say, with carpet) as the screws may spoil any surface artwork.

10 Fascia – figure 7.12

A) As previously mentioned, fascias are as varied in character as are types of flooring: the example illustrated here cannot be described as being 'normal' or 'typical' – no such beast exists. This unit represents the support columns and ventilation grills below the veranda of a timber-built house. The grill effect is achieved by having two layers of 12 mm ply (½"): one has slats cut vertically; the other's slats are horizontal. Both are screwed together. The columns are a simple construction of timber and ply boxing-out, clad with decorative 18 mm MDF 'quoins'. An overhanging floor unit hides the top edge, and the possibility of rear access allows for the use of pin-hinges to fit the fascia to a batten let in to the floor.

RAKED FLOORING AND DEVELOPMENT

Raked flooring can be confusing to draw unless certain fundamental principles are borne in mind. The first drawings to undertake are a plan view and a side section taken along the direction of the rake. The **direction of rake** and the **angle of rake** need to be established. From these drawings, other views may be developed, including the projected view that is the 'true view' on the top surface (the true view is the view taken at 90 degrees to the raking surface plane).

Given that most floors are decked with sheets of plywood, and that those plywood sheets come in stock sizes, it is essential to realise that the sheets need to be drawn in the side section – say, 2440 mm (8') along the raking surface – in order to find the plan-view dimensions of the supporting rostra. Put simply, remember that the plan view on a raking plane is *not* a true view of that surface.

(Note that the two drawings discussed are wholly metric, because to include imperial dimensions would have made them unreadable. The dimensions do not matter here, the method is more important than the size in question.)

The following **methodology** should apply to drawing most raked floors:

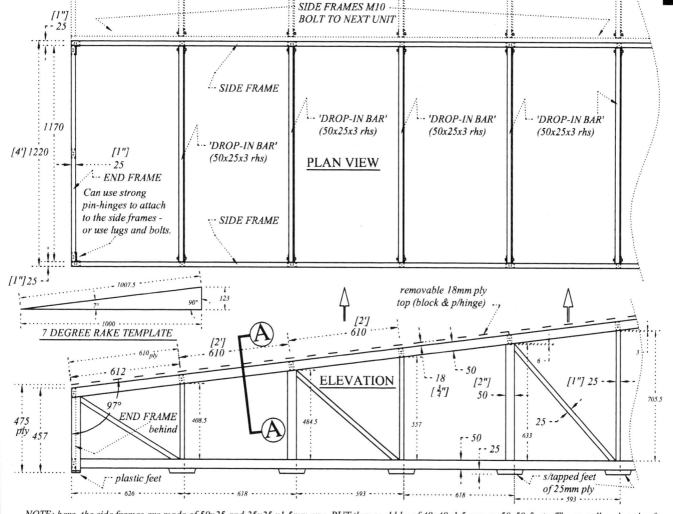

SIDE FRAMES M10 BOLT TO NEXT UNIT

SIDE FRAME

'DROP-IN BAR' (50x25x3 rhs)

'DROP-IN BAR' (50x25x3 rhs)

'DROP-IN BAR' (50x25x3 rhs)

'DROP-IN BAR' (50x25x3 rhs)

PLAN VIEW

[1"] 25

1170

[4'] 1220

[1"] 25

END FRAME
Can use strong
pin-hinges to attach
to the side frames -
or use lugs and bolts.

SIDE FRAME

[1"] 25

7 DEGREE RAKE TEMPLATE

1007.5
7°
1000
90°
123

removable 18mm ply top (block & p/hinge)

[2'] 610

[2'] 610

ELEVATION

610 ply
612
97°

END FRAME behind

408.5

484.5

557

475 ply 457

plastic feet

626   618   593   618   593

18 [³⁄₄"]
50
[2"] 50
25
50
25
633
6
3
[1"] 25
705.5

s/tapped feet of 25mm ply

NOTE: here, the side frames are made of 50x25 and 25x25 x1.5mm erw, BUT they could be of 40x40x1.5 erw, or 50x50 & etc. The overall <u>length</u> of the side frames is decided by either the get-in size, truck size, or convenience of handling - add centre frames to very long frames, say every 3600mm.

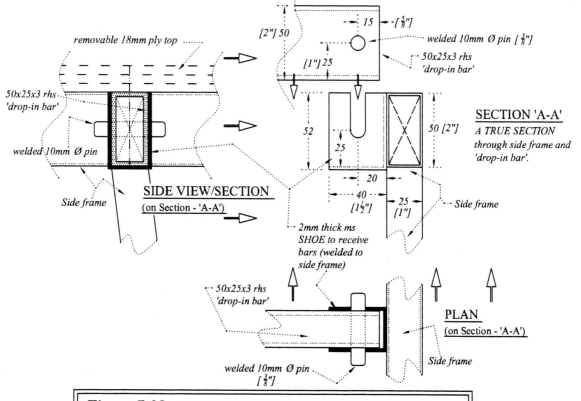

removable 18mm ply top

50x25x3 rhs 'drop-in bar'

welded 10mm Ø pin

Side frame

SIDE VIEW/SECTION
(on Section - 'A-A')

[2"] 50
15   [⁵⁄₈"]
welded 10mm Ø pin [³⁄₈"]
50x25x3 rhs 'drop-in bar'
[1"] 25
52
25
50 [2"]
20
40 [1½"]
25 [1"]
Side frame

SECTION 'A-A'
A TRUE SECTION
through side frame and
'drop-in bar'.

2mm thick ms
SHOE to receive
bars (welded to
side frame)

50x25x3 rhs 'drop-in bar'

PLAN
(on Section - 'A-A')

Side frame

welded 10mm Ø pin [³⁄₈"]

Figure 7-08 - STEEL 'DROP-IN BAR' SYSTEM OF FLOORING
Steel <u>side frames</u> are connected by two <u>end frames</u> and <u>removable bars</u>. Plywood tops
are removable (blocked and pin-hinged from below). THIS VERSION IS RAKED.

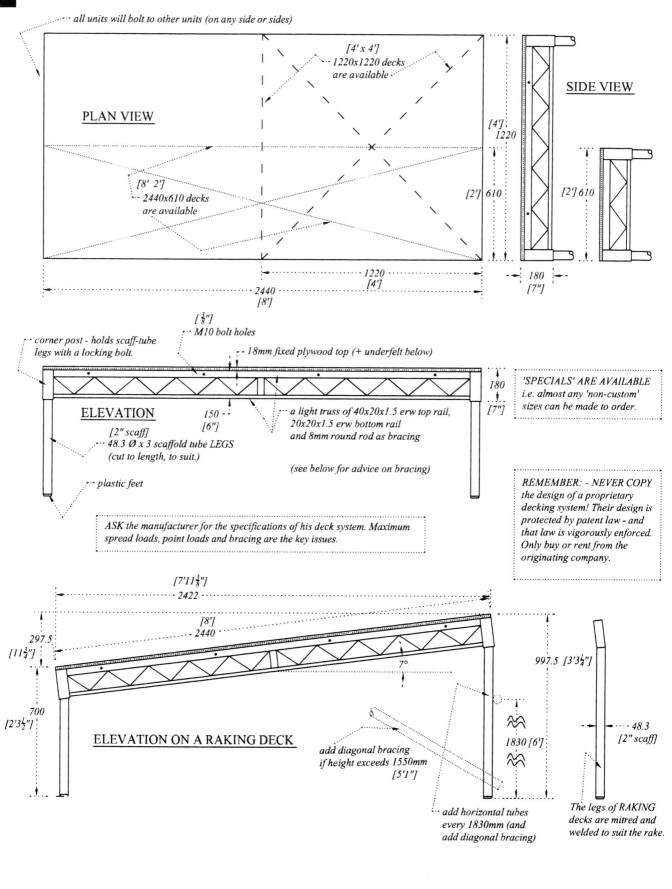

all units will bolt to other units (on any side or sides)

PLAN VIEW

[4' x 4']
1220x1220 decks
are available

[4']
1220

[8' 2']
2440x610 decks
are available

[2'] 610

SIDE VIEW

[2'] 610

1220
[4']

2440
[8']

180
[7"]

[⅜"]
M10 bolt holes

corner post - holds scaff-tube
legs with a locking bolt.

18mm fixed plywood top (+ underfelt below)

180
[7"]

'SPECIALS' ARE AVAILABLE
i.e. almost any 'non-custom'
sizes can be made to order.

ELEVATION

150
[6"]

[2" scaff]
48.3 Ø x 3 scaffold tube LEGS
(cut to length, to suit.)

a light truss of 40x20x1.5 erw top rail,
20x20x1.5 erw bottom rail
and 8mm round rod as bracing

(see below for advice on bracing)

plastic feet

REMEMBER: - NEVER COPY
the design of a proprietary
decking system! Their design is
protected by patent law - and
that law is vigorously enforced.
Only buy or rent from the
originating company.

ASK the manufacturer for the specifications of his deck system. Maximum
spread loads, point loads and bracing are the key issues.

[7'11⅜"]
2422

[8']
2440

297.5
[11¾"]

7°

997.5 [3'3¼"]

700
[2'3½"]

ELEVATION ON A RAKING DECK

add diagonal bracing
if height exceeds 1550mm
[5'1"]

1830 [6']

48.3
[2" scaff]

add horizontal tubes
every 1830mm (and
add diagonal bracing)

The legs of RAKING
decks are mitred and
welded to suit the rake.

Figure 7-09 - PROPRIETARY 'DECKING' SYSTEM

Many types of 'buy-or-hire' decking systems exist - this one is popular in
the UK and the USA. **Steeldeck**® is a registered trade name.

(With thanks to Philip Parsons of *Steeldeck*, London.)

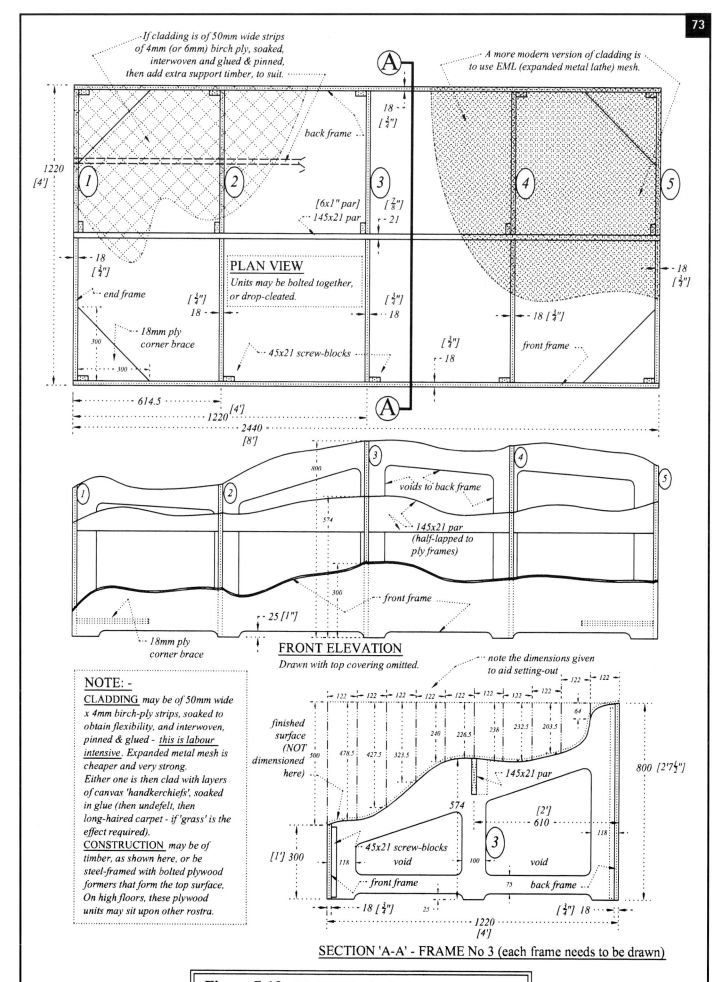

If cladding is of 50mm wide strips
of 4mm (or 6mm) birch ply, soaked,
interwoven and glued & pinned,
then add extra support timber, to suit.

A more modern version of cladding is
to use EML (expanded metal lathe) mesh.

(A)

back frame

18 -
[³/₄"]

1220
[4']

①   ②   ③   ④   ⑤

[6x1" par]   [⁷/₈"]
145x21 par   - 21

- 18
[³/₄"]   - 18
                                                          [³/₄"]

PLAN VIEW
*Units may be bolted together,
or drop-cleated.*

end frame   [³/₄"]   [³/₄"]
                              18 -   - 18

300   ── 18mm ply   [³/₄"]   front frame
             corner brace   - 18

── 300   45x21 screw-blocks

614.5
1220 [4']

2440
[8']

(A)

③   ④
800   ⑤

①   ⑤
②

voids to back frame

574   145x21 par
                         (half-lapped to
                         ply frames)

300   front frame

-- 25 [1"]

── 18mm ply
corner brace

FRONT ELEVATION
Drawn with top covering omitted.

note the dimensions given
to aid setting-out

|← 122 →|← 122 →|← 122 →|← 122 →|← 122 →|← 122 →|← 122 →|← 122 →| 122 | 122 |

NOTE: -

CLADDING *may be of 50mm wide
x 4mm birch-ply strips, soaked to
obtain flexibility, and interwoven,
pinned & glued - this is labour
intensive. Expanded metal mesh is
cheaper and very strong.
Either one is then clad with layers
of canvas 'handkerchiefs', soaked
in glue (then undefelt, then
long-haired carpet - if 'grass' is the
effect required).*
CONSTRUCTION *may be of
timber, as shown here, or be
steel-framed with bolted plywood
formers that form the top surface,
On high floors, these plywood
units may sit upon other rostra.*

finished
surface
(NOT
dimensioned
here)

64

500   478.5   427.5   323.5   240   226.5   238   232.5   203.5

800 [2'7½"]

574

145x21 par

[2']
610   118

[1'] 300   45x21 screw-blocks
                 void   100   void

118   118

front frame   75   back frame

-- 18 [³/₄"]   25   [³/₄"] 18 --

1220
[4']

SECTION 'A-A' - FRAME No 3 (each frame needs to be drawn)

Figure 7-10 - PROFILED, OR SHAPED, FLOORING
Flooring that has an 'organic' shape to its upper surface.

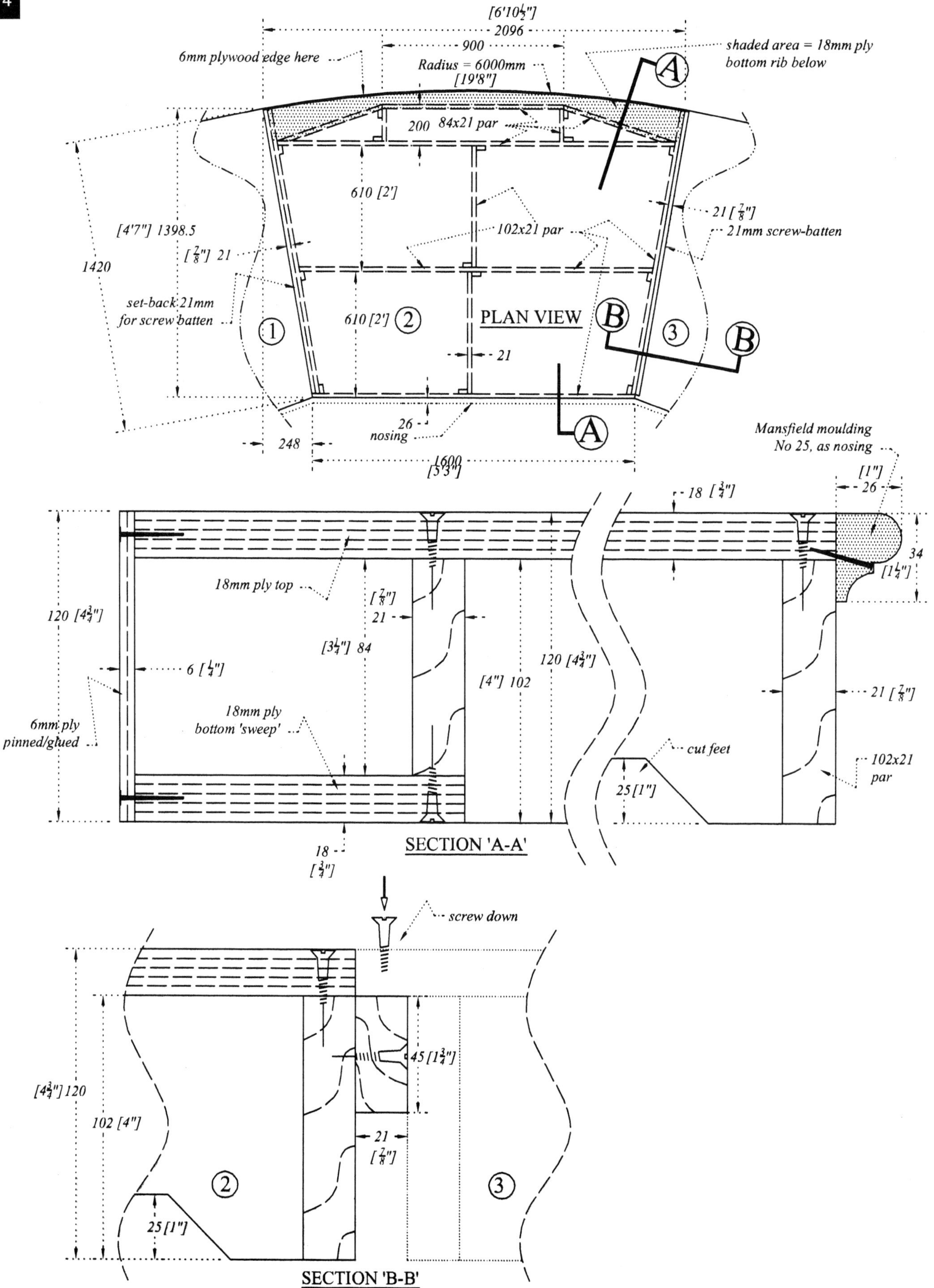

74

[6'10½"]
2096
900
6mm plywood edge here
Radius = 6000mm
[19'8"]
shaded area = 18mm ply
bottom rib below

Ⓐ

200 84x21 par

610 [2']

[4'7"] 1398.5

1420

[⅞"] 21

102x21 par

21 [⅞"]
21mm screw-batten

set-back 21mm
for screw batten

① 610 [2'] ② PLAN VIEW Ⓑ ③ Ⓑ

21

26
nosing

Mansfield moulding
No 25, as nosing

[1"]
26

248

1600
[5'3"]

Ⓐ

18 [¾"]

34
[1¼"]

18mm ply top

[⅞"]
21

120 [4¾"]

[3¼"] 84

120 [4¾"]

6 [¼"]

[4"] 102

21 [⅞"]

6mm ply
pinned/glued

18mm ply
bottom 'sweep'

cut feet

25 [1"]

102x21
par

18
[¾"]

SECTION 'A-A'

screw down

[4¾"] 120

45 [1¾"]

102 [4"]

21
[⅞"]

②

③

25 [1"]

SECTION 'B-B'
Screw-battens (used if top surface is to be covered with, say, carpet.)

Figure 7-11 - 'CURVED-IN-PLAN-VIEW' FLOORING
Where visible, the edges of curved floors require a plywood facing.

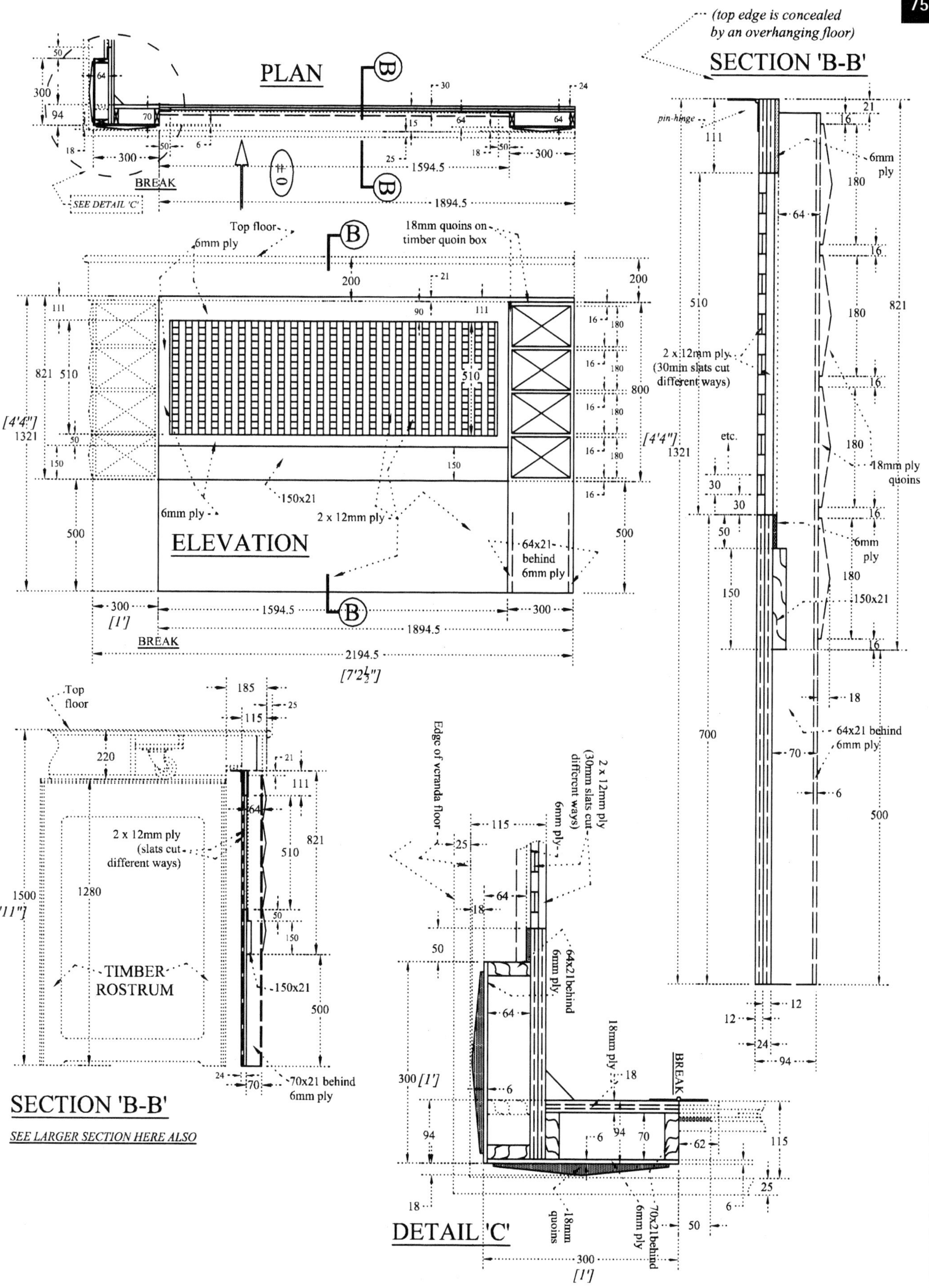

PLAN

(top edge is concealed by an overhanging floor)

SECTION 'B-B'

BREAK
SEE DETAIL 'C'

Top floor
6mm ply

18mm quoins on timber quoin box

pin-hinge

2 x 12mm ply
(30mm slats cut different ways)

6mm ply

18mm ply quoins

etc.

64x21 behind 6mm ply

150x21

6mm ply

2 x 12mm ply

ELEVATION

64x21 behind 6mm ply

BREAK

[4'4"] 1321

[1']

[7'2½"]

Top floor

2 x 12mm ply (slats cut different ways)

1500 [4'11"]

TIMBER ROSTRUM

150x21

70x21 behind 6mm ply

SECTION 'B-B'

SEE LARGER SECTION HERE ALSO

Edge of veranda floor

2 x 12mm ply (30mm slats cut different ways)
6mm ply

64x21 behind 6mm ply

18mm ply

BREAK

18mm quoins
6mm ply
70x21 behind 6mm ply

DETAIL 'C'

[1']

Figure 7-12 - A FASCIA

One example only, many types are used.
Only key dimensions have been shown in Imperial sizes:
the principle, rather than the size, is what matters here.

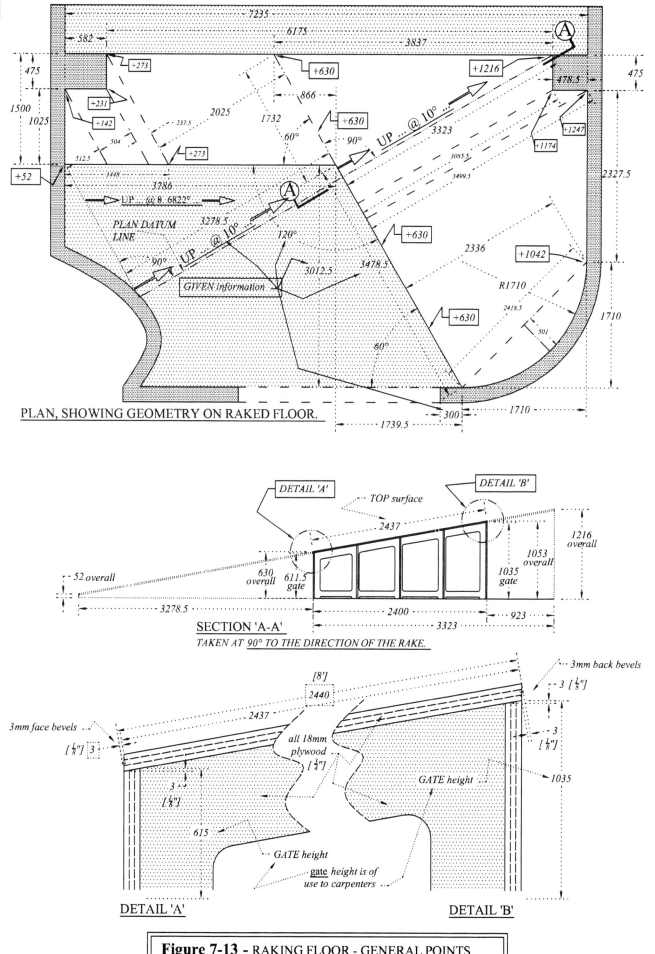

PLAN, SHOWING GEOMETRY ON RAKED FLOOR.

SECTION 'A-A'
TAKEN AT 90° TO THE DIRECTION OF THE RAKE.

DETAIL 'A'

DETAIL 'B'

Figure 7-13 - RAKING FLOOR - GENERAL POINTS

Also see drawing 07-13a ....

Note that metric is used here: the *principle* is more important than the random shape illustrated - the dimensions *needed* are shown.

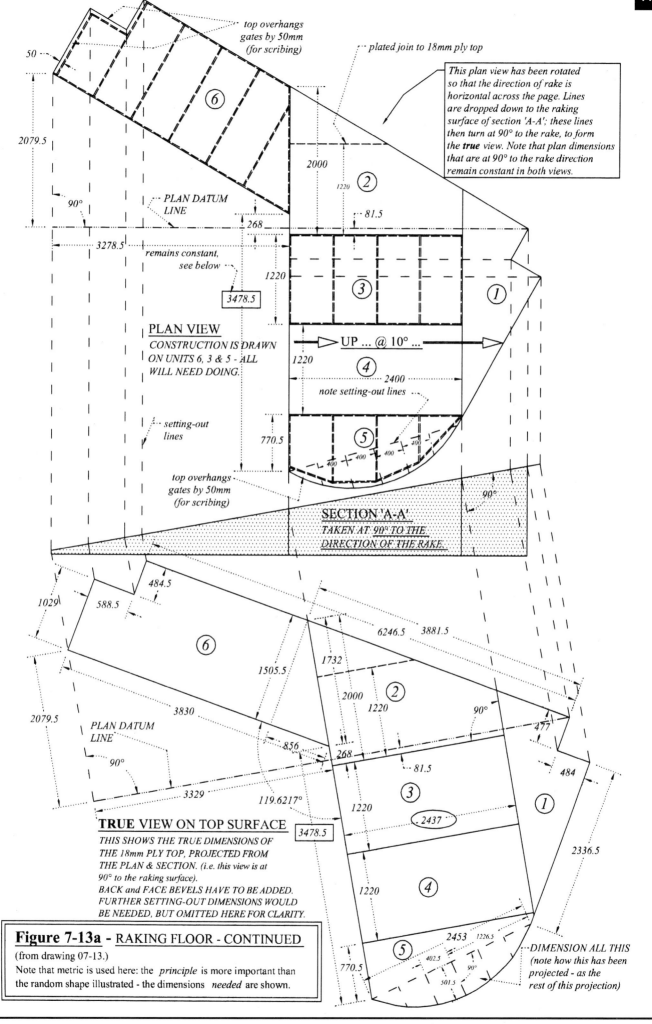

top overhangs
gates by 50mm
(for scribing)

50

2079.5

plated join to 18mm ply top

This plan view has been rotated
so that the direction of rake is
horizontal across the page. Lines
are dropped down to the raking
surface of section 'A-A'; these lines
then turn at 90° to the rake, to form
the **true** view. Note that plan dimensions
that are at 90° to the rake direction
remain constant in both views.

90°

PLAN DATUM
LINE

2000

1220

②

81.5

268

3278.5

remains constant,
see below

3478.5

1220

③

①

PLAN VIEW
*CONSTRUCTION IS DRAWN
ON UNITS 6, 3 & 5 - ALL
WILL NEED DOING.*

⟶ UP ... @ 10° ... ⟶

1220

④

2400

note setting-out lines

setting-out
lines

770.5

⑤

400 400 400 400

top overhangs
gates by 50mm
(for scribing)

90°

SECTION 'A-A'
*TAKEN AT 90° TO THE
DIRECTION OF THE RAKE.*

484.5

1029

588.5

⑥

6246.5   3881.5

1505.5

1732

2000

②

1220

90°

477

2079.5

PLAN DATUM
LINE

90°

3830

856

268

81.5

484

3329

119.6217°

3478.5

③

2437

①

TRUE VIEW ON TOP SURFACE
*THIS SHOWS THE TRUE DIMENSIONS OF
THE 18mm PLY TOP, PROJECTED FROM
THE PLAN & SECTION. (i.e. this view is at
90° to the raking surface).
BACK and FACE BEVELS HAVE TO BE ADDED.
FURTHER SETTING-OUT DIMENSIONS WOULD
BE NEEDED, BUT OMITTED HERE FOR CLARITY.*

1220

1220

④

2336.5

2453   1226.5

402.5   90°

⑤

770.5

501.5

DIMENSION ALL THIS
(note how this has been
projected - as the
rest of this projection)

Figure 7-13a - RAKING FLOOR - CONTINUED
(from drawing 07-13.)
Note that metric is used here: the *principle* is more important than
the random shape illustrated - the dimensions *needed* are shown.

A) Begin the overall plan view of the proposed floor (see **figure 7.13**) and, as soon as is practical, establish and indicate the direction of rake, the angle of rake and the key overall height dimensions.

B) Then draw a side section (**figure 7.13**, Section 'A-A') that is aligned to the direction of rake and draw the top plywood sheets. This will establish the plan-view dimensions of the flooring units upon which the sheets sit – *subject to detailing!* Details 'A' and 'B' show that, in this case, a 3 mm (⅛") bevel reduces the actual top surface of the sheet to 2437 mm, giving a plan-view dimension of 2400 mm for the support rostrum. (Note that Section 'A-A' should be drawn off-set – i.e. parallel – to the 'plan datum line' shown on the plan. Lack of space here has meant that the section has been placed below the plan.)

C) Decide upon the *type* of rostra to be used and complete the side section and details 'A' and 'B'. You may need to add further detail at this stage, such as split-battens, screw-battens, connections and tracks. Here, simple 18 mm plywood block rostra have been shown.

D) Complete the plan view, showing the construction of the support rostra and the positions of the ply sheets (see **figure 7.13a**).

E) Bear in mind that, in plan view, any line at 90° to the direction of rake represents a contour line – in the sense that the **height of the floor will be constant** along that line.

F) Develop the plan view into a 'True View On Top Surface' – a view of the top surface drawn at 90° to that plane, as shown in **figure 7.13a**. This view is constructed by developing the plan view, via Section 'A-A'. The notes and drawings in **figures 7.13 and 7.13a** illustrate how this is done. **Understanding this form of simple projection, or development, is essential.**

G) Compound rakes tend to confuse the mind and often generate more detailing of individual rostra. However, they are only marginally more difficult to comprehend than a regular raked floor. A compound rake is merely a rake that, in plan view, has a direction of rake *not* at 90° to the downstage edge (or any 'obvious' edge): for example, the direction of rake may be from corner to corner.

On a large compound-raked floor, consider the possibility of having the rostra arranged so that they still lay along the direction of rake. If you think about this, and bear in mind point 'E' above, you will see that it simplifies the drawing of, and the building of, each rostrum. In effect, they become identical to 'normal' raked rostra – having parallel end and middle gates, and only the side gates needing to be raked. (In **figure 7.13a**, units 2, 3, 4 and 5 have parallel end and centre gates.)

Unit No. 6 is a compound-raked flooring unit – *all* its gates have raking upper edges.

H) Once the main, given direction of rake is plotted, rakes can be established for any direction desired using straightforward geometry. In **figure 7.13**, the main direction of rake is shown as being 10°; another angle of rake has been established that applies to the direction going across the page (shown as 'UP ... @ 8.6822° ...' beneath the '3786' dimension, below where unit No. 6 is to be). This angle is easily found (note that actual dimensions are used for calculating, not the rounded-off dimensions plotted): along 3785.8798 mm ('3786'), the floor rises from +51.8824 mm ('52') to +630 mm; it is rising 578.1176 mm. Therefore, 578.1176 ÷ 3785.8798 = 0.1527036. Press 'Inv', 'Tan', '=', on the calculator, and you get an answer of 8.6822033°. Various rake-angles may need to be found to suit the 'direction' of any given gate.

8 • Flattage and Walls

In the theatre, most structures consist of **flattage** – frames (**flats**) that connect to their neighbours, forming the overall desired shape. A flat consists of a light but strong framework that is usually clad with a lightweight sheet material, say thin plywood or canvas. It may be strengthened by the use of **stiffeners** – on-edge timber battens fitted to the back of the flat. Conventionally, flats were made of timber, but steel flats have been in common use for many years now.

Flats may be used to form almost any structure; this chapter concentrates on their use as walls, but do bear in mind that the principles of flat construction apply whether the flat is being used as a wall, ceiling, roof or any piece of set. Other types of wall construction follow the more scenic ones: stud partitioning, for museum and exhibition work, and exhibition walls that have lift-off, laminated panels.

Trusses and beams are included in this chapter because they often form part of a flattage structure, providing additional strength: they may even be *made* of flattage. Trusses and beams span between support points; they may simply need to 'self-support' (bear their own load only – without sagging), or they may carry a load, such as a floor above.

NOTES ON FLATTAGE AND WALLS

1 The finished, visible surface

A) Some flats have no cladding – they are open frames, often called **space-frames**. Flats like this may be used 'out of view', acting as braces to the flats that are 'in view'. An example of this would be a tall, 'facing' flat – i.e. one that is seen by the audience – with a back space-frame of similar dimensions 'spaced back' from it by a pair of side frames, a top frame and a few intermediate horizontal frames. The single facing flat is now part of a strong three-dimensional structure. Space-frames always require braces within the flat, because if they have no plywood cladding, they possess no inherent bracing.

B) The face material most commonly used for theatre and trade-show flats is 4 mm plywood ($\frac{1}{8}$" or $\frac{5}{32}$"). If greater surface strength is required then 6 mm ply ($\frac{1}{4}$") may be used – the weight of the flat increases. The stock sizes of plywood will often dictate where rails are positioned within the flat – the usual sizes being 2440 x 1220 mm (8' x 4') and 3050 x 1525 mm (10' x5').

Plywood cladding acts as its own brace – when pinned and glued to the flat, the flat is held square, so bracing need not always be added. However, brace all steel frames. Facing ply should be flameproof.

As a general rule, 4 mm ply ($\frac{1}{8}$" or $\frac{5}{32}$") should not be unsupported for more than 9 square feet (say, 900 x 900 mm) of its surface: ideally, make it *less* than this – I prefer 8 square feet (say, 1200 x 600 mm). This means that the flat's rails must be placed close enough together to suit – they are commonly spaced at 610 mm centres (2').

On large flats the outer rails may be 25 mm (1") thick, while the inner rails – toggle rails for example – are 21 mm thick ($\frac{7}{8}$"). When clad with plywood, the inner rails must be set flush to the face of the outer rails.

The plywood facing may be painted; it may be clad with cloth that is wrapped around the flat; or it may have calico or canvas glued to its surface, acting as a paint 'key'.

C) **Canvas** is frequently used as a face material because it is lightweight and forms a good surface for painting. It is stretched tight and glued and tacked to the timber flat. 'Canvas flats', as they are known, always require bracing, as the canvas alone will not brace the flat.

The flats should have outer rails of a thicker material than the inner rails, and the inner rails must be set flush to the *back* of the outer rails. This is so that the canvas is stretched cleanly across the whole face of the flat without being touched by the inner rails. If this is forgotten, the painted surface of the canvas will begin to 'show' the rails behind – particularly after a tour, when dust and wear will generate a ghosting or shadow of the toggle-rails.

D) **Travel breaks** in a run of flattage will be dictated by the design. Always position the breaks to follow a natural architectural feature and avoid placing a break-line on a plain surface – it *will* show, and show more and more with age.

E) **Mouldings and décor** may well be fitted to the face of the flats. Ensure that support rails are placed behind the plywood facing if the size of the moulding warrants it. Remember that flats will not fold face-to-face if they have fixed mouldings upon them – if necessary consider having removable mouldings. Peg-plates, step-hooks, etc. may be used to fit large mouldings: **figure 8.09**, Section 'A-A' has an example of a 'dummy' beam fitted with peg-plates.

F) **Panels** may be fitted to flats or exhibition walls. Many varied types of panels are possible, but all tend to need to be secretly fixed to the flat. They may be fitted from the rear or be hooked on with drop-cleats or similar. For example, graphic panels have photographic images sealed to their face – clearly, they cannot be face-screwed to the flat – so take care to ensure that the method of fitting is considered and solved during the drawing process. Cloth-wrapped panels and laminated or veneered panels all present the same problem.

G) **Showcases** may be fitted to the face of flats and walls or be let-in to them. *Access* is the problem that most troubles the draughtsman: access will be needed in order to maintain the exhibit and to change light bulbs (and some may have air-treatment systems that will clearly need maintenance). Lockable, front-access showcases are sometimes used (bought as proprietary items), but it is more common for showcases to be designed and built as 'one-off' units – and it is these that need special care. It is usually far neater and cheaper to have rear access designed into this type of unit. Consider the possibility of having double walls (i.e. instead of having a single wall that is viewed from both sides, have two walls, leaving an access corridor between).

H) **Plasterboard** is commonly used to face stud-partitioned walls; it may be 'skimmed' with a thin layer of plaster or be 'dry-lined' – filled and sanded only. The local Fire Regulations will dictate whether or not *both* sides of the wall need cladding and/or whether the plasterboard needs to be double-skinned, having the board-joints overlapping (*see* **figure 8.15**).

2 Bracing

A) All flats and frames need to be braced in order to maintain their shape. Timber flattage needs braces fitted within the framing where no plywood cladding is to be applied – as on a canvas flat or space-frame. The braces can be of 45 x 21 mm (2" x 1" par) or 70 x 21 mm (3" x 1" par) and may be screwed, half-lapped or have mortise and tenon joints. Plywood cladding will act as its own brace, so the flats need no internal braces.

B) Steel flats should always have steel braces, regardless of whether or not the flat is clad with plywood. This is because it is less likely that thin plywood would hold the shape sufficiently – the ply has to be self-tapped and could be pulled out from these fixings by a powerful external force.

3 Support

A) Clearly, all walls and flats require support: they will not stand up alone unless the inherent plan-view shape allows them to do so. This is so obvious, and yet one frequently sees design drawings showing a solitary flat, with no support or French brace in sight. Flats can have French braces fitted to the back (*see* **figure 8.01**), or space-frames, or other flats may create a final shape which is inherently self-supporting.

B) Exhibition walls can pose problems, particularly if their tops do not fit directly to an overhead beam, ceiling or similar. Under-floor **'cruciform'** steel support posts may be of help; each consists of a welded steel unit having an 'X' shape in plan view with a vertical post rising from the centre. The 'X' shape is fixed and concealed below a false floor, leaving an upright steel column protruding through it – the timber wall framing is bolted to this column. The columns are set *between* the wall flats, so that the facing material covers and hides them. When correctly placed along a line of wall flats, these columns will prevent the wall from being pushed over.

SOME TYPES OF FLATTAGE/WALLING

1 Conventional 3" x 1", mortise and tenon, theatre flattage

A) **Figure 8.01** illustrates a typical 8' x 4' (2440 x 1220 mm) theatre flat built in the conventional style. The timber outer framing has mortise and tenon joints, shown in 'Detail X' – *note that the top and bottom rails run*

through: the stiles run between them. This ensures that when the flat is 'run' by the crew (slid across the floor), no end-grain is pointing down, touching the floor. If it were in contact with the floor there would be a very real danger of the end-grain snagging and causing the stile to split apart.

B) **Toggle-rails** are used to span between the stiles; always span across the shortest distance (here, the 4' dimension is the shorter, not the 8'). The toggle-rail consists of a rail that has a mortise and tenon joint at each end attaching it to two toggle-shoes. The toggle-shoes are then screwed to the inner edge of the stiles, using two stout, size 14 screws. Toggle-shoes are always of 70 x 21 mm (3" x 1" par) cut down to 68 mm (2 $^{11}/_{16}$") – the carpenters cut them down in order to guarantee that they are all of a consistent size.

C) The left-hand side of the elevation and Section 'A-A' indicate that the flat is clad with 4 mm plywood (⅛" or $^5/_{32}$") and that all flattage timber is 21 mm thick (⅞") – a perfectly normal method of construction. The right-hand side and Section 'B-B' illustrate a similar flat, but this version is clad with canvas: it has 25 mm (1") outer rails, 21 mm (⅞") toggle-rails and 45 x 21 mm (2" x 1" par) corner braces.

D) A **French brace** is shown hinged to the back of the flat. When travelling, the brace is folded back and attached to the flat with a 'block and turn button'. When open and being used as a brace, the stage crew add a stage-weight to the back end of it – the 100 mm (4") 'toe'. The brace could be fitted with pin-hinges, thus making it removable. Note that this brace is quite small, so the centre rail is fitted using stub-tenon joints. However, a larger French brace may have several centre-rails, and – if each were to be fitted in a similar fashion – having so many mortises cut into it would weaken the stile. In cases such as this, the centre-rails are fitted with toggle-shoes, as indicated.

2 Ply-plated flattage ('dog and biscuit' flats)

A) **Figure 8.02** has in its top-left corner an elevation of a conventional ply-plated flat – often known colloquially as a 'dog and biscuit' flat. This type of construction avoids using mortise and tenon joints, which are labour-intensive (and therefore expensive) to produce. The flat uses the same material for its rails and stiles as described above, but the joints are achieved with the use of timber-connectors (*dogs*) and ply-plates (*biscuits*) that are glued and pinned to the back of the flat. Flats with mortise and tenon joints are stronger and deemed more professional, but ply-plates are common enough to be perfectly acceptable in film, TV and trade-show work. Budget often dictates that they are also used in theatre productions.

B) Ply-plates are usually of 4 mm or 6 mm plywood ($^5/_{32}$" or ¼") and the usual dimensions are shown in **figure 8.02**. Occasionally, when extra strength is needed, 9 mm ply (⅜") is used, this being screwed and glued to the flat.

C) Note that the ply-plates are set back from the edge of the flat by 25 mm (1") in order to allow for other flats to butt to the back of the flat in a clean fashion.

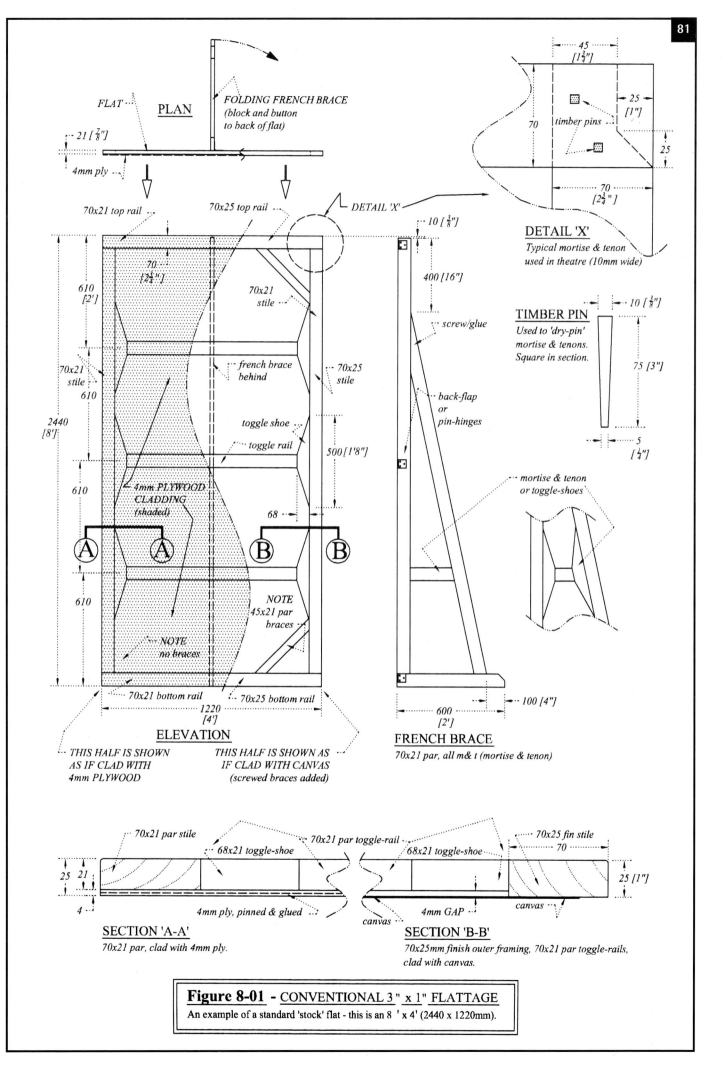

PLAN

FLAT

FOLDING FRENCH BRACE
(block and button
to back of flat)

21 [⅞"]

4mm ply

70x21 top rail

70x25 top rail

DETAIL 'X'

DETAIL 'X'
Typical mortise & tenon
used in theatre (10mm wide)

45 [1¾"]

25 [1"]

70

timber pins

25

70 [2¾"]

610 [2']

70 [2¾"]

70x21 stile

french brace behind

70x21 stile

70x25 stile

610

70x25 stile

toggle shoe

toggle rail

2440 [8']

610

500 [1'8"]

68

4mm PLYWOOD CLADDING (shaded)

Ⓐ   Ⓐ   Ⓑ   Ⓑ

610

NOTE
45x21 par braces

610

NOTE
no braces

70x21 bottom rail

70x25 bottom rail

1220 [4']

ELEVATION

THIS HALF IS SHOWN
AS IF CLAD WITH
4mm PLYWOOD

THIS HALF IS SHOWN AS
IF CLAD WITH CANVAS
(screwed braces added)

10 [⅜"]

400 [16"]

screw/glue

back-flap
or
pin-hinges

mortise & tenon
or toggle-shoes

100 [4"]

600 [2']

FRENCH BRACE
70x21 par, all m& t (mortise & tenon)

TIMBER PIN
Used to 'dry-pin'
mortise & tenons.
Square in section.

10 [⅜"]

75 [3"]

5 [¼"]

70x21 par stile

68x21 toggle-shoe

70x21 par toggle-rail

70x25 fin stile

70

68x21 toggle-shoe

25 21

4

4mm ply, pinned & glued

canvas

4mm GAP

canvas

25 [1"]

SECTION 'A-A'
70x21 par, clad with 4mm ply.

SECTION 'B-B'
70x25mm finish outer framing, 70x21 par toggle-rails,
clad with canvas.

Figure 8-01 - CONVENTIONAL 3 " x 1" FLATTAGE
An example of a standard 'stock' flat - this is an 8 ' x 4' (2440 x 1220mm).

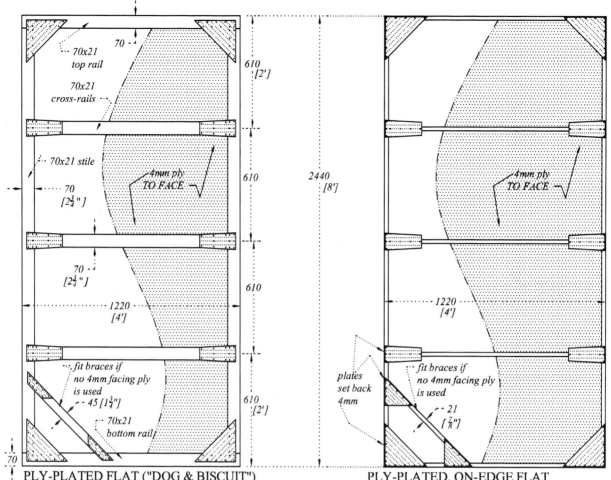

PLY-PLATED FLAT ("DOG & BISCUIT")
VIEWED FROM THE BACK

70x21 par, clad with 4mm ply with 6mm (or 4mm) plates.

70x21 top rail

70x21 cross-rails

70x21 stile

70 [2¾"]

70 [2¾"]

4mm ply TO FACE

610 [2']

610

610

610 [2']

2440 [8']

1220 [4']

fit braces if no 4mm facing ply is used

45 [1¾"]

70x21 bottom rail

70

PLY-PLATED, ON-EDGE FLAT
VIEWED FROM THE BACK

70x21 (or 45x21), clad with 4mm ply with 6mm (or 4mm) plates.

4mm ply TO FACE

1220 [4']

plates set back 4mm

fit braces if no 4mm facing ply is used

21 [⅞"]

PLY-PLATES ("BISCUITS")

6mm (or 4mm) plates, pinned & glued.

200 [8"]

[2¾"] 70

[3 9/16"] 90

gap to clear any flats that abut

"DOGS" = a pair of serrated steel timber-connectors below ply plates

note grain direction

[1"] 25

45

230 [9"]

200 [8"]

[4⅜"] 110

230 [9"]

45 [1¾"]

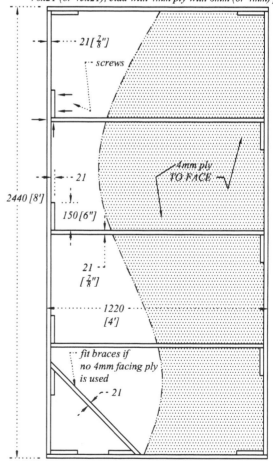

21 [⅞"]

screws

4mm ply TO FACE

21

150 [6"]

2440 [8']

21 [⅞"]

1220 [4']

fit braces if no 4mm facing ply is used

21

BLOCKED, ON-EDGE FLAT
VIEWED FROM THE BACK

70x21 (or 45x21), clad with 4mm ply with 21mm screw-blocks.

Figure 8-02 - PLY-PLATED FLATS
AND ON-EDGE FLATS

Example of standard 'stock' flats, 8 ' x 4' (2440 x 1220mm).

83

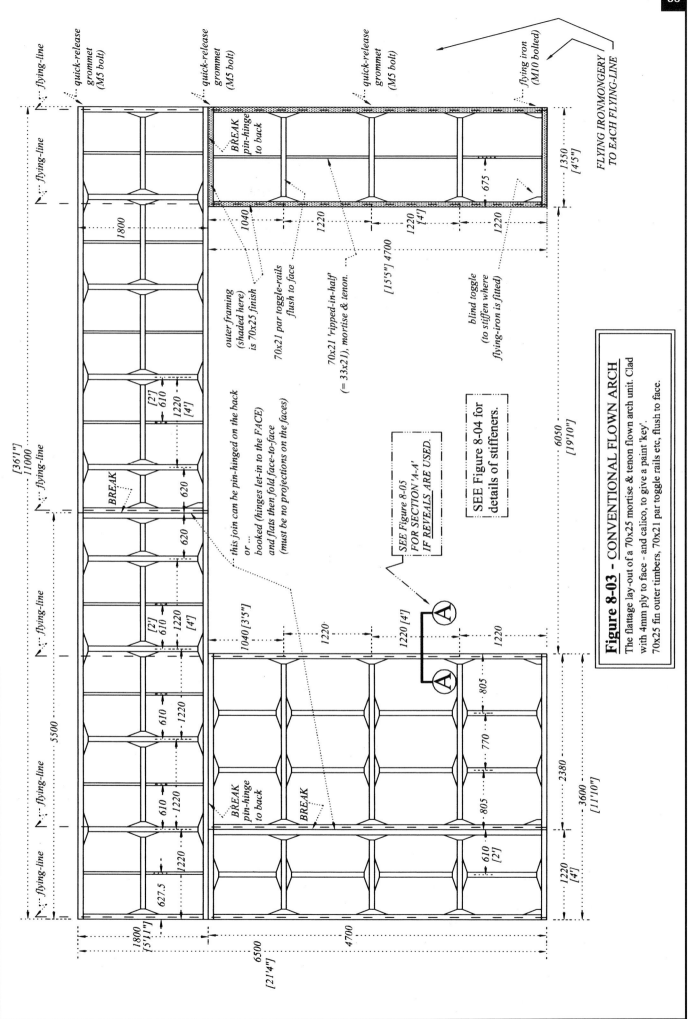

Figure 8-03 – CONVENTIONAL FLOWN ARCH

The flattage lay-out of a 70x25 mortise & tenon flown arch unit. Clad with 4mm ply to face - and calico, to give a paint 'key'. 70x25 fin outer timbers, 70x21 par toggle rails etc, flush to face.

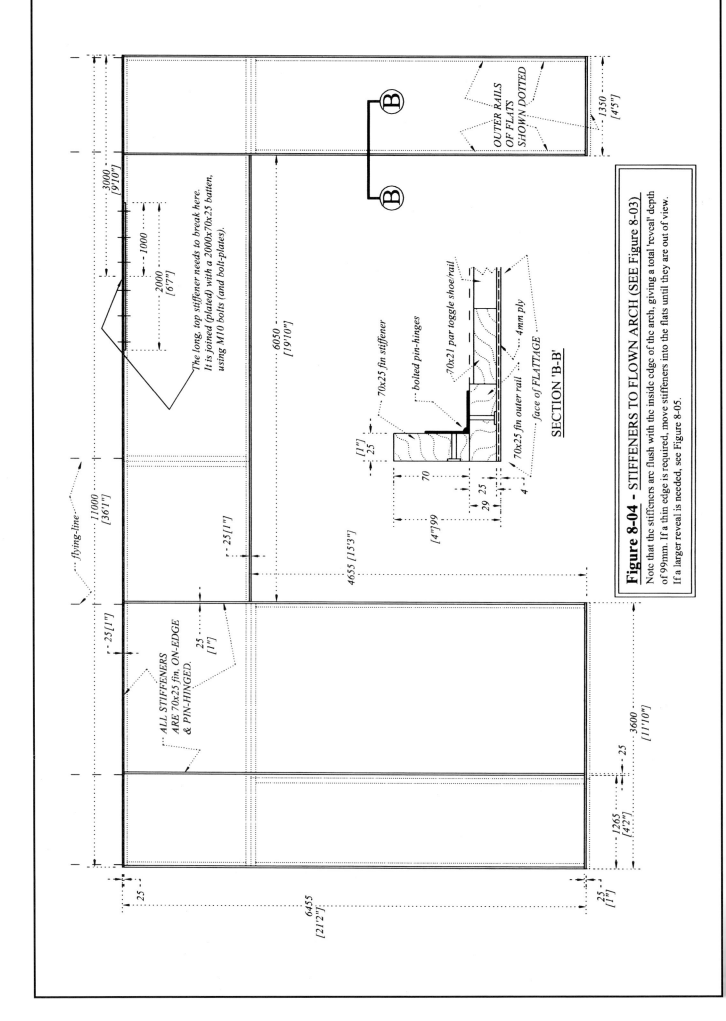

3000
[9'10"]

1000

2000
[6'7"]

The long, top stiffener needs to break here. It is joined (plated) with a 2000x70x25 batten, using M10 bolts (and bolt-plates).

6050
[19'10"]

25 [1"]

4655 [15'3"]

flying-line

11000
[36'1"]

25 [1"]

25
[1"]

ALL STIFFENERS ARE 70x25 fin, ON-EDGE & PIN-HINGED.

25 [1"]

25

3600
[11'10"]

1265
[4'2"]

25

6455
[21'2"]

1350
[4'5"]

OUTER RAILS OF FLATS SHOWN DOTTED

70x25 fin stiffener

70x21 par toggle shoe/rail

bolted pin-hinges

4mm ply

70x25 fin outer rail

face of FLATTAGE

[1"]
25

70

29 25

4

[4"]99

SECTION 'B-B'

Figure 8-04 - STIFFENERS TO FLOWN ARCH (SEE Figure 8-03)

Note that the stiffeners are flush with the inside edge of the arch, giving a total 'reveal' depth of 99mm. If a thin edge is required, move stiffeners into the flats until they are out of view. If a larger reveal is needed, see Figure 8-05.

3 'On-edge' flattage

Flats can be built using the timber 'on-edge', i.e. having the narrow side of the timber rails seen in elevation. Clearly, the thickness of the flat increases and this has a great advantage from a structural point of view: the flat has more inherent stiffness. This method of construction can obviate the need for stiffeners to be added to the back of flattage. Connections are also simple – just bolt flats together with M10 bolts (⅜").

Trade shows tend to favour on-edge flattage made of 45 x 21 mm (2" x 1" par), whereas theatre always uses 70 x 21 mm (3" x 1" par). This is because trade-show flats are usually used for a short period only and need to be light-weight and cheaper to build.

Mortise and tenon joints are not practical for on-edge flattage and so two methods of joining the timbers have evolved, both of which are quick and cheap to produce. **Figure 8.02** illustrates the two types of on-edge flats:

(i) **Blocked, on-edge flats** have joints secured by the use of 'two-way' screw-blocks, as shown. The inner rails are screwed through the stiles and then screwed into the blocks (which are themselves screwed and glued), giving screws in *two* directions – making it less likely that the rail could be pulled out. Note the positions of the blocks at the top and bottom of the flat; again, they are placed so as to ensure that screws are placed in two directions.

(ii) **Ply-plated, on-edge flats** are occasionally used, but blocked construction is preferable, being less 'fussy' and having no protrusions at the back.

4 Flown flattage

A) Flown flats are suspended by wire cables from the theatre's flying-bars ('pipes' in the USA). The lines are attached to flying-irons bolted to the bottom rail of the flats (*see* also 'Ironmongery', pp. 162–63), and the lines are held to the back of the flats with bolted or quick-release grommets. (These allow the line to be removed without having to unbolt the grommet.) Lines should only be attached to the *top* of flats if the flattage is of steel construction. Always consider whether flown flattage needs stiffeners to the back face. A large area of flattage, consisting of several individual flats, will be laid face-down on the stage by the crew, the lines attached and the top lifted until the unit is vertical. This places great strain on the centre of the flats when the unit is half-way raised at 45°. Vertical stiffeners will prevent failure at this point; they also help to tie the flats together, again reducing the possibility of structural failure. A tall flat stored in the grid for a lengthy period will be inclined to bend in the middle when viewed from the side – the centre will tend to bend downstage. Vertical stiffening will prevent this. Horizontal stiffeners help in keeping a series of flats straight in plan view (although, in truth, the flying-bar and lines also assist in this regard).

Ensure that nothing can lift off and fall from flown flattage. Flying flats often pass very close to one another and a very real danger exists that one may dislodge items from its neighbour. Doors and windows must be locked in a closed position for flying (sliding bolts on the back face usually suffice) and must never be hung on lift-off hinges. Ensure that any item – such as a large cornice – that is attached to the flat with a lift-off device (drop-cleats or

pelmet clips, etc.) has a locking mechanism to prevent accidental removal. Flown flats with door openings should have sill-irons (again, *see* pp. 162–63) bolted to the timber.

B) **Figure 8.03** shows a simplified elevation of a flown arch constructed in the traditional manner – of 3" x 1" mortise-and-tenon flattage, clad with 4 mm ply (⅛" or ⁵⁄₃₂"). Outer rails are all 25 mm thick (1"); inner rails are 21 mm (⅞") set flush to the face. The five flats are joined to one another by pin-hinges to their back face. Six flying lines and associated ironmongery are used to fly this piece.

Note the positions of the **inner rails** of each flat: the main toggle-rails always run across the shortest distance; the space remaining is then sub-divided by either more toggle-rails or by 3" x 1" ripped-in-half (using stub tenons). The spacing of the inner rails ensures that the facing ply is not unsupported for more than nine square feet of its surface and that its edges fall upon the centre of a rail. (It is also common to use 45 x 21 mm (2" x 1" par) instead of 3" x 1" ripped-in-half.) If the flats were to be clad with **canvas**, not ply, no sub-divisions would be required – the main toggle-rails plus braces would be sufficient. A 'blind toggle' is fitted to the corner where flying-irons are placed, helping to strengthen this crucial joint.

Section 'A-A' refers to reveals – *see* point 'D' below.

Stiffeners are necessary for flattage of this type, but showing them on the flat-construction elevation would be confusing to the eye. So, for the sake of clarity, always draw a separate stiffener layout (it can be at a smaller scale). **Figure 8.04** shows this drawing.

C) **Figure 8.04** indicates that the stiffener layout to the flown arch in question has five vertical stiffeners of the same length and four horizontal stiffeners of varying lengths. The top stiffener is very long and so is 'plated' with a bolted timber batten, called a plate, allowing the piece to break into two or three pieces.

All the stiffeners are on-edge 70 x 25 fin (2¾" x 1" fin) and are fitted to the flats and to each other by bolted pin-hinges. Note that the stiffeners may have to be moved away from the archway if the designer desires a thinner profile. It is normal to have the bottom stiffener set flush with the top of the flat's bottom rail – leaving a gap between the stiffener and the stage when the flat is landed. This helps to prevent the flat 'riding' on any stage detritus beneath it, but it is particularly useful for flats landing upon a raking stage – the stiffener, being set up from the bottom of the flat, should clear the rake.

D) **Reveals** are used as a method of giving a visible thickness to the edge of flattage. Two types are indicated in **figure 8.05**; both would be Section 'A-A' from **figure 8.03**, one being fixed, the other a removable version.

(i) A **fixed reveal** is shown as being 18 mm ply (¾") screwed into the *edge* of the flat's stile. Note that the facing plywood of the flat also covers the edge of the reveal, hiding a potential 'raw' edge. Triangular plywood formers hold the reveal in place – these are screwed into the flat's toggle-rails and fitted to the reveal with a screw-batten. The formers should be fitted every 1000–1220 mm (3–4') around the reveal.

(ii) A **removable reveal** is frequently necessary, and these tend to be fitted entirely to the *back* of the flattage. The triangular plywood formers are usually fitted to the

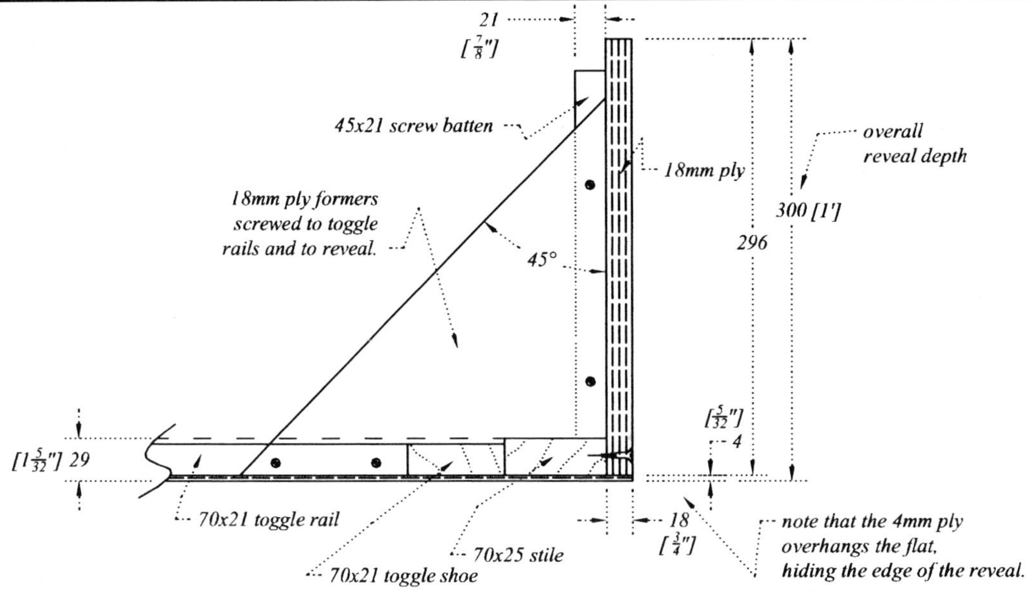
21
[7/8"]
45x21 screw batten
18mm ply formers
screwed to toggle
rails and to reveal.
45°
18mm ply
overall
reveal depth
300 [1']
296
[1 5/32"] 29
[5/32"]
4
70x21 toggle rail
70x25 stile
70x21 toggle shoe
18
[3/4"]
note that the 4mm ply
overhangs the flat,
hiding the edge of the reveal.

SECTION 'A-A' - FROM Figure 8-03 - A FIXED REVEAL

This type of reveal is screwed/glue to the flat.
NOTE that the flat's dimensions are reduced by 18mm ... and the reveal reduced by 4mm.
A fixed reveal will act as a good stiffener. Ply-plate the reveal to obtain the desired length.

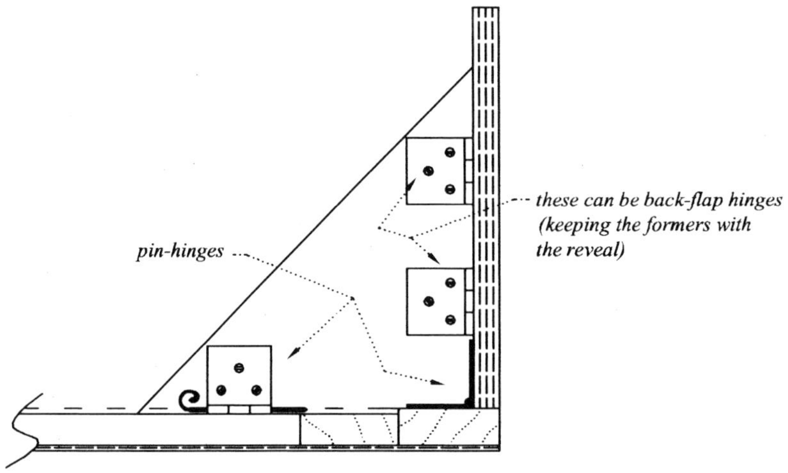
pin-hinges
these can be back-flap hinges
(keeping the formers with
the reveal)

SECTION 'A-A' - FROM Figure 8-03 - A REMOVABLE REVEAL

This type of reveal is pin-hinged to the flat. The 18mm ply formers may be fitted to the reveal with back-flap hinges instead of pin-hinges, ensuring they they do not get lost.

Figure 8-05 - REVEALS
PLEASE REFER TO Figure 8-03, SECTION 'A-A'.

reveal with back-flap (fixed) hinges, and fitted to the flat with pin-hinges – ensuring that when the unit is struck from the flat, the formers remain with the reveal, thus reducing the chance of their being misplaced on tour.

Plywood reveals are plated to achieve lengths longer than the ply sheet size.

E) **Figure 8.06** illustrates another version of the flown arch under discussion, built of four 3" x 1" on-edge, blocked-and-screwed flats. Note that the main cross rails still run across the shortest distance – the width of each flat – and the intermediate rails are of 45 x 21 mm (2" x 1" par) on-edge. On-edge flattage requires less stiffening: a top stiffener is shown that ties the flats together and a second stiffener is placed across the top of the open arch. Note that solid corner-blocks are fitted where the flying-irons are bolted.

5 Finished view, decor and mouldings – figs 8-07–8.09

A) The carpenters require finished views so that they are aware of how to add décor to the completed flat. These drawings will inevitably include sections through mouldings, usually at a larger scale.

B) **Figure 8.07** shows an elevation and section of part of a 'period' style set. A recessed bookcase is flanked by a doorway and a fibreglass Doric column set back from the bookcase. For clarity, much of the information originally given upon these drawing has been omitted. This unit contains most of the types of architectural mouldings in common use, including skirting, dado – or chair – rail, picture rail and cornice (obviously, many versions of each type exist).

C) **Figure 8.08** illustrates the details of Section 'X-X' at a larger scale. Note that for fixing purposes, the flat has

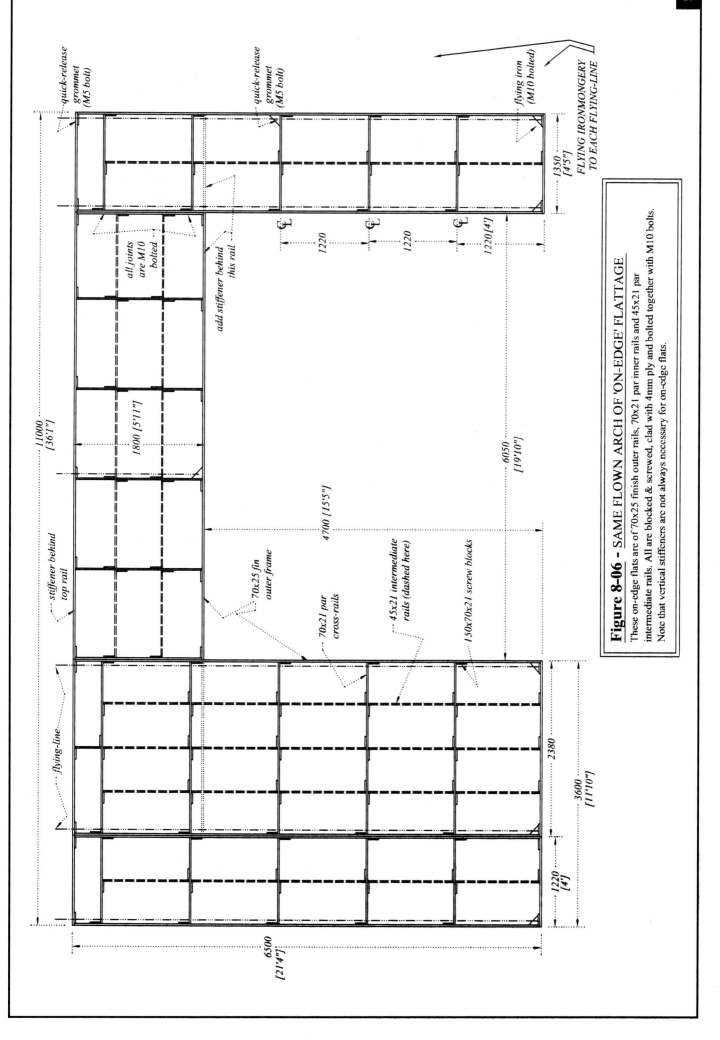

Figure 8-06 – SAME FLOWN ARCH OF 'ON-EDGE' FLATTAGE

These on-edge flats are of 70x25 finish outer rails, 70x21 par inner rails and 45x21 par intermediate rails. All are blocked & screwed, clad with 4mm ply and bolted together with M10 bolts. Note that vertical stiffeners are not always necessary for on-edge flats.

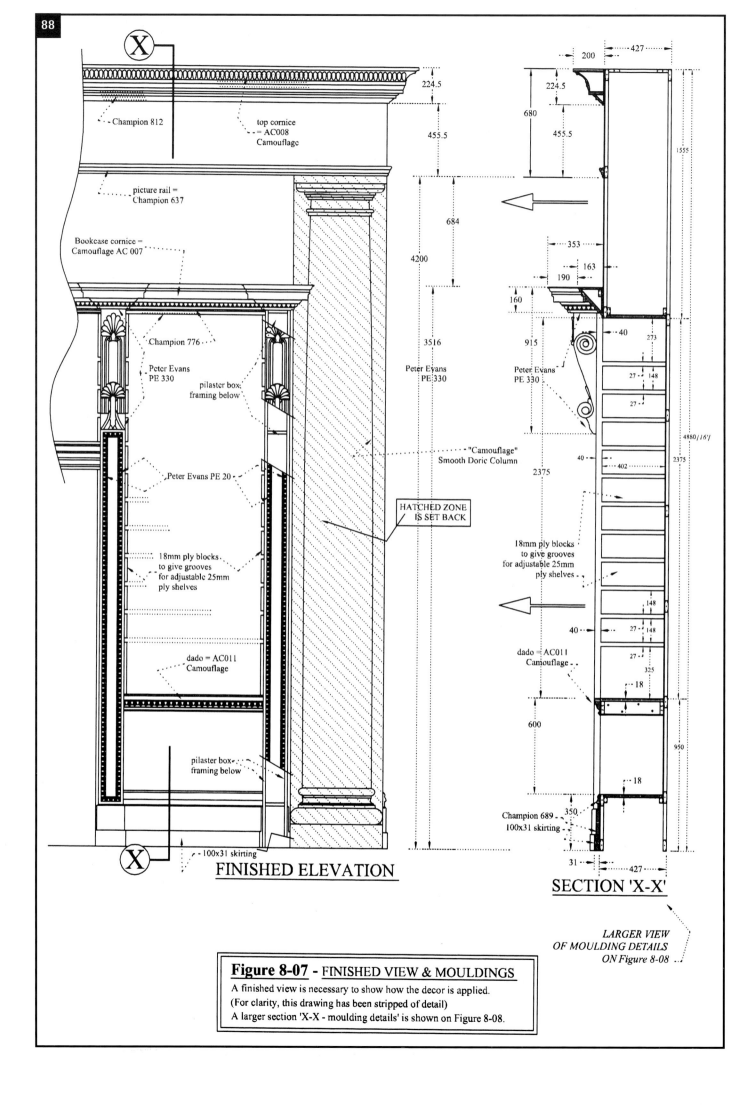

88

FINISHED ELEVATION

Champion 812

top cornice = AC008 Camouflage

picture rail = Champion 637

Bookcase cornice = Camouflage AC 007

Champion 776

Peter Evans PE 330

pilaster box framing below

Peter Evans PE 20

18mm ply blocks to give grooves for adjustable 25mm ply shelves

dado = AC011 Camouflage

pilaster box framing below

100x31 skirting

"Camouflage" Smooth Doric Column

HATCHED ZONE IS SET BACK

SECTION 'X-X'

Peter Evans PE 330

Peter Evans PE 330

18mm ply blocks to give grooves for adjustable 25mm ply shelves

dado = AC011 Camouflage

Champion 689
100x31 skirting

224.5
455.5
684
4200
3516
2375
600

200   427
224.5
680
455.5
1555
353
163
190
160
915
40
273
27   148
27
4880/16'
2375
402
40
148
40   27   148
27
325
18
950
18
350
31   427

LARGER VIEW OF MOULDING DETAILS ON Figure 8-08

Figure 8-07 - FINISHED VIEW & MOULDINGS

A finished view is necessary to show how the decor is applied.
(For clarity, this drawing has been stripped of detail)
A larger section 'X-X - moulding details' is shown on Figure 8-08.

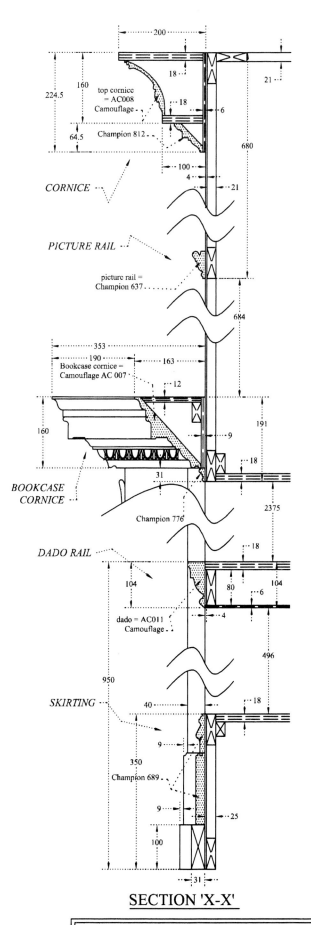

200

18

160
224.5
top cornice
= AC008
Camouflage
18
6

64.5
Champion 812

21

680

CORNICE

100
4
21

PICTURE RAIL

picture rail =
Champion 637

684

353
190
163
Bookcase cornice =
Camouflage AC 007
12

160
9
191

BOOKCASE
CORNICE
31
18

Champion 776
2375

DADO RAIL
18
104
80
104
6
dado = AC011
Camouflage
4

496

SKIRTING
40
18
950
9
350
Champion 689
9
25
100
31

SECTION 'X-X'

Figure 8-08 - MOULDING DETAILS
This is section 'X-X' from Figure 8-07.

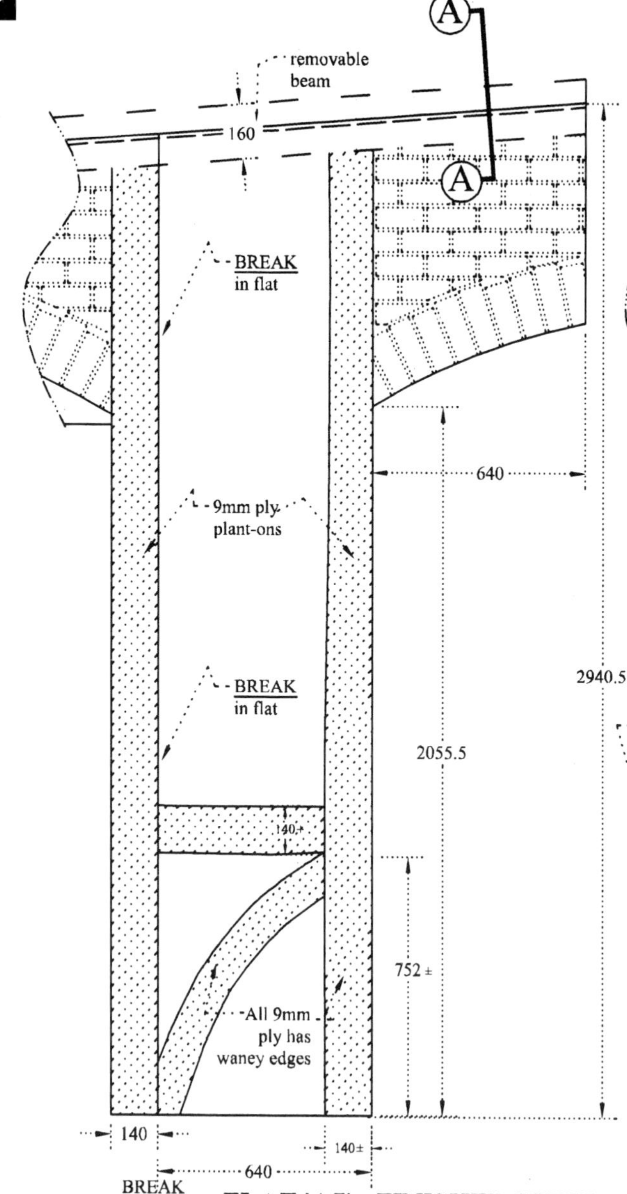

FLAT 'A7' - FINISHED VIEW

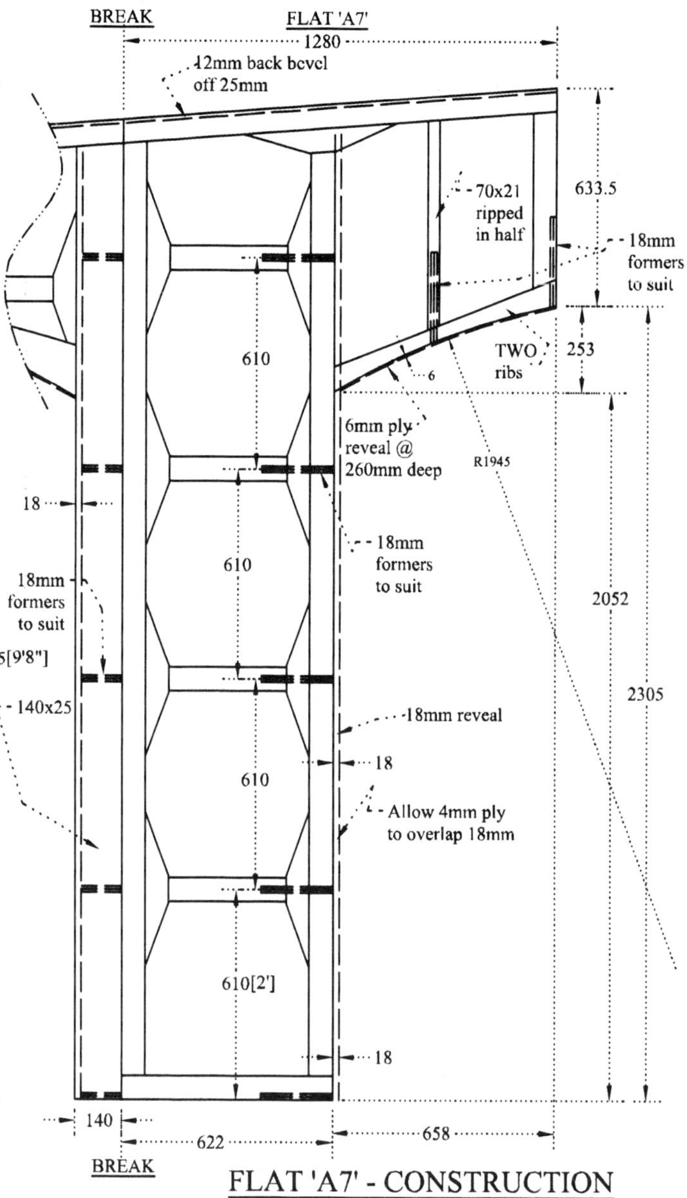

- A
- A

removable beam

160

BREAK in flat

9mm ply plant-ons

BREAK in flat

640

2055.5

140

752 ±

All 9mm ply has waney edges

140

140 ±

640

BREAK

BREAK

FLAT 'A7' - CONSTRUCTION

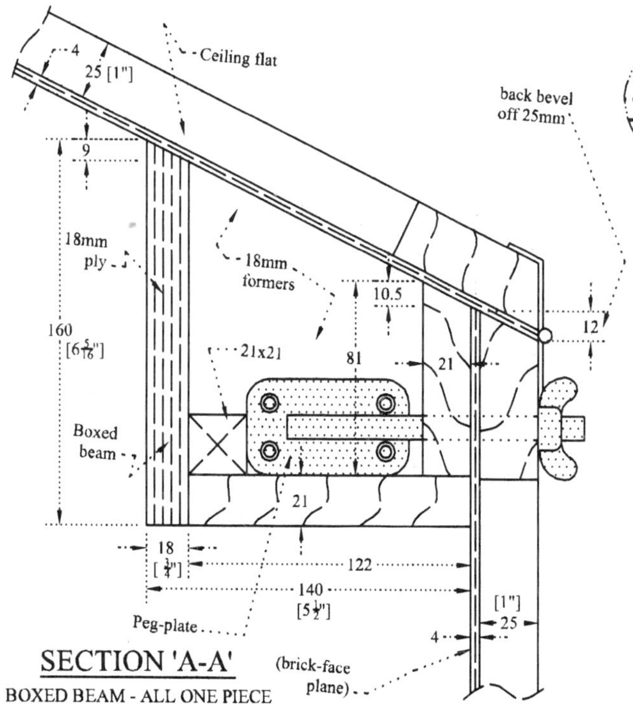

BREAK

FLAT 'A7'

1280

12mm back bevel off 25mm

70x21 ripped in half

633.5

18mm formers to suit

610

6mm ply reveal @ 260mm deep

TWO ribs

6

253

R1945

18

18mm formers to suit

610

18mm formers to suit

18mm formers to suit

2940.5[9'8"]

140x25

610

18mm reveal

18

610

Allow 4mm ply to overlap 18mm

2052

2305

610[2']

18

140

622

658

BREAK

SECTION 'A-A'
BOXED BEAM - ALL ONE PIECE
(PEG-PLATES TO FLATS 'A')

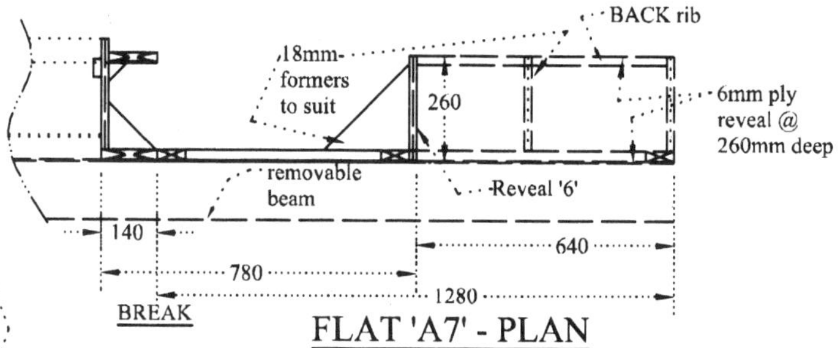

4

25 [1"]

Ceiling flat

back bevel off 25mm

9

18mm ply

18mm formers

10.5

12

160 [6 5/16"]

21x21

81

21

Boxed beam

21

18 [3/4"]

122

140 [5 1/2"]

[1"]

25

Peg-plate

(brick-face plane)

4

FLAT 'A7' - PLAN

BACK rib

18mm formers to suit

260

6mm ply reveal @ 260mm deep

removable beam

Reveal '6'

140

780

640

1280

BREAK

Figure 8-09 - ARCH FLAT & REVEAL
A simple flat containing half an arch with a reveal.

rails behind certain mouldings. The top cornice is an example of a built-up moulding: plywood boxing-out has bought-moulding applied to its face.

D) **Figure 8.09** shows a finished view of a truncated archway flat with brickwork and mock-Tudor style timber and plaster to its face. The timber is replicated by using 9 mm (³/₈") plywood and its design has allowed for the placing of a secret **break-point** to the run of flats. The plaster effect will be painted and textured by the scenic artists; the bricks will be either vac-formed plastic or thin plywood rectangles dressed by the artists.

A removable beam is indicated at Section 'A-A' acting as a continuous face stiffener to the run of flattage that includes this arch. It is attached to the flats with peg-plates and, as can be seen, butts to a raking ceiling flat.

The archway has a **reveal**, 260 mm deep overall (10¼"). The vertical part of the reveal is of 18 mm ply (¾") but the upper, **curved reveal** is 6 mm plywood (¼") bent around two ribs; one forms part of the flat as seen in elevation, the other is set behind it, flush to the *back* of the reveal. All is held in place with 18 mm ply formers, blocked and screwed to the back of the flat; the pair of formers shown above the curved top of the reveal would be notched to take and hold the rear rib.

6 Curved-in-plan flats – figure 8.10

A) Flats that curve in plan view can either be made of steel, rolled to the desired radius, or of timber and plywood. **Figure 8.10** includes a plan/section of a curving wall constructed of a steel core with hook-on timber flats to each face; the overall height is 4825 mm (16'). A plan/section of the end detail is shown in Detail 'X' and a broken vertical section indicates the basic method of construction. Clearly, not all curved walls need a steel core, but this example is useful as it indicates both steel and timber in one piece.

B) **Curved walls having more than one radius** are frequently necessary; this means that in plan view the desired shape comprises of, say, two arcs, each having a different radius. For the whole curve to be completely smooth it is *essential* that the correct geometry be employed. If it is not, the change-of-radius point will be clearly visible on the wall as a straight vertical line – especially if the surface material has a shine to it, like laminate. Designers tend to ignore this simple fact and it is the construction draughtsman who has to correct the anomaly. A sketch included in **figure 8.10** is intended as a reminder of how to achieve the perfect join between different curves: the point where the change of radius occurs *must* be on the end of the extended line that joins the centre points of the two circles used.

C) The **steel core** is of 50 x 50 x 1.5 mm erw (2" x 2" x ¹/₁₆"). The entire frame is not shown here, but it consists of three vertical posts capped with a rolled head and four further rolled, horizontal members that are cut between the three posts. (The posts of this unit actually fitted to an under-floor socket and spigot system, not shown here. The wall was a 'stand-alone' piece on a stand at a Paris Motor Show; the top was not visible.) A separate steel drawing was supplied for this unit, showing an elevation and a plan indicating the radius to the centre-line and the chord dimensions of the posts.

D) The **four timber flats** are constructed of 18 mm (¾") plywood 'sweeps' – ribs shaped to the required curve – cut between timber uprights and fitted to them with screw-blocks (not shown here). The face is clad with 6 mm (¼") plywood and laminate. The laminate had to have a maximum width of 1200 mm (4') to suit the graphics that would be applied. The setting-out of this whole unit was based upon the fact that two equal laminated panels were required on the 'back face' – the outer face – of the curve. Therefore, the unit's size was dictated by the fact that the arc length on the outer, longer face was restricted to 2400 mm (two sheets of 1200 mm) – the chord length is shown as being 1199.5 mm. The inner-face flats have a shorter arc length, being based upon a smaller radius (shown as R9660 mm), but one 'full' laminated panel was paired with a 'cut' one – the full one still having its laminate 1200 mm wide as an arc (chord is shown as 1199 mm).

Always show the radius, overall chords and lesser chords when drawing curved work. Mention arc dimensions if it clarifies the logic of the setting-out.

The vertical section shows that the inner facing flats are fitted with screw-blocks that screw to the steel with self-tapping screws. The outer flats are fitted by being lowered onto proprietary plastic clips and are held at the top by being self-tapped into the upper member of steel. The clips are not drawn here – they fit to both the steel and the flat – but they were used because drop-cleats are difficult to work with when placed on curved work.

Detail 'X' shows that the timber flats overhang the steel at the ends of the wall – both flats touch on the centre-line – allowing for the flats to be self-tapped to the steel upright. A laminated 12 mm (½") plywood end-capping is fitted to the flats, via 12 mm drop-cleats, leaving 'shadow-gaps' to each face.

E) **Shadow-gaps**, here shown as being 12 x 12 mm (½" x ½"), are simply grooves that are deliberately introduced in order to create a clean line between adjoining pieces. Commonly, shadow gaps are seen where showcases or wall panels butt to one another; if these items are full-height, then a shadow-gap is placed between their tops and the ceiling itself. They are usually painted black or dark grey and as a consequence are ideal for disguising secret screws – in fact they can hide a multitude of sins!

7 Steel flattage

A) As previously mentioned, this book cannot encompass the vast topic of engineering. In fact, it attempts no engineering at all; let engineers do that. The fact is that scenic draughtsmen *do* draw many items in steel, but what they would normally be drawing cannot be construed as 'engineering' – metalwork, as in 'school metalwork', would be more apt. Generally in our business, simple steel frames are drawn; some stairs, elementary trusses and other basic structures may be attempted, but only as experience allows. When true engineering is required, proper engineers should draw the job; the steel contractor would usually prefer to produce their own drawings (they should, they are responsible for the job!).

A whole book could be filled with drawings and comments on steel flats and walls, but as with timber flattage, a few examples can still give a satisfactory grounding in the basics of the matter. Accept that the shape of the flats

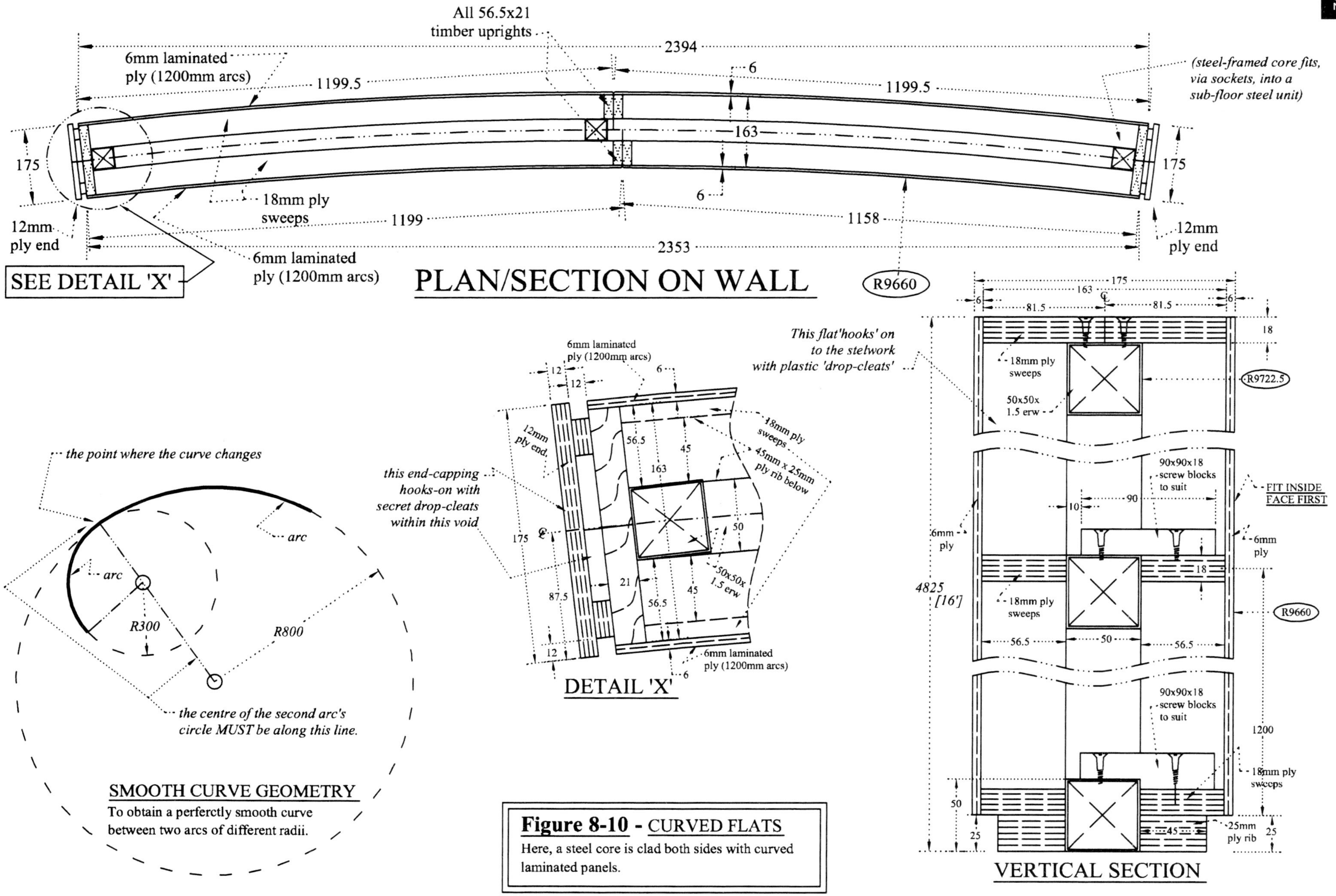

PLAN/SECTION ON WALL

(steel-framed core fits, via sockets, into a sub-floor steel unit)

175

12mm ply end

1199.5

6

163

6

2394

R9660

2353

1199

18mm ply sweeps

6mm laminated ply (1200mm arcs)

6mm laminated ply (1200mm arcs)

1158

All 56.5x21 timber uprights

175

12mm ply end

SEE DETAIL 'X'

VERTICAL SECTION

18

6

81.5

(R9722.5)

175

163

81.5

6

18mm ply sweeps

50x50x 1.5 crw

FIT INSIDE FACE FIRST

90x90x18 screw blocks to suit

6mm ply

18

90

10

50

(R9660)

18mm ply sweeps

56.5

6mm ply

4825 [167]

56.5

90x90x18 screw blocks to suit

1200

18mm ply sweeps

25mm ply rib

18mm ply sweeps

25

45

50

25

This flat 'hooks' on to the stelwork with plastic 'drop-cleats'

DETAIL 'X'

18mm ply sweeps

45mm x 25mm ply rib below

6mm laminated ply (1200mm arcs)

50

45

50x50x 1.5 crw

45

163

56.5

56.5

6

6mm laminated ply (1200mm arcs)

6

12mm ply end

12

12

21

87.5

175

this end-capping hooks-on with secret drop-cleats within this void

6mm laminated ply (1200mm arcs)

Figure 8-10 - CURVED FLATS

Here, a steel core is clad both sides with curved laminated panels.

SMOOTH CURVE GEOMETRY

To obtain a perfectly smooth curve between two arcs of different radii.

the point where the curve changes

arc

arc

R800

R300

the centre of the second arc's circle MUST be along this line.

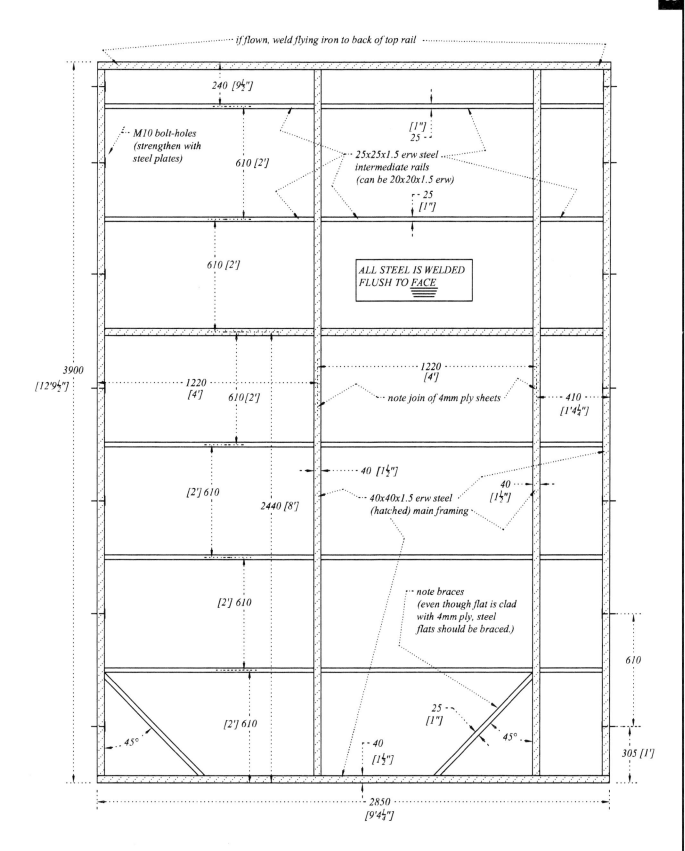

if flown, weld flying iron to back of top rail

240 [9½"]

M10 bolt-holes
(strengthen with
steel plates)

610 [2']

[1"]
25

25x25x1.5 erw steel
intermediate rails
(can be 20x20x1.5 erw)

25
[1"]

610 [2']

ALL STEEL IS WELDED
FLUSH TO FACE

3900
[12'9½"]

1220
[4']

610[2']

1220
[4']

note join of 4mm ply sheets

410
[1'4¼"]

40 [1½"]

[2'] 610

2440 [8']

40x40x1.5 erw steel
(hatched) main framing

40
[1½"]

[2'] 610

note braces
(even though flat is clad
with 4mm ply, steel
flats should be braced.)

610

[2'] 610

25
[1"]

45°

45°

40
[1½"]

305 [1']

2850
[9'4¼"]

Figure 8-11 - A STEEL FLAT

An example of a steel flat that is to be clad with 4mm plywood (40x40x1.5 erw is used as the
main framing steel - it could be 50x25, 25x25 etc, according to needs.)
Flown steel flats may have their flying-irons welded to the *top* rail - they hang better this way.
Note that it is always prudent to weld braces to steel flats (where possible), even when they are
clad with plywood.

SEE FLYING LUGS BELOW

BREAK

[10'8½"]
3260

40x40x6
M.S. angle
flying lug
SEE DETAIL 'Y'

1220

1220

1220

1220

820

1000mm long Unistrut
welded to top rail

610

610

610

610

610

610

610

610

610

610

M10
bolts

40x40x1.5 crw

585

BREAK

40x40x1.5
stiffener
behind SEE
DETAIL 'Z'

40x40x1.5
stiffener
behind SEE
DETAIL 'Z'

Stiffener
behind SEE
DETAIL 'Z'

40x40x1.5 crw

610

3025
[9'11"]

[9'8"]
2945

5700
[18'8¾"]

20x20x1.5

610

2440

2360
[7'9"]

40x40x1.5 crw

610

SEE
STIFFENER
BELOW

610

PORTAL HEADER/BORDER No. 4

25

(For clarity, many details/dimensions
have been omitted here)

BREAK
C̶L

DECOR LAY-OUT

(The plywood and plastic mirror discs
require their own drawing. Dimensions
have been omitted here for clarity)

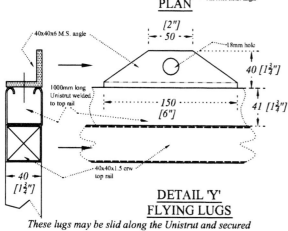

[6"]
150

[1¾"]
40

DETAIL OF
STIFFENERS

4mm ply
+ canvas

100
[4"]

50x6

17 [¾"]
C̶L

+ M11 hole
C̶L

50

M11 holes

[1'8"] 500

200 [8"]

PLAN

40x40x6 M.S. angle

40
[1¾"]

40x40x
1.5 crw
stiffener

40x40x
1.5 crw

40x40x6 M.S. angle

[2"]
50

18mm hole

BREAK

40 [1¾"]

200 [8"]

1000mm long
Unistrut welded
to top rail

150
[6"]

41 [1¾"]

40x40x1.5 crw
top rail

M11 hole

50x6

40
[1¾"]

DETAIL 'Y'
FLYING LUGS

*These lugs may be slid along the Unistrut and secured
in position - ensuring plumb flying-lines. Add stops to Unistrut.*

50x6

40x40x
1.5 crw
stiffener

PLAN ON
STIFFENERS

50x6

Figure 8-12 - A FLOWN STEEL BORDER FLAT

Here, the S/L half of a steel border is shown; applied decor would be drawn
separately and detailed. An example of steel stiffeners is drawn. The
adjustable flying lugs are detailed (*with thanks to Kimpton Walker Ltd*).

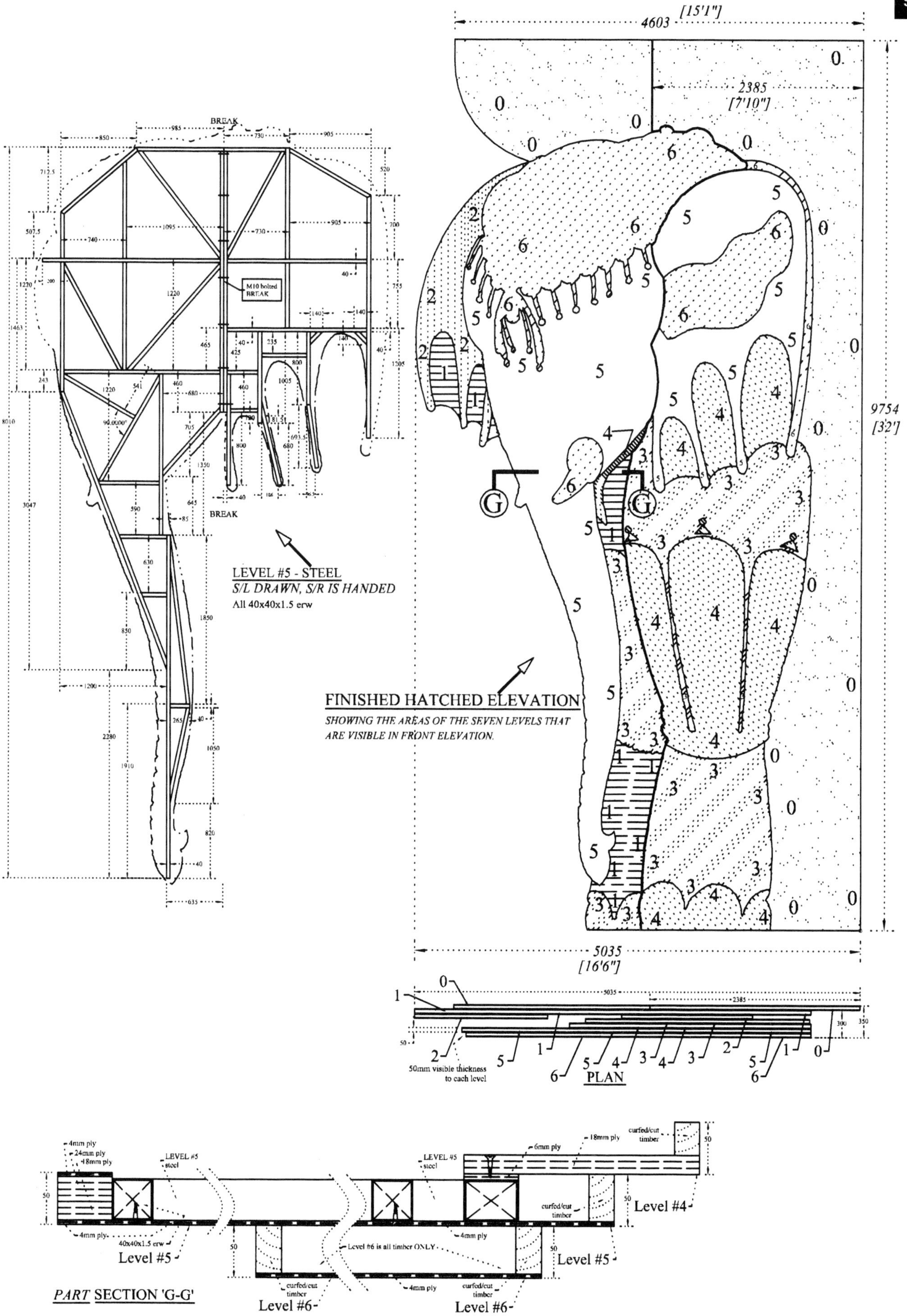

4603 [15'1"]
2385 [7'10"]
9754 [32']
5035 [16'6"]
BREAK
M10 bolted BREAK
LEVEL #5 - STEEL
S/L DRAWN, S/R IS HANDED
All 40x40x1.5 erw
FINISHED HATCHED ELEVATION
SHOWING THE AREAS OF THE SEVEN LEVELS THAT ARE VISIBLE IN FRONT ELEVATION.
G
50mm visible thickness to each level
PLAN
4mm ply
24mm ply
18mm ply
6mm ply
LEVEL #5 steel
40x40x1.5 erw
Level #6 is all timber ONLY
curfed/cut timber
Level #4
Level #5
Level #6
PART SECTION 'G-G'

Figure 8-13 - A STEEL FLAT ('*ELEPHANT LEG FLAT*')

This complicated flat has seven levels, each being 50mm thick. Four levels are of steel, three timber. Steel level No 5 is drawn. Four pairs of these legs were required, plus another pair that were *curved in plan*.

and the sizes of the members used to construct it will alter from job to job.

The following few drawings are intended to show that steel flattage or frames are, in essence, very similar to timber flattage – they have to obey the same rules. (A great advantage is that one does not have to know or worry about the intricacies of timber joints, grain and shrinkage because joints are simply welded.)

B) A **basic steel flat** – figure 8.11 – is drawn in elevation. It is a simple, braced steel frame that is to be clad with 4 mm plywood (⅛" or ⁵/₃₂"). It is fairly large (its width would only just fit into a high-sided road truck) and so needs *more than one sheet* of cladding plywood. This important fact dictates where the inner rails are placed, because the plywood sheets must meet on the centre of a rail, and the thin ply also needs the correct intermediate support (*see* also page 79 on 4 mm ply).

For the **outer framing**, 40 x 40 x 1.5 erw (1½" x 1½" x ¹/₁₆") is used. It is also used for any rails where the plywood sheets meet– this material is shown hatched on the drawing. Remember that the carpenters need to self-tap the plywood to the steel, so if they are fitting two sheets that meet on a rail they need enough steel to do that: here, they have 20 mm. The sheet size is assumed to be 2440 x 1220 mm (8' x 4').

The **intermediate rails** are of 25 x 25 x 1.5 erw (1" x 1" x ¹/₁₆"), flush to the face of the main, outer framing and spaced to suit the 4 mm ply cladding. **Braces** are also of 25 x 25x 1.5 erw (1" x 1" x ¹/₁₆"), flush to the face of the main, outer framing.

Bolt connections are shown along the stiles (uprights) of the main frame, suggesting that this flat is part of a larger structure. M10 bolts are used (⅜"). A square plate of 3 mm (⅛") steel, drilled to take the bolt, should be welded to the inside edge of the stile at each bolt-hole. The thin wall of erw tube – here 1.5 mm (¹/₁₆") – necessitates the use of this bolt-plate; without it an over-enthusiastic turn of the spanner could crush and buckle the steel walls of the box-section.

C) A **flown steel flat** is illustrated in **figure 8.12**: it is a partial elevation, showing the stage-left half of a large steel border flat, clad with 4 mm plywood. For the sake of clarity, many dimensions and details have been omitted here. The entire piece is made of five steel frames: two lower flats join on the centre-line, and three slim flats bolt to the top of these. The upper slim flats are split into three in order to avoid having a continuous join up the centre-line which would weaken the whole structure – staggered joins always add to the overall integrity of the whole piece.

A decorative border is shown to the bottom edge of the unit, dotted on the elevation and drawn again below it as 'Décor Lay-out'. It is permanently fixed to the flattage and is constructed of plywood, timber battens and plastic-mirror discs. This décor would be fully detailed and all relevant dimensions given.

Flying lugs are detailed at a larger scale. Normally, each suspension point on a steel flat consists of a thick plate (say, 8 mm – ⁵/₁₆") welded to the back of the frame; the plate has an 18 mm (¾") hole through which is fitted the shackle at the end of the steel cable. However, the method drawn here allows for adjustment, ensuring that the line is exactly plumb (many thanks to *Kimpton Walker*

Ltd for this idea). A piece of *Unistrut®* is welded to the top rail of the flat and a flying lug of thick angle-iron is slid along it and bolted when in the correct position. The lug may be turned around, placing the pick-up point upstage or downstage of the plan centre-line, thereby adjusting the centre of gravity.

Unistrut® is a proprietary system used world-wide in the construction industry as a simple but strong method of fixing or hanging items within the structure of the building. It would normally be used the other way up compared to how it is drawn here, and consists of a uniquely shaped steel channel having strong bolt-connections that can slide along inside the channel. When something is bolted to the connection it remains locked in that position. The connectors will take studding, as well as bolts of course (studding is a length of round-threaded bar). Do obtain a brochure from *Unistrut®* – this economic system has many uses.

Steel stiffeners are also detailed. These particular ones are very short, connecting as they do to the slim, upper flats. However, the method of fixing is shown and this is fairly standard to stiffeners of any length. The stiffener is a square or rectangular steel tube upon which are welded lugs of 50 x 6 mm flat bar (2" x ¼"); the lugs are bolted to the flat. Here, the plan view indicates that double lugs are fitted, one each side of the stiffener, although it is quite common to use single lugs with a bolt-plate welded to the flat's steel. The longer the stiffener and the more lugs added (within reason!), the more the flat is stiffened.

D) A **steel leg flat** is shown in **figure 8.13**. A leg is a vertical unit, or flat, or piece of cloth usually placed in an offstage position and having a 'handed' twin on the other side of the stage. Legs act as both scenery and masking – and they usually have a header, or border, suspended between them above the centre of the stage. The border may be placed downstage of the legs, hiding the tops of the legs and any track being used.

Sometimes the legs may be 'sliders' – they track on and off the stage by being suspended from a track that is hidden behind the header flat or border. The bottom of the sliders may be guided by a track in the stage, or simply by fixed wheels hidden within, or upstage of, the slider flat. Here, four pairs of the sliding leg units shown were placed onstage, with a fifth pair placed downstage of the iron curtain. Both of these forestage flats were curved in plan view.

The **finished elevation and the plan** give a broad idea of how these units appeared (stage-left is drawn, stage-right being handed). The entire unit is large – 9754 mm high and 5035 mm wide (32' by 16' 6") – and made up of seven layers, each 50 mm thick (2"). The layers are shaded and numbered and the unit's break-line is indicated with a thicker line. Each layer was drawn overlaid on to a grid so that the scenic artists could draw the desired shapes upon 4 mm plywood (⅛" or ⁵/₃₂"). The grid used was 200 x 200 mm (8" x 8").

Layers 0, 1, 3 and 5 are made of 40 x 40 x 1.5 mm erw steel framing (1½" x 1½" x ¹/₁₆"), each frame attached to its upstage neighbour with welded stubs of steel. Each steel layer is clad with 4 mm plywood that overhangs the steel and has its visible edges thickened to 50 mm. Layers 2, 4 and 6 are all timber and ply (although some areas of layer 4 were concealing sound speakers and so were clad with steel mesh and painted gauze to allow the sound through).

The steelwork to Level No. 5 is shown in elevation and, when read in conjunction with part-Section 'G-G', the general idea should be understood.

8 Exhibition walls – figure 8.14

A) Exhibition walls can involve any number of varied construction methods because every new project has its own individual design and environment. The example shown here is fairly typical, where the surface of the wall is to be made of laminated panels. This particular example was used on the upper floor of a 'double-decker' stand at a motor show; stands like this tend to have a strong steel core or 'grid' that is dressed with walls, showcases, graphics, etc. The drawing shows side sections, one on the steel, one on the finished wall and two details of the top and bottom of the wall.

B) **The steel section** indicates that the main steel joists of the first floor level are 'I' beams – or 'universal beams' – supported with square posts at relevant points (the ground floor is not seen here). Further posts rise from the flooring beams/joists, supplying support for the timber walls on the first floor, and tied together at the top with rectangular box steel ('roof ties'). Frequently, a cloth ceiling is stretched over the roof ties, diffusing the light that scatters from above in a large exhibition hall.

Note that **only an engineer** can specify the steel members used for the **grid** of a double-decked stand (written calculations that 'prove' the structural integrity of the stand are required by the show's organiser). The posts would have large square plates as feet (base-plates), each of which is connected to its neighbours with steel under-floor ties – both feet and ties being concealed by the timber platform that would usually be used to form the ground floor of the stand. The engineer will want to cross-brace the grid by bracing one bay in both directions. These braces may complicate the timber wall cladding, so establish which bays are to be cross-braced before planning the walls, openings, dressings and showcases. The grid will include details of the staircases and provide stairwell information.

A **construction draughtsman** can take the finished engineer's drawing of the grid, obtain the final design drawings and proceed to draw the entire stand, including steel, timber and glass. As ever, the devil lies in the details – spend time on the *detail* of the construction before drawing too much. This small, partial drawing – **figure 8.14** – includes details 'A' and 'C'; these confirm how all walls will meet at the first-floor level and at the top, roof level. Once this type of detail is considered, drawn and approved, whole areas of walls can be quickly drawn and completed.

C) **The timberwork section and details** show that the first floor is clad with 25 mm (1") plywood and carpet. A laminated fascia hides the main floor joists, fitted by being screwed from the inside of the stand, through the web of the joist – a false ceiling is fitted to the top of the lower flange, hiding a multitude of sins.

A **fascia box** conceals the roof ties. This type is pushed up from below and secured at the top with steel straps screwed to both timber and steel. It acts as a stiffener to the wall frames, but it can comfortably span any open areas or behave as a header to framed glass walls.

The wall frames drawn here are of 45 x 45 mm timber (2" x 2" par), but any suitable size can be considered. Remember that the *overall thickness* of the wall is important; these walls are required to butt to the steel posts, not pass over and conceal them, therefore this size of framing was adequate. The frames can be made in bay-long lengths, running from post to post, or as a series of narrower frames that screw together in units to suit the width of the wall panels. A continuous packer is shown to the top of the frame, but this may be fitted to the bottom – it allows for any discrepancies that may arise on-site and can be trimmed to suit.

The wall cladding consists of sheets of 15 mm laminated panels that drop-cleat to the frame using 12 mm (½") MDF split-battens. Note that lift-off panels require a shadow-gap at the top to allow for the panel to lift clear of the drop-cleats.

Note that the overall thickness of the walls is 99 mm (4"), made-up of the 45 mm frame, two 12 mm drop-cleat zones and two 15 mm panels. The steel posts are 120 mm square, so the walls butt between the posts (the posts are powder-coated with a colour to suit the design).

9 Stud partitioning – figure 8.15

A) Stud partitioning is used throughout the construction industry to place walls within buildings. Museum and exhibition work may often include this type of wall. The construction involves a timber or steel frame consisting of a sole plate (on the floor), studs (vertical members, spaced with their centre-lines at 406.5 mm – 16"), noggins (cross-members fitted *between* the studs) and a top rail. The frame is clad with plasterboard in a manner that suits the local fire regulations and may be skimmed with a thin coat of finished-plaster or be filled and sanded only – known as dry-lining.

B) **The elevation** illustrates part of a typical stud wall. Here, timber framing is drawn and the joints are shown as being 'housed' – often the joints are simply 'tosh-nailed' (pairs of nails placed at an angle), but this is not good practice. The noggins are shown as being placed horizontally every 1220 mm (4') and extra ones can be added to suit, as shown. The timber used here is 95 x 45 mm (4" x 2" par), but it can be rough-sawn, and smaller walls may use 70 x 45 mm (3" x 2" par). Note that the positioning of the studs and noggins ensure that the joints of the plasterboard fall on the centre of timber; if drawing these walls, always ascertain the size of the plasterboard to be used because both metric and imperial sizes may be obtained.

C) **Steel studding** is a proprietary system consisting of pressed-steel members – a plan/section detail is shown on one stud. Please be aware that these are available in various sizes so it is advisable, as ever, to obtain a brochure from the manufacturers or the stud-wall contractor – the thickness of the wall may be relevant to the rest of the job.

D) **Plasterboard** is available in many sizes; obtain a brochure to find out more. The fire regulations may insist on the *back* face of the studding being clad (even if it is not to be seen) and specify that more than one layer of plasterboard is used to both faces. When using plasterboard 'double-skinned', the joints of each layer must overlap the previous layer and must not be in line with them.

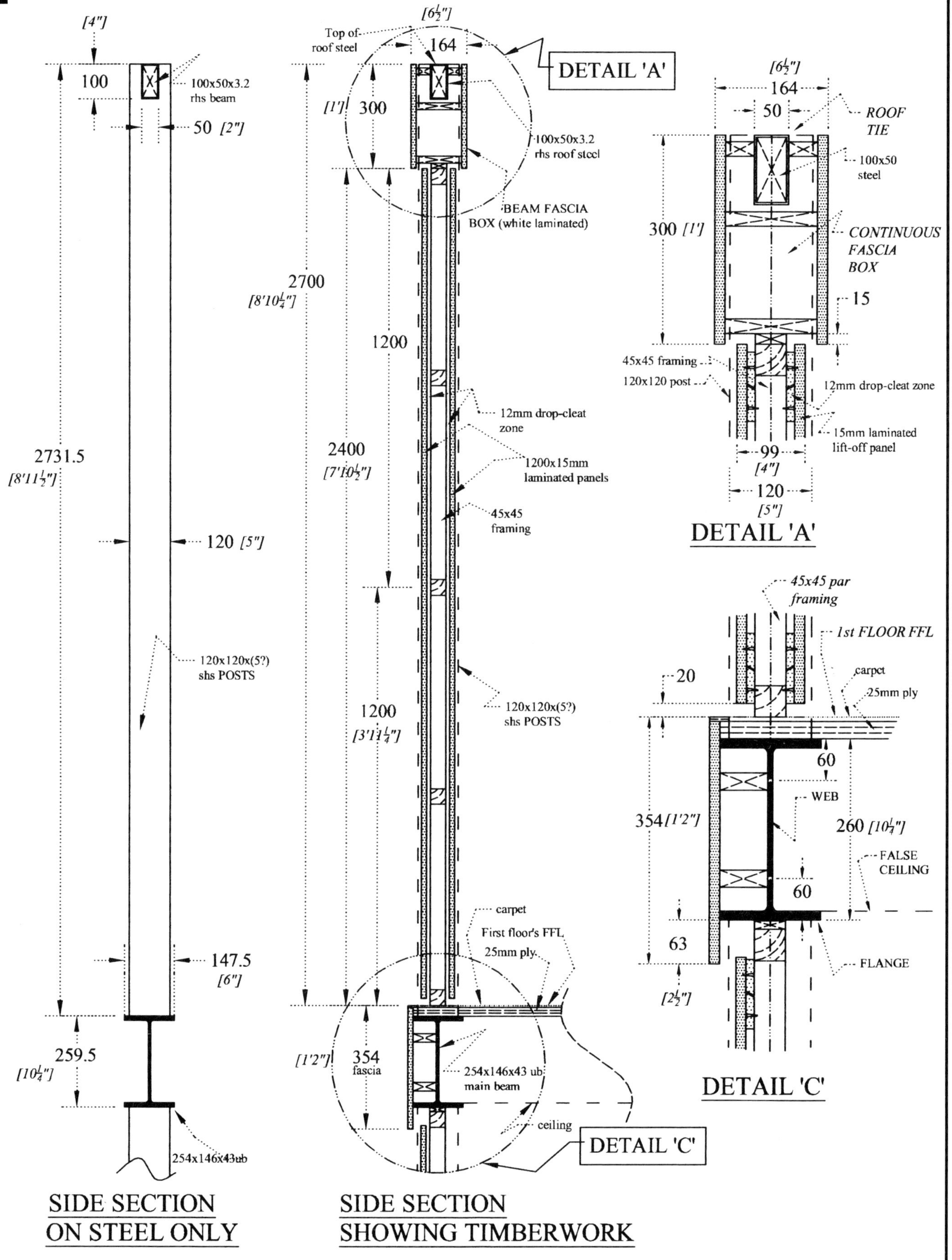

[4"]

100

50 [2"]

100x50x3.2 rhs beam

[6½"]

164

Top of roof steel

DETAIL 'A'

[1'] 300

100x50x3.2 rhs roof steel

BEAM FASCIA BOX (white laminated)

2700
[8'10¼"]

1200

2400
[7'10½"]

12mm drop-cleat zone

1200x15mm laminated panels

45x45 framing

2731.5
[8'11½"]

120 [5"]

120x120x(5?) shs POSTS

1200
[3'11¼"]

120x120x(5?) shs POSTS

147.5
[6"]

carpet

First floor's FFL

25mm ply.

259.5
[10¼"]

254x146x43ub

354 fascia

[1'2"]

254x146x43 ub main beam

ceiling

DETAIL 'C'

SIDE SECTION
ON STEEL ONLY

SIDE SECTION
SHOWING TIMBERWORK

[6½"]

164

50

ROOF TIE

100x50 steel

300 [1']

CONTINUOUS FASCIA BOX

15

45x45 framing

120x120 post

12mm drop-cleat zone

15mm laminated lift-off panel

99
[4"]

120
[5"]

DETAIL 'A'

45x45 par framing

1st FLOOR FFL

carpet

25mm ply

20

60

WEB

354 [1'2"]

260 [10¼"]

FALSE CEILING

60

63

FLANGE

[2½"]

DETAIL 'C'

Figure 8-14 - AN EXHIBITION WALL

Here, laminated lift-off panels are fitted to 45x45 par timber framing.

The sides of this framing are bolted to the steel posts shown.

The top is stiffened by a continuous fascia that is concealing a steel member.

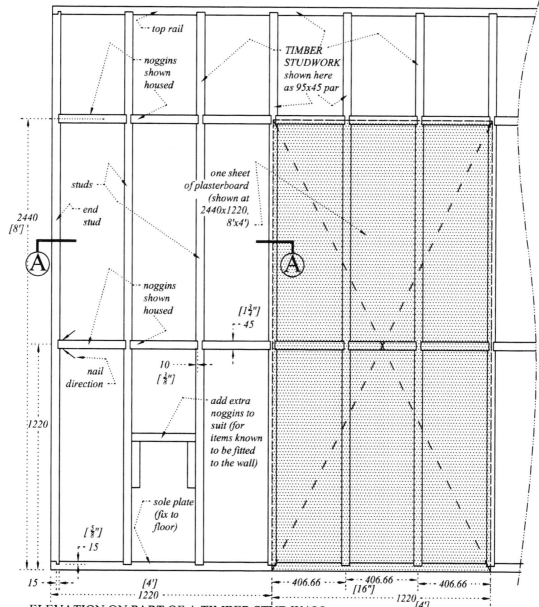

top rail

noggins shown housed

TIMBER STUDWORK shown here as 95x45 par

studs

end stud

one sheet of plasterboard (shown at 2440x1220, 8'x4')

2440 [8']

Ⓐ

Ⓐ

noggins shown housed

[1¾"] 45

nail direction

10 [⅜"]

add extra noggins to suit (for items known to be fitted to the wall)

1220

sole plate (fix to floor)

[⅝"] 15

15

[4'] 1220

406.66 · 406.66 · 406.66
[16"]

1220 [4']

ELEVATION ON PART OF A TIMBER STUD WALL

TIMBER may be 100x50 rough-sawn, 95x45 par (shown here), 75x50 r/sawn, 70x45 par & etc.
TIMBER is often just nailed together (poor quality) - housing is better.
METAL STUDWORK is available - and is used more than timber, by partitioning contractors.
PLASTERBOARD is made in various sheet sizes and thicknesses - check your local supplier BEFORE drawing the studwork.
FIRE REGULATIONS, local to the job, will specify whether BOTH faces of the studwork is to be clad (whether seen or not)
and/or whether TWO SKINS of plasterboard are required to each face (with overlapping joints - to seal against fire)

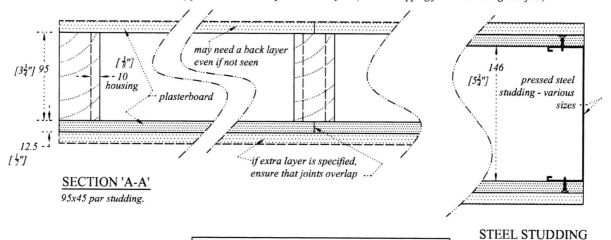

[3¾"] 95

[⅜"] 10 housing

may need a back layer even if not seen

plasterboard

146 [5¾"]

pressed steel studding - various sizes

12.5 [½"]

if extra layer is specified, ensure that joints overlap

SECTION 'A-A'
95x45 par studding.

STEEL STUDDING

Figure 8-15 - STUD PARTITIONING
Walls used in the building trade, museum work & etc.

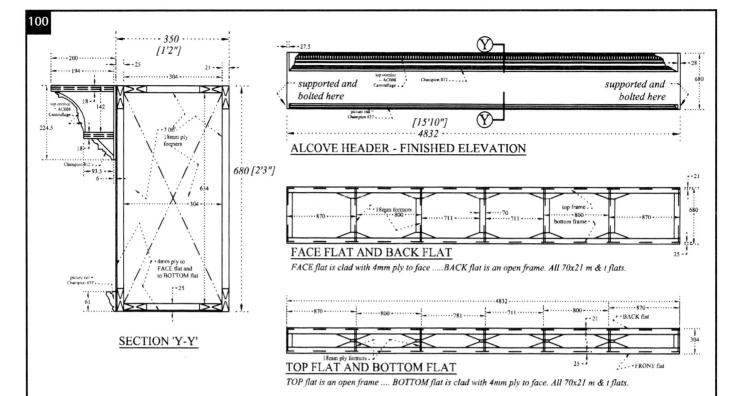

SECTION 'Y-Y'

ALCOVE HEADER - FINISHED ELEVATION

supported and bolted here   *supported and bolted here*

FACE FLAT AND BACK FLAT

FACE flat is clad with 4mm ply to face .....BACK flat is an open frame. All 70x21 m & t flats.

TOP FLAT AND BOTTOM FLAT

TOP flat is an open frame .... BOTTOM flat is clad with 4mm ply to face. All 70x21 m & t flats.

A TIMBER 'TRUSS' - *This unit had to span a considerable distance. The audience could only see the front and bottom faces, however, a back and top flat was added in order to form a strong 3D truss unit that included seven 18mm ply formers.*

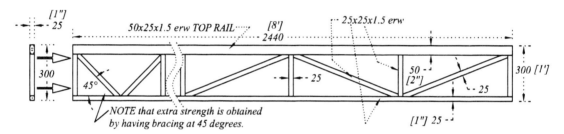

NOTE *that extra strength is obtained by having bracing at 45 degrees.*

A STEEL '2D' TRUSS, OR 'LADDER BEAM' - *A braced steel frame having no depth other than its own thickness - it can take 'down-loads' and span reasonable distances without deflecting downwards, but may buckle in plan if the span is too great (stiffen the back.)*

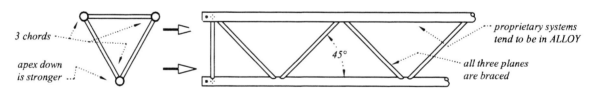

3 chords

apex down is stronger

proprietary systems tend to be in ALLOY

all three planes are braced

A TRIANGULAR STEEL ('3D') TRUSS - *A braced steel frame having three chords. Optimum strength is obtained by using it 'apex-down', as drawn here. Lengths of truss are joined with steel pins to form long lengths. Many proprietary systems exist.*

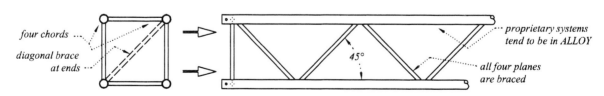

four chords

diagonal brace at ends

proprietary systems tend to be in ALLOY

all four planes are braced

A RECTANGULAR STEEL ('3D') TRUSS - *Braced steel framing having four chords. Many proprietary systems exist - always obtain brochures from the suppliers in order to obtain the size and strength of the truss. They can be made to suit.*

Figure 8-16 - TRUSSES AND BEAMS
Beams and trusses are used to span distances and/or take loads.

10 Trusses and beams in timber and steel – figure 8.16

A) A **timber truss** is shown at the top of this drawing: it is simply a rectangular box, consisting of four conventional flats screwed together and tied with 18 mm ply formers. This particular piece was only visible to the audience on its front and bottom faces, but, as it had to span 4832 mm (15' 10"), a truss was chosen as the construction method – supplying greater strength and stability than the face and bottom flats alone would have done. As with all trusses and beams, the deeper it is, the stronger it will be (i.e. in front elevation, extra height gives extra strength).

B) A **steel ladder beam** is shown. This is a two-dimensional truss, having only one plane of steel. Note that greater strength is obtained if the bracing is all at 45°. The top chord is shown as being a larger steel section than is the bottom chord. This is because, when a load is applied, the top chord is under compression and the bottom is in tension ... and steel is stronger in tension than in compression.

C) A **triangular truss** is sketched having circular alloy chords and braces. All three planes are braced. Trusses like this are usually rented or bought from specialist companies; they come in many sizes and individual units connect together to form long trusses. Optimum strength is obtained by using them 'apex-down', as shown.

D) A **rectangular truss** is shown, made from similar materials to the above. All four sides are braced and the two ends have diagonal braces. Large structures may have rectangular trusses that include a maintenance walkway, allowing for lamps, etc. to be accessible from within the truss. These units tend to have alloy 'walkway mesh' attached to joists welded between the bottom chords.

E) **Bridges** used in our business (to link units of scenery, or used as public access in large exhibition work) frequently consist of two trusses as the main members that sit beneath the walkway surface. The trusses are linked with joists that run across the width of the bridge. Each truss can be extended upwards to include the handrail and balustrade of the bridge, and this increase in height will greatly increase the load that can be taken. This method is ideal if there is any restriction on the amount of structure that can be placed below the walkway surface. Modern architectural design often incorporates the structural strength of glass into pedestrian bridges – when using balustrades of sheet glass and steel, the glass is acting as a brace (only engineers can draw and specify such structures).

9 • Windows

In the real world – the world outside stages and exhibitions – windows are constructed to high specifications due to the relentless nature of the elements. Rain, frost, sunshine and wind have ensured the ongoing development of window construction; special joints have now been devised that reduce the risk of timber rot or failure. Metal windows have followed an equally sophisticated 'learning curve'.

Fortunately, our business merely has to replicate the *look* of a certain window; we produce a facsimile that has no need to combat the weather. Stage windows are simply frames that resemble a desired window-type. Consequently, there is no real need to learn the intricacies of the carpentry or engineering involved in building genuine windows. As ever, the best way of acquiring knowledge is to begin consciously to notice real windows – look at all types from all eras and get a 'feel' for their proportions, their mouldings and the sizes of the sections used. Brochures are ideal for reference use. It also helps to have an architectural reference book – one that shows windows throughout the ages.

NOTES ON WINDOWS

1 Genuine windows

A) **Traditional wood** windows consist of timber sections with a rebate for glass on the outside face and an ovolo, or similar moulding, on the inside face. **Figure 16.17** on page 164 has an example of a 'sash stile' and a 'sash bar' – glass and putty have been indicated.

B) **Note that the glass, and therefore the rebate, faces the outside.** Even if rain were to penetrate the putty, it would still have to struggle to breach the rebate. Occasionally, one may see this rule reversed: some doors have glass panels with the moulding – the ovolo – on the outside, for decorative purposes. Some work may include a 'bead', or small timber section, to the outside that mimics the inside moulding.

C) The depth, or **thickness of the material** is usually 45 mm (1¾"), whereas its width can vary – the bottom rail usually being wider than the stiles and the top rail.

D) Stiles 'run through' on window sashes: the top and bottom rails cut into the stiles (leaving the long edges 'clean' of end-grain). *This is the reverse of flattage construction*, where the top and bottom rails run through.

E) **French windows** are, of course, doors, but their traditional construction still incorporates timber sections that resemble the sash stile and sash bar shown. The stiles and top rail would be wider, the bottom rail wider still.

F) **'Drips'** are methods employed to ensure that rain will drip off the window at certain points. Drips may be in the form of applied mouldings that encourage water to shed along a line. **Figure 16.17** shows a door-drip moulding – it forces rainwater off the face of the door (for

example), protecting the vulnerable end-grain at the bottom of the stiles (end-grain absorbs water, leading to rotting). The bottom edge of this moulding has a half-round groove, known as a **drip-groove**. Drip-grooves ensure that when raindrops are blown inwards they will be made to drip off at this point. Windowsills have them; sash stiles and bottom rails may have them.

Be aware of the existence of drips in *real* windows, but also be aware that applying drip-grooves to the sashes of theatrical, stage windows would be somewhat indulgent. If they can't be seen, don't put them on.

G) **Metal windows** can be of alloy or galvanised steel. Obtain brochures to see the various sections used. These are usually simple to replicate in timber or ply, for use in the theatre.

H) **Double-glazed windows** can be of timber or metal-framed construction. Alloy double-glazed units are frequently used in exhibition and museum work: they have a neat appearance and are practical in reducing unwanted noise from adjoining areas (and they travel quite easily too). When introducing such units into a drawing, ensure you ask the *manufacturer* for all the relevant details. You might find these in a brochure, but always confirm that the specification is correct for the size of window being used.

I) **Glass** may be used in exhibition and museum work. *Always obtain the correct glass specification from a qualified glazier*: many types of glass are available, and only a professional should choose the thickness of each type relevant to the task in hand. Note that some 'unbreakable' types of glass are surprisingly fragile when handled – the slightest tap on a corner may shatter the pane – so always order spares for a touring show.

2 Theatrical stage windows

A) **Glass** is never used in stage windows: the stage environment is too hazardous. Also, the weight of real glass is considerable (approximately 2.5 kg per 1 mm thickness, per square metre) compared to its substitutes.

B) **Clear PVC** (such as *Darvic*) is an ideal substitute for glass: it is flameproof, lightweight and not too expensive. Its sheet size is approximately 2440 x 1220 mm (8' x 4') and it is sold in various thicknesses, 4 mm being common for the average window (⁵⁄₃₂"). Be aware that some commercial PVC has a bluish tint that can be noticeable under stage lighting – ask for samples.

C) Clear **polycarbonate** may also be used as window-pane material. It is more expensive than PVC, but is sold in larger sheets and is very tough and strong.

D) **Film** may be applied to the PVC or polycarbonate in order to give an effect such as a colour tint, or a 'frost', or to provide a surface upon which to project images.

E) Stage windows can be **'practical' or 'non-practical'**: they open or they don't. If practical, ensure that the actors' intended movements and actions are known. Check, for example, that they can safely climb through the window, if required. Ensure that flown practical windows are lockable; they need to be locked closed before flying begins, in order to avoid the danger of their opening in the grid and being torn from the flat.

Non-practical windows can be made entirely of vac-formed PVC or ABS. These moulds are lightweight and are ideal for use on flown scenery.

F) Note that on a real window the **ovolo moulding** (or similar) that is part of the window sash would appear to be **mitred**. It is not – it is a scribed joint – but it looks as though it were. However, stage carpenters would be more likely to apply the ovolo to the finished frame with an electric router ... and this leaves a 'quarter-round' finish to the ovolo at internal corners. Some designers hate this rounded detail, so ensure that the carpenters 'ease' the joint with a sharp chisel, recreating the mitred look. (Often, the audience would need eyes like hawks to be able to spot this tiny transgression from conventionality, but then attention to detail *is* a part of our job.)

SOME TYPES OF WINDOWS

1 Sliding sash windows – figure 9.01

A) This drawing shows an elevation of the two non-practical sashes used to form a window unit. The sashes are simple frames of 21 mm thick timber (1", par, ⅞") with an ovolo routed to one face and material added to the back face – fly-screen to the lower sash, calico and black backing-cloth to the upper. Stage sashes tend to be thinner than real ones because the audience cannot usually 'read' the thickness of the framing.

B) Plan Section 'A-A' and Section 'B-B' show that the window frame is simply an 18 mm ply (¾") reveal fitted to the surrounding flat, having a boxed-out dummy sill and a boxed-out window surround (architrave). Above the window, a boxed moulding is added to the window surround. The two sashes are fixed as shown. A parting bead and a staff bead are fitted to the window frame.

C) Practical sliding sashes for the stage can be achieved by counter-weighting the sashes, as in real life. However, this method is quite complicated, involving pulleys, lines, weights and weight-boxes, and has the further drawback of being too noisy for the theatre – as the set is moved, the weights tend to bang around in their boxes. A far easier method is to use 'false springs': the sashes are made to clear the sides of the frame by about 3 mm (⅛") and each sash is fitted with two sprung-steel plates that grip the frame, but allow for sliding. The sprung plate can be a strip cut from a broken band-saw blade – say 75 mm (3") long – with screw-holes drilled at the ends. It is let in and screwed to the sash in such a fashion that the centre of the steel strip is bowing away from the sash in a shallow 'C' shape. Amazingly, this simple device has sufficient friction to allow the sash to remain in any position, yet still be slid up or down with ease.

2 A bay window and opening sash – figure 9.02

A) A front elevation, a section on centre and Plan Section 'D-D' show a bay window and window seat. The seat unit is a simple plywood box with recessed panels to the downstage faces. The three window frames are 25 mm (1") thick timber

and have mouldings attached to their faces. A 12 mm (½") plywood top is indicated on the side section, helping to tie the whole window unit together into one strong piece.

The two large centre panes are opening sashes, as indicated on the plan view. The other, fixed panes have clear PVC fitted to the back of the frames ... and false 'leading' is applied to the PVC by the prop department.

B) One of the opening sashes is drawn as a separate elevation and part Section 'A-A' illustrates its somewhat unusual construction. The frame of the sash is simply a piece of voided 18 mm plywood (¾") and it is faced with 8 mm polycarbonate (⁵⁄₁₆"). To use such thick, expensive material is rare on windows of this size, but here it is employed so that the breakable 'sugar-glass' panes can be housed or rebated into it (held in place with clear adhesive tape). An actor has to break three of these panes two or three times per show ('sugar-glass' is literally that: a thin pane of clear melted sugar that will shatter without cutting any skin). The scenic artists need to paint the sash's frame onto the *face* of the polycarbonate – only the centre stiles are visible when the window is closed.

C) Details 'E', 'F' and 'G' illustrate how the window frames, mouldings, fixed windows and opening sashes are detailed.

3 A steel-cored window – figure 9.03

A) At first glance, looking at the window elevation, this appears to be a straightforward piece of scenery – an ecclesiastical-type window. However, 13 of the window panes have to fall out of the frame, on cue; each has to 'pop out' of the window (which is plumb).

B) The solution used on this particular production was to have a steel window unit that bolted to neighbouring flattage (not shown on the drawing). This steel window was clad with timber, MDF and plywood to achieve the design. The steel elevation indicates the steelwork: it has outer framing of 40 x 40 x 1.5 erw (1½" x 1½") and inner framing of 20 x 20 x 1.5 erw (¾" x ¾"). Fixing-lugs are welded to the outer framing.

C) Sections 'B-B' and 'Y-Y' show how the steelwork was clad in order to satisfy the design. The lighter, inner steel was clad with 18 mm MDF (¾") to *both* faces, creating the moulding and the rebate for the PVC panes. The MDF was housed to receive the steel members. The outer steel framing was clad to form the architrave and sill, as shown.

D) The mechanism is indicated in Sections 'B-B' and 'Y-Y' (more detail was provided for the actual show; here things have been simplified for clarity). Each of the square, inner cross-rails of the window contains a round steel tube that can rotate within it – PTFE bushes help to reduce friction. These round tubes protrude through the main frame and have welded lugs and a cable-clamp fitted to each end. The steel elevation shows these lugs; the bottom three are placed plumb above one another and the upper two are in line. As can be imagined, a cable system was devised that allowed for one pull on the cable to rotate each of the round tubes simultaneously.

The upper part of Section 'Y-Y' shows one of the falling panes in its 'held' position, before activation of the cable. Next to this is shown the same pane after activation. Notice that the round tube has a small lug fitted to it that passes through a slot in the square tube. This lug holds the pane, then pushes it out as the round tube is rotated.

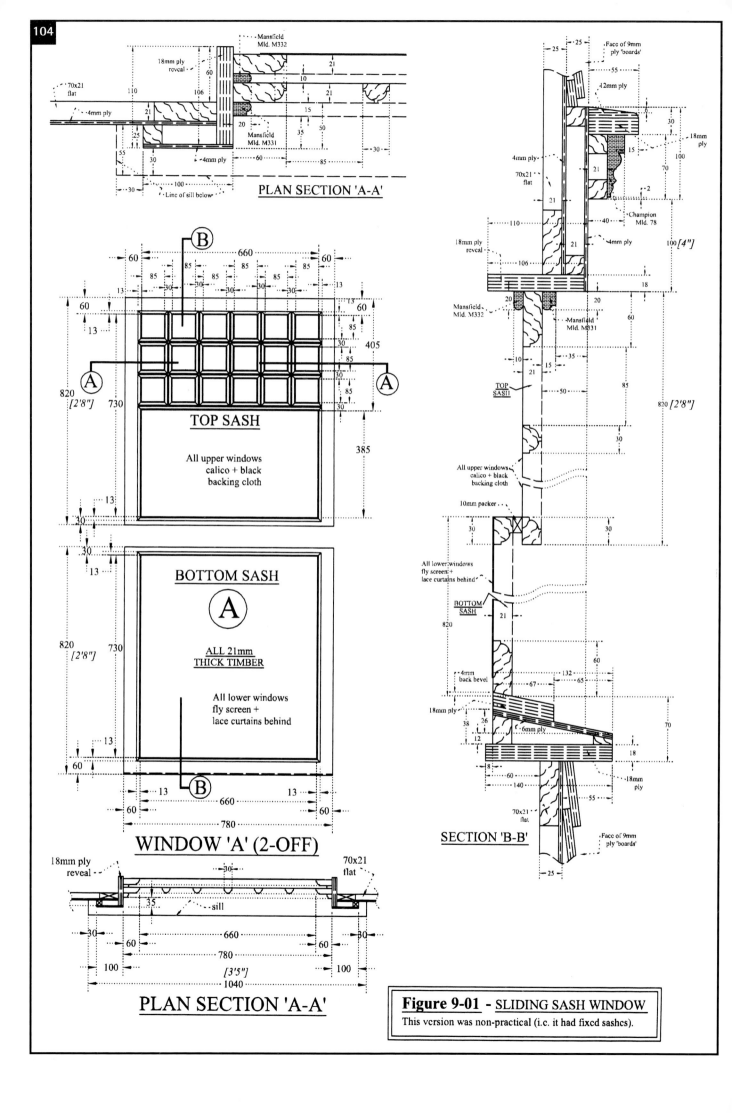

PLAN SECTION 'A-A'

TOP SASH

All upper windows
calico + black
backing cloth

WINDOW 'A' (2-OFF)

BOTTOM SASH

A

ALL 21mm
THICK TIMBER

All lower windows
fly screen +
lace curtains behind

PLAN SECTION 'A-A'

SECTION 'B-B'

Figure 9-01 – SLIDING SASH WINDOW
This version was non-practical (i.e. it had fixed sashes).

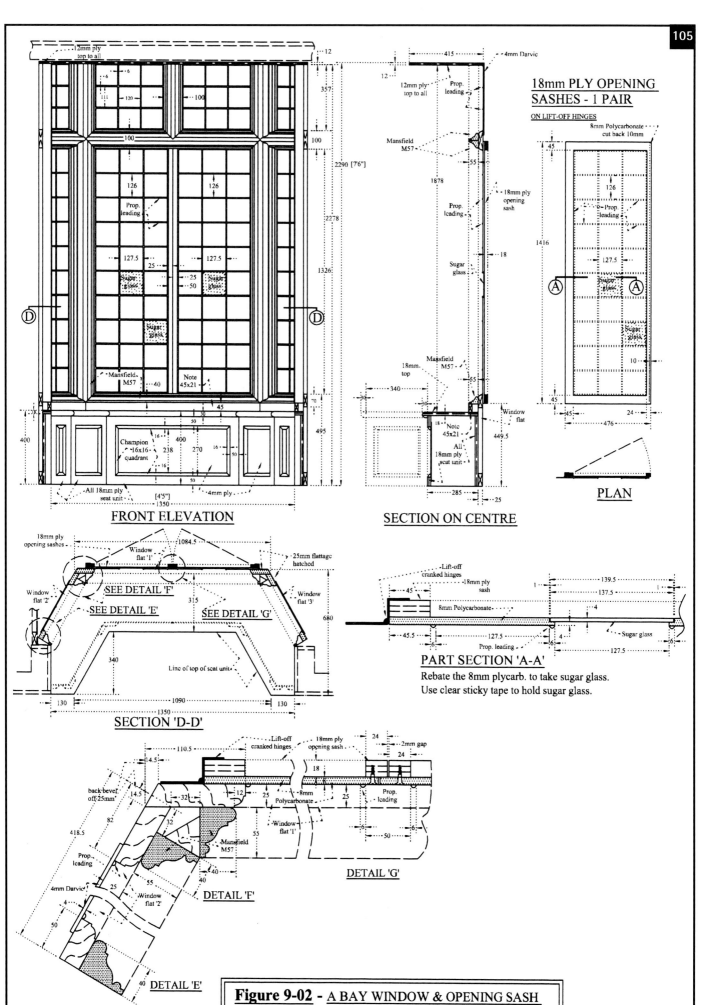

FRONT ELEVATION

SECTION ON CENTRE

18mm PLY OPENING
SASHES - 1 PAIR

ON LIFT-OFF HINGES

PLAN

SECTION 'D-D'

PART SECTION 'A-A'
Rebate the 8mm plycarb. to take sugar glass.
Use clear sticky tape to hold sugar glass.

DETAIL 'F'

DETAIL 'G'

DETAIL 'E'

Figure 9-02 - A BAY WINDOW & OPENING SASH
The opening sashes contain breakable sugar-glass panes - these break two
or three times during each show, each pane being replaced each time.

106

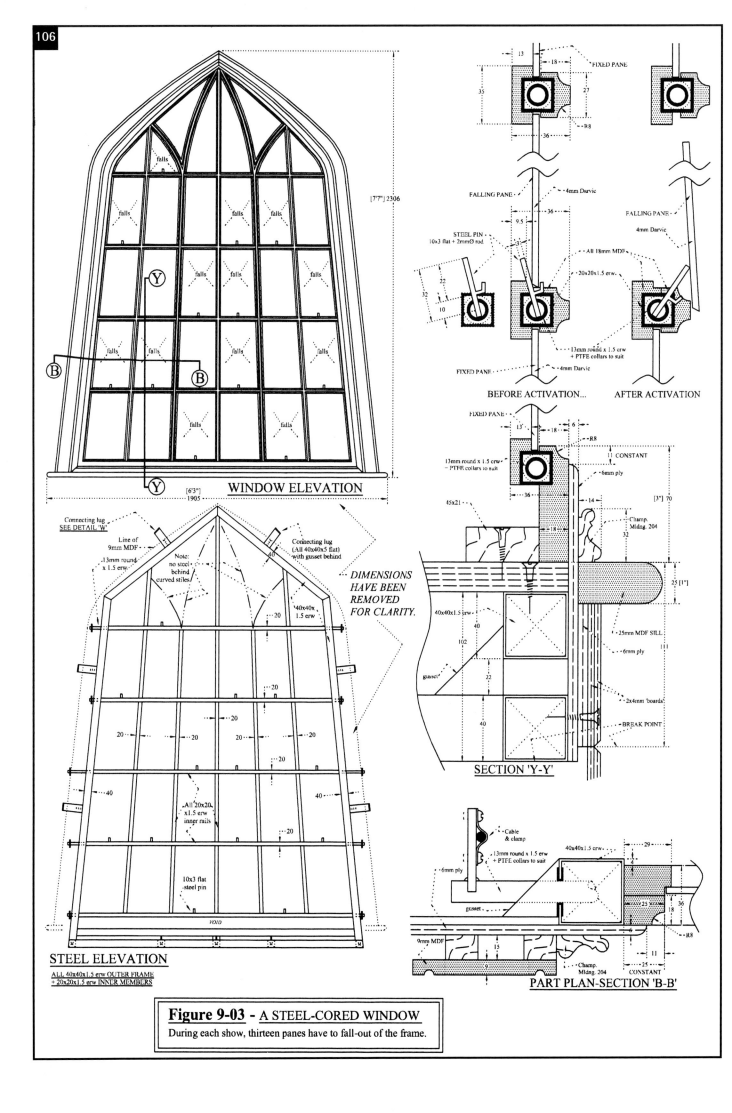

WINDOW ELEVATION

[7'7"] 2306

[6'3"] 1905

STEEL ELEVATION
ALL 40x40x1.5 erw OUTER FRAME
+ 20x20x1.5 erw INNER MEMBERS

Connecting lug
SEE DETAIL 'W'
Line of
9mm MDF
13mm round
x 1.5 erw
Note:
no steel
behind
curved stiles
Connecting lug
(All 40x40x5 flat)
with gusset behind
40
40x40x
1.5 erw

DIMENSIONS
HAVE BEEN
REMOVED
FOR CLARITY.

All 20x20
x1.5 erw inner rails

10x3 flat
steel pin

VOID

FIXED PANE

FALLING PANE
4mm Darvic

STEEL PIN
10x3 flat + 2mmØ rod

FALLING PANE
4mm Darvic

All 18mm MDF
20x20x1.5 erw.

13mm round x 1.5 erw
+ PTFE collars to suit
4mm Darvic

FIXED PANE

BEFORE ACTIVATION...   AFTER ACTIVATION

FIXED PANE

13mm round x 1.5 erw
– PTFE collars to suit

R8
CONSTANT
6mm ply

45x21
Clamp.
Mldng. 204
[3"] 70

40x40x1.5 erw
40
102
gusset
22
40

25 [1"]

25mm MDF SILL
6mm ply

2x4mm 'boards'

BREAK POINT

SECTION 'Y-Y'

Cable
& clamp
13mm round x 1.5 erw
+ PTFE collars to suit
6mm ply
gusset
9mm MDF
40x40x1.5 erw
29
36
18
R8
11
CONSTANT
Champ.
Mldng. 204

PART PLAN-SECTION 'B-B'

Figure 9-03 - A STEEL-CORED WINDOW
During each show, thirteen panes have to fall-out of the frame.

10 • Doors

As with windows, doors come in a vast variety of styles: the draughtsman ought to make a conscious effort to study and understand their different uses and their proportions as they have evolved through history. Door manufacturers supply excellent brochures that include dozens of types with their specifications. Many old, traditional types of door remain in constant supply.

Museum and exhibition work tends to involve bought doors, while the theatre usually has them built as bespoke items by the carpenters – for reasons explained below.

NOTES ON DOORS

1 Non-theatrical

A) Timber doors may be divided into two types: 'flush' doors and 'framed' doors. **Flush doors** are made of on-edge timber framing, faced *on both sides* with plywood. Between the timber framing they can be hollow, filled with 'egg-box' type cardboard, or be solid. The hollow and egg-box variety are lightweight and easy to handle. The solid type (usually fire-resistant doors) can be bought in standard sizes or as 'door-blanks' – large slabs that are cut down to suit the relevant doorway. Flush doors tend to be very good at holding their shape, with less tendency to buckle and bend or to 'go in wind' (where one corner, in elevation, moves back – or forwards – in relation to the others. Pronounced as in 'wind my watch').

B) **Framed doors** are constructed of a stout timber frame, usually consisting of two stiles; a top and bottom rail; and a lock, or middle, rail. As with window sashes, the stiles 'run through' – they go from top to bottom and have the rails cut between them, making it easier to plane the edges. The frame can be clad with boards on one side, or have panels or glass fitted between the frame's voids.

Figure 7.01 on page 61 shows a framed, ledge and braced door. The subject of this drawing is the theory of bracing, but it is worth looking at the proportions of the timber framing of the door. Notice that the stiles are the same width as the top rail (here, 95 mm or 3¾"), the lock rail is wider (145 mm or 5¾"), and the bottom rail is even wider (195 mm or 7¾"). On some 'period' doors, the lock rail can be as wide as, or even wider than, the bottom rail. The draughtsman should always ensure that doors are proportionate to their type; many designers make a guess at drawing a door's main framing and are often grateful if their design is corrected (after they have been consulted, naturally).

Being made of so much solid timber, framed doors are more prone to distortion than are flush doors. Each piece of the frame wants to bend its own way as the timber fibres absorb or shed moisture. This can put the door 'in wind' (*see* 'A' above). The dry heat emitted by stage lighting can cause havoc with solid-framed doors and so theatrical doors are built in a special fashion.

C) **Standard sizes** for domestic and workplace doors include:

1981 x 762 x 44 mm (6' 6" x 2' 6" x 1³/₄")
– the standard domestic door
1981 x 838 x 44 mm (6' 6" x 2' 9" x 1³/₄")
2032 x 813 x 44 mm (6' 8" x 2' 8" x 1³/₄")
2000 x 807 x 44 mm
– 'metric' (6' 6³/₄" x 2' 7³/₄" x 1³/₄")

D) **Fire doors** are designated so by the Local Authority and the Fire Department. They may be 'half-hour' or 'one hour' fire-check doors (the time for which they should contain a fire). *Always obtain the correct specification for doors of this type.* They are usually of solid, flush-door construction. They may have to have intumescent strips around their edges, which swell during a fire and seal the gap around doors. Any glass panels may have to be in wired Georgian glass. They may require specific, sprung door-closers. The door frame may need solid, inherent door-stops (not planted-on, but moulded from the frame material itself) of a minimum thickness of 25 mm (1"). Crash-bars may be fitted to fire-exit doors.

Fire doors through which people pass when moving from one area of a building to another are fitted and hung so that they are *pushed* open. This allows egress towards the outside of the building.

Double-doors will usually require rebated closing stiles – i.e. the doors rebate into one another, closing any gaps. This necessitates the opening of one door before the other is free to open (normally, a person's right hand should *push* open the right-hand door).

E) **Health & Safety** issues apply to doors, as with everything. Glass viewing panels should be added to any door when there is a danger of it opening into the path of a passer-by – better still, mask the swinging door with a wall. Doorways that need to open into corridors should be set back into a small vestibule, allowing the doors to open against a wall and not into the corridor. Door furniture, such as handles and locks, must be chosen so that the user's hand cannot be trapped (against the door-stop, for example, when turning a round handle that is set too close to the edge of the door).

F) The **hanging** of doors – the direction in which they swing open – can be a matter of choice if they are not subject to fire and safety issues. Custom has it that in a domestic dwelling, a door opening into a room should protect the privacy of the room. This ensures that a person in the room sees the door open before the visitor comes into view; the person entering the room cannot see much of the room until the door has been opened and passed. However, modern custom often reverses this 'privacy' rule; it may look neater in plan view and create the illusion of more space within the room, but a home's cosiness is sacrificed when this is done.

Offices and public areas are different environments and they may benefit from a reversal of the privacy rule. The point is, carefully consider the hanging of all doors. The theatre tends to hang its doors in a fashion best-suited to the action of the play and to help in the masking of off-stage areas.

G) **Steel doors** are used in many circumstances. An example is shown on **figure 7.01** (*see* page 61) of a familiar type of gate: notice the bracing and remember that all steel-framed doors should carry braces.

H) **Alloy doors** may be used in the office, industrial or home environment. They are usually complete units, containing door frame and door, sliding or opening, and the manufacturer's brochure will provide the details. Exhibition and museum projects will often include these double-glazed units – the soundproofing qualities are attractive to shows of this type.

2   Theatrical doors and door frames

A) It has been mentioned that the stage environment, with its hot lights, makes it inadvisable to use solid-framed timber doors in a theatre set. More importantly, solid-framed doors are too heavy and too costly for use in scenery. Scenery doors tend to be requested in non-standard sizes and are therefore made individually, to order – so to make them solid would be pointless and counter-productive. Consequently, stage doors are made using hollow construction methods: a light, on-edge frame is clad with thin plywood to recreate the designed door pattern. Versions of this method are illustrated and described below.

B) **Doors contained within flown scenery** must be locked and secured before flying commences. Avoid using lift-off hinges on flown doors.

C) **Hinges (butts)** are produced in many styles to suit a variety of uses. The average domestic door has two hinges that are placed 'six inches down, nine inches up' (*see* **figure 7.01** – the top hinge is 150 mm down from the top of the door and the bottom hinge is 225 mm up from the bottom). Exterior doors and high-quality doors – say in hardwood – have a third hinge placed between the two.

Lift-off hinges are popular for obvious reasons: it is simple to remove or add the door to the frame.

Removable-pin hinges are useful as they allow for the door's removal, but only if a tool-kit is to hand – the pin needs to be tapped out of the hinge, separating the two leaves. Remember that almost any hinge can be made into this type; the hinge's pin can be ground off at the top and then the pin can be forced out of the knuckle.

Rising-butt hinges are of the lift-off variety, designed so that as the door opens it is lifted upwards by about 10 mm (⅜"), clearing the carpet. Remember that when the door is open at 90 degrees it will want to close itself on these hinges (as long as the door frame is fitted plumb). Doors on rising butts want to close themselves. **Falling-butt** hinges are very similar, except that their design dictates that the door wants to remain open at 90 degrees – the door falls by about 10 mm when open. These are often used in the cubicles of public toilets; an unused cubicle is easily visible because its door swings open when not locked shut.

Sprung hinges are self-explanatory: they include springs that encourage the door to open or close.

Bomber hinges allow for doors to swing in both directions – like a saloon door in the Wild West. They are clever, but can be bulky in appearance.

Floor springs are rarely used in the theatre, but may be found in exhibition and museum work. They consist of a metal box containing the spring mechanism that is let into the floor below the door – the door is fitted to a shoe on the box and a pivot at the top. These units allow for the adjustment of the closing speed.

Doors can be made to **pivot**, rather than be hinged, and the theatre business uses many home-made versions of pivot mechanisms.

Door-closers are not hinges – they are fitted in addition to hinges – but they control the closing action of the door. Some types are hidden from view by being entirely let-in to the frame and door.

SOME TYPES OF DOORS

1   A panelled door, theatre-style
– figure 10.01

A) This drawing shows a conventional panelled door that is constructed in the theatre style. A light framework of on-edge timber is clad with thin plywood and the panels and mouldings are added to suit. Note that the frame includes two 'hinge-blocks' that strengthen where the hinges are to be placed, and a 'lock-block' that provides solid timber where the lock or latch is to be fitted.

B) Plan Section 'A-A' indicates that this door is single-sided – the back face is clad with a plain sheet of ply. An alternative section is included that shows how the door would be if it were double-sided – the panels should be housed into the framing.

2   A removable door-frame unit
– figure 10.01

A) Doors and door frames or reveals may be constructed as one unit. Here, a door-reveal unit is made to be removable from its adjoining flattage. The 18 mm ply (¾") reveal is built to include the architrave, door frame, door stops and the door – the bottom of the unit is held by two 'reveal irons' (steel straps bolted to the reveals).

B) When pushed into the opening in the flattage, the architrave butts to the face of the flats and the unit is secured by folding-down hinge-flaps made of 18 mm ply. These flaps trap the unit in position – three flaps per stile and one at the top would suffice.

3   French doors – figure 10.02

A) The left-hand elevation shows a finished view; the right shows the framing used in its construction; and the Section explains how the cladding, mouldings and clear PVC 'glass' are fitted. The curved timbers of the top rail would be 'curfed' (scored with regularly spaced saw-cuts, allowing the timber to bend). This type of door has been included to illustrate that using solid timber framing is never a good option for stage doors: even doors like this are built using hollow construction methods.

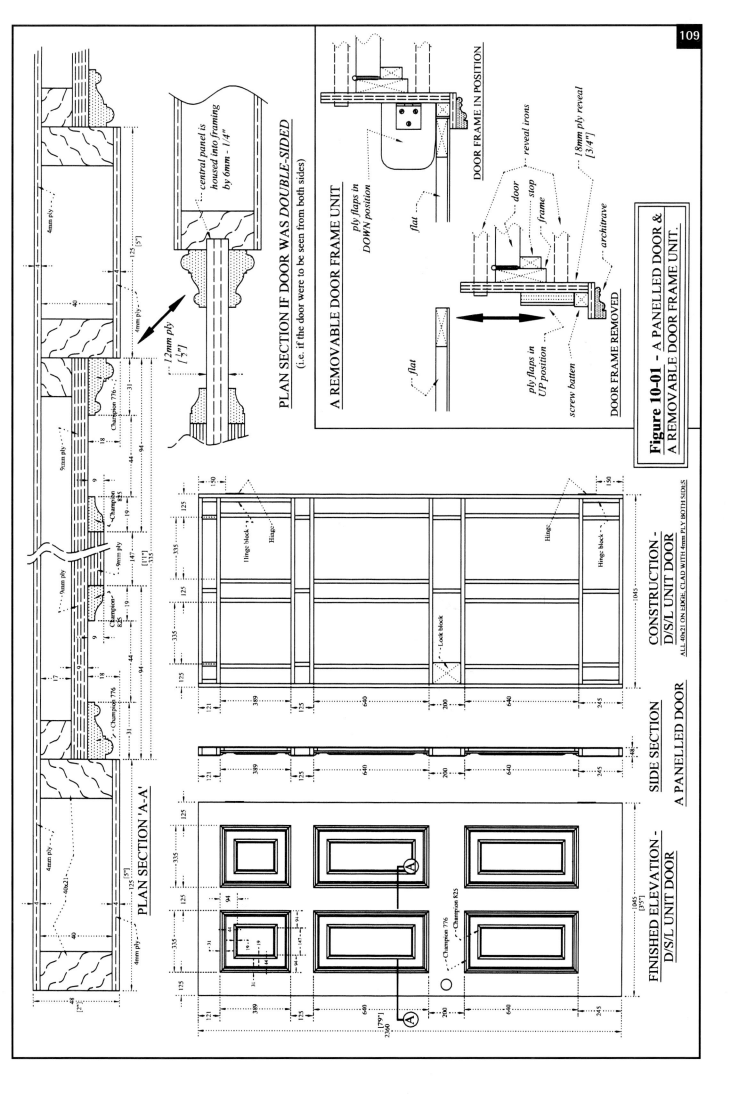

PLAN SECTION 'A-A'

central panel is housed into framing by 6mm - 1/4"

PLAN SECTION IF DOOR WAS DOUBLE-SIDED
(i.e. if the door were to be seen from both sides)

12mm ply [1/2"]

A REMOVABLE DOOR FRAME UNIT

DOOR FRAME IN POSITION

ply flaps in DOWN position

flat

door
stop
frame
reveal irons

flat

18mm ply reveal [3/4"]

ply flaps in UP position

screw batten

architrave

DOOR FRAME REMOVED

Figure 10-01 - A PANELLED DOOR & A REMOVABLE DOOR FRAME UNIT.

CONSTRUCTION - D/S/L UNIT DOOR

Hinge block

Hinge

Lock block

Hinge

Hinge block

ALL 40x21 ON EDGE. CLAD WITH 4mm PLY BOTH SIDES

SIDE SECTION
A PANELLED DOOR

FINISHED ELEVATION - D/S/L UNIT DOOR

Champion 776
Champion 825

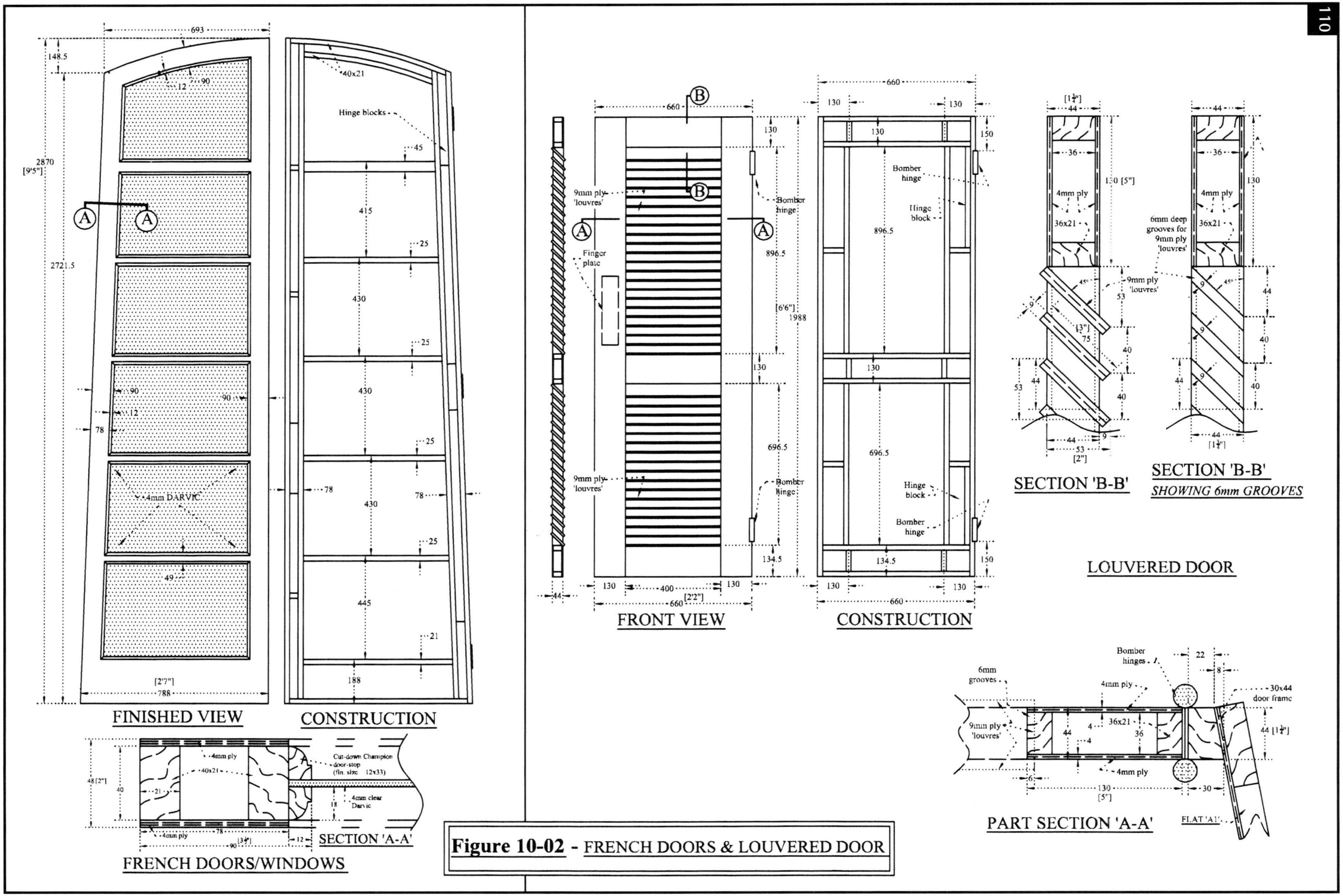
FINISHED VIEW
CONSTRUCTION
FRENCH DOORS/WINDOWS
SECTION 'A-A'
4mm DARVIC
Hinge blocks
40x21
4mm ply
Cut-down Champion door-stop (fin. size 12x33)
4mm clear Darvic
FRONT VIEW
CONSTRUCTION
LOUVERED DOOR
SECTION 'B-B'
SECTION 'B-B'
SHOWING 6mm GROOVES
PART SECTION 'A-A'
FLAT 'A1'
9mm ply 'louvres'
Finger plate
Bomber hinge
Hinge block
6mm deep grooves for 9mm ply 'louvres'
36x21
Bomber hinges
30x44 door frame
6mm grooves

Figure 10-02 - FRENCH DOORS & LOUVERED DOOR

4 A louvered door – figure 10.02

A) This door is again constructed using the hollow-core method. The louvers are of 9 mm ply (⅜") and are housed into the framing by 6 mm (¼"). Place louvers with care – ensure that it is not possible to see through them – and remember that when replicating exterior window shutters or louvered doors, the louvers would be positioned so that rain runs off them (not pouring straight in, as they would if reversed).

Louvered doors with curved top rails are quite tricky and time-consuming for the carpenters, so bear in mind the increased labour costs.

B) Part Section 'A-A' indicates that this door is hung on bomber hinges, allowing it to swing in both directions. Notice that these hinges have two sprung 'knuckles', one each side of the door, and that they fit to a batten that ensures that the door will clear any obstructions on the adjacent wall flat.

11 • Trucks

Trucks are wheeled units that carry scenery or people, or both. They range from simple stage 'dollies', used by the stage-crew to assist in shifting awkward items of set, to complex, remote-controlled units that can move an entire set ... or an audience seating block.

NOTES ON TRUCKS

1 Construction

A) **Timber and plywood trucks** are commonly used for their simplicity. They are lightweight and cost-effective. There are numerous types, some of which are illustrated in this chapter, but they all consist of simple frames fitted with castors – just flooring on wheels.

A large moving truck – containing an entire set, for example – will consist of a number of individual trucked units, each truck being bolted or drop-cleated to its neighbours. Large units such as this are prone to squeak and groan when being danced upon or while being moved; lubrication, such as candle-grease or *WD40*, will help this problem.

B) **Always add underfelt to trucks that are to be acted upon**, whether the trucks are made of steel or timber and plywood. The underfelt is stapled to the underside of the plywood top and helps to deaden unwanted noise.

C) **Steel trucks** have a greater inherent rigidity than timber ones and so they are often quieter (the heavier the truck, the quieter it runs – up to a point). Again, their basic construction is invariably simple – frames on wheels – and they may often bolt to neighbouring trucks to form part of a large moving platform. It is common to use steel trucks to form a large, strong skeleton upon which timber units are laid that flesh-out the scenic elements of the set.

D) **Drop-bolts** are used to hold a truck in a given position on stage. These can vary from simple, bought 'shoot-bolts' to tailor-made units having large, removable pins with handles for ease of use.

2 Castors

A) Some trucks have no need to be guided along any given path. **Swivel castors** allow the crew to move them anywhere they wish, making handling quite simple. Swivel castors for stage use tend to have 'poly tyres' (polyurethane), and can be single- or double-wheeled. Many sizes are manufactured (get a brochure); the small twin-wheeled variety are relatively compact and can carry decent loads. Keeping the height of the truck *low* is the common problem: the selected castor has to be sufficient for the loads that it must carry and therefore one's choice is limited to the castors available that meet the specification.

Swivel castors are free to swing in all directions but have an inherent problem. In plan view, each wheel is positioned off-centre to its fixing plate, allowing it to rotate and be 'dragged' into the ideal position for smooth running. The unfortunate consequence of this is that if a truck is pushed along a straight line and stopped, the castors each have to make a 180° turn before the truck can be reversed, causing it to swing about in an awkward fashion before resuming a smooth reverse. Additionally, it will be found that the truck has moved off-line: it follows a different path when returning (fixed castors would not do this – *see* below). In an effort to solve this problem, some engineering companies have invented clever, three-wheeled units, sometimes known as 'triplex' castors. Here, *three* swivel castors are fitted to a large 'ball-race' beneath the fixing-plate, so that each unit consists of three swivel castors on a rotating plate. This type of wheel-unit makes the truck behave better, but is expensive, large and usually only used on sizeable steel trucks.

B) **Fixed-wheel castors** allow free movement, forwards and backwards, along a certain path only. A truck employing such wheels will travel in the desired direction, but with no guiding mechanism it will tend to wander slightly off-course. A stage revolve may use fixed castors, each wheel-unit being fitted in relation to the centre-point of the revolve.

Trucks using fixed castors are awkward for the crew to handle in offstage situations – the truck insists on moving one-way only. Occasionally, **slave-trucks** are built in an effort to overcome this problem: the fixed-wheel truck is stored upon a simple truck that has swivel castors, allowing both to be moved at will (for safety's sake some form of connection, such as drop-bolts, needs to be made between the two trucks).

C) **Locking swivel-castors** provide the solution to many of the problems that are encountered with truck movements. These units are swivel castors that can be locked-off, by flicking a simple lever, into one of four fixed positions. By definition, hand access is required to each castor – to switch each unit from fixed to swivel mode – and this is not always possible. They are more expensive than normal swivel or fixed castors.

D) **Grooved wheels** are often fitted to trucks to act as guide wheels – *see* **figure 7.02** on page 62. They run along a track like the wheels of a train, guiding the truck on a certain path. A large truck may have two guide-wheels in addition to a number of fixed or swivel castors – the guide wheels coerce the others into line.

E) As a general rule, **the larger the wheel, the smoother the ride**. Big trucks, carrying a set and using 8" wheels, seem to glide far better than do smaller units.

3 Guides

A) Tracks can be made that guide a truck along a certain path (*see* above, and figure 7.02 on page 62). They can be recessed into the show-floor, as shown, or be placed upon the surface. Surface-mounted tracks should be fitted using boss-plates and bolts to allow for accurate re-laying of the track.

B) Spades are steel, nylon or polycarbonate plates that bolt to a truck and protrude down through the show-floor into a guide track – *see* figure 7.02 on page 62. A truck would have fixed castors and a pair of spades. The spade allows for the truck to be fitted with underfloor cables as shown, so that the truck can be moved across the stage with no visible means of propulsion. A spade that is not fitted to cables is a guide-spade: it holds one end of the truck on-course.

C) High-tech guiding systems can be used in large, big-budget productions. 'Magic eye' technology may be employed: the truck has a unit that 'reads' and follows wires let-in to the show-floor. Radio-controlled units (and infra-red, I believe) are also utilised. Signal interference is the main problem – theatres are packed with electronic equipment, so they are not ideal venues for some of these systems. However, given that guiding mechanisms of this type are proprietary, the manufacturer or supplier should be the one taking responsibility. The stage draughtsman merely obtains the relevant details and draws the truck movements.

4 The motive power

A) 'Mandraulic' power (stage slang for anything pushed or pulled by people) will frequently be the main method of driving trucks. Push-sticks and snap-on lines may assist the crew in doing this. When drawing manually driven trucks, ensure that the crew *can* safely pull and push from the desired points. On raking stages 'dead-lines' may be fitted – these are of cable or rope and are snapped onto the truck and secured to a fixed object in the theatre, reducing the danger of a truck rolling into the audience of its own volition.

B) Cable-driven trucks, having an underfloor cable/spade system, are often driven by a simple hand-winch. The cable passes from the winch, via diverting pulleys, to the spade, on to a return pulley and back to the winch – ensuring that the winch can drive the truck forwards *and* backwards. Clearly, the winch and all pulleys need good fixings down to the stage (*do* confirm that these fixings are allowed by the venue).

C) Motor-driven trucks are common: a motorised winch can replace the hand-winch described above, or trucks can carry an on-board motor that directly drives a 'drive-wheel'. Hydraulic motors may also be used, being quieter than most. Cable management becomes an issue with these systems.

5 Health & Safety

A) Any moving objects on a stage carry a potential risk to the staff. The draughtsman must try to reduce any likely danger by whatever means possible. Trucks can generate accidents. Expect only professional cast and crew to perform specific movements in order to avoid danger. They can rehearse the movements in full light and are under the watchful eye of stage management.

B) Foot-traps must be avoided – it is horribly easy to trap feet beneath a moving platform. Either fit a skirt to the edges of the truck, leaving a 15 mm clearance gap ($^5/_8$"), or have the structure high enough not to be a danger to feet.

C) Finger-traps must be considered. Ensure that items such as secret trap-doors, drop-bolts, connecting hinges, etc. are positioned so that a crew member has no danger of trapping a hand, should the truck be moving.

D) Fit safety lines – or dead-lines – where appropriate, as mentioned above.

E) The paging of cables can be difficult. Surface-mounted drive-cables and pulleys are *very* likely to cause people to trip and fall – try and mark these, if possible, with coloured and/or luminous tape. Alternatively, supply ramps that allow passage over the cables at certain points. Electrical cables that connect to trucks need paging to ensure that the wheels of the truck do not cut the cable. The electricians will try and bunch the cables into a 'loom', making it necessary for only one, single cable to be man-handled to safety. The drawings should include a path for the cables, ensuring that their paging is practical (and out of view, usually).

F) Headroom must be maintained. A moving truck may be carrying members of the cast, crew or audience and the movement will probably be taking place in low-light conditions – with some smoke thrown in for good measure. *It is essential for the draughtsman to ensure that headroom be maintained for all passengers, throughout the whole journey.* Remember to allow for the 'odd' things that people do (they are not odd, we all do them), such as putting children on their shoulders, standing on a chair in order to see better, or jumping up and down – all these activities increase the headroom.

SOME TYPES OF TRUCKS

1 Timber trucks – figure 11.01

A) A folding-gate rostrum on castor plates is shown in plan and sectional view at the top of this drawing. This is a very simple form of truck that has the advantage of breaking down into small, manageable parts that will pack and travel with ease. Two pieces of timber (the 'plates' – 145 x 25 mm, or 6" x 1"), each carrying two bolted castors, are pin-hinged to the bottom of a folding-gate rostrum. Notice that in this example, the downstage gate of the rostrum is extended down to form a fascia, concealing the wheels from view, whereas the other gates sit *upon* the castor plates. The castor plates must be fitted in a fashion that ensures that the swivel radius of each castor will clear any obstructions, such as the gates.

B) An 18 mm (¾") plywood truck is shown in a part-plan and Section 'B-B'. The castors are bolted to boxes whose sole function is to adjust the overall height of the truck. A spade is shown bolted to the rostrum, normally duplicated at the other end of the truck. Remember that hand-access is needed in order to attach the spade to the truck, either from the side or from a trap in the top.

C) Section 'B-B' using 145 x 25 mm (6" x 1") as the truck's framing is shown as an example. The choice of castors becomes more limited as the required height of the truck lowers – here, 100 mm (4") wheels can be used with ease. A drop-bolt is indicated on the upstage edge of the truck. Notice the 'easy-to-see-and-use' pin, which would be 10 mm (⅜") steel bar, with a tapered, rounded end that eases the pin into the locating hole in the stage.

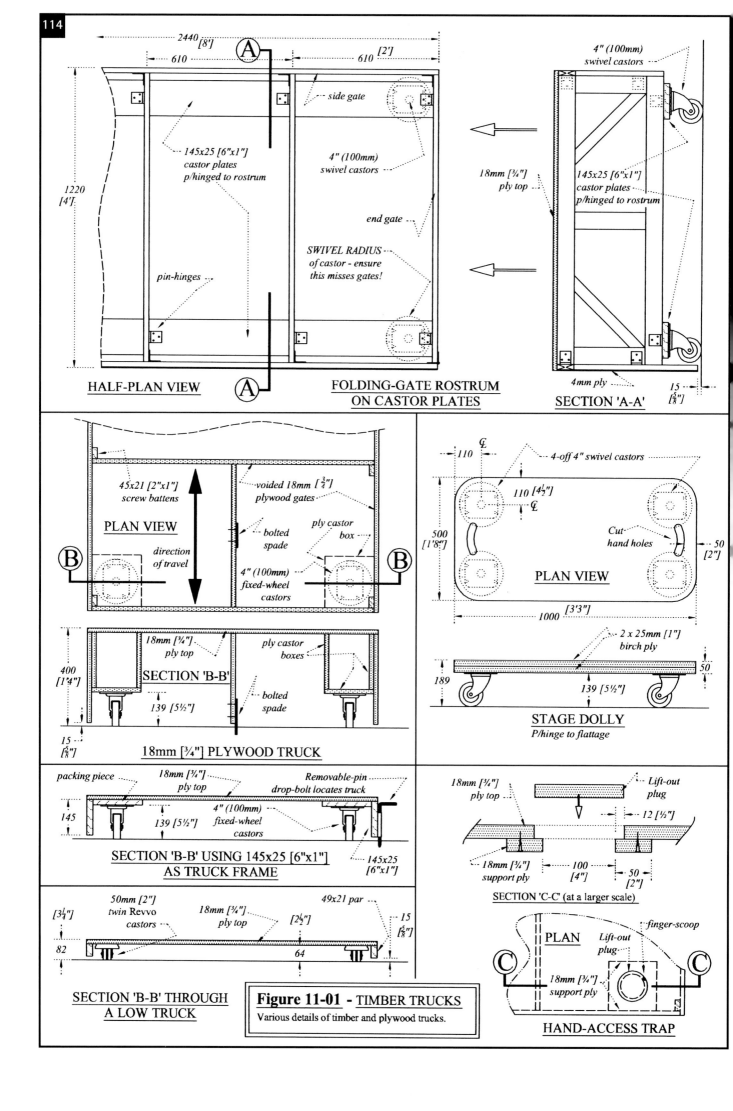

114

HALF-PLAN VIEW

2440 [8']
610
610 [2']

1220 [4']

145x25 [6"x1"] castor plates p/hinged to rostrum

side gate

4" (100mm) swivel castors

end gate

SWIVEL RADIUS of castor - ensure this misses gates!

pin-hinges

FOLDING-GATE ROSTRUM ON CASTOR PLATES

4" (100mm) swivel castors

18mm [¾"] ply top

145x25 [6"x1"] castor plates p/hinged to rostrum

4mm ply

15 [⅝"]

SECTION 'A-A'

45x21 [2"x1"] screw battens

voided 18mm [¾"] plywood gates

PLAN VIEW

direction of travel

bolted spade

ply castor box

4" (100mm) fixed-wheel castors

18mm [¾"] ply top

SECTION 'B-B'

ply castor boxes

400 [1'4"]

bolted spade

139 [5½"]

15 [⅝"]

18mm [¾"] PLYWOOD TRUCK

110
110 [4½"]
500 [1'8"]

4-off 4" swivel castors

Cut hand holes

50 [2"]

PLAN VIEW

1000 [3'3"]

2 x 25mm [1"] birch ply

189

139 [5½"]

50

STAGE DOLLY
P/hinge to flattage

packing piece

18mm [¾"] ply top

Removable-pin drop-bolt locates truck

145

4" (100mm) fixed-wheel castors

139 [5½"]

145x25 [6"x1"]

SECTION 'B-B' USING 145x25 [6"x1"] AS TRUCK FRAME

18mm [¾"] ply top

Lift-out plug

12 [½"]

18mm [¾"] support ply

100 [4"]

50 [2"]

SECTION 'C-C' (at a larger scale)

50mm [2"] twin Revvo castors

18mm [¾"] ply top

49x21 par

[3¼"]

[2½"]

15 [⅝"]

82

64

SECTION 'B-B' THROUGH A LOW TRUCK

finger-scoop

PLAN

Lift-out plug

18mm [¾"] support ply

C   C

HAND-ACCESS TRAP

Figure 11-01 - TIMBER TRUCKS
Various details of timber and plywood trucks.

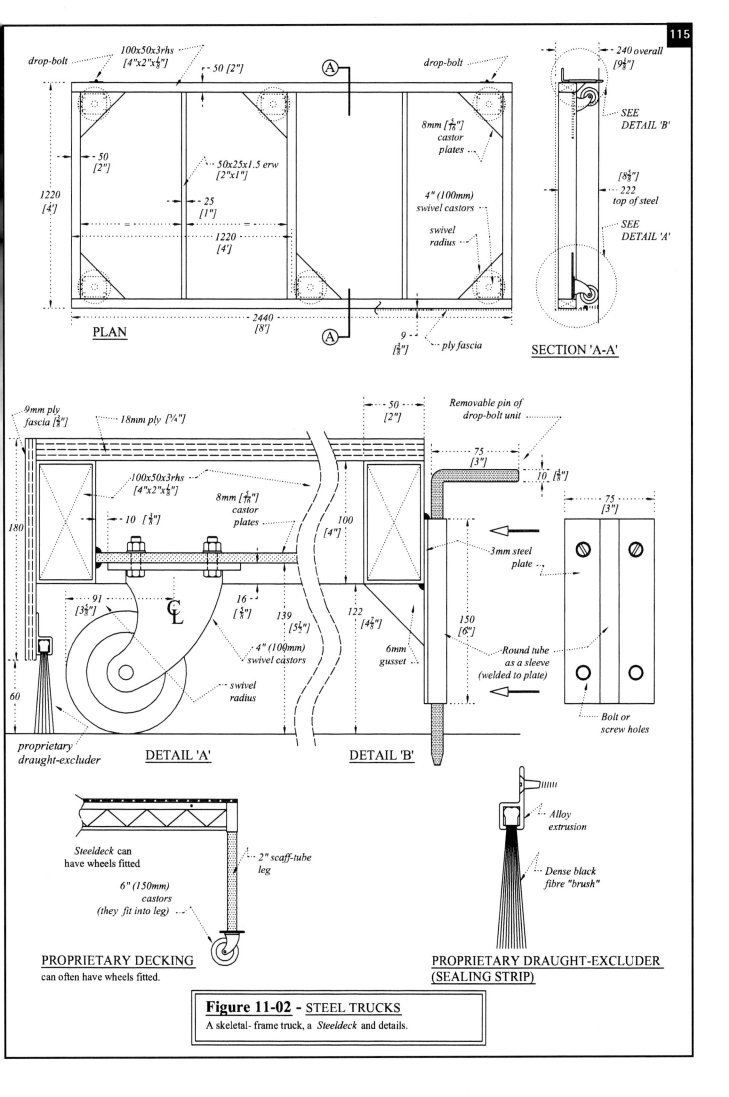

drop-bolt
100x50x3rhs [4"x2"x⅛"]
50 [2"]
A
drop-bolt

8mm [⁵⁄₁₆"] castor plates

50 [2"]
50x25x1.5 erw [2"x1"]
25 [1"]
=   1220 [4']   =

4" (100mm) swivel castors

swivel radius

1220 [4']

240 overall [9½"]

SEE DETAIL 'B'

[8⅝"]
222 top of steel

SEE DETAIL 'A'

2440 [8']
PLAN
A
9 [⅜"]
ply fascia

SECTION 'A-A'

9mm ply fascia [⅜"]
18mm ply [¾"]

50 [2"]

Removable pin of drop-bolt unit

75 [3"]
10 [⅜"]

75 [3"]

100x50x3rhs [4"x2"x⅛"]
8mm [⁵⁄₁₆"] castor plates

10 [⅜"]

180

100 [4"]

3mm steel plate

91 [3⅝"]
C L

16 [⅝"]
139 [5½"]

122 [4⅞"]

150 [6"]

Round tube as a sleeve (welded to plate)

4" (100mm) swivel castors

swivel radius

6mm gusset

60

proprietary draught-excluder

DETAIL 'A'

DETAIL 'B'

Bolt or screw holes

Steeldeck can have wheels fitted

6" (150mm) castors (they fit into leg)

2" scaff-tube leg

PROPRIETARY DECKING
can often have wheels fitted.

Alloy extrusion

Dense black fibre "brush"

PROPRIETARY DRAUGHT-EXCLUDER (SEALING STRIP)

Figure 11-02 - STEEL TRUCKS
A skeletal- frame truck, a *Steeldeck* and details.

D) Section 'B-B' through a low truck is also shown. Twin-wheeled swivel castors are bolted directly to the underside of the truck's 18 mm (¾") plywood top, giving an overall height of 82 mm (3¼"). These small castors have a pair of 50 mm (2") polyurethane-tyre wheels, carrying a load of up to 160 kg (350 lb) – it is difficult to find stronger castors with such minimal height. The castor unit can be used as a fixed-wheel unit by the addition of a locking-bolt (*Revvo* make these).

This truck would not be *very* strong, despite having strong castors, because the height of the support framing is so low – 49 mm (2"). If the truck is to have awkward loads imposed upon it, consider using steel instead of timber framing. Alternatively, add more castors – but remember that they are not cheap items.

E) A 'stage-dolly' is also sketched. These units are ubiquitous, and their uses backstage hardly need expanding upon. Some are covered with underfelt to protect the flattage being carried. Always cut hand-holes, as these strong units are awkward to manhandle without them.

F) A hand-access trap is shown in plan and section. This is a typical method of allowing secret access to the inside of a truck. The minimum diameter of the *actual void* should be 100 mm (4"). One part of the removable plug should have a small finger-scoop – a semicircular void – to facilitate its removal, and it is common to attach a chord to the underside and to the truck, preventing the plug being lost on tour.

2 Steel trucks – figure 11.02

A) A conventional steel truck is shown in plan view, Section 'A-A' and at details 'A' and 'B'. This is a skeletal truck base, comprising of a simple steel frame on wheels. Notice that the heavier members, the 100 x 50 x 3 mm rhs (4" x 2"), support the castors plates and that the lighter steel, the 50 x 25 x 1.5 erw (2" x 1"), is placed to support the 18 mm (¾") plywood top.

B) A sealing strip is indicated in detail 'A' and is also shown at a larger scale. These proprietary draught-excluders are very useful in sealing light-leaks on moving pieces of set. When placed below a truck, as shown, the black bristles appear to close the gap beneath the truck's fascia; when the truck is moving, the brush appears to 'flow' over any tracks or other protrusions on the stage. The brush also allows the fascia to be kept well short of the stage, avoiding potential foot-traps. These strips are available in many sizes and styles.

C) A drop-bolt and pin are shown in detail 'B'. These home-made units are far superior to proprietary 'shoot-bolts' (the type used to bolt doors). As drawn, the lower pair of fixing holes are not being used, but a 6 mm (¼") gusset plate is welded to the back, for strength.

D) Proprietary decking systems can be fitted with castors. Here, a *Steeldeck®* unit has 150 mm (6") nylon wheels fitted to each of its scaffold-tube legs. Sometimes, castors are put on these units for use during change-overs – the crew can stack and transport a 'pack' of decks upon another that is fitted with castors.

12 • Staircases

At first sight, a staircase seems such a simple concept. It is only when one comes to try and *make* one that certain problems begin to surface. Luckily, it is easier to draw a stair than to build one – and drawing is our subject here. Clearly, a certain amount of basic construction knowledge is required before attempting a drawing of a staircase, but, more importantly, it is vital to be aware of the rules and regulations governing the final proportions.

This chapter includes illustrations of some of the elementary types of staircases commonly encountered in the theatre and exhibition industries. Lack of space restricts the number of types, but it is hoped that the examples chosen will provide a good grounding in the subject.

NOTES ON STAIRCASES

1 Regulations and Health & Safety

A) Most areas of the world have regulations governing the sizes and proportions of staircases, covering handrails, balustrades and matters relating to headroom. It is imperative that the draughtsman be familiar with relevant local rules; a touring exhibition will require its stairs to conform to the most stringent regulations encountered on that tour. **Do remember** that if a person is injured through using a faulty stair, the legal machinery may well trace the error back to the draughtsman. Nobody wants to be the cause of an accident, or to spend days in court, so, *be aware of these regulations!*

Figure 12.01 is a distillation of the main points of the British regulations for public staircases – these are adequate for most other countries. **It is important to be familiar with all the points raised in this drawing** – some of the following notes expand upon them.

B) **Tread proportions** are shown in points 1–6. Hundreds of years of experience have taught us that stairs must follow ergonomic logic: the stair must fit with the human shape and its natural stride. Each tread (or going) and each riser must be identical to its neighbours or a person *will* trip. Two rules – the proportions shown in point 2 (*one tread plus two risers must equal 500–700 mm – 1'9¾" to 2' 3½"*) and the maximum pitch angle of 38° – both help to shape the stairs so that they conform to the needs of the human frame.

Notice that nosings are often added to the edge of the treads. Provided that they are applied to *every* tread, including the landing, they do not interfere with the human stride. When present, they place the riser further away from the climber's toes, making the stair easier to climb. A 25 mm (1") nosing is common; an over-large nosing can cause the user to trip. Their presence moves the 'nosing line' (the nosing line touches the top, front edge of each tread – the top, front edge of the nosings, if the treads have them).

Open flights of stairs have no risers – they have a rise, of course, but no solid ris*er*. Ensure that the treads are not slippery and that they each have an overhang, or nosing of approximately 25 mm (1") – the front of each tread overhangs the back of the tread below it. If polished timber treads are used, then add proprietary non-slip strip(s) to suit.

Visibility is an issue for many stairs used in our business because low-light conditions are so frequently encountered. Backstage treads should have white edging-strips applied to the edges of all treads, landings and handrails ('low-tech' white gaffer-tape will suffice). Small blue lamps can be used to give some light. For stairs used by the public, proprietary non-slip strips can be obtained that are made of white rubber and alloy – as used in cinemas.

C) **Handrails and balustrades** are included in **figure 12.01**. Remember that these regulations are for *public* stairs; domestic staircases may have lower handrails (often 900 mm or 3') and need not conform to the '100 mm (4") ball' rule. Notice that the height of the **raking handrail** must be 840–1000 mm (between 2' 9" and 3' 3⅜") when measured *plumb* above the nosing line – this is often ignored by inexperienced designers and is usually rectified by the construction draughtsman. This regulation ensures that the handrail is neither too low, nor too high, but it does place the position of the mitred join between the level landing-handrail and the raking one (this position is *not* always plumb above the top nosing – as in this drawing).

Finger-traps must be avoided on handrails – allow a minimum clearance of 40 mm (1½") between any wall (or any fixed object) and the outer edge of the handrail.

The '100 mm (4") ball' rule is applicable to public balustrades. Put simply, this means that a ball having a diameter of 100 mm must not be able to pass through the balustrade – children's heads stuck in railings leap to mind here.

Pocket-traps must be avoided when designing handrails (*see* **figure 12.05**, which shows an 'anti-pocket trap'). Many counties have regulations that forbid a handrail to just 'end', pointing into space. It must either return to a wall, another handrail or post, or be turned downwards so that anyone escaping a fire cannot catch their pockets on the rail.

D) **Landings** are often 'quarter-spaced' (the stair-user turns through 90° upon a square landing) or 'half-spaced' (the stair-user turns through 180°. A dog-leg stair has these landings: one flight comes up to the landing and another rises from the same edge of the landing – the gap between them being the open-well of the staircase). Do not add a step to a half-spaced landing because people will trip upon it. The minimum width for a landing should be the width of the staircase(s) involved.

E) **Headroom clearance** is measured in two ways: one is measured at 90 degrees to the nosing line (minimum of

1500 mm, or 5') and the other is measured *plumb* above the nosing line (minimum of 2000 mm, or 6' 6¾"). *Both* must be adhered to.

F) The **safest type of staircase** has a generous going or tread of say, 300 mm (1') and a reasonably low rise, say 150 mm (6"). It has nosings, solid risers and full (not cut) strings with a good nosing-line width (the top of the string is well above the nosing line). It has handrails to both sides and the user feels comfortable when climbing or descending – part of the comfort being drawn from the fact that the stair encloses them. No gaps exist; gaps invite accidents. Obviously, other types of stair are not necessarily unsafe but open flights (no risers) or flights having cut-strings (shaped to the treads) have more potentially dangerous gaps and so extra attention must be paid to ensure that they are safe.

G) **Curving stairs, spiral stairs** and **stairs using winders** have the inherent safety problem of having non-parallel treads. The plan-view centre-line of the staircase is used as the basis for obtaining the correct going-to-rise-ratio – this centre-line is halfway between the centre of the newel and the outer edge of the treads. It is along this line that the regulations apply.

Winders are three, shaped treads that turn the stair-user through 90 degrees (they are sometimes known as 'kites', since the centre tread is kite-shaped). When drawing stairs of an average width, try to maintain three treads here, not four or two – four usually gives an inadequate going (measured on the plan centre-line of the flight) and two often gives an over-generous going (this being equally dangerous).

2 Drawing staircases

A) **Draw the entire staircase** before detailing any particular flight. Stairs that continue past landings or on through various floor levels must all have the same rise and going, so ensure that each flight is drawn in 'simplistic' terms (showing each rise and going) before starting any detail. Do not have different risers between each floor level, i.e. the risers between the ground and first-floor level must be maintained throughout all floor levels.

B) **When starting to draw a flight of stairs**, begin by dividing the *overall rise* into a number of individual risers, say 14 risers of 180 mm (7"), then sketch in plan view how much room 13 suitable treads (goings) will take up. It may then be necessary to adjust the going and tread size to suit the available space – always remaining firmly within the regulations.

C) **Add landings** to suit, remembering that no individual flight should exceed 16 risers and that a maximum of 12 is more usual. Long, unbroken flights are tiring to use and are potentially more dangerous; falling headlong down 16 risers would be quite unpleasant. A landing placed along a flight of stairs (in the same direction of the stair) should be as wide as the stairs and at least as long as it is wide.

D) **Handrails** are all too easy to draw incorrectly! Figure 12.04 expands upon this matter: it is horribly easy to draw *impossible mitres*. When drawing stairs with landings, guarded on both sides by handrails, ensure that elevations are drawn of each handrail – many mistakes occur as a result of this omission. Inexperienced draughtsmen may be tempted to draw the outer elevation only,

forgetting that the inner handrail may well be doing something else entirely. This is particularly true of dog-leg stairs and spiral or curved stairs. Always consider *both* handrails.

E) **Stair construction** is tackled after the geometry and regulations have been settled. The following drawings provide some construction examples. Once the construction method has been established, it is worth detailing the top and bottom of each flight in order to resolve the *connections*. A flight of stairs is like a large ladder: the bottom needs good, secure attachment and the top requires a solid platform against which it leans and connects. Like a ladder, it exerts a horizontal force against the top landing as well as a downward force, so ensure that landings can take both.

F) **Bearers and extra strings** may be introduced to wide stairs. Bearers (or carriage-pieces) are beams that touch and support the underside of the treads and risers – taking the 'bounce' out of the treads. An extra string – a cut-string – that supports the centre of the staircase can be used instead.

SOME TYPES OF STAIRCASES

1 Plywood stairs – figure 12.02

A) The upper part of this drawing illustrates a simple plywood stair rostrum, typically used in theatres as 'get-offs'. Notice that the strings, treads and the bottom riser are of 18 mm plywood (¾"). Thinner ply is used for the risers and timber is used on the back face, adding strength and providing structural bracing. On tour, the crew may well lift the unit by this brace, so ensure that it is well fixed (some theatre get-ins require that such items are tied to a rope and hauled up and into the backstage area – this brace is an obvious tying-off point). The timber rail that supports the back of the top tread may be used to bolt to the rostrum.

The strings are voided (to lighten the unit) and feet are cut to prevent rocking. If the stair were wider, a centre-string could be added – on a very wide stair, these should be spaced every 750 mm (2' 6").

B) The lower part of the drawing shows a plywood flight of stairs that spans from the floor at the bottom to the rostrum at the top. The width of the string is important: being a cut-string, enough room must be left for the 'waist' to be able to support the unit adequately.

The larger-scale section indicates a commonly used method of 'hooking' the stair to the rostrum: the top timber support sits upon a batten bolted to the rostrum and is held in place by flushing plates. As indicated, if no nosings are to be added, the thin plywood riser should have its top edge bevelled to prevent it being accidentally kicked away.

C) A folding handrail is also shown here. These are for backstage use in theatres, allowing for the handrail to be folded away and stored with the whole stair unit, reducing the chance of the crew losing vital pieces.

2 Finished view, naming parts and showing décor – figure 12.03

A) This drawing is mainly included to specify the naming of parts. It shows part of a traditional 'domestic' staircase used in a theatre set; it was built as a truck that

STAIRCASES IN PUBLIC PLACES:
BUILDING REGULATIONS

1. Between consecutive floors, every step must have an equal going *for every parallel step* and have an equal rise. NEVER DEVIATE FROM THIS! EVEN IF THE STAIRS ARE FOR THE USE OF 'BACKSTAGE STAFF' ONLY - SOMEONE *WILL* TRIP, AND MAY SUE **YOU**!!

2. Tread plus 2 x riser must = 550 to 700mm [1'9¾" to 2'3½"]

3. Maximum riser = 190mm [7½"]

4. Minimum tread = 230mm [9"]

5. Maximum pitch angle = 38°.

6. No more than 16 risers per flight (add landings to prevent this). 12 are more usual.

7. If a stairway rises more than 600mm [2'], and its width is 1000mm or more [3'3"], <u>each</u> side must be guarded by a wall or balustrade (to minimum sizes shown below). Under 1000mm wide, only one side needs guarding.

8. 'Standard' width for British houses = 900mm [3'].

9. <u>Do not</u> *divide a half space landing into two quarter space landings by use of a* <u>riser</u> *- people will trip on this!*

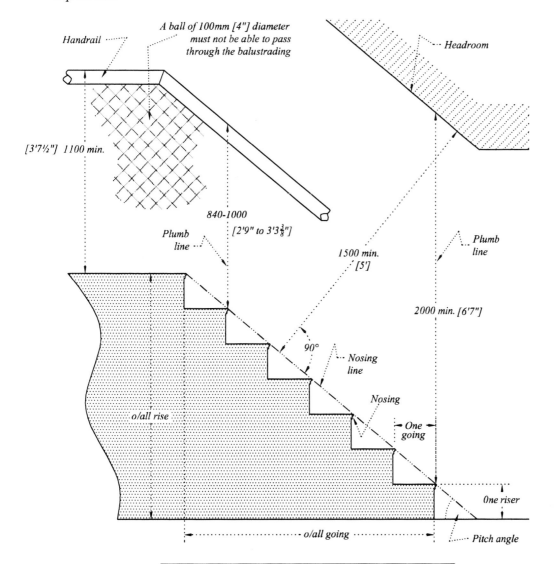

NOTE:- These rules are for *PUBLIC* buildings.
Private/domestic dwellings are slightly different

(Theatre, and stage shows in general, do not always strictly adhere to some of these rules e.g. handrail heights and '100mm ball rule' for balustrades. But, if the public are to use the stairs, then they MUST comply with the above. Dispensation <u>can</u> *be sought in order to deviate from the regulations, but beware!)*

Figure 12-01 - STAIRCASES - UK BUILDING REGULATIONS

Some of the main issues relating to staircase safety are listed here - UK only.

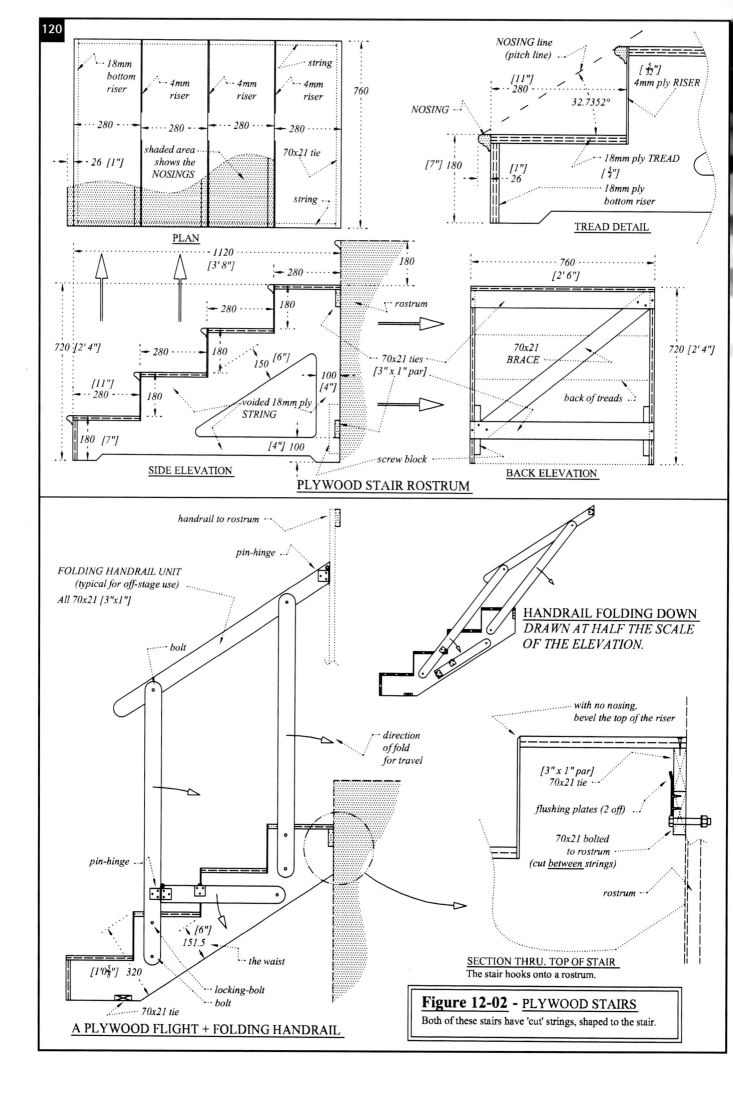

PLAN

18mm bottom riser
4mm riser
4mm riser
4mm riser
string
760
280
280
280
280
26 [1"]
shaded area shows the NOSINGS
70x21 tie
string

TREAD DETAIL

NOSING line (pitch line)
[11"] 280
32.7352°
[5/32"] 4mm ply RISER
NOSING
[7"] 180
[1"] 26
18mm ply TREAD [3/4"]
18mm ply bottom riser

SIDE ELEVATION

1120 [3' 8"]
280
180
rostrum
280
180
720 [2' 4"]
280
180
150 [6"]
100 [4"]
[11"] 280
180
voided 18mm ply STRING
70x21 ties [3" x 1" par]
180 [7"]
[4"] 100
screw block

BACK ELEVATION

760 [2' 6"]
70x21 BRACE
720 [2' 4"]
back of treads

PLYWOOD STAIR ROSTRUM

A PLYWOOD FLIGHT + FOLDING HANDRAIL

handrail to rostrum
pin-hinge
FOLDING HANDRAIL UNIT (typical for off-stage use)
All 70x21 [3"x1"]
bolt
pin-hinge
[6"] 151.5
the waist
[1'0 5/8"] 320
locking-bolt
bolt
70x21 tie
direction of fold for travel

HANDRAIL FOLDING DOWN
DRAWN AT HALF THE SCALE OF THE ELEVATION.

with no nosing, bevel the top of the riser
[3" x 1" par] 70x21 tie
flushing plates (2 off)
70x21 bolted to rostrum (cut between strings)
rostrum

SECTION THRU. TOP OF STAIR
The stair hooks onto a rostrum.

Figure 12-02 - PLYWOOD STAIRS
Both of these stairs have 'cut' strings, shaped to the stair.

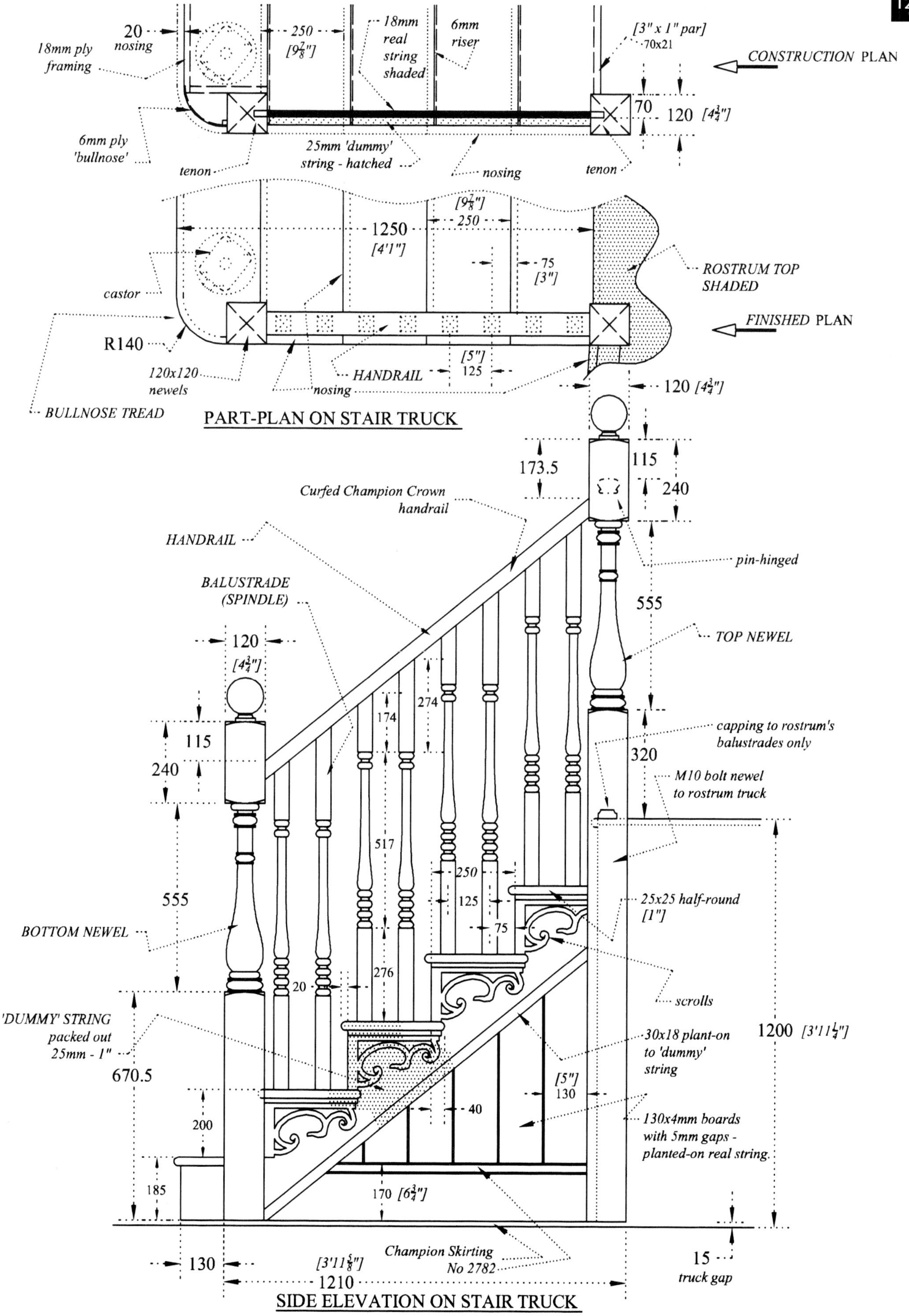

CONSTRUCTION PLAN

18mm ply framing
20 nosing
250 [9⅞"]
18mm real string shaded
6mm riser
[3" x 1" par] 70x21
70
120 [4¾"]

6mm ply 'bullnose'
tenon
25mm 'dummy' string - hatched
nosing
tenon

FINISHED PLAN

castor
1250 [4'1"]
[9⅞"] 250
75 [3"]
ROSTRUM TOP SHADED

R140
120x120 newels
HANDRAIL
nosing
[5"] 125
120 [4¾"]

BULLNOSE TREAD

PART-PLAN ON STAIR TRUCK

Curfed Champion Crown handrail
173.5
115
240
pin-hinged

HANDRAIL
TOP NEWEL

BALUSTRADE (SPINDLE)
555

120 [4¾"]
274
174
capping to rostrum's balustrades only

115
240
320
M10 bolt newel to rostrum truck

517
25x25 half-round [1"]

555
250
125
75

BOTTOM NEWEL
276
20
scrolls

'DUMMY' STRING packed out 25mm - 1"
30x18 plant-on to 'dummy' string

670.5
[5"] 130
1200 [3'11¼"]

200
40
130x4mm boards with 5mm gaps - planted-on real string.

185
170 [6¾"]
15 truck gap

130
Champion Skirting No 2782
1210
[3'11⅝"]

SIDE ELEVATION ON STAIR TRUCK

Figure 12-03 - NEWELS, HANDRAIL, BALUSTRADES & DECOR

This stair was trucked, connecting to a trucked rostrum that was notched to take the newel.

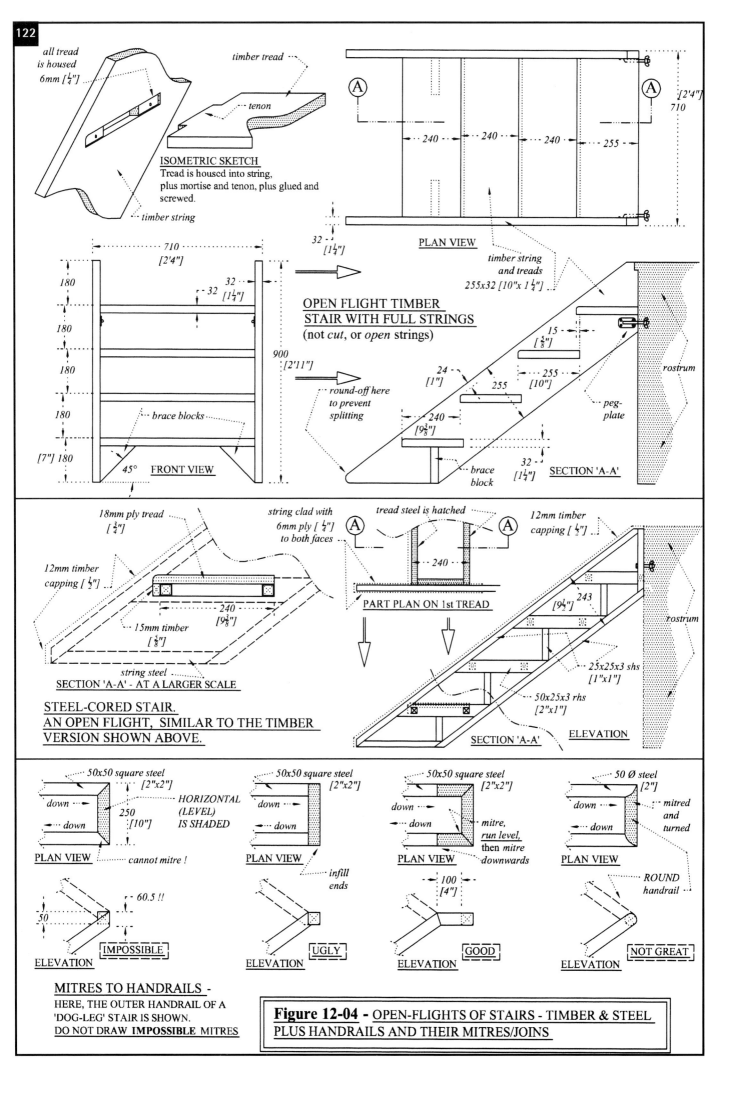

122

ISOMETRIC SKETCH
Tread is housed into string,
plus mortise and tenon, plus glued and
screwed.

all tread
is housed
6mm [¼"]

timber tread

tenon

timber string

PLAN VIEW

240 · · 240 · · 240 · · 255

[2'4"] 710

32 [1¼"]

timber string
and treads
255x32 [10" x 1¼"]

710 [2'4"]

180

32

32 [1¼"]

180

180

180

180 [7"]

45° FRONT VIEW

brace blocks

900 [2'11"]

**OPEN FLIGHT TIMBER
STAIR WITH FULL STRINGS**
(not *cut*, or *open* strings)

round-off here
to prevent
splitting

15 [⅝"]

24 [1"]

255

255 [10"]

240 [9⅜"]

brace
block

32 [1¼"]

rostrum

peg-
plate

SECTION 'A-A'

18mm ply tread [¾"]

12mm timber
capping [½"]

240 [9⅜"]

15mm timber [⅝"]

string steel

SECTION 'A-A' - AT A LARGER SCALE

**STEEL-CORED STAIR.
AN OPEN FLIGHT, SIMILAR TO THE TIMBER
VERSION SHOWN ABOVE.**

string clad with
6mm ply [¼"]
to both faces

tread steel is hatched

240

PART PLAN ON 1st TREAD

12mm timber
capping [½"]

243

[9½"]

25x25x3 shs [1"x1"]

50x25x3 rhs [2"x1"]

rostrum

SECTION 'A-A'   ELEVATION

50x50 square steel [2"x2"]

down

down

250 [10"]

*HORIZONTAL
(LEVEL)
IS SHADED*

PLAN VIEW   cannot mitre !

50

60.5 !!

ELEVATION   IMPOSSIBLE

50x50 square steel [2"x2"]

down

down

PLAN VIEW

infill
ends

ELEVATION   UGLY

50x50 square steel [2"x2"]

down

down

*mitre,
run level,*
then *mitre
downwards*

PLAN VIEW

100 [4"]

ELEVATION   GOOD

50 Ø steel [2"]

down

down

*mitred
and
turned*

PLAN VIEW

*ROUND
handrail*

ELEVATION   NOT GREAT

MITRES TO HANDRAILS -
HERE, THE OUTER HANDRAIL OF A
'DOG-LEG' STAIR IS SHOWN.
DO NOT DRAW **IMPOSSIBLE** MITRES

Figure 12-04 - OPEN-FLIGHTS OF STAIRS - TIMBER & STEEL
PLUS HANDRAILS AND THEIR MITRES/JOINS

connected to a larger, wheeled section of scenery, hence the clearance gap below it all. This 'finished' elevation is necessary to illustrate to those building the stair how the finished result is to appear – construction drawings have been omitted here.

B) The construction plan indicates that the unit was built as a conventional plywood stair, very similar to the top staircase drawn in **figure 12.02**, with the addition of castors, a bull-nose tread and a 'dummy' string. The side of the 'real' 18 mm plywood string is clad with boards and a piece of skirting, so the dummy string is necessary: it is packed off from the real string by 25 mm (1"). The decorative scrolls are fretted 6 mm ply (¼") and were drawn at full-size for the carpenters to use as a template.

C) When designing stairs such as these, ensure that all mouldings, treads and nosings run *into* the newel posts: they do not overhang the width of the newels in plan view.

3 A timber, open flight of stairs – figure 12.04

A) This type of stair is common; the one shown is built entirely from 255 x 32 mm timber (10" x 1¼") and is peg-plated to the adjoining rostrum. Stage get-offs are often built in this fashion, though lighter timbers would usually be employed. Having no risers, the treads are completely unsupported in the centre and so require adequate thickness. The top leading edge of each tread is 'softened' by introducing a 'pencil-round'.

B) Brace blocks are shown on this flight. The front view helps to illustrate why these are required: with no risers, the stair carries no inherent cross-bracing and needs these to prevent it racking from side to side. The bracing can be made less visible – by using steel brackets, for example – but this is a matter of design choice.

C) Notice that the upper edge of the string is rounded off at the bottom of the flight. This is an important detail to include in strings of solid timber that are part of a touring staircase: without this detail, as the string dries and after constant handling, this point would be prone to splitting.

4 A steel-cored, open flight – figure 12.04

A) Here, the above-described stair has been drawn using 25 mm (1") thick steel as its central skeleton. The side elevation/section indicates that the string is a simple two-dimensional truss that is to be clad with timber and plywood. The string is bolted to the rostrum.

B) Steel treads are invariably made as rectangular frames that weld to corresponding steels within the strings. The timber tread and nosing carry the familiar 'pencil-round' detail.

C) Cladding the *inside* face of the strings with thin ply is very difficult and time-consuming, involving cutting around each tread. It is for this reason that the string has 50 mm wide (2") steel bearers that support the treads: this extra width provides a face to which the ply cladding is self-tapped – above and below the tread steel.

D) Stairs like this, though common, are very labour-intensive and therefore expensive to build. First, the engineers have to build the steel skeleton and then the carpenters have to clad and finish it.

5 Mitres to handrails – figure 12.04

A) Starting on the left, a series of four plans and elevations illustrate 'impossible' mitres, ugly mitres and two acceptable ways of dealing with the junctions between raking and level handrails. The plans show the outer handrails to a dog-leg stair (we are looking down a stairwell: the upper handrail is raking down and meets a level handrail – shaded – and the lower handrail rakes down from this level piece).

B) 'Impossible mitres' are all too easy to draw. Given that the handrail material is square in section (50 x 50 mm, or 2"), this plan view is impossible to achieve: *the mitres drawn in plan cannot be true mitres.* A glance at the elevation illustrates why these mitres do not work – the raking tubes present a larger face at the mitre than does the level tube. This simple geometric fact applies to *all* sections of handrail (only round material can be made to work in this fashion and is mentioned here later).

As they are drawn, there is no satisfactory way of making these handrails work ... so, will designers please stop drawing them? I have seen whole stairwells, two storeys high, being stripped of their steel balustrades, having them rebuilt and fitted again because of this error – nobody spotted it until the carpenter was assigned to fit the heavily moulded oak handrail. Understandably perhaps, the horrified architect demanded that the mitre be *attempted*, just so he could see for himself what an impossibility he had drawn. Again, I know – I *was* that carpenter.

'Wreathed handrails' are used in traditional expensive work. These are solid pieces of timber that are inserted at mitre points such as those shown; they curve in plan view while maintaining the moulded shape 'plumb' to the user's hand. They are carved shapes that successfully turn a complex raking handrail through 90 degrees to a level section. Joinery brochures contain illustrations of various types.

C) An 'ugly version' of a similarly shaped handrail is drawn to the right of the previous sketch. Here, provided that the handrail is simple in section – square or rectangular – the join can be made to work. The elevation shows how the raking pieces can be cut to meet the continuous horizontal tube, the ends of which require in-filling. This is not an impossible join, just ugly ... and it does provide hard, awkward edges that the user's hand may rap against.

D) A correct version of solving this problem is shown next. This method is comfortable to use and will work for handrails of any section: the raking handrails are mitred to level before they again mitre to turn through 90 degrees. The user's hand will run smoothly along its entire length. Clearly, each mitre could be replaced by curved sections that would round-off the plan and elevation – frequently, only the plan-view mitres are rounded-off. (Rounding-off is expensive, more so when complex timber sections are used.)

E) Circular-tube handrail *can* be made to mitre at this particular junction: the final sketch, on the extreme right, shows how this can be achieved. Imagine that the upper handrail is laid flat and mitred at 90 degrees to the short, level piece; the upper handrail is lifted to its raked position, thereby rotating the level piece; it can be seen that this may now be mitred to the lower raking piece. The mitres are turned in relation to one another, presenting slightly different plan views. I have (somewhat arrogantly) indicated that this method is 'not great' … and the reason is that it, like the 'ugly' method, can be uncomfortable in practice. The user of the handrail is liable to rap their fingers at the sudden change of direction, whereas the previous, correct method provides warning of a change of direction with a change of rake.

6 A simple steel spiral stair – figure 12.05

A) This drawing has been included to give the geometric principles involved in drawing curving or spiral stairs – here, drawing space has dictated that it be a small stair. The stair is constructed using a central, round newel-post to which three tread-plate treads are welded (each tread is crimped: they have folded edges). Each tread has a central support in the form of a shaped fin of 6 mm steel (¼"), and both tread and fin are welded to a flat-steel string of 220 x 6 mm (8¼" x ¼"). This string has to be 'rolled' to shape in engineer's rollers. The simple circular handrail is connected by shaped round-rod to the three balustrades; this rod allows the user's fingers a clear journey along the handrail. Anti-pocket traps are shown at the ends of the handrail – the handrail curves downwards.

B) The geometry of the stair is simple to establish – and *it is the geometry that the stair-builder requires*. First, the overall rise is established and the plan view is drawn. Please note that this small stair *does not* conform to the regulations: on plan centre-line, the going is only 188.5 mm and as the rise is 180 mm (7") the pitch angle is an excessive 43.5°. At the outer part of the treads, the going becomes a more respectable 340 mm (1' 1⅜"), creating a pitch angle of 27.9°. For the sake of sanity, let us assume that this stair is used in a set, for one actor at a time: it is not for public use.

C) 'Unrolled-to-flat' elevations are always required when drawing curving stairs: these are elevations of items that are curved in plan, but have been unrolled so that they are drawn 'flat'. As shown on the plan, the line chosen to 'unroll' is the *inside* face of the string, which is also the centre-line of the handrail (Section 'A-A' and detail 'X' both confirm this). By having the string and handrail share a plan line, one 'unrolled' drawing will accurately portray both items: if they did not share a plan line, an unrolled drawing of each would be required.

When drawing unrolled elevations, all heights are true dimensions and all horizontal lines are *arcs on the plan* that have been unrolled and drawn flat. For example, on plan, the arc made by each tread's outer going (where it touches the inside face of the string) is shown as being 340.5 mm (1' 1⅜"); that same arc dimension transfers to the unrolled elevation as a horizontal line, the going.

Draw each rise and going first; add the nosing or overhang; decide upon the nosing line and the string's width; and then draw the entire string. (For clarity, this elevation has a bare minimum of information. In real life, however, it is better to dimension the string *along* it. In other words, dimensions are shown parallel to the top edge of the string and others are at 90° to it, helping the builder, who has the string material laid along the workbench.)

This drawing of the string could be cut out, then curved (in plan) to the correct radius. It would then be a scaled model representing the inside face of the string. Imagine a cylindrical can of beans: this string would be a ribbon forming a helix cut from the can. A helix is a line drawn on a cylinder: if the cylinder rotated at a constant rate of speed and a pen moved vertically at a constant speed, a helix is drawn around the cylinder. The nosing line, the string and the handrail each form a helix.

7 Two steel, public stairs – figure 12.06

A) The two staircases shown here were used in large exhibition stands (designed by *Imagination Ltd*) and were for public use. The regulations relating to exhibition stairs are most rigorous; the organiser will have a set of written instructions that must be adhered to. Attention to detail and a high-quality finish are prerequisite for work such as this; expensive materials are used and the margin for error is minimal.

B) The steel stair with glass balustrade is shown in the upper half of the drawing as a partial elevation and Section 'A-A'. The strings are of large steel channel that is powder-coated. The strings are connected by a steel tie-bar concealed by the show-floor (shaded). Patterned steel treads with crimped edges are connected to the strings by a shaped piece of angle – treads 2 and 3 are shown here. The section shows that these angle supports are hidden within the channel of the strings.

The glass balustrades are rectangular panes of toughened glass, bolted to the strings with cylindrical stainless steel fittings. Note that a tiny gap of 3–6 mm (⅛"–¼") needs to be left between each pane. (Clear silicone sealant was not wanted here – this stair toured.)

The stainless-steel handrail connects via stainless-steel rod to glass fittings similar to those used at the string. (At the top of this stair, not shown here, one channel string – the one drawn – mitred and continued horizontally to form the fascia of the first-floor level. The handrail and glass followed. *See* **figure 3.04**, page 30, 'South Elevation'.)

C) A steel stair with timber treads is shown as a partial elevation and a tread detail. The strings are of rectangular steel box-section with steel fins welded to their top edges, on plan centre-line. The bottom of the strings are tied by underfloor ties as in the previous example; the top is tied by a large steel angle that bolts to the main 'I' beam of the first floor level.

The tread detail indicates that solid maple treads are fitted to a steel flat-bar tie that joins each pair of fins. (The tie was drilled and countersunk from below. The treads also had non-slip strips let into them, not shown here.)

Although this particular flight was quite narrow, this style of 'string-and-fin' does lend itself for use on a wide staircase, where extra strings are required. Extra strings can be added with ease. The previous example of a string could *not* be added to the centre of a flight, because the top of the string is *above* the nosing line – an undercarriage would have to be added (that would probably resemble this 'string-and-fin' style of construction).

The handrail, posts and rails are of circular steel tube (the fittings have not been detailed here). Note that the '100 mm ball' rule has been ignored with spectacular abandon! In fact, the whole flight was contained within a solid stairwell – the walls were a couple of inches away from the outer edge of the handrail – so nobody could fall through the balustrade.

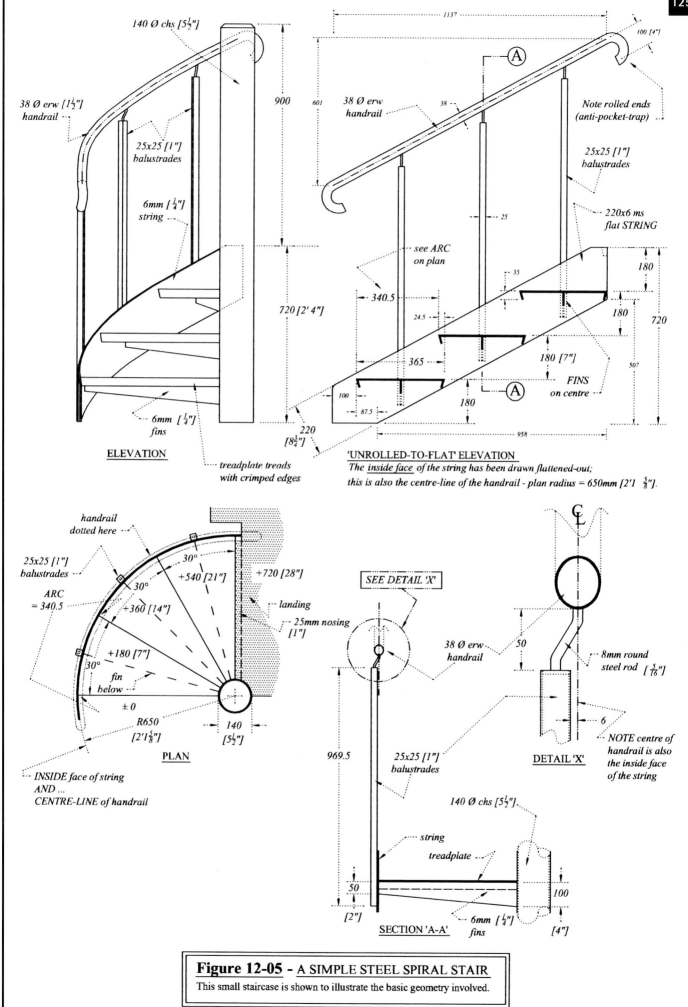

140 Ø chs [5½"]

38 Ø erw [1½"]
handrail

25x25 [1"]
balustrades

6mm [¼"]
string

6mm [¼"]
fins

ELEVATION

treadplate treads
with crimped edges

1137

100 [4"]

601

38 Ø erw
handrail

38

Note rolled ends
(anti-pocket-trap)

25x25 [1"]
balustrades

900

A

25

35

340.5

see ARC
on plan

24.5

365

100

87.5

220
[8¾"]

180

180

180 [7"]

180

958

220x6 ms
flat STRING

180

180

720

507

FINS
on centre

'UNROLLED-TO-FLAT ELEVATION
The inside face of the string has been drawn flattened-out;
this is also the centre-line of the handrail - plan radius = 650mm [2'1 ⅝"].

handrail
dotted here

25x25 [1"]
balustrades

30°

30°

30°

ARC
= 340.5

+540 [21"]

+720 [28"]

+360 [14"]

landing

25mm nosing
[1"]

+180 [7"]

fin
below

± 0

R650
[2'1⅝"]

140
[5½"]

PLAN

INSIDE face of string
AND ...
CENTRE-LINE of handrail

SEE DETAIL 'X'

38 Ø erw
handrail

25x25 [1"]
balustrades

969.5

50

C L

50

8mm round
steel rod [5/16 "]

6

NOTE centre of
handrail is also
the inside face
of the string

DETAIL 'X'

140 Ø chs [5½"]

string

treadplate

50

[2"]

SECTION 'A-A'

6mm [¼"]
fins

100

[4"]

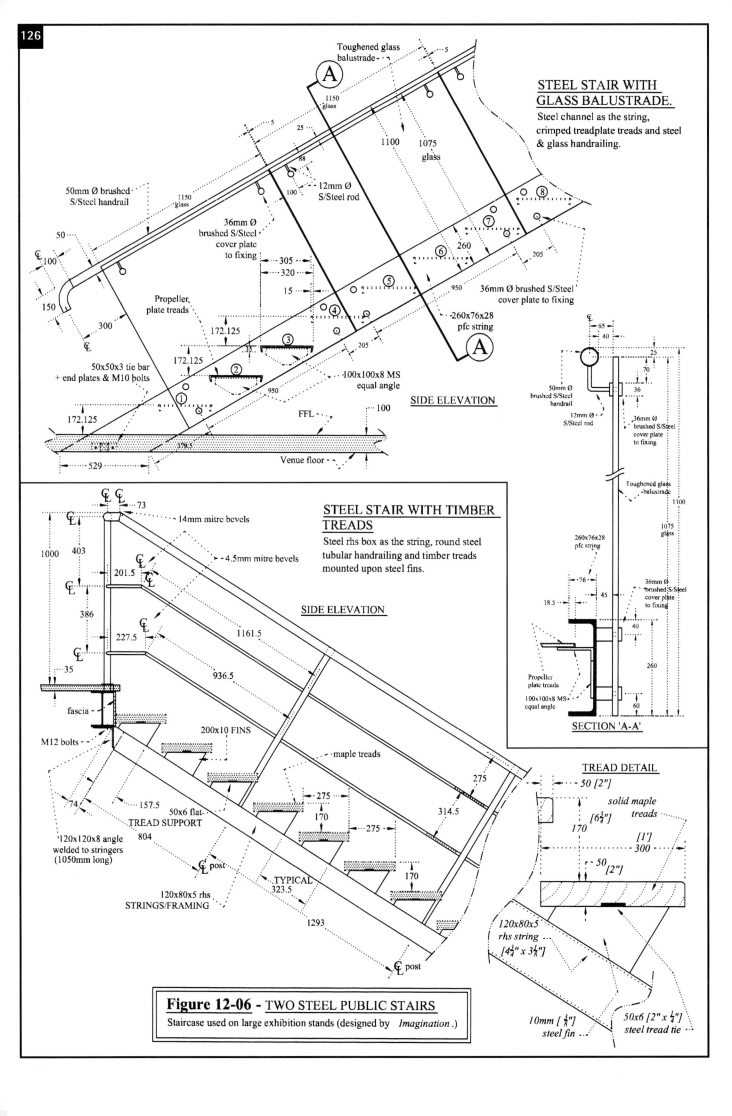

Figure 12-06 - TWO STEEL PUBLIC STAIRS
Staircase used on large exhibition stands (designed by *Imagination*.)

13 • Roofs and Ceilings

The subject of roofing can, and does, fill volumes. Outside the world of scenery construction, there exists a huge variety of roof structures involving many materials. Sets tend to reproduce facsimiles of genuine roofs, rather than faithful copies, so there is little point in learning the finer details of roof construction. However, the construction draughtsman may well benefit from a book that illustrates traditional roofing methods (as with any architectural matter, designers will research the subject to suit their design, as and when they need to).

Given that it is impossible to predict all the varying roof structures that one may be asked to replicate (and accepting the limitations of space here), time is better spent learning the *basic geometry* that allows for most roofs to be set-out and built. Roofing geometry has evolved over centuries; generations of carpenters faced the problem of how to cut and shape all the timbers on the ground, before erecting them in position. 'Roofing squares' became the carpenter's 'calculators': steel squares, marked with calibrations that help to establish all the cutting angles and lengths of each roof member. The draughtsman has no need of roofing squares: to *draw* a roof one needs only a certain amount of basic geometry, as shown here.

If roof geometry is understood, any roof can be drawn and built. The roof of a stage set is likely to consist of traditional flattage rather than a series of rafters, but if the draughtsman is cognisant with the necessary geometry, *it does not matter what the roof is made of* – it can still be drawn with ease. Interestingly, roof geometry often solves problems completely unrelated to roofs; after all, the geometry deals with sets of inclined planes, and those planes could represent anything.

Therefore, the brevity of this chapter is no accident: learn the geometry and the subject will then resolve itself into a simple matter of choosing materials and of ensuring that the roof is structurally sound.

NOTES ON ROOFS AND CEILINGS

1 Health & Safety

A) Roofs carry potential for danger on a number of fronts. First, the safety of those *erecting* the roof must be considered, so safe working access must be supplied. Second, those *using* the roof need protection: the security of maintenance workers or actors must be scrutinised (snap-on safety lines and other equipment should be discussed). Thirdly, care must be taken that items cannot fall from the roof and cause injury below (in real life, thousands of people are killed by falling tiles: don't let art imitate life).

B) 'Walk-on zones' of a roof are sections that are safe to walk upon. The problem is that, by definition, there are also areas that will not support a person – and that *is* dangerous. Walk-on zones must be marked in a clear fashion.

Consider marking the zone with luminous tape: working in semi-darkness is an inescapable fact of life in show conditions and must be borne in mind.

C) People who maintain museum or long-term exhibition sets may be unaware of an in-built weakness in a structure. Therefore, never draw a 'false' structure – a flat roof, for example – that would, quite reasonably, tempt someone to walk upon it. If someone is *likely* to step on something, make it strong enough for them to do so, or prevent access.

2 Roofs

A) The simplest form of roof is a **flat roof**. It *is* flat, but *not* level – if it were, rainwater would not run to the gutter. The minimum pitch is about three-quarters of a degree (copper, lead, zinc covered), rising to six degrees for asphalt or corrugated cladding material. Flat roofs need good support from joists or beams below; they should always be able to take the weight of a person. (Always? Even when they form part of a set? Well, no ... but ensure that the whole crew is aware of any weakness.)

B) A **lean-to roof** is a single plane inclined at a pitch (usually 30 degrees) to a wall. A double lean-to (or pent, or V-roof) is where two lean-to roofs form a 'V' shape, with a gutter between them; the top of each section usually meets a parapet wall (hiding the roof from the street).

C) The following roofs can be pitched at a variety of **angles**: it is the type of roof *covering* that governs the minimum pitch that is used (in the real world). Some examples are:

Large slates 22°
Shingles and glazing 27°
Average slates 27°
Stone slating and small slates 34°
Pantiles 24°
Plain tiles and thatch 45°

D) A **couple roof** can best be described as being typical of many garden sheds: two inclined planes meet at a central ridge. Rafters rake up from the walls to a ridge timber. This type of roof, though familiar to all, is very limited in its scope because the down-weight of the roof tends to spread the walls apart: the rafters are transferring the load at an angle against the walls. Unless the walls are particularly strong, roofs like this are not used if the span exceeds 3600 mm (12′).

E) **Close-couple and collar roofs** are used throughout the construction industry: they resolve the shortcomings of a simple couple roof by tying each pair of rafters together – each pair forms a rigid *triangle* – removing the tendency to spread the walls.

A **close-couple roof** has ties fitted very near the bottom of the rafters. When the underside of the ties form the ceiling structure to the rooms below, they are called 'ceiling joists'. 'Hangers' hang down from the rafters to support the ceiling joists (hangers do not support the rafters, they support the joist from the rafters). The maximum span for roofs like this is about 6000 mm (20').

A **collar roof** is similar to a close-couple roof, except that the ties are moved upwards (anywhere from near the bottom of the rafters to a maximum of halfway up the rise, or height of the roof). These ties are now called collars – one is indicated at the top, right corner of **figure 13.01**. The maximum economical span for roofs such as this is 4800 mm (16').

F) **Double roofs** (roofs with purlins) are stronger and should be considered when the span exceeds about 6000 mm (20'). Purlins are strong timbers that provide support to the rafters of a roof – one is indicated at the top right-hand corner of **figure 13.01**.

G) **Avoid twisting planes.** Most roofs consist of a number of inclined planes, and those planes should be kept as true, flat planes and not be twisted or bent 'out-of-true'. The roof of an ancient barn may well have a more organic-looking roof – subsidence, weather and age contribute to that process – but, *when built*, it would have had true planes. It is horribly easy to draw the plan view of a roof that makes no geometric sense: the ridge should be parallel to the eave for most roofs; if it is not, and the walls at the eaves are horizontal (level), then the ridge becomes raked in side elevation. Raking ridges are not unknown, but don't create one unwittingly.

3 Ceilings

A) **In the theatre,** ceilings tend to be made of conventional flattage that may or may not require beams to achieve adequate support. Obviously, beams may be visible and part of the design, or they may be secretly introduced, out of view – above the ceiling, for example.

Ceilings carry an inherent drawback when used on stage: they present the lighting designer with the problem of how to light the set and cast. Inexperienced set designers are forever proposing ceilings that would occlude all light from the acting space (where do they learn their trade! Who teaches them?). As a result, the production manager and lighting designer will usually 'apply the scalpel' to the model – or send the designer back to work upon a re-design. There *are* ways to design around some of these problems: the ceiling can be fitted with large, cross-stage beams that have an open upstage face; lamps are fitted within the beam, allowing light into the rear of the set. The ceiling can also 'step-up' at a certain point – the upstage part of the ceiling being higher than the downstage section – allowing light through the slot created. Skylights (windows) can be designed into the ceiling. Cloth ceilings can be backlit, providing an even spread of ambient light from above. None of this is rocket-science; one would imagine it to be screamingly obvious.

B) **Exhibition ceilings** often consist of 'casement' – a single piece of cloth that is stretched tight across the space. Alternatively, a ceiling contractor may supply a conventional 'office-type' of ceiling, consisting of a light steel grid and removable mineral-board **ceiling tiles**. Both types are alluded to in the text that accompanies **figure 8.14** (*see* page 100) – cloth merely requires some timber to which it

may be stapled, proprietary ceiling grid-systems need something from which to suspend. Permanent exhibitions may, of course, have a **plaster ceiling**: skimmed plasterboard fitted to joists above.

Very large cloth ceilings tend to belly, but this can be rectified by the use of tennis balls – yes, tennis balls – and clever riggers. A tennis ball is pushed, from below, up into the cloth and a cable-tie, or string, is tied tightly around the bottom – the ball is wrapped in the cloth and cannot escape. The wrapped balls are then tied to pick-up lines and hauled up into position. The final effect is of an upholstered ceiling; the imagination can play with the various patterns achievable.

Fibrous plaster ceilings are made and fitted by specialist contractors and provide a very clean, crisp ceiling that can include complex plaster moulding details. They are made in a factory in panel form and are fitted and filled on-site. This type of ceiling is 'permanent' and would probably only be encountered in museum projects or permanent exhibitions. The contractor will advise as to what he needs in the way of hangers, etc. from which to suspend his structure.

Spray-painted MDF ceilings are common. The sheet joins should carry a 'quirk' – such as a small, chamfered 'vee' – that *accentuates* the join: trying to fill and paint the joins is a useless exercise because, in time, natural shrinkage and the structure's imperceptible movements will reveal the joins as cracks. The old adage, 'if you can't hide it, make a feature of it,' is most profound and should ring in the ears of all designers.

C) **Lamp access** must be considered where downlights are fitted to a ceiling. Although most bulbs can be changed from below, wiring access may be needed from above. Lighting-coves – or **lighting-pelmets** – are commonly used to 'spill' light across a ceiling from a light source hidden within a cornice or pelmet. Again, lamp access must be considered.

SOME TYPES OF ROOFS AND CEILINGS

1 Roof geometry – figure 13.01

A) This drawing contains a sketch in the bottom-left that names the parts; the direction of the shading indicates the direction that rafters would run on a real roof. Notice that a hip is an 'external' edge where two planes meet, and a valley is an 'internal' edge: geometrically they are identical, just inverted, and so the geometry that follows regarding hips also applies to valleys.

B) Main rafters and their bevels are established quite simply. The upper section of this drawing has a part-plan view and an end elevation of a roof. The elevation can also be seen as a section through the main part of the roof, and the sketch named, 'Elevation on rafter V-W' is a half-section. This allows the 'plumb bevel' and the 'foot bevel' to be drawn, as shown.

Once these bevels are established, the *detail* of the particular roof must be drawn in order to arrive at the true lengths and shape of the rafters (or roof flats possibly, if in a theatre set). The sketch at bottom-right called 'Ridge and eave detail' shows a scenic version of this, using flattage as the roof structure. It can be seen that at the ridge, half the ridge thickness must be deducted from the geometry line, and that the eave must be detailed in order to show the material needed *extra* to the geometric setting-out line.

C) A hip rafter is placed where two roof planes meet at an 'external' edge. The true length of the hip is established by using the method shown on the plan: the hip 'A-B' is *laid over* on the plan – the hatched zone – by drawing the height (or rise) from 'B' at 90 degrees to line 'A-B'. 'A-D' is the true length of hip rafter 'A-B' (true *geometric* length, that is: ridge and eave detailing will again adjust this). The plumb bevel and foot bevel are found this way.

D) The 'backing bevel' (or the dihedral angle) is a very important and useful piece of geometry to understand – *its uses far exceed those related to roofing alone*. A simple isometric sketch is drawn that shows a hip rafter, a jack rafter and the plane of the main roof and the plane of the hip roof. The top of the hip rafter has a V-shaped bevel and that is the backing, or dihedral angle. It can be seen that each bevel is aligned to the adjoining plane – so that a batten (a tile batten) can be laid along the plane of either roof and be mitred at the centre of the hip to continue along the other plane. (Picture a 'straight-edge', laid across either plane, touching the top edge of the main rafters and extending over the hip: it would touch the top of the backing bevel on the hip rafter and be resting upon the bevel.)

The drawing titled, 'Hip backing bevel as applied to flattage' is a section through the hip of a roof made of conventional ply-clad flattage, each plane of the roof consisting of one flat. It is a view that is 'looking up' the hip. A *real* hip rafter is not shown, or needed, on this section, but it can be seen that the angle at which the two flats meet *is* the dihedral angle – it determines how much of a back-bevel is cut from the edge of each flat. It can also be seen that the carpenters need to know this bevel in order to build the roof flats. They also need it to cut and pre-fit the timber support batten that is screwed to one flat. (Remember, as with all flattage, to indicate the back-bevel – or face bevel – on the flattage drawing as being '6 mm off of 21 mm timber', or whatever the sizes are. Don't just supply an angular dimension – show it as a dimension that is cut from the thickness of the material being used.)

To obtain the dihedral angle, refer to the plan: a line is drawn anywhere along line 'A-B' (the hip plan) at 90 degrees to it, crossing the eaves at points 'F' and 'G'. Line 'F-G' crosses line 'A-B' at point 'E'. From 'E' draw a line that meets 'A-D' (the true view of the hip) at 90 degrees to it: line 'E-H' is perpendicular to 'A-D'. From 'E' draw an arc (of length 'E-H') from 'H' to cross line 'A-B' at point 'I' (i.e. 'E-H' = 'E-I'). Angle 'FIG' is the dihedral angle.

E) 'Jack rafters' are rafters that are trimmed to meet a hip or valley rafter (they are not full-length, main rafters). One is indicated here, jack rafter 'X-Y', and the method of obtaining its true length and its edge bevel is shown on the plan. An arc is drawn that is centred upon point 'A' and runs from point 'D' to cross the ridge plan at 'J'. (line 'C-J' = 'A-D'). Join 'C-J' and extend line 'X-Y' to intersect it at point 'K'. Line 'X-K' is the true length of the jack rafter. Angle 'X-K-C' is the true edge bevel.

F) The uses to which the above geometry can be applied are many and varied. Bear all this in mind when dealing with other plane geometry problems. If drawing by hand, the dimensions have to be calculated using maths (*not* by scaling); CAD systems automate the dimensioning process. Either way, the correct geometry – the setting-out – is prerequisite.

2 An example of a show's roof – figure 13.02

A) This drawing contains views of a roof also shown in **figure 3.01**, 'A Proposal Drawing' (*see* page 22) and **3.03**, 'An Elevation and Side View' (*see* page 28). (Downstage is to the right of this drawing.) The main bulk of the roof was built as one piece, 6780 mm long (22' 3"), and – on 'change-over' days in the repertoire – it was hinged down for storage.

B) The 'S/R end view' shows a gable-end to the roof resting upon one of the veranda's main boxed-beams. (For this show, the gable-end was a flat that 'plugged in' beneath the roof flats.) Decorative, shaped 'rafter-ends' protrude from the face of the panelled beam. There were three up-and-downstage beams, one at each end and one in the centre.

C) 'Section A-A' shows this (plain-sided) centre beam. It is fixed to the main downstage beam and carries a timber frame that is let into the centre of it – as shown in 'Section D-D'; each up-and-downstage beam had a similar frame. Both sections show a continuous ridge member and two other continuous timbers, referred to as purlins (somewhat loosely, the pedant would point out).

D) 'The roof frames' drawing shows the three timber frames, notched to receive the ridge and purlins.

E) The roof flats are not drawn fully here, but can be seen in the two sections. They were conventional ply-clad flats, the downstage one being a simple rectangle, the upstage one being shaped around the bay window that is drawn dotted.

3 A flown ceiling – figure 13.03

A) This drawing has views of a large flown ceiling that rested upon the walls of a theatre set. The walls are omitted here, for clarity's sake, but the ceiling was supported around its outside edges when in position. Vertical black flats sat upon the ceiling flats, a little way back from the inner edge ... and they required French braces and space-frames in order to tie the whole structure into an independent flying unit. All flats were pin-hinged to one another.

B) The ceiling flats are shown dashed on the plan view and are identified as 'A' to 'D'. One flat, 'B', is shaded on the plan and shown separately below it. Each of these four conventional, ply-faced flats carried a moulded detail to their downstage and on-stage edges – as shown in 'Section Y-Y'.

C) The vertical, black flats and their supporting French braces and space-frames are shown in a heavy line on the plan and can be seen in 'Section A-A', where one of the black flats, 'No. 8', is shown shaded in elevation. One of the French braces has been drawn separately.

D) The flying points are marked as 'F' on the plan, eight points to two bars. The positions of the two bars can be inferred: one downstage, where two pick-up points are behind each of flats '1' and '11'; the other, upstage bar, being where the four flying points are shown along the back of the cross-stage, vertical flats, '6' and '7'.

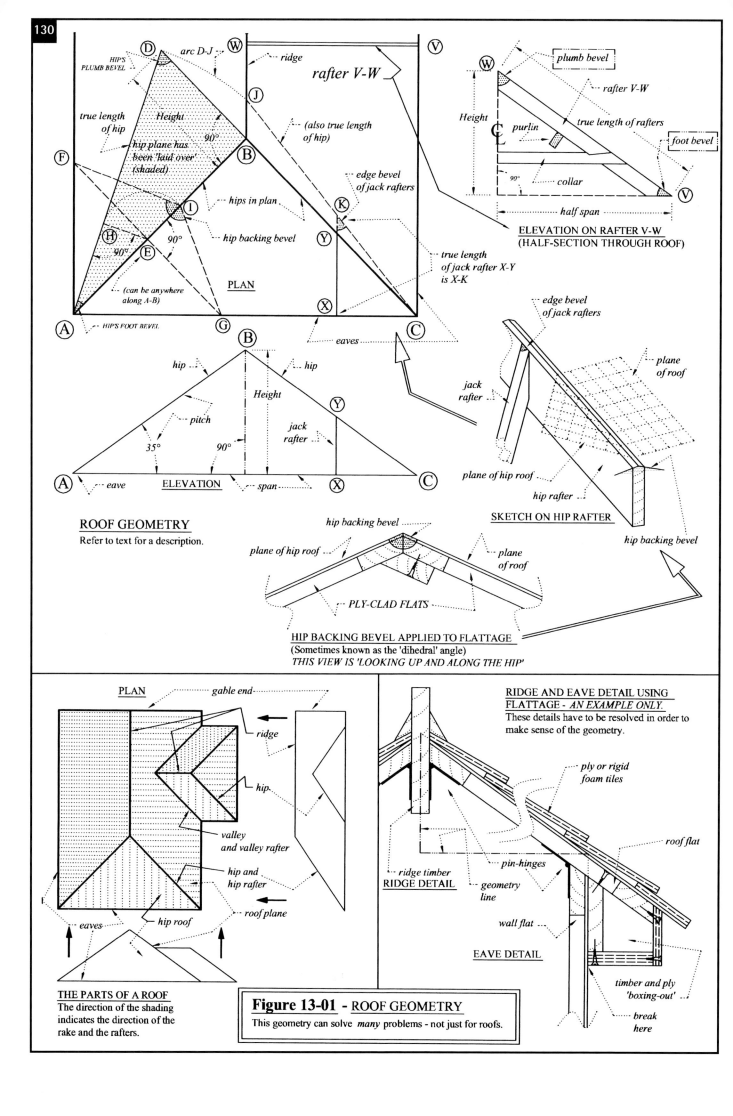

130

PLAN

HIP'S PLUMB BEVEL

arc D-J

ridge

rafter V-W

true length of hip

Height

hip plane has been 'laid over' (shaded)

90°

(also true length of hip)

edge bevel of jack rafters

hips in plan

hip backing bevel

true length of jack rafter X-Y is X-K

90°

90°

(can be anywhere along A-B)

HIP'S FOOT BEVEL.

eaves

plumb bevel

rafter V-W

Height

purlin

true length of rafters

foot bevel

90°

collar

half span

ELEVATION ON RAFTER V-W
(HALF-SECTION THROUGH ROOF)

ELEVATION

hip

hip

Height

pitch

jack rafter

35°

90°

eave

span

ROOF GEOMETRY
Refer to text for a description.

edge bevel of jack rafters

plane of roof

jack rafter

plane of hip roof

hip rafter

hip backing bevel

SKETCH ON HIP RAFTER

hip backing bevel

plane of hip roof

plane of roof

PLY-CLAD FLATS

HIP BACKING BEVEL APPLIED TO FLATTAGE
(Sometimes known as the 'dihedral' angle)
THIS VIEW IS 'LOOKING UP AND ALONG THE HIP'

PLAN

gable end

ridge

hip

valley and valley rafter

hip and hip rafter

roof plane

eaves

hip roof

THE PARTS OF A ROOF
The direction of the shading indicates the direction of the rake and the rafters.

RIDGE AND EAVE DETAIL USING FLATTAGE - *AN EXAMPLE ONLY.*
These details have to be resolved in order to make sense of the geometry.

ply or rigid foam tiles

roof flat

ridge timber
RIDGE DETAIL

pin-hinges

geometry line

wall flat

EAVE DETAIL

timber and ply 'boxing-out'

break here

Figure 13-01 - ROOF GEOMETRY
This geometry can solve *many* problems - not just for roofs.

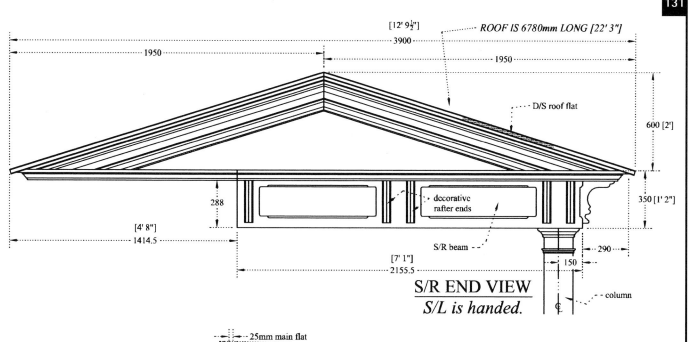

[12' 9½"]
3900
1950 · 1950

ROOF IS 6780mm LONG [22' 3"]

D/S roof flat

600 [2']

288

350 [1' 2"]

decorative
rafter ends

[4' 8"]
1414.5

S/R beam

[7' 1"]
2155.5

290

150

column

S/R END VIEW
S/L is handed.

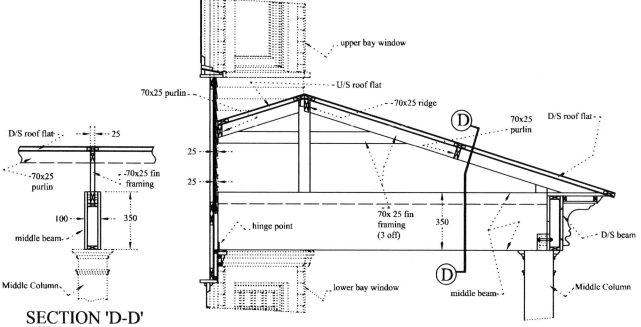

25mm main flat

upper bay window

U/S roof flat

70x25 purlin

70x25 ridge

70x25
purlin

D/S roof flat

D/S roof flat

25

70x25
purlin

70x25 fin
framing

100

350

middle beam

25

25

70 x 25 fin
framing
(3 off)

350

hinge point

D/S beam

Middle Column

lower bay window

middle beam

Middle Column

SECTION 'D-D'

SECTION 'A-A' - ON CENTRE BEAM (OF THREE)

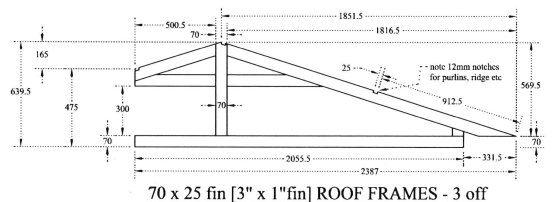

500.5

1851.5

70

1816.5

165

639.5

475

300

70

70

25

note 12mm notches
for purlins, ridge etc

569.5

912.5

2055.5

331.5

70

2387

70 x 25 fin [3" x 1"fin] ROOF FRAMES - 3 off

Ensure all is well glued screwed and m & t.

Figure 13-02 - AN EXAMPLE OF A SHOW'S ROOF

This roof unit was made to fold down - *see* **figure 3-01.**

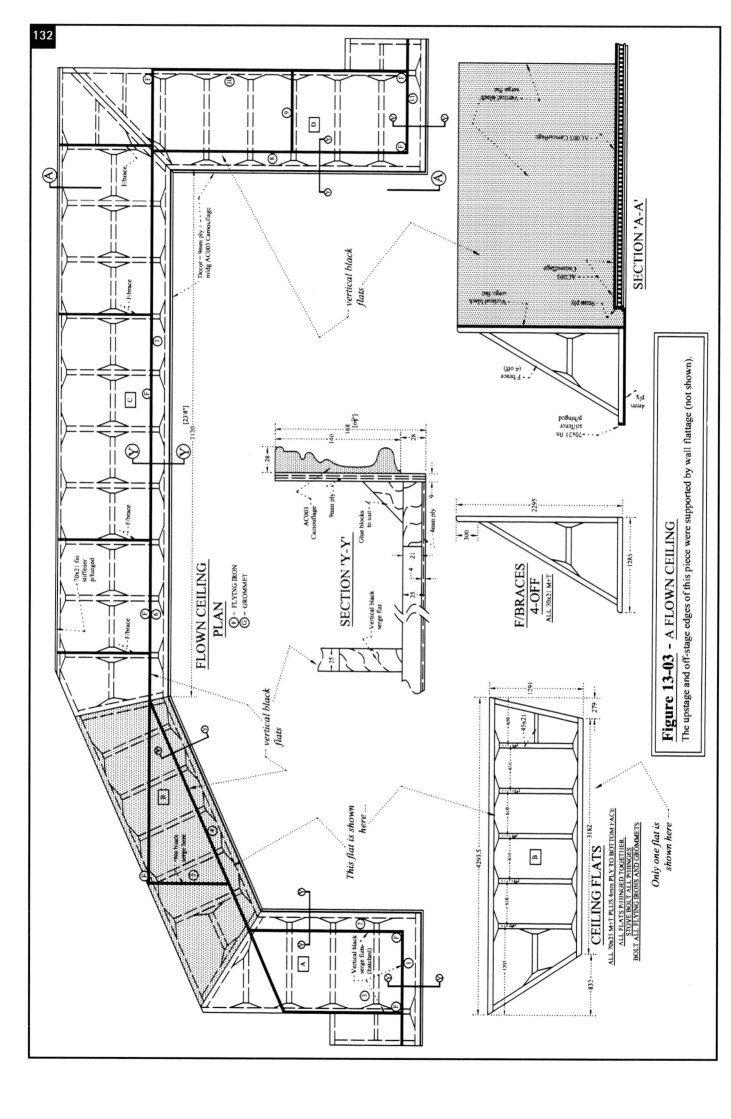

Figure 13-03 - A FLOWN CEILING

The upstage and off-stage edges of this piece were supported by wall flattage (not shown).

14 • Revolves

A revolve, or turntable, is a rotating disc or ring upon which items of set and/or cast can be turned through space. Although they can be built of timber and plywood, most revolves are of steel construction, with plywood tops. Consequently, engineering contractors tend to be the experts on revolves and they will either build them to suit each job or hire out stock-revolves for short-term use. Small turntables are readily available to hire for use with cars – car shows always seem to use revolves.

Very basic information is supplied here, but it is advisable to discuss any proposed revolve structure directly with the engineers involved.

NOTES ON REVOLVES

1 Health & Safety

A) All moving objects are potentially hazardous and revolve design must be approached in a fashion that considers and eliminates any conceivable risks. The revolve manufacturer must be informed of the load to be carried and the series of movements that are planned. Musical productions often employ hoards of cast spinning about the place and it is important to ensure that their movements cannot bring them into accidental contact with pieces of the set. Scene changes, where flying scenery is on the move, present an obvious danger.

B) Cable-driven revolves must have their cables housed safely away from passing people. Backstage, in semi-darkness, exposed, moving cables snaking across the floor are a real hazard; clearly marked walkways and ramps must be built to eradicate the problem.

C) A 'dead man's button', or emergency stop button, should be fitted at a point where a member of stage-management is placed, such as the prompt corner. The operator needs a clear view of the revolve and its surroundings.

D) Revolves, especially car revolves, are sometimes designed to be placed in awkward positions – high up, or tilted at an angle – and consideration must be given as to how the crew can get the car into position. There are, in fact, professional teams of car handlers, expert at shifting vehicles – their experience is invaluable and their help should be sought.

E) Revolves used by the public are quite common in museum work, exhibitions and trade shows. Clearly, safe handrails are needed, as well as extra emergency-stop buttons. It is also usual – and advisable – to have a trained attendant with the public at all times. The attendant sees that the public are 'loaded' and 'unloaded' safely and tends to cue the operation of the revolve. Sufficient lighting must be supplied to suit local regulations.

2 Construction

A) Cable-driven revolves are common: a continuous cable runs from the 'drum' of a motor (or hand-winch) around the revolve structure and back. Diverter pulleys are strategically placed to enable the cable to run where it is wanted. A simple cable-tightening mechanism is required. Ideally, the revolve should carry a 'V' shaped member – call it a 'drive rail' – in which the cable runs. This helps the cable to grip the structure, and is usually set just back and below from the outer edge of the overhanging top plywood disc.

B) Friction-drive revolves do not use cable. Instead, a static, motor-driven wheel pushes against a drive rail made of rolled steel and set beneath the revolve's top: the revolve is being driven by the motor, using friction. A mechanism allows for adjustment of the amount of friction being applied.

C) Rack and pinion drives are sometimes used. Here a static, motor-driven toothed wheel engages with a drive rail that has grooves or notches to take each tooth. A form of chain may be welded to the face of a piece of rolled box-steel, and the wheel's teeth locate with the chain.

D) Fixed castors are fitted to the underside of the revolve – they are positioned square to radial lines. They should run upon a continuous steel flat-bar track, circular in plan view, whose job is to provide a smooth running surface that will reduce vibration and unnecessary noise.

E) For the sake of economy, a revolve structure contains as few rolled members as possible. All the steel framing can be of straight tubes, the outer edge being facetted – the overhanging plywood top is cut to a true circle. Only the above-mentioned drive rail and the tracks need to be rolled.

F) Limit switches can be fitted that stop the revolve at predetermined positions. These are small mechanical switches that are 'tripped' by coming into contact with an arm fitted to a part of the revolve's structure. The positions at which the revolve must stop are called 'deads'.

G) Hand winches can have mechanical 'counters' fitted that supply a visible read-out of the number of turns taken upon the winch. The operator has to make a note of the individual numbers displayed at each dead: during the show, he stops turning the winch when a relevant number appears in the window of the counter. (This is not very accurate: the cable can stretch and the counters are fairly primitive. It is better for the operator to have a full view of the revolve's surface and to place surreptitious marks around the revolve that he can 'line up' with a fixed mark placed outside the revolve. Don't bother to attempt to put coloured tape around the cable at relevant points – it will fall off or slide along the cable.)

H) 'Doughnut', or ring, revolves are frequently used – they are simply in the form of a ring rather than a disc. When using multiples of these – as in figure 14.01 – one is faced with the problem of ensuring that the inner

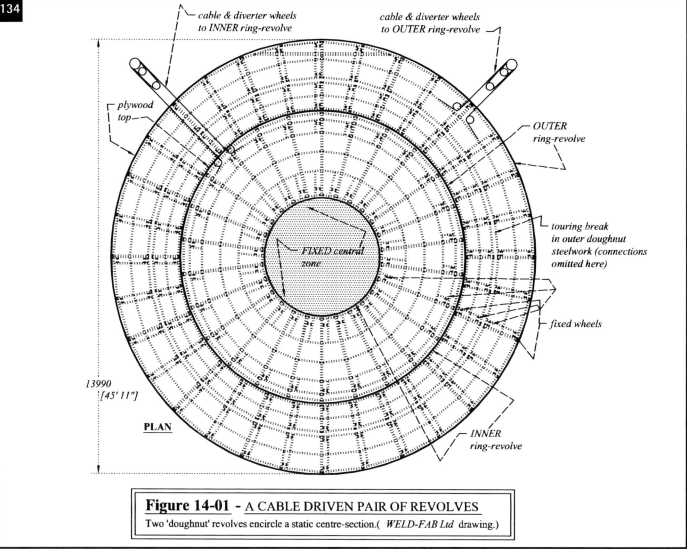

cable & diverter wheels to INNER ring-revolve

cable & diverter wheels to OUTER ring-revolve

plywood top

OUTER ring-revolve

FIXED central zone

touring break in outer doughnut steelwork (connections omitted here)

fixed wheels

13990 [45' 11"]

PLAN

INNER ring-revolve

Figure 14-01 - A CABLE DRIVEN PAIR OF REVOLVES
Two 'doughnut' revolves encircle a static centre-section.(*WELD-FAB Ltd* drawing.)

revolve's drive-cables (and LX cables, perhaps) are not trapped by the wheels of the outer unit. A little extra *over-all* height can help to solve this.

I) **Raked revolves** are quite common. It may sound obvious, but be very aware that a revolve that sits upon a raking stage is *elliptical in plan view*. This can be particularly relevant when either the revolve or the surrounding floor rises and/or falls during a show, because fascias then have to be introduced– and their plan-view shape is elliptical. The revolve *cannot* be circular in plan view, only in 'true-view'.

SOME TYPES OF REVOLVES

1 A cable-driven pair of revolves – figure 14.01

A) This small drawing shows a pair of ring-revolves concentric to a fixed central disc. The cable-route to the inner revolve is indicated as running from the top left of the drawing; clearly, these cables must pass *beneath* the wheels and track of the outer revolve.

B) The outer revolve has a clear break in its steel-work: this is a touring break – some dates of the tour

required a smaller overall unit. The steelwork has connections - not shown here - that join the two halves of the outer revolve when required. Clearly, two sets of plywood top-cladding would have been made for the tour.

C) Concentric revolves such as this have horizontal guide wheels fitted (not shown here) that hold the units the correct distance apart.

2 A 'doughnut' revolve – figure 14.02

A) The left-hand plan shows the steel framing of a ring-revolve that encircles a hydraulically driven scissor-lift. The scissor-lift has an upper platform in the shape of a disc. Wheel positions are marked and the drive rail is indicated. This revolve is driven by two friction-drive motors, it's not cable-driven.

B) The right-hand plan has the 'spider frame' drawn: this frame is both a track for the wheels of the revolve and a mounting-frame for the two motors.

C) The sections indicate how this unit operates, the spider frame being supported by steel rostra that provide a well in which the scissor-lift is concealed. One guide wheel is indicated: these roll against the guide rail, holding the revolve in its true position.

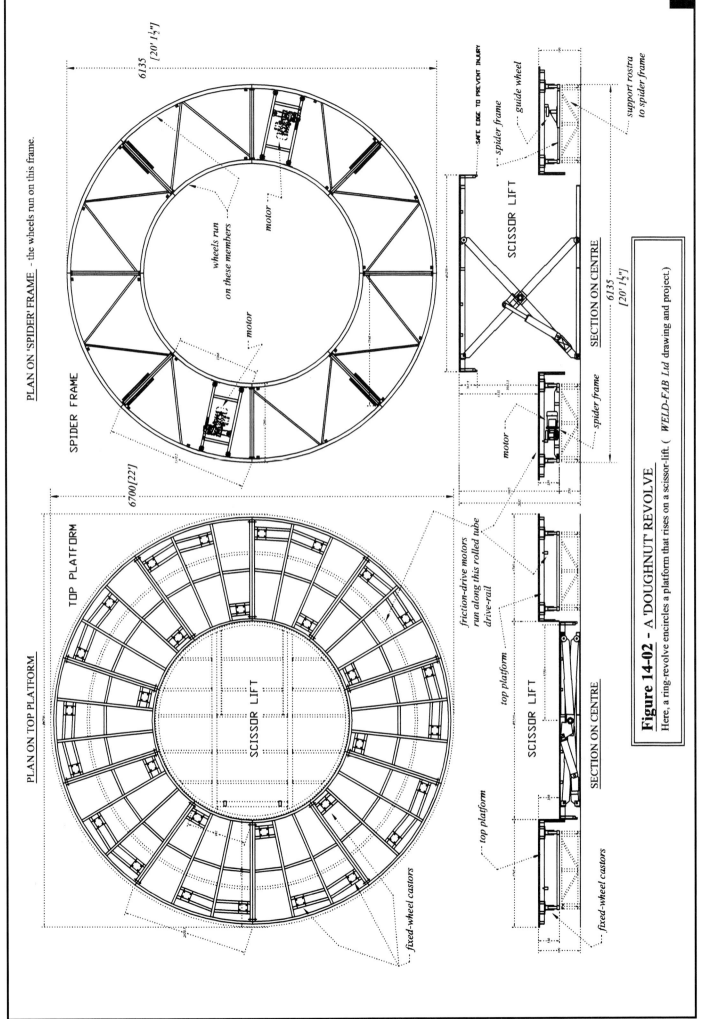

PLAN ON 'SPIDER FRAME' - the wheels run on this frame.

6135 [20' 1½"]

SPIDER FRAME

wheels run
on these members

motor

motor

SCISSOR LIFT

SECTION ON CENTRE
6135
[20' 1½"]

spider frame

guide wheel

SAFE EDGE TO PREVENT INJURY

support rostra
to spider frame

spider frame

motor

PLAN ON TOP PLATFORM

6700 [22']

TOP PLATFORM

SCISSOR LIFT

friction-drive motors
run along this rolled tube
drive-rail

top platform

top platform

SCISSOR LIFT

SCISSOR LIFT

SECTION ON CENTRE

top platform

fixed-wheel castors

fixed-wheel castors

Figure 14-02 – A 'DOUGHNUT' REVOLVE
Here, a ring-revolve encircles a platform that rises on a scissor-lift. (*WELD-FAB Ltd* drawing and project.)

Part Three:
AN EXAMPLE OF A DESIGN DRAWING PACKAGE

The production featured in this chapter has been deliberately chosen for its 'normality' – normality, that is, from the *set-builder's* point of view and not necessarily from that of the audience or from an aesthetic stance. It is a trade-show set built to play one performance only and was seen by an audience for just two-and-a-half minutes before being destroyed. Such a brief life expectancy obviously coloured the way in which this show was drawn and constructed.

It is hoped that by reproducing all four of the drawings here, a useful record of a design-drawing package is preserved for reference. This design package, when read in conjunction with the accompanying text, will illustrate the information that the designer must supply to both the set-builder and the production staff in order to achieve the successful implementation of his design.

I would certainly not suggest that this was a perfect, complete package (one can *always* improve upon what has gone before); nor would I imply that the methods employed in drawing and construction were the only methods worth considering.

15 • Design Drawings for a Trade-Show Set

'Bar Scene', at the Rai Centre, Amsterdam
Designed by John Blurton; built by *Creative Construction*

With sincere thanks to: Andy Peat of *Peat Bellkins Ltd*,
Richard McCabe of *Creative Construction*,
and to the ultimate client, an American film company.

Trade shows come in all guises: they are all, by defini-tion, *commercial* productions as opposed to *theatre* productions – even though, logically, many or most theatre shows are produced commercially (it needs to be accepted as a somewhat quirky definition, used and understood col-loquially). Trade shows may be of the conference-set type or they may be exhibitions, stage shows, car launches, or any other promotional public event imaginable – and such potential variety is part of the attraction to those working in the business. Each type of trade show requires similar skills from its production staff. It is common knowledge that those skills originated in the theatre; many have now been developed further, separate to theatre, but they all 'speak the same language' – and all demand drawings that are clear and precise.

This particular production was a stage-show set within an existing, purpose-built auditorium. It carried the fol-lowing **brief**:

A live stage show was needed during one of the days that films were being shown at the Amsterdam Film Festival. The venue, the Rai Centre, was familiar to all involved, having been used for several previous productions staged there on behalf of the film company.

The cinema screen would fly out at a pertinent moment, ending a segment of film that showed trailers; the live show would last approximately two-and-a-half minutes and the screen would fly back in and the trailers continue. The audio speakers behind the cinema screen would have to be struck for the live section of the show and returned to position in time for the trailers to recommence.

The live show was to be a song-and-dance routine, played within a modern and vibrant American bar setting – the bar's design was to suggest an earthy, 'streetwise' quality. The bar would need to contain a dance podium, as well as steel posts along the bar-top for use by the dancers during their routine. There were to be approximately ten dancers and a cast of 15–20 playing the bar's customers.

The design of the bar was to be similar to, but *not a copy* of, a bar featured in the film trailer that was to be interrupted by this live show. The designer was sent a video containing the relevant film clips, for reference. It was more important to convey the 'feel' of the type of bar than to attempt to replicate it exactly.

A neon sign, displaying the name of the bar, was to be made to an existing design (as in the film). The design ref-erence would follow after the set was designed.

A prop buyer would be purchasing the goods required to 'dress' the bar (bottles, glasses, optics, wall posters and pic-tures, etc.). That dressing would take place during the four night-shifts available to build, light and rehearse the show. (Note that this point is relevant to the designer: prop dress-ing need not be researched and drawn.)

The set budget would be quite low, reflecting the short time that it would be seen. Nevertheless, the set had to cover a considerable area of stage.

The set design, production management, and set con-struction were to originate in the UK and be approved by the client prior to the production period in Amsterdam. The venue's stage crew were also available for the production period.

The following **final-issue drawings** were the result of this brief:

Drw. '01A' – General Arrangement – 1:50 @ A1

A) This drawing shows a plan view and a side section on centre-line. It shows the relevant parts of the venue, the set (without detail), flying plot, cinema screen and its maskings, speaker stacks, and black leg maskings.

The side section often appears to be somewhat bereft of interest, but it is vital for checking sight-lines and for sub-sequent use by the lighting designer. Always remember that the next person – often the *only* person – who will work upon and develop this drawing, will be the lighting designer. Subsequent drawings will detail the set; the gen-eral arrangement only needs the main outlines of the set, its 'foot-print'.

(It may be noted that a front elevation is not shown here; normally, I would prefer to see it on this drawing. However, in this particular case I placed the front elevation on the following drawing, at a larger scale. My reasons were influenced by the fact that I had only four days to design and draw this show and the fact that the venue was familiar to all – a dark cinema environment.)

B) This drawing only shows **dimensions that are necessary** to place everything in the correct positions within the venue. **It will be the key drawing used during the fit-up.** The actual set need not be dimensioned because those dimensions appear on subsequent drawings devoted to the set itself; this general arrangement requires dimensions that show where to place the completed items of set.

C) Note that the dimensions spring from two datum lines. It is simpler for all concerned if only two datum lines are used: the likelihood of errors being made on stage rises proportionately with each additional datum line. The two datum lines used here are:

(i) The **downstage edge of the venue's stage** is used as a datum line supplying the up-and-downstage dimensions to key points. This is a fixed, very obvious and unmistakable point from which to measure. (Beware of using lines that are close to other natural lines – make sure the crew know where to measure from.)

(ii) The **stage centre-line** is the second datum line used, supplying a baseline from which to measure the on-and-off-stage dimensions. This is a datum line that apparently 'does not exist', so it could be asked whether this line is too ethereal to be of use; however, it is the *best* line to use. This is because most venues will have marks (brass nails or studs are common) that show a downstage centre-point and an upstage one – a chalk-line is used to 'ping' a centre-line at each fit-up. Remember also, fearing the worst, that if the venue's centre-line is wrong, at least the whole set is 'wrong together', meaning that the set will still work as a complete whole, but it may have shifted over to one side within the proscenium, hopefully by an imperceptible amount. Obviously, if the set dictates that the centre-line must be *exactly* on centre of the downstage edge and *exactly* at 90 degrees to that edge, then say so on the drawing.

D) The **venue**, as previously mentioned, was a familiar one. The Rai Centre sent their drawings of the venue to me by e-mail – I then 'fine-tuned' them to suit the on-site surveys that I had taken in previous years. With this particular production, at this particular venue, there was no need to show the whole of the auditorium in plan and section: previous shows had included that information in the drawing package, and, more importantly, the whole production team knew the venue (and knew that the circle was not to be used by the audience). When I began this drawing, I did place the extreme seats of the whole venue in position – they would be outside the borders of this drawing – in order that I could plot the key sight-lines.

E) The **iron curtain**, as in most venues, has to be kept free of any potential obstructions and its position must therefore be clearly delineated.

F) The **flying plot** has been shown and all flown pieces relevant to this show have been named and a bar number allocated to them. (A large note, placed upstage right on the plan, asks the crew to check and confirm these allocated bar numbers. I did this because I was unsure as to the exact spacing of the in-house bars. The dimensions given would allow for the correct placing of the items regardless of the actual number of the bar. If in any doubt, never be afraid to signal any uncertainties that may exist – the in-house crew, who clearly know the venue better than anyone else, can sort out the bar numbers providing that dimensions have been given.)

G) The **end seats** are included so that sight-lines can be proved.

H) **Maskings** have been placed and sightlines 'proved'. Remember that soft black legs need to have dimensions: the crew can simply place chalk marks on the stage, bring in the empty bar, tie the legs to it and fly it out. If dimensions are *not* given (and sight-lines *not* 'proved' upon the drawing), the crew will have to keep flying the bar back in, move the leg along the bar and then check whether or not the leg does its masking job.

Once the main body of the set is placed, it is often very awkward – if not impossible – to fly the bars back in for adjustment. Nobody would be too thrilled at the prospect of striking the set merely to adjust a wrongly placed leg on a bar.

I) The **cinema screen** and **speaker stacks** have been positioned on this drawing: they are an inherent part of 'our' live show because of the fact that they need to be removed before the show can begin and then need replacing afterwards. The speaker stacks are drawn sitting on wheeled *Steeldeck*® units in order that the crew can push them offstage, paging the cables as they go. (Normally, when showing full-length films in this venue, five stacks are used; however, it was agreed that three could be used for the trailer sequence in order to ease the problem of striking and re-setting for the live show. Two further stacks were added before the next full film was shown.)

J) All sorts of **show staff** will use this general arrangement drawing, including the choreographer, who will want to see the clear space that is available for the dance routine. Stage management may need to mark out a rehearsal room with the foot-print of the set. Keep this in mind when drawing the 'GA'.

In truth, another drawing was issued, not shown here, that only showed the set *at the time of the show* – i.e. stripped of everything except the venue, the set and settings. In CAD this is easy to accomplish by turning off certain layers and then printing and issuing that version as a new drawing.

K) The **set** is shown in position, each wall given a reference number, and salient **setting dimensions** shown. The bar and the dance podium are shown and labelled.

L) **Set dressings** ('props') are indicated; here they consist of the flown neon sign and the (rented) tables and chairs. Their positions may well be changed later to suit the dance routine.

Rehearsals, not drawings, finally fix the positions of props. The function of the drawing here is to show that they will indeed fit into the space. Once drawn and placed, it is obvious that the tables and chairs could be moved to numerous positions, each satisfactory as far as the set and sight-lines permit. Only rehearsals will place them finally; the drawing indicates one of many possibilities, but does illustrate how a certain number of items fit within the acting area.

M) This drawing, you may notice is '01A'. It was revised because early rehearsals with a good show-management team, coupled with prompt feedback from the production manager, *allowed* it to be changed in time for re-issuing to those who needed it.

The **revisions** included moving the tables and changing their type (because the hired tables had been found and their sizes known). Following a 'recce' by the production manager, the screen and speaker stacks were slightly shifted, which then allowed the set to shift downstage. The bar was then sent downstage in relation to the back wall of the set, allowing more room for dancers behind the bar. The dance podium was placed to suit the dance routine.

Drw. '02' – Front Elevation + Bar Details – 1:20 @ A1 'stretched'

A) This is a 'stretched' A1 drawing: it is the height of A1 paper in landscape format, 594 mm, but its length has grown by about 85 mm from the standard length of 841 mm. 'Stretching' is a useful weapon in the CAD armoury – an A1 roll-feed plotter can print a drawing 50000 mm wide (!) by 594 mm high. Those who receive only a paper copy of the drawing *can* experience difficulties trying to obtain further copies, but this problem may be avoided if the whole drawing, like this one, can be fitted onto A0 paper.

B) The **design** is mentioned beneath the title, 'Front Elevation – 1:20 – without prop dressing!'. It reads: 'The "feel" of the set is: an ex-industrial unit, below ground level, that has been converted to become a rather tacky, "grunge" type of bar. The paint-work, though simple, should look a bit dirty.'

The walls of the set incorporate six vertical 'steel I beams' coated with silver metallic paint. The walls have a skirting and dado rail, between which are vertical boards. Above this is painted vac-form brickwork that will be peppered with posters, cards and pictures by the prop buyer/dresser. Round conduit occasionally runs vertically up the walls, disguising the flat breaks. A false, non-practical fire-exit doorway is on stage-left.

The top of the brickwork ends at a protruding 'concrete beam', above which is an area of plain walling that is punctured by old 'steel-framed' windows, protected by rusty two-inch *Weldmesh* (a welded 50 x 50 mm grid of 3 mm round rod). Everything above the concrete beam is to be very grubby and dirty in appearance.

The wall behind the bar consists of four bays of shelving and four bays of 'mirror'. The mirror is '*Gerriets* transparent silver' material – this has mirror to one side but can be back-lit so as to make it transparent.

The bar unit has a shiny aluminium framework of scaffold-type tubes for use by the dancers. The face of the bar has inset perforated steel panels, through which back-light can pour.

Lighting is obviously the responsibility of the lighting designer, but the set designer must allow for lamps – more than that, the designer's mental image of the set must be 'under light'. If certain items are designed to incorporate specific lighting effects, then a note should be made on the drawing.

This set carries within it some lighting opportunities that may, or may not, be utilised. The grubby set of top windows are backed with thin, dirty cotton: they could, for example, be back-lit with a cold, dawn light; then, during the dancing, they could pulse with strong light. The 'mirrors' behind the bar can switch to being banks of back-light, throwing the dancers into silhouette. The bar itself can contain lamps facing downstage that push light through the mesh panels, lamps facing upstage that up-light the rear wall, or lamps pointing up at the dancers (the bar top would need holes cut that were covered with clear, rigid PVC).

The lighting designer will also organise the 'front' lighting of the set. He can use the flown bars for his lamps as well as various front-of-house positions available in this venue. He could also have lamp stands placed downstage left and right, masked by legs.

Certain parts of the set will naturally 'pick up the light' because of their surface finish: the aluminium scaffold poles, the vertical 'steel I beams' and the mesh panels along the front of the bar (the last two items are painted with silver *Hammerite*, or similar – a metallic finish).

C) The **front elevation** is drawn in the upper half of the drawing. A glance at the plan view (**Drw 01A**) will confirm that flats No. 2, 4 and 6 are angled to our viewpoint.

The drawing of the front elevation of a set is frequently somewhat 'underwhelming' as an image; this is because an elevation is *not* a 'true view'. In life, looking at the set, one would be viewing it in perspective so that all recesses – such as windows and door frames – are properly 'read' by the eye. An elevation, however, draws each item 'straight on', regardless of its height or position – omitting all of the 3D effects that the viewer's eye will see. This does inhibit the impact of the drawing, and that is why 'visuals' are usually supplied (coloured artist's impressions of the set, drawn as a true, lifelike view, incorporating perspective, lights, smoke and 'atmosphere').

D) This elevation was originally drawn as part of drawing **01A**, completing the holy trinity of **plan, section and elevation**: one should always draw these three views while they are in a strict relationship to one another on the paper or screen. It is only due to CAD that I was later able to choose to enlarge the scale and place the elevation on this drawing.

E) **Artwork references** have been placed upon the elevation. These give details such as the paint colours (here referring to RAL colours, but any convenient reference is fine), the type of vac-form brickwork wanted, mesh specification, mirror type and scaffold reference.

Note that the **neon sign** – 'A Large Neon' – is clearly marked as being, 'to be to the client's design (reference) – <u>NOT</u> as drawn here.' This is because, at the time of drawing, I did not have the correct reference for this sign. It was an important issue because it related to the title of the film and so the calligraphy, or font, had to be correct. I drew it, adding the above note, in order to show that the sign had a 'home': it had been considered (neon will not be ignored!) and a place been allocated for it. Leaving the neon off the drawing, however inaccurately it has been depicted, would be wrong, because those reading the drawing need to be aware that neon of some description will be in the area shown. (For example, neon requires an emergency 'fireman's switch', normally placed in the prompt corner, or wherever stage management will be in attendance during the show.)

F) The **bar unit** has been drawn in the lower half of this drawing. A plan, elevation and section have been drawn at 1:20, an enlarged section is shown at 1:5 scale and a 1:1 detail and specification of the perforated steel is included. Do remember that these are *design*, not construction, drawings – but even so, enough construction detail has been suggested in order to illustrate how the set can be made in an economic fashion. The set-builder may construct this item in another way. That is his affair: he is responsible for the safe and accurate interpretation of the design represented here. However, *the designer must design* *to the budget*, and in order for him to 'get-more-for-the-money' he must be aware of the economic impact of everything drawn and should, therefore, suggest cheap methods of construction.

The design must also utilise the size of materials in an effort to be economic. Such reasoning has dictated that this bar has four 'eight-by-four' (feet, that is) decking units as its core. Given that this is a one-off show, it would be idiotic to design the bar to be of a size that would involve 'special' units being made. The design has to work inherently with the budget.

The budget has dictated that this unit is simple in design. The structure consists of *Steeldeck®*, or a similar rented decking system, faced with straightforward facing flats. The size of the perforated steel panels is determined by using the steel-sheet size in an economic way.

If rehearsals proved that this structure needed stiffening, the steel scaffold-tube legs of the decking system would provide adequate and simple connection-points for additional scaffold bracing. Bracing could spread upstage, where convenient – the audience cannot see it below the bar-top. The set-builder would be aware of all this.

Drw. '03' – Back Wall (No. 3), Column Detail and Podium Detail – 1:20 @ A1

A) The back, or upstage, wall of the set is shown in plan, elevation and section; this wall is flat '3' on the general arrangement drawing.

Again, the design has maintained full economic use of materials. Bearing in mind that plywood and most 'stock' flattage (flats that set-builders may have in store) are 4' wide, 1220 mm, it can be seen that this large wall is divided by its design, *by intent*, into bays 1220 mm wide.

Two full-height flats form the ends of the wall; they are 610 mm wide by 4880 mm high (2' x 16'). Eight vertical flats form the bulk of the wall, each being 1220 mm wide by 3660 mm (4' x 12'), and are 'topped off' by a horizontal flat that ties them together, which is 1220 mm wide by 9760 mm (4' x 32').

Flattage is drawn as on-edge 45 x 21 mm par (2" x 1") faced with 4 mm ply. This is standard construction for one-off trade-show work.

Four of the vertical flats are partially covered with 'transparent' mirror material in order that, during the dance routine, back-light may be pumped through, thereby placing some dancers into silhouette. Clearly, it was important that I knew the width of this material *before* I designed further (it is 1370 mm wide, which allows for enough material to wrap-around the flat).

As previously mentioned, note that the 'A Large Neon' sign is an indication *only* – a full design reference was to follow from the client.

B) The **column detail** is drawn at 1:2 scale. It shows the proposed flattage construction as well as the column detail. The column is to represent a steel 'I' beam and is to be painted in silver metallic paint, hence the use of MDF for its construction: MDF has a smooth, hard, grain-free surface (even when shaped with a router) ideal for accepting a clean paint finish.

C) The **dance podium section**, also at 1:2 scale, shows enough detail to fully indicate what is wanted. Note that the steel decking units are to be faced with 4mm hardboard on the top surface: this provides an ideal surface for dancing. A black plastic angle-strip hides the joint between the 12 mm side fascias and the top.

Drw. '04' – Walls 1, 2, 4, 5 and 6 – 1:20 @ A1

A) The remaining walls of the set are drawn here. Flat 4 is a 'handed' version of flat 2 – meaning that it is a 'mirrored' version of flat 2, as drawn.

B) Sections 'B-B', 'C-C', 'D-D' and 'E-E' have been carefully selected to indicate the necessary details, but in a fashion that involves the least drawing. 'B-B' and 'C-C' show the skirting, dado and vertical board details. 'D-D' indicates the window, its sill and the steel grills. 'E-E' illustrates the 'dummy' fire-exit doorway in flat 6.

C) Wall No. 6 includes a recessed section of 'brickwork' and 'steel' above the dummy fire-exit door. The drawing indicates this recessed area in three ways: firstly, the elevation has marked the area by having two diagonal lines and a note that says '*all set back*'. *Two* plan sections are then drawn above the elevation; one is the upper section, the other shows a lower section. Lastly, detail 'E-E' clearly shows that the dummy fire-exit door is to the *back* of the flattage and that an MDF strip, representing steel, is inserted all around the recess.

In conclusion, these four drawings were sufficient for the production to be built and produced.

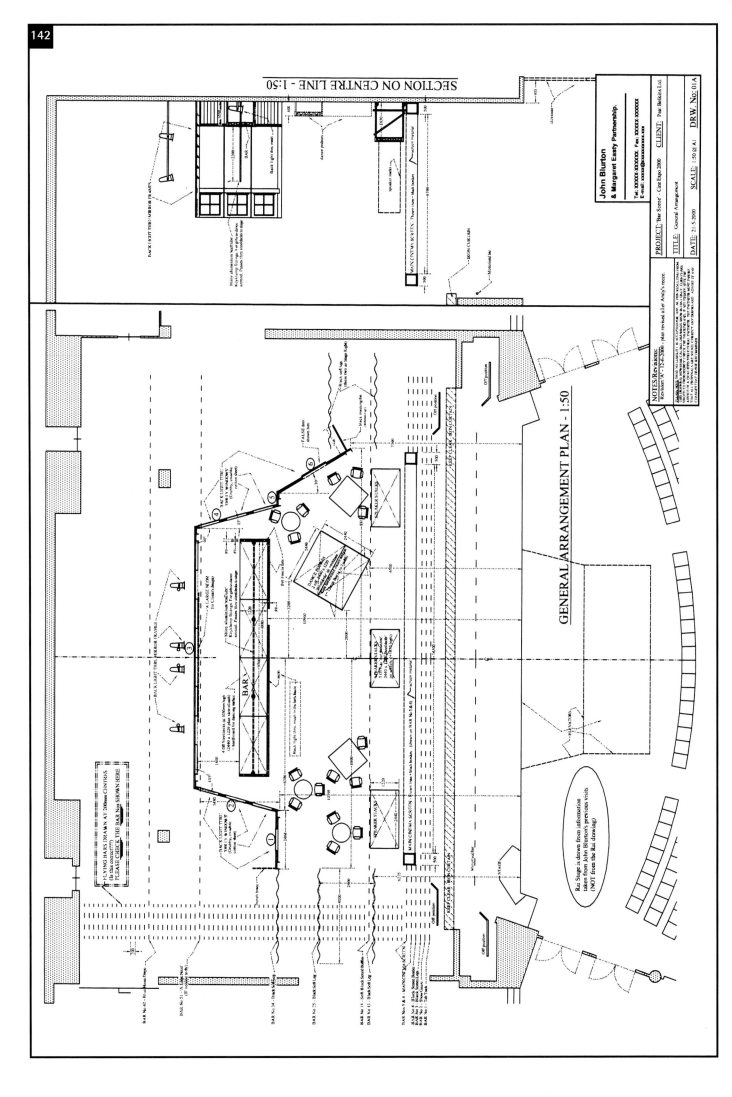

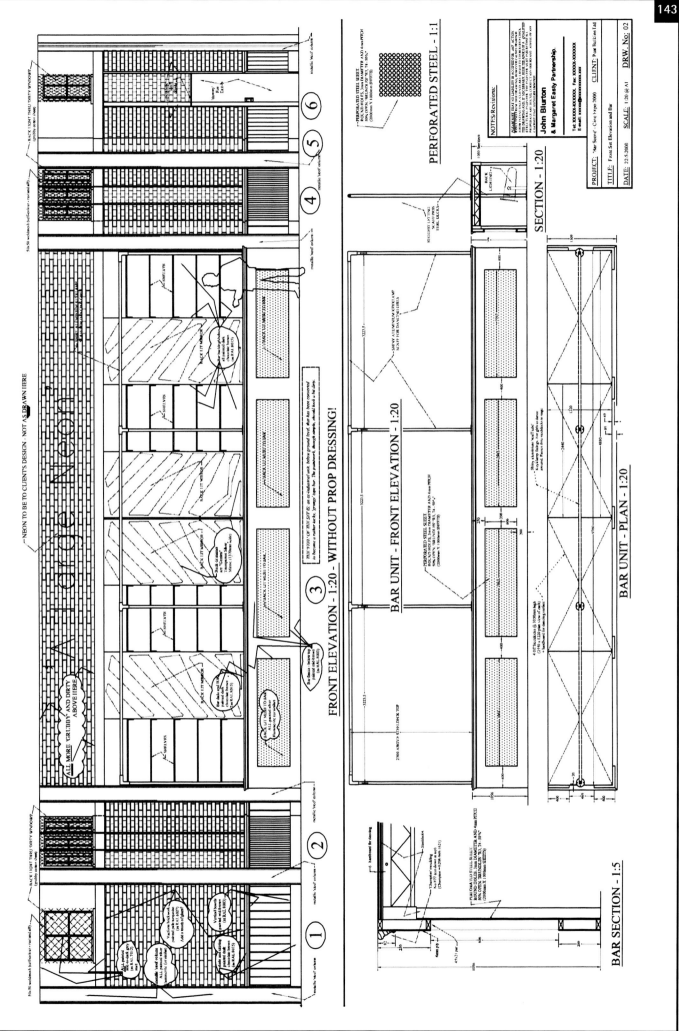

143

NEON TO BE TO CLIENT'S DESIGN - NOT AS DRAWN HERE

Bar Large Neon

ALL MORE GRUBBY AND DIRTY ABOVE HERE

FRONT ELEVATION - 1:20 - WITHOUT PROP DRESSING!

PERFORATED STEEL - 1:1

BAR UNIT - FRONT ELEVATION - 1:20

BAR UNIT - PLAN - 1:20

SECTION - 1:20

BAR SECTION - 1:5

NOTES/Revisions:

John Blurton
& Margaret Easty Partnership.

Tel: xxxxx-xxxxxx Fax: xxxxx-xxxxxx
E-mail: xxxxxx@xxxxxxxx

PROJECT: 'Bar Scene' - Circ Expo 2000   CLIENT: Post Boilers Ltd

TITLE: Front Set Elevation and Bar

DATE: 22-5-2000   SCALE: 1:20 @ A1   DRW. No: 02

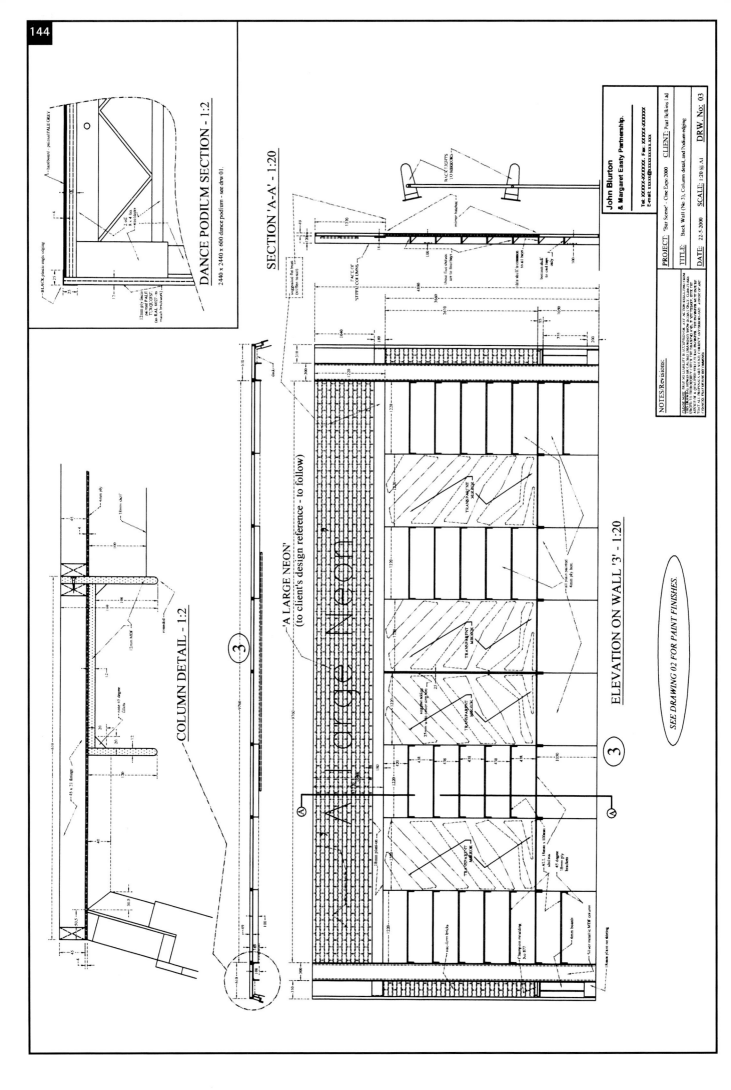

144

DANCE PODIUM SECTION - 1:2

2440 x 2440 x 600 dance podium - see drw 01.

SECTION 'A-A' - 1:20

COLUMN DETAIL - 1:2

'A LARGE NEON'
(to client's design reference - to follow)

A Large Neon

ELEVATION ON WALL '3' - 1:20

SEE DRAWING 02 FOR PAINT FINISHES.

John Blurton
& Margaret Easty Partnership.

Tel: XXXXX-XXXXXX, Fax: XXXXX-XXXXXX
E-mail: xxxxx@xxxxxxxxxx.xx

NOTES/Revisions:

PROJECT: 'Bar Scene' - Cine Expo 2000   CLIENT: Pearl Bellini Ltd

TITLE: Back Wall (No. 3), Column detail, and Podium edging

DATE: 22-5-2000   SCALE: 1:20 @ A1   DRW. No: 03

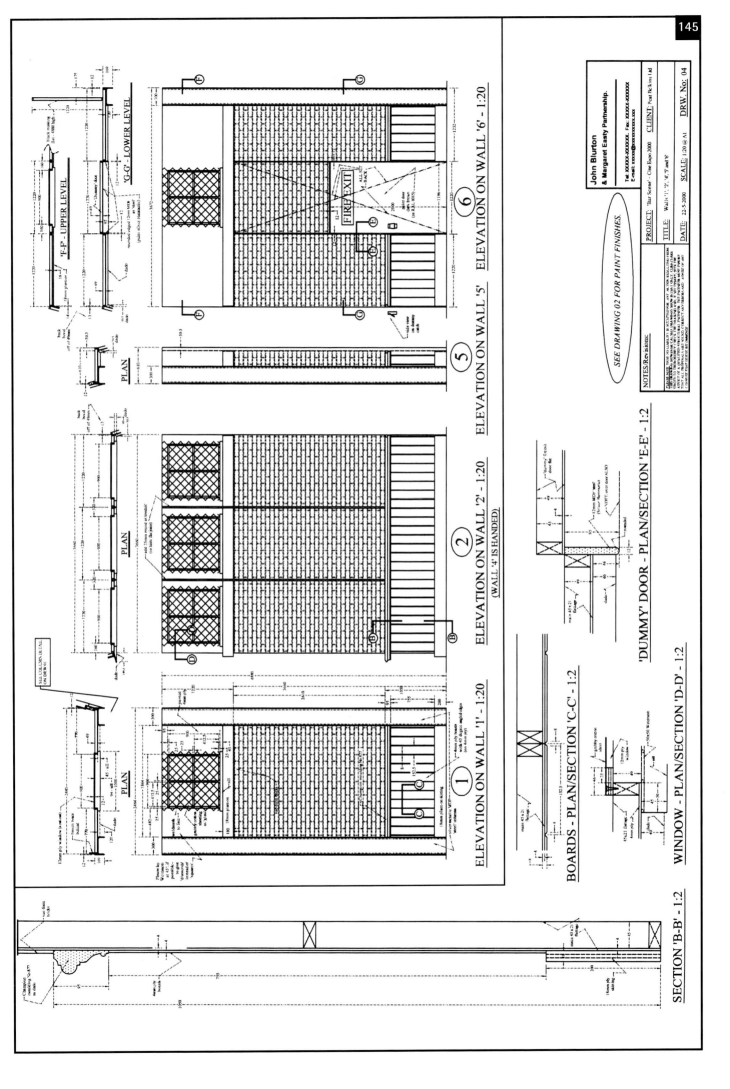

ELEVATION ON WALL '1' - 1:20

ELEVATION ON WALL '2' - 1:20
(WALL '4' IS HANDED)

ELEVATION ON WALL '5'

ELEVATION ON WALL '6' - 1:20

SECTION 'B-B' - 1:2

BOARDS - PLAN/SECTION 'C-C' - 1:2

WINDOW - PLAN/SECTION 'D-D' - 1:2

'DUMMY' DOOR - PLAN/SECTION 'E-E' - 1:2

'F-F' - UPPER LEVEL

'G-G' - LOWER LEVEL

John Blurton
& Margaret Easty Partnership.

Tel: xxxxx-xxxxxxx.   Fax: xxxxx-xxxxxxx
E-mail: xxxxx@xxxxxxxxx.xxx

CLIENT: Post Relk ins Ltd

PROJECT: 'Bar Scene' - Cine Expo 2000

TITLE: Walls '1', '2', '4', '5' and '6'

DATE: 22-5-2000   SCALE: 1:20 @ A1   DRW. No: 04

SEE DRAWING 02 FOR PAINT FINISHES.

NOTES/Revisions:

Part Four:
USEFUL DATA

The following pages contain information relating to geometry, maths and industry data.

Regrettably, the author can accept no responsibility for any errors, omissions, misprints, etc that may appear within this document.

CONVERSION FACTORS

IMPERIAL			METRIC				IMPERIAL
Inches	X	25.4	=	Millimetres	X	0.0394	=	Inches
Feet	X	0.3048	=	Metres	X	3.281	=	Feet
Yards	X	0.9144	=	Metres	X	1.094	=	Yards
Miles	X	1.609	=	Kilometres	X	0.6214	=	Miles
Sq. feet	X	0.0929	=	Sq. metres	X	10.764	=	Sq. feet
Sq. yards	X	0.8361	=	Sq. metres	X	1.196	=	Sq. yards
Acres	X	0.4047	=	Hectares	X	2.471	=	Acres
Cubic feet	X	0.0283	=	Cu. metres	X	35.315	=	Cubic feet
Cubic yards	X	0.765	=	Cu. metres	X	1.308	=	Cubic yards
Pints	X	0.568	=	Litres	X	1.76	=	Pints
Gallons	X	4.5460	=	Litres	X	0.22	=	Gallons
Pounds	X	0.4536	=	Kilograms	X	2.2046	=	Pounds
Tons	X	1.01605	=	Tonnes	X	0.9841	=	Tons
Lbs. sq. in.	X	0.0703	=	Kilos. sq. cm.	X	14.223	=	Lbs. sq. in.
Lbs. sq. ft.	X	4.882	=	Kilos. sq. m.	X	0.2048	=	Lbs. sq. ft.
Lbs. cu. ft.	X	16.019	=	Kilos. cu. m.	X	0.0624	=	Lbs. cu. ft.
Lbs. cu. yard	X	0.5933	=	Kilos. cu. m.	X	1.6860	=	Lbs. cu. yard
Price sq. ft.	X	10.764	=	Price sq. m.	X	0.0929	=	Price sq. ft.
Price 100 sq. ft.	X	1.0764	=	Price 10 sq. m.	X	0.929	=	Price 100 sq. ft.

WEIGHTS.
Approximate weights of materials:

PLYWOOD:- 18mm thick Far Eastern ply:- 2440 x 1220 = 35k per sheet.
3050 x 1525 = 54k per sheet,
or 11.6k per square metre.
18mm Douglas Fir ply:- 9.8k per square metre.
Add 10% for flameproof ply.

12mm thick Far Eastern ply:- 7.74k per square metre. (8.5k flameproof.)

6mm thick flameproof ply:- 2440 x 1220 = 11.52k per sheet.
3050 x 1525 = 18k per sheet,
or 3.87 per square metre.

4mm thick flameproof ply:- 2440 x 1220 = 8k per sheet.
3050 x 1525 = 12.6k per sheet,
or 2.7k per square metre.
4mm Birch ply:- 3.2k per square metre.

MDF:- 6mm MDF:- 2440 x 1220 = 13k per sheet or 4.37k per square metre.
25mm MDF:- 2440 x 1220 = 54.2k per sheet or 18.2k per square metre.

TIMBER:- 45 x 21 par:- 0.56k per metre.
70 x 21 par:- 0.85k per metre.
45 x 45 par:- 1.13k per metre .
Add 10% for flameproof.

GLASS:- 2.5k per 1mm thick, per square metre.

POLYCARBONATE:- 1.2k per 1mm thick, per square metre.

AEROLAM:- 14 x 2440 x 1220 'M' board:- 13.69k per sheet.
14 x 2440 x 1220 'F' board:- 9.168k per sheet.
25 x 2440 x 1220 'F' board:- 12.5k per sheet.

STEEL:- 20 x 20 x 1.5:- 0.857k per metre.
25 x 25 x 1.5:- 1.09k per metre.
40 x 40 x 1.5:- 1.828k per metre.
40 x 40 x 3:- 3.44k per metre.

SHEET STEEL:- 7.85k per 1mm thick, per square metre.

> **1 kg force = 9.807N**
> **1N = 0.1019Kg force**
> **therefore 1 KN = 101.9 kg force**

Figure 16-01 - CONVERSION FACTORS & APPROXIMATE WEIGHTS OF MATERIALS

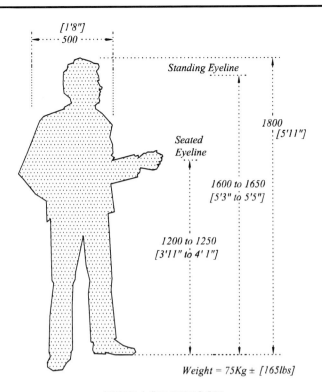

[1'8"]
500

Standing Eyeline

1800
[5'11"]

Seated
Eyeline

1600 to 1650
[5'3" to 5'5"]

1200 to 1250
[3'11" to 4'1"]

Weight = 75Kg ± [165lbs]

AVERAGE PERSON

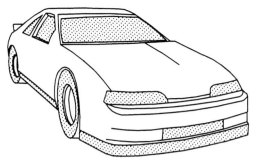

AVERAGE CAR

4500mm Long x1700mm Wide x 1350mm High
[14'9" Long x 5'7" Wide x 4'5" High]

Note:
1) Always confirm weight of car.
2) Check if width includes wing mirrors.

SHIPPING CONTAINERS

Inside dimensions of an average 20' unit =
2387h x 2337w x 5890 long [7'10"h x 7'8"w x 19'4" long]
Door size =
2286h x 2337w [7'6"h x 7'8"w]
Containers are *smaller* than the road trucks used by our industry!

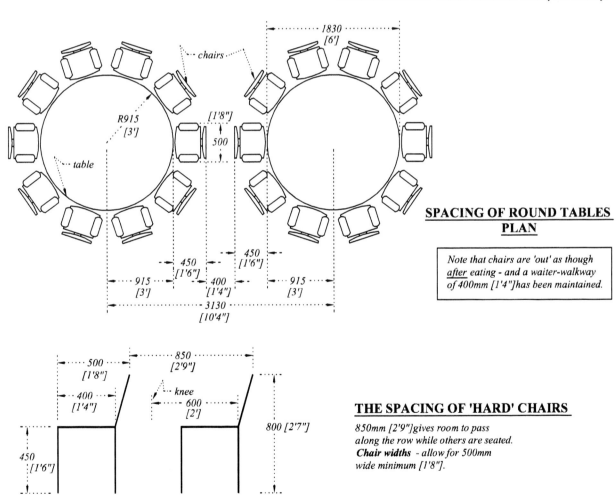

chairs

1830
[6']

R915
[3']

[1'8"]
500

table

450
[1'6"]

450
[1'6"]

915
[3']

400
[1'4"]

915
[3']

3130
[10'4"]

SPACING OF ROUND TABLES
PLAN

Note that chairs are 'out' as though
after eating - and a waiter-walkway
of 400mm [1'4"]has been maintained.

500
[1'8"]

850
[2'9"]

400
[1'4"]

knee

600
[2']

800 [2'7"]

450
[1'6"]

THE SPACING OF 'HARD' CHAIRS

850mm [2'9"]gives room to pass
along the row while others are seated.
Chair widths *- allow for 500mm*
wide minimum [1'8"].

SIDE VIEW
(Approximate sizes only)

Figure 16-02 - RANDOM DATA
Average car, average person, tables & chairs.

SCREEN/SLIDE/VIDEO/TV/FILM - DATA

1) 35mm SLIDE SCREEN:

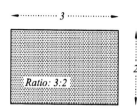

***Throw** (m)* = $\dfrac{\text{Lens focal length (mm) x screen width (m)}}{\text{Aperture width (mm) e.g. 34.8 'normal' slide}}$ ÷

Typical lenses = 45mm/60mm/90mm and 70-125mm zoom, etc.
Square slides are available, e.g. 37.3mm sq.
(Superslide = 46mm x 46mm)

Always confirm throw with AV supplier and allow room for the projector(s).

2) VIDEO SCREEN:

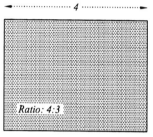

(Other ratios available, e.g. 16:9)

Throw = *VARIABLE according to lens + projector type.*
(Confirm with AV supplier.) 1.5 x screen width is average.
Examples: -
GE projector = 1.5:1 x screen width *(minimum lens.)*
(Other lenses = 3:1, 5:1, &etc.)
BARCO 5000 projector = 1.49 x screen width (m) x Z + 0.123
(Z is a variable: video = 1, graphics = 1.181)
BARCO 9200 projector = 1.2:1 x screen width - *(minimum lens.)*

Note:
A) *Allow for projector being 1200 long x 800 wide [4' x 2'8"].*
B) *Viewer should not be closer than 2 x screen width.*
C) *Viewer should be no further away from screen than 8 x screen width - to read graphics.*

3) TV MONITORS:

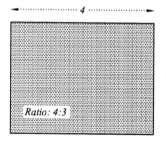

Monitor size is given as the diagonal of screen: -
e.g. 24" (610mm) = 488mm wide x 366mm high.
Remember: exact image size is slightly *less* than screen size.
Note: Other TV ratios are now available.

4) FILM:

The exact screen ratio is slightly less important when film is involved because a thin metal mask is cut (by the projectionist) that 'adjusts' the image to fit the screen (within reason, of course!)
Always *discuss ratio and throw with the projection company.*
Screen ratios that I have encountered include: -
35mm film = 2.358 : 1
70mm film = 2.21 : 1

Figure 16-03 - DATA FOR SCREENS, SLIDES,VIDEO,TV and FILM

RIGHT ANGLED TRIANGLES:-

One angle equal to 90°
Perimeter = A + O + H
Area = ½ AO

$$\text{SIN angle} = \frac{\text{opposite side}}{\text{hypotenuse}} \quad \text{(SOH)}$$

$$\text{COS angle} = \frac{\text{adjacent side}}{\text{hypotenuse}} \quad \text{(CAH)}$$

$$\text{TAN angle} = \frac{\text{opposite side}}{\text{adjacent side}} \quad \text{(TOA)}$$

(SOH,CAH,TOA)

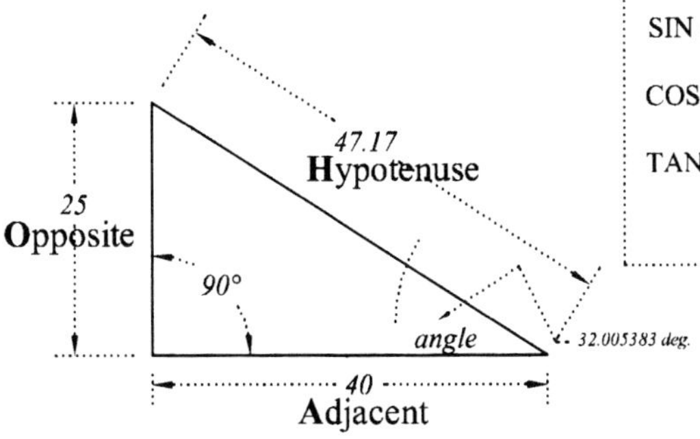

47.17
Hypotenuse
25
Opposite
90°
angle — 32.005383 deg.
40
Adjacent

EXAMPLE TRIANGLE USED HERE

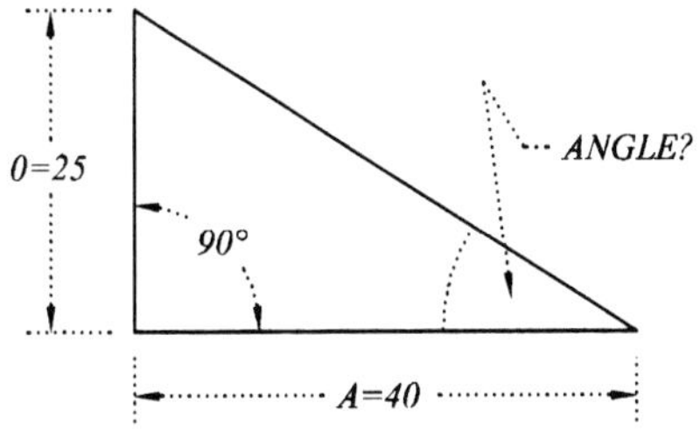

O=25
90°
ANGLE?
A=40

O given and A given:-

Angle = $\frac{25}{40}$ = Inv Tan = 32.005383°

(Inv is sometimes Shift on calculator)

H = $\sqrt{(25^2 + 40^2)}$ = 47.17

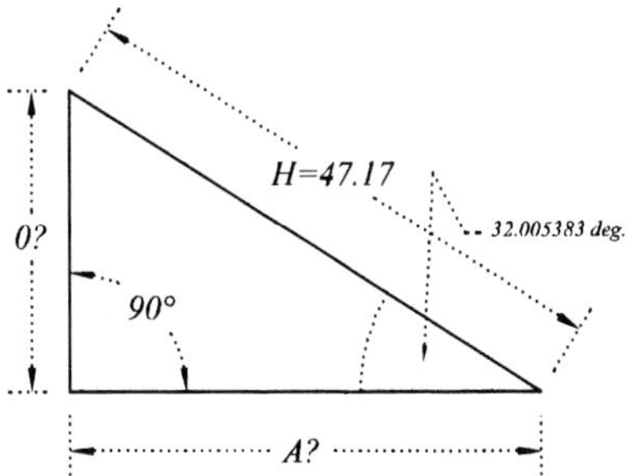

H=47.17
O?
90°
32.005383 deg.
A?

H given and Angle given:-

A = 47.17 x Cos 32.005383 = 40
O = 47.17 x Sin 32.005383 = 25

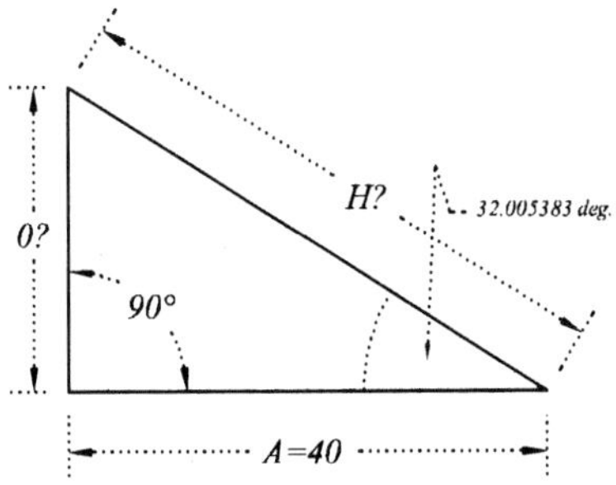

O?
H?
90°
32.005383 deg.
A=40

A given and Angle given:-

H = $\frac{40}{\text{Cos } 32.005383}$ = 47.17

O = 40 x Tan 32.005383 = 25

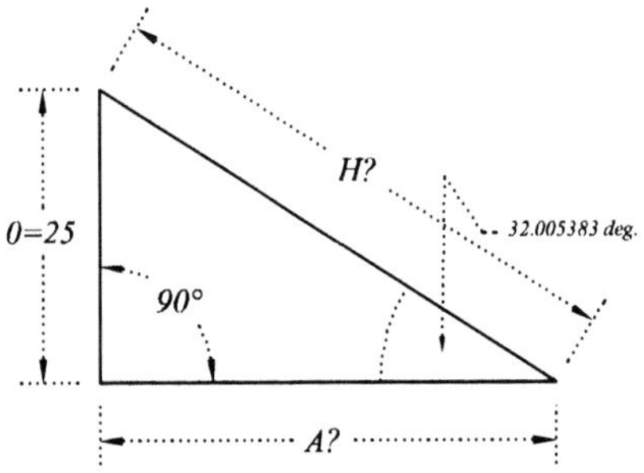

O=25
H?
90°
32.005383 deg.
A?

O given and Angle given:-

H = $\frac{25}{\text{Sin } 32.005383}$ = 47.17

O = $\frac{25}{\text{Tan}32.005383}$ = 40

TO DRAW A RIGHT-ANGLED TRIANGLE:-
GIVEN THE LENGTH OF THE HYPOTENUSE (150mm)
AND ONE OTHER SIDE (90mm)

1) Draw A - B, (150mm long) and bisect it at point X.
2) Draw a semi-circle of diameter A - B (radius = X-A)
3) Draw an arc of radius 90mm from Point A, intersecting the semi-circle at C.
4) ACB = a right-angled triangle.

R90
C
90°
A
X
B
150

5
5
5
hypotenuse
5
3
B
3
opposite to angle
3
A
angle
90°
4
C
adjacent to angle
4
4

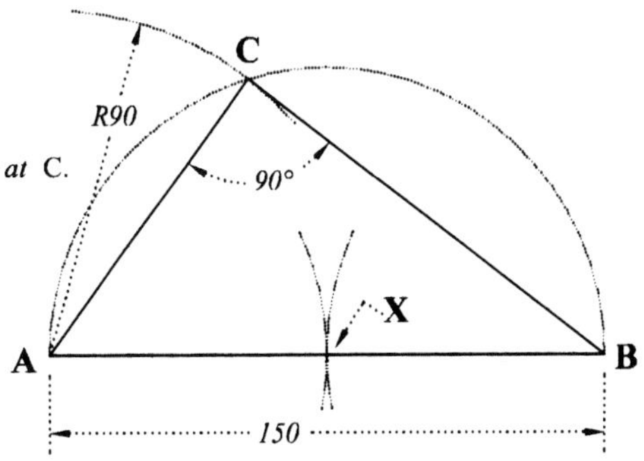

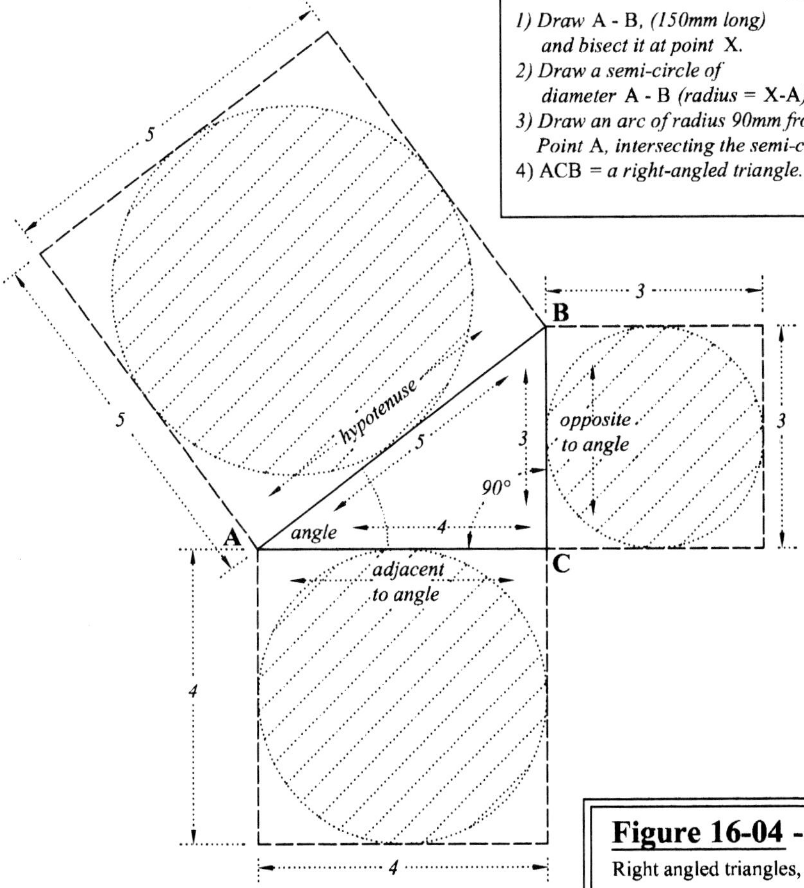

PYTHAGORAS' THEOREM:

In a right-angled triangle (a triangle containing a 90° angle,) the square on the hypotenuse is equal to the square on the other two sides.

OR: $AB^2 = AC^2 + BC^2$

OR: $5^2 = 4^2 + 3^2$

(As shown here - 25=16+9)

(Also, the area of circle 5-5 equals the sum of the areas 4-4 & 3-3.)

Figure 16-04 - RIGHT-ANGLED TRIANGLES

Right angled triangles, sines/cosines/tangents, Pythagoras and general data.

SOLUTION OF OBLIQUE-ANGLED TRIANGLES: ANGLES.

GIVEN:	TO BE FOUND:		
	ANGLE A:	**ANGLE B:**	**ANGLE C:**
abc	$\dfrac{b^2+c^2-a^2}{2bc} = cosA$	$\dfrac{a^2+c^2-b^2}{2ac} = cosB$	$\dfrac{a^2+b^2-c^2}{2ab} = cosC$
$\dfrac{bc}{\text{Angle A}}$		$\dfrac{bsinA}{c-bcosA} = tanB$	$\dfrac{csinA}{b-ccosA} = tanC$
$\dfrac{ac}{\text{Angle B}}$	$\dfrac{asinB}{c-acosB} = tanA$		$\dfrac{csinB}{a-ccosB} = tanC$
$\dfrac{ab}{\text{Angle C}}$	$\dfrac{asinC}{b-acosC} = tanA$	$\dfrac{bsinC}{b-acosC} = tanB$	
$\dfrac{ab}{\text{Angle A}}$		$\dfrac{bsinA}{a} = sinB$	$180° - (A+B)$
$\dfrac{ab}{\text{Angle B}}$	$\dfrac{asinB}{b} = sinA$		$180° - (A+B)$
$\dfrac{ac}{\text{Angle A}}$		$180° - (A+C)$	$\dfrac{csinA}{a} = sinC$
$\dfrac{ac}{\text{Angle C}}$	$\dfrac{asinC}{c} = sinA$	$180° - (A+C)$	
$\dfrac{bc}{\text{Angle B}}$	$180° - (B+C)$		$\dfrac{csinB}{b} = sinC$
$\dfrac{a}{\text{Angles AB}}$			$180° - (A+B)$
$\dfrac{a}{\text{Angles AC}}$		$180° - (A+C)$	
$\dfrac{a}{\text{Angles BC}}$	$180° - (B+C)$		
$\dfrac{b}{\text{Angles AB}}$			$180° - (A+B)$
$\dfrac{b}{\text{Angles AC}}$		$180° - (A+C)$	
$\dfrac{b}{\text{Angles BC}}$	$180° - (B+C)$		
$\dfrac{bc}{\text{Angle C}}$	$180° - (B+C)$	$\dfrac{bsinC}{c} = sinB$	
$\dfrac{c}{\text{Angles AB}}$			$180° - (A+B)$
$\dfrac{c}{\text{Angles AC}}$		$180° - (A+C)$	

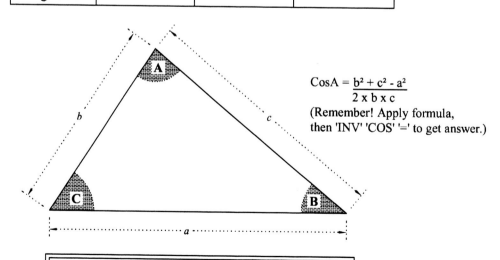

$CosA = \dfrac{b^2 + c^2 - a^2}{2 \times b \times c}$

(Remember! Apply formula, then 'INV' 'COS' '=' to get answer.)

Figure 16-05 - OBLIQUE ANGLED TRIANGLES
To find <u>ANGLES.</u>

SOLUTION OF OBLIQUE-ANGLED TRIANGLES: SIDES.

GIVEN:	TO BE FOUND:		
	SIDE a:	SIDE b:	SIDE c:
$\dfrac{bc}{\text{Angle A}}$	$\sqrt{b^2 + c^2 - 2bc\,cosA}$		
$\dfrac{ac}{\text{Angle B}}$		$\sqrt{a^2 + c^2 - 2ac\,cosB}$	
$\dfrac{ab}{\text{Angle C}}$			$\sqrt{a^2 + b^2 - 2ab\,cosC}$
$\dfrac{ab}{\text{Angle A}}$			$\dfrac{asinC}{sinA}$
$\dfrac{ab}{\text{Angle B}}$			$\dfrac{bsinC}{sinB}$
$\dfrac{ac}{\text{Angle A}}$		$\dfrac{asinB}{sinA}$	
$\dfrac{ac}{\text{Angle C}}$		$\dfrac{csinB}{sinC}$	
$\dfrac{bc}{\text{Angle B}}$	$\dfrac{bsinA}{sinB}$		
$\dfrac{bc}{\text{Angle C}}$	$\dfrac{csinA}{sinC}$		
$\dfrac{a}{\text{Angles AB}}$		$\dfrac{asinB}{sinA}$	$\dfrac{asinC}{sinA}$
$\dfrac{a}{\text{Angles AC}}$		$\dfrac{asinB}{sinA}$	$\dfrac{asinC}{sinA}$
$\dfrac{a}{\text{Angles BC}}$		$\dfrac{asinB}{sinA}$	$\dfrac{asinC}{sinA}$
$\dfrac{b}{\text{Angles AB}}$	$\dfrac{bsinA}{sinB}$		$\dfrac{bsinC}{sinB}$
$\dfrac{b}{\text{Angles AC}}$	$\dfrac{bsinA}{sinB}$		$\dfrac{bsinC}{sinB}$
$\dfrac{b}{\text{Angles BC}}$	$\dfrac{bsinA}{sinB}$		$\dfrac{bsinC}{sinB}$
$\dfrac{c}{\text{Angles AB}}$	$\dfrac{csinA}{sinC}$	$\dfrac{csinB}{sinC}$	
$\dfrac{c}{\text{Angles AC}}$	$\dfrac{csinA}{sinC}$	$\dfrac{csinB}{sinC}$	
$\dfrac{c}{\text{Angles BC}}$	$\dfrac{csinA}{sinC}$	$\dfrac{csinB}{sinC}$	

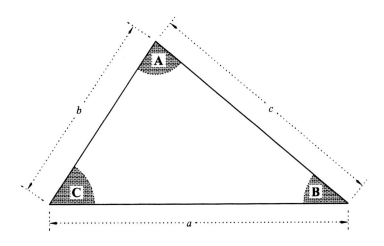

Figure 16-06 - OBLIQUE ANGLED TRIANGLES
To find SIDES.

154

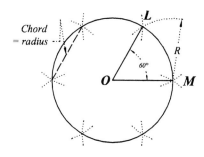

Chord = radius

60°

O R L M

The radius of a circle can be 'stepped off' around the circumference exactly six times. (The six chords would form a hexagon.) Therefore, the angle L - O - M is 60° (360° ÷ 6)

TO DRAW A 60° ANGLE

TO DRAW A CIRCLE GIVEN 3 POINTS

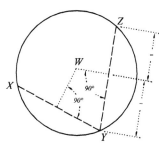

Join X & Y and Y & Z.
Bisect XY and YZ.
Use Centre point W and strike circle through X, Y and Z.

TO DRAW A TANGENT TO A CIRCLE FROM A POINT OUTSIDE THE CIRCLE

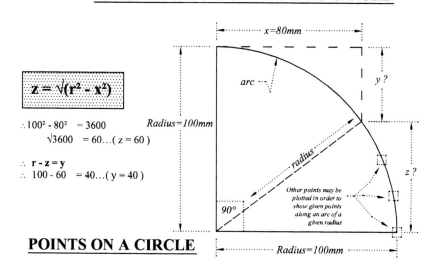

1) Join points A & B and bisect it at point C.
2) Draw a circle from centre point C, with radius C-B. This cuts the original given circle at D.
3) Line D-B is tangential to the circle. Line A-D is normal to the tangent.

$$z = \sqrt{(r^2 - x^2)}$$

∴ 100² - 80² = 3600
√3600 = 60...(z = 60)

∴ **r - z = y**
∴ 100 - 60 = 40...(y = 40)

POINTS ON A CIRCLE

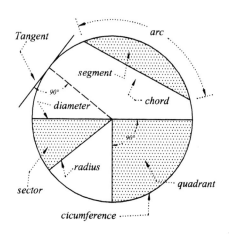

Tangent, arc, segment, chord, diameter, radius, sector, quadrant, cicumference

Circle:-
π = 3.1416 (approx.)
2πR = circumference.
πD = circumference.
D = 2R
πR² = area.
D² x π/4 = area.
⁴⁄₃πR³ = volume of sphere.
4πR² = surface area of sphere.

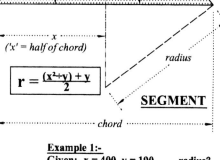

RING
Area = π(R² - r²)

SECTOR
Length of arc = πRa ÷ 180
Area = a/360 πR²

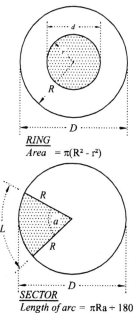

SEGMENT

$$r = \frac{(x^2 \div y) + y}{2}$$

('x' = half of chord)

Example 1:-
Given:- x = 400, y = 190, ...radius?
400 x 400 = 160000
160000 ÷ 190 = 842.1052
842.1052 + 190 = 1032.1052
1032.1052 ÷ 2 = **516.0526 (radius)**

Example 2:-
Given:- y = 190, rad = 516.0526,........x?
516.0526 x 2 = 1032.1052
1032.1052 - 190 = 842.1052
842.1052 x 190 = 160000
√160000 = **400 (x)**

Figure 16-07 - CIRCLES,CHORDS, ARCS & TANGENTS
General properties of circles.

MINOR AXIS   **A** = 40mm (given)
MAJOR AXIS   **B** = 60mm (given)
GIVEN   **40mm**
WHAT IS?   **C ?**

FIRST... FIND 'D'

- by describing a semi-circle whose radius
equals the major axis of the ellipse in question
- in this case, *a radius of 60mm ('B')*.
'D' can then be found:- $60^2 - 40^2 = D^2$,
which gives 'D' as..... **44.72mm.**

FORMULA:- $\boxed{C = \frac{A}{B}D}$

Or, $40 \div 60 = 0.6666666$
$0.6666666 \times 44.72 = \textbf{29.81mm}$
C = 29.81mm.

ESTABLISHING POINTS ON AN ELLIPSE.

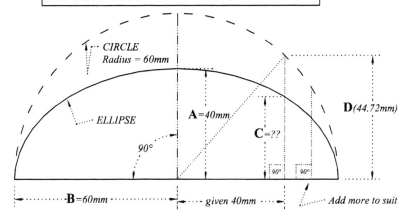

FINDING POINTS ON AN ELLIPSE, GIVEN ONLY THE MAJOR AND MINOR AXES AND ONE ANGLE.

$$\boxed{\frac{0^2}{61^2} + \frac{A^2}{54^2} = 1}$$

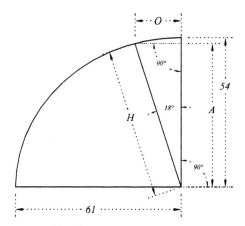

Therefore......

$$\frac{H^2 \sin 18^2}{61^2} + \frac{H^2 \cos 18^2}{54^2} = 1$$

$$H^2\left(\frac{\sin 18^2}{61^2} + \frac{\cos 18^2}{54^2}\right) = 1$$

$$H^2\left(\frac{-0.587785252}{3721} + \frac{0.809016994}{2916}\right) = 1$$

$$H^2\left(-0.0001579643246 + 0.0002774406701\right) = 1$$

$$H^2\left(0.0001194763455\right) = 1$$

$H^2 = \dfrac{1}{0.0001194763455}$

$H^2 = 0.0001194763455$ (press "1/X" button)
$H^2 = 8369.857613$
$H = \sqrt{8369.857613}$
$H = 91.48692591$, *or* 91.49

DRAWING AN ELLIPSE BY TRAMMEL METHOD.

Step 1

a) Set out major and minor axes.

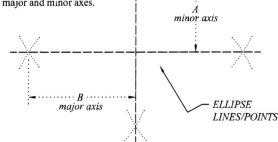

b) Mark a rod/batten/paper as shown.

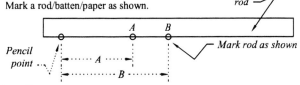

Step 2

Lay rod upon setting-out; Keep A on the major axis and B on the minor axis;
Mark pencil points; Join up pencil points with a flexible batten.

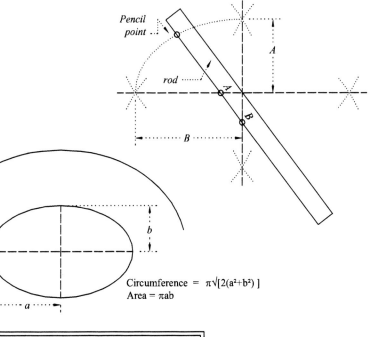

Circumference = $\pi\sqrt{[2(a^2+b^2)]}$
Area = πab

Figure 16-08 - THE ELLIPSE
Ellipse data, points on an ellipse, drawing by trammel method.

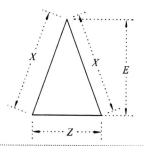

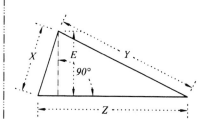

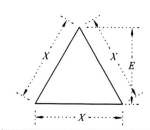

Isosceles triangle:-
Two equal sides and two equal angles
Perimeter = X + X + Z
Area = ½ ZE

Scalene triangle:-
No equal sides or equal angles
Perimeter = X + Y + Z
Area = ½ ZE

Equilateral triangle:-
Three equal sides and three equal angles
Perimeter = 3X
Area = ½ XE
Height = $\frac{X}{2}\sqrt{3}$

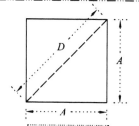

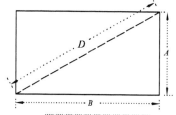

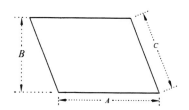

Square:-
Perimeter = 4A
Area = A²
Diagonal = A √2
Side = ½D √2

Rectangle:-
Perimeter = 2(A+B)
Area = AB
Diagonal = √(A²+B²)

Rhomboid (parallelogram):-
Perimeter = 2(A+C)
Area = A B

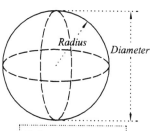

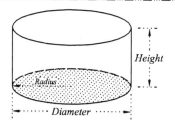

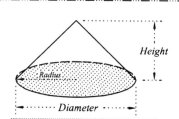

Sphere:-
Volume = $\frac{4}{3}\pi R^3$
Surface Area = 4 π R²

Cylinder:-
πr²h   = volume **(where h = height)**
2πrh   = curved surface area.
2πrh + 2πr² = total surface area
2πr(r+h)   =   ditto

Cone:
Volume = $\frac{1}{3}(\pi R^2)$ H
Surface Area of slant = ½ π DH

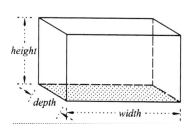

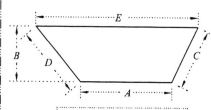

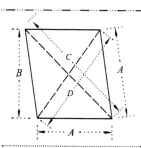

Rectangular solid:-
Volume = W D H
Surface Area = (2WD)+(2WH)+2(HD)

Trapezoid:-
Perimeter = C + D + A + E
Area = ½B(A + E)

Rhomboid (equilateral parallelogram):-
Perimeter = 4A
Area = AB *OR* = ½DC

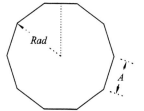

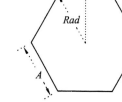

Regular Polygon:-
(n = number of sides)
Perimeter = nA
Area = ½(nA) $\sqrt{R^2 - \frac{A^2}{4}}$
Radius = $\sqrt{R^2 - \frac{A^2}{4}}$

Regular Hexagon:-
Perimeter = 6A
Radius = A (when hexagon is inscribed in circle)
Radius = $\frac{A}{2}\sqrt{3}$ (when hexagon is conscribed in circle)
Area = $\frac{3A^2}{2}\sqrt{3}$

Figure 16-09 - GEOMETRIC SHAPES
General data.

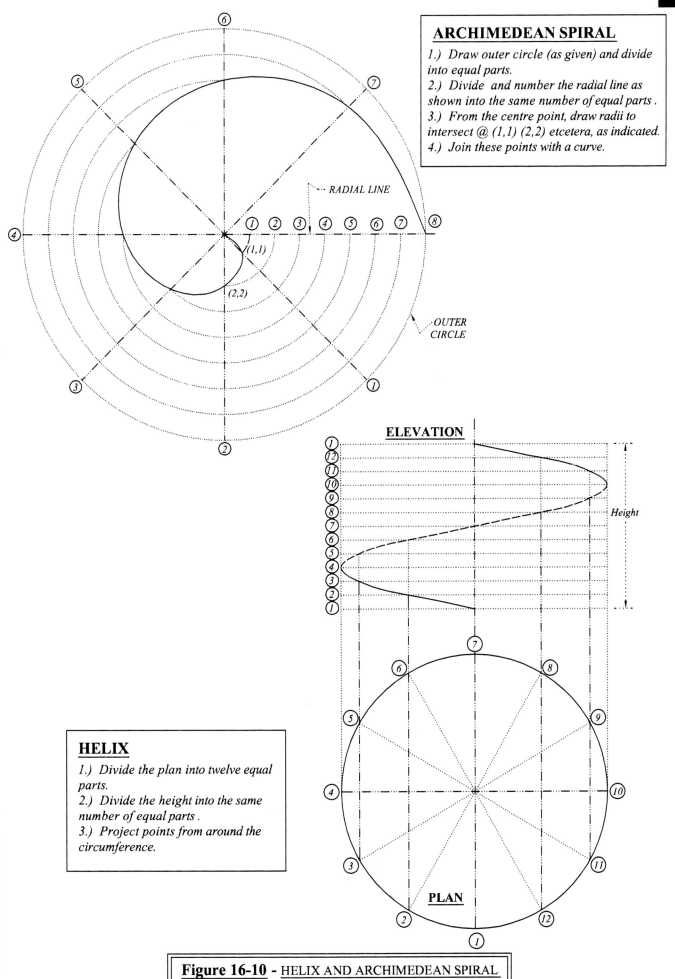

ARCHIMEDEAN SPIRAL

1.) Draw outer circle (as given) and divide into equal parts.
2.) Divide and number the radial line as shown into the same number of equal parts.
3.) From the centre point, draw radii to intersect @ (1,1) (2,2) etcetera, as indicated.
4.) Join these points with a curve.

RADIAL LINE

(1,1)

(2,2)

OUTER CIRCLE

ELEVATION

Height

HELIX

1.) Divide the plan into twelve equal parts.
2.) Divide the height into the same number of equal parts.
3.) Project points from around the circumference.

PLAN

Figure 16-10 - HELIX AND ARCHIMEDEAN SPIRAL

How to draw a helix and an Archimedean spiral.

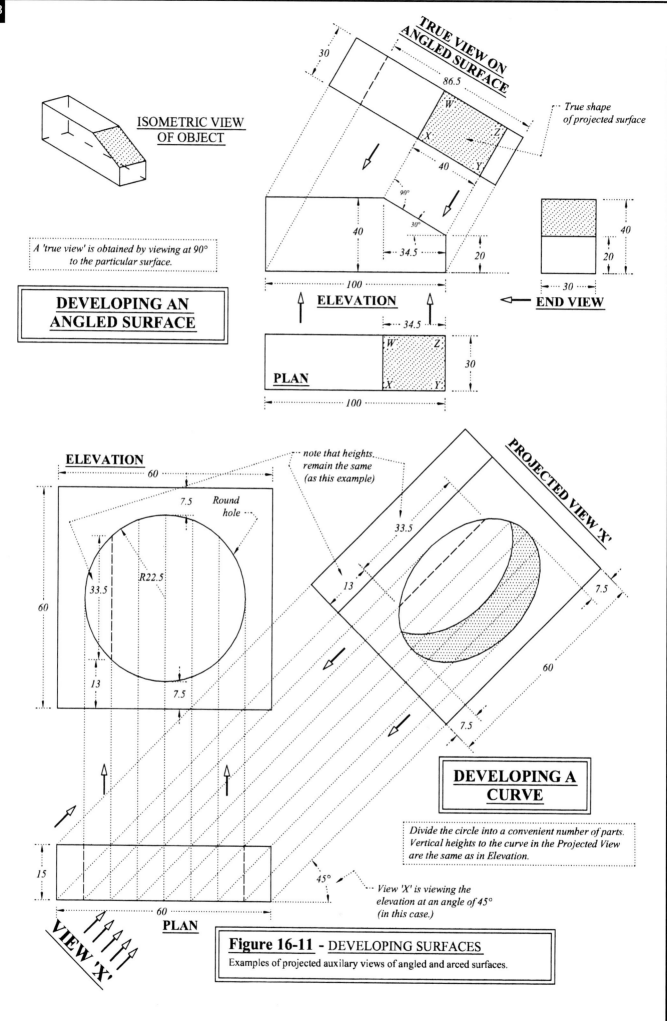

ISOMETRIC VIEW
OF OBJECT

TRUE VIEW ON
ANGLED SURFACE

True shape
of projected surface

A 'true view' is obtained by viewing at 90°
to the particular surface.

**DEVELOPING AN
ANGLED SURFACE**

ELEVATION

END VIEW

PLAN

ELEVATION

note that heights
remain the same
(as this example)

PROJECTED VIEW 'X'

Round
hole

R22.5

**DEVELOPING A
CURVE**

Divide the circle into a convenient number of parts.
Vertical heights to the curve in the Projected View
are the same as in Elevation.

View 'X' is viewing the
elevation at an angle of 45°
(in this case.)

PLAN

VIEW 'X'

Figure 16-11 - DEVELOPING SURFACES
Examples of projected auxilary views of angled and arced surfaces.

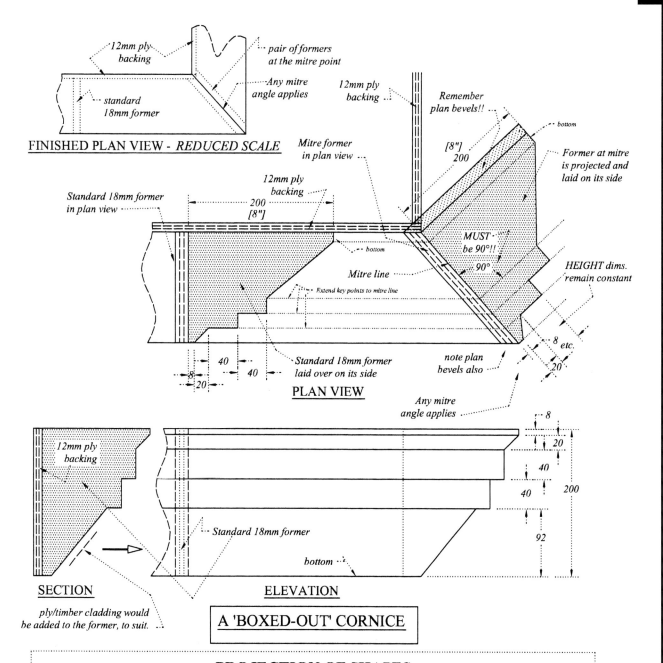

FINISHED PLAN VIEW - *REDUCED SCALE*

PLAN VIEW

SECTION

ELEVATION

A 'BOXED-OUT' CORNICE

PROJECTION OF SHAPES:

The above shows part of a scenic cornice; it is a 'boxed-out' construction i.e. plywood formers are shaped to suit the desired section and fixed to a plywood backing piece - the formers would then be clad with thin ply.

The problem *to solve is how to project the shape of a 'standard' former to form the shape of the formers that are required at the mitre. (The mitre angle can be any angle).*

The solution:

Set-out the plan view as shown and lay the standard former on its side. Extend its relevant points across to the mitre line and then turn those lines at 90° to the mitre line and extend them. Mark the relevant height dimensions of the standard former from the mitre line along the new extended lines and the correct shape is obtained.

You can see that the shape obtained is a 'stretched' version of a standard former that now fits at the mitre line.

Remember to allow for the plan view bevel of the thickness of plywood, as indicated (the former is cut bevelled in order to give a flat surface where it will be clad). Two formers are used at the mitre, but only one has been shown here, for clarity.

Figure 16-12 - PROJECTION......OF FORMERS.

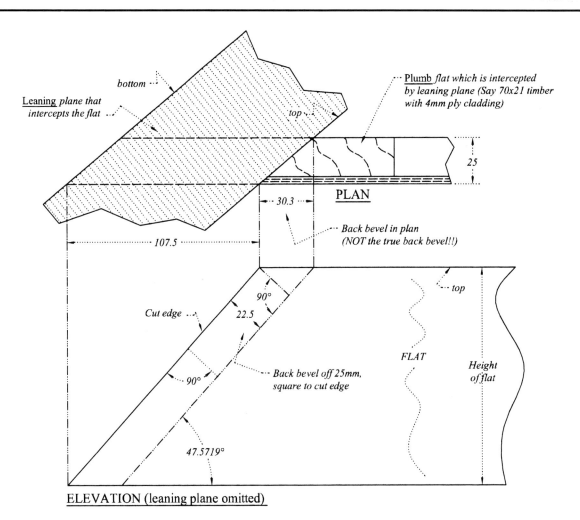

bottom

Leaning *plane that intercepts the flat*

Plumb *flat which is intercepted by leaning plane (Say 70x21 timber with 4mm ply cladding)*

top

25

PLAN

30.3

Back bevel in plan
(NOT the true back bevel!!)

107.5

90°

22.5

Cut edge

top

FLAT

Height
of flat

Back bevel off 25mm,
square to cut edge

90°

47.5719°

ELEVATION (leaning plane omitted)

A PLUMB FLAT MEETS LEANING PLANE

*This shows how to obtain the true back bevel of the cut, angled edge of the flat.
(The whole back bevel is shown here - however, the carpenters would prefer to
be given the back bevel off the 21mm thickness of the flat only. See below.)*

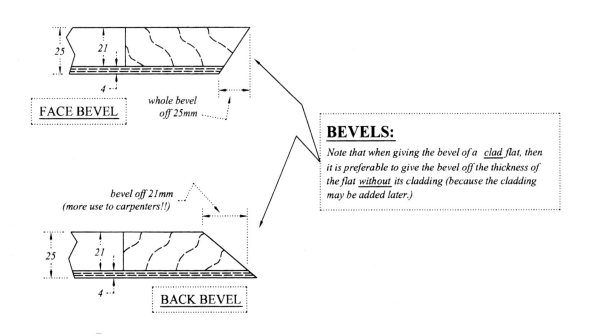

25   21

4

FACE BEVEL

*whole bevel
off 25mm*

BEVELS:

*Note that when giving the bevel of a clad flat, then
it is preferable to give the bevel off the thickness of
the flat without its cladding (because the cladding
may be added later.)*

*bevel off 21mm
(more use to carpenters!!)*

25   21

4

BACK BEVEL

Figure 16-13 - BEVELS: WHEN A PLUMB FLAT MEETS LEANING PLANE .

TO DRAW A PERPENDICULAR FROM A GIVEN POINT 'C' TO A GIVEN LINE 'A-B'

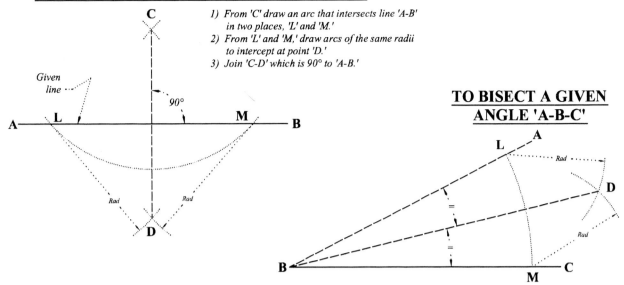

1) From 'C' draw an arc that intersects line 'A-B' in two places, 'L' and 'M.'
2) From 'L' and 'M,' draw arcs of the same radii to intercept at point 'D.'
3) Join 'C-D' which is 90° to 'A-B.'

TO BISECT A GIVEN ANGLE 'A-B-C'

1) From 'B' draw an arc that intersects A-B and C-B at points L and M.
2) From L and M, draw arcs of the same radii to intersect at point D.
3) Join 'B-D.' Angle 'A-B-D' is identical to angle 'D-B-C.'

TO DRAW A REGULAR POLYGON, GIVEN THE LENGTH OF ONE SIDE

(EXAMPLE GIVEN IS A PENTAGON, EACH SIDE TO BE 100mm)

1) Draw 'A-B,' 100mm long and a semi-circle of radius 100mm from point 'A.'
2) Divide the semi-circle into the same number of parts as the desired polygon has sides - 5 in this case.
3) Line 'A2' is the second side of the polygon.
4) Draw extended lines 'A3' and 'A4.'
5) From point '2' draw an arc of radius 100mm, to intersect extended line 'A3' at 'D.'
6) From either point 'D' or point 'B', draw an arc of radius 100mm to cross extended line 'A4' at 'C.'

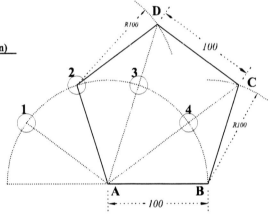

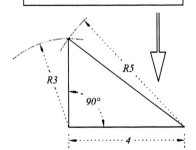

'3-4-5' TRIANGLE

To obtain an accurate 90° angle: - set-out a triangle whose sides are 3, 4 and 5 units in length.

PYTHAGORAS' THEOREM:

$3^2 + 4^2 = 5^2$ *in a right angled triangle.* (9+16=25)

TO DRAW A LINE PERPENDICULAR TO A GIVEN LINE 'A-B'

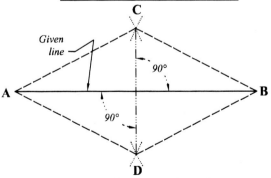

1) From 'A' strike two arcs (of any radius larger than half 'A-B' as shown.)
2) Do the same from 'B' using the same radius.
3) Join 'C-D' which is 90° to 'A-B.'

Figure 16-14 - RANDOM GEOMETRIC DATA

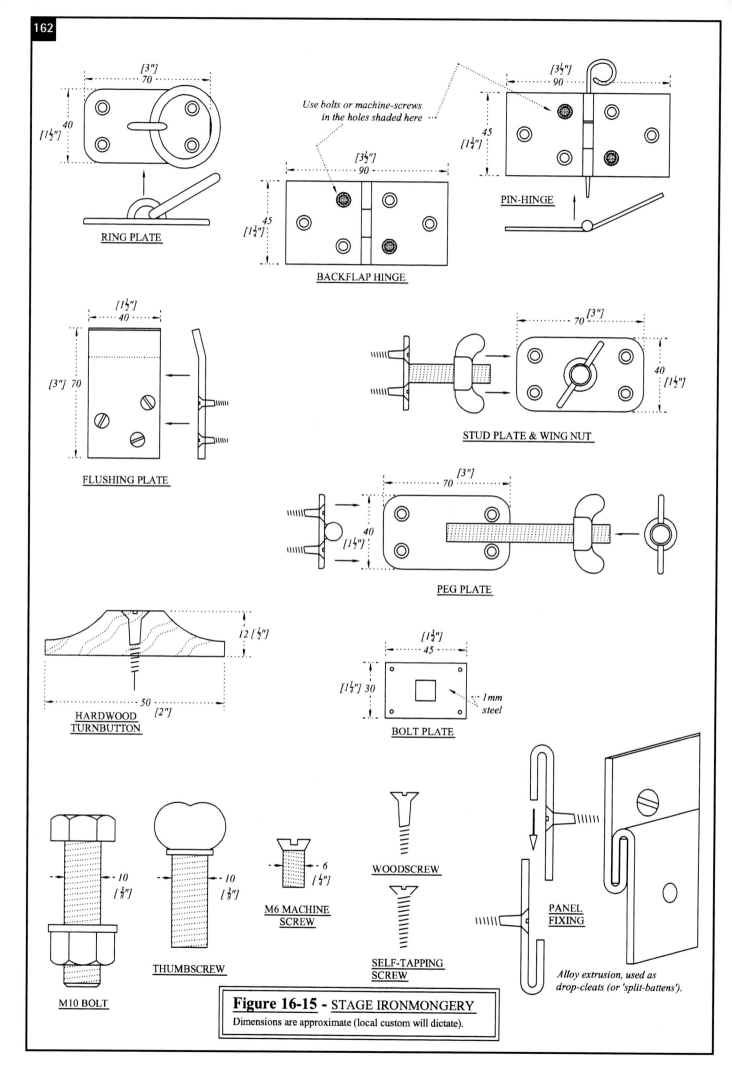

[3"]
70

40
[1½"]

RING PLATE

Use bolts or machine-screws
in the holes shaded here ···

[3½"]
90

45
[1¼"]

BACKFLAP HINGE

[3½"]
90

45
[1¾"]

PIN-HINGE

[1½"]
40

[3"] 70

FLUSHING PLATE

70 [3"]

40
[1½"]

STUD PLATE & WING NUT

[3"]
70

40
[1½"]

PEG PLATE

12 [½"]

50

[2"]

**HARDWOOD
TURNBUTTON**

[1¾"]
45

[1¼"] 30

1mm
steel

BOLT PLATE

10
[⅜"]

M10 BOLT

10
[⅜"]

THUMBSCREW

6
[¼"]

**M6 MACHINE
SCREW**

WOODSCREW

**SELF-TAPPING
SCREW**

**PANEL
FIXING**

*Alloy extrusion, used as
drop-cleats (or 'split-battens').*

Figure 16-15 - STAGE IRONMONGERY
Dimensions are approximate (local custom will dictate).

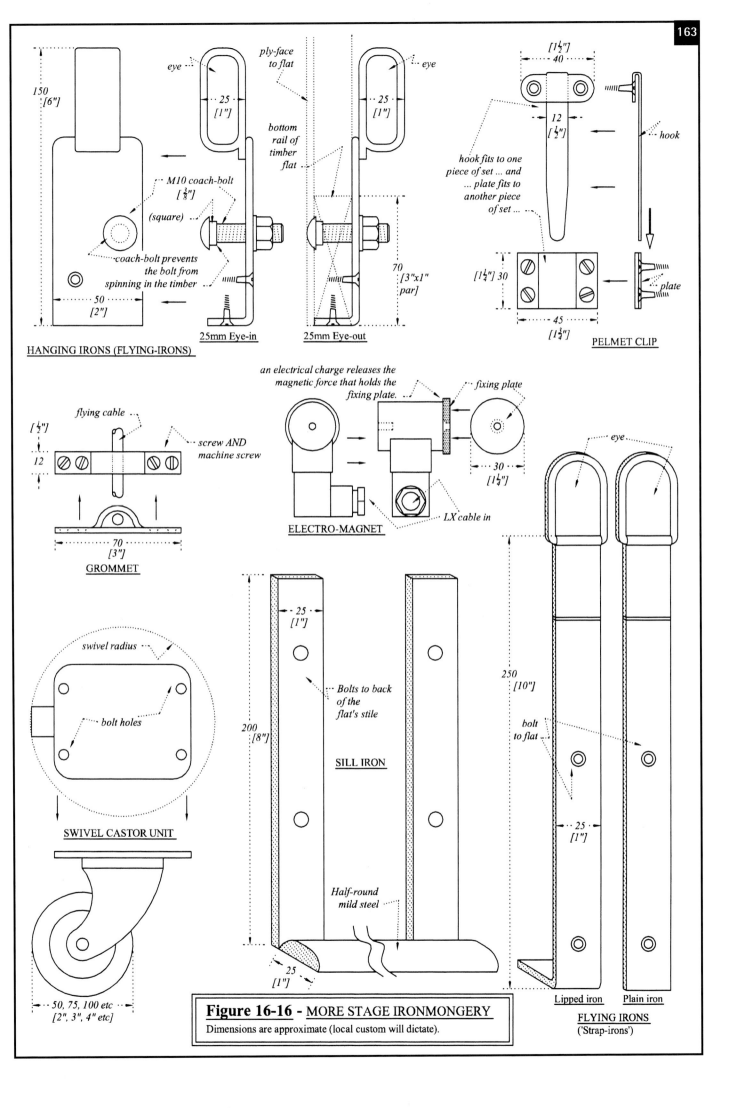

HANGING IRONS (FLYING-IRONS)

150
[6"]

eye

25
[1"]

ply-face
to flat

bottom
rail of
timber
flat

25
[1"]

eye

M10 coach-bolt
[3/8"]

(square)

coach-bolt prevents
the bolt from
spinning in the timber

50
[2"]

25mm Eye-in

70
[3"x1"
par]

25mm Eye-out

[1½"]
40

12
[½"]

hook fits to one
piece of set ... and
... plate fits to
another piece
of set ...

[1¼"] 30

45
[1¾"]

hook

plate

PELMET CLIP

[½"]
12

flying cable

screw AND
machine screw

70
[3"]

GROMMET

an electrical charge releases the
magnetic force that holds the
fixing plate.

fixing plate

30
[1½"]

LX cable in

ELECTRO-MAGNET

swivel radius

bolt holes

SWIVEL CASTOR UNIT

50, 75, 100 etc
[2", 3", 4" etc]

25
[1"]

Bolts to back
of the
flat's stile

200
[8"]

SILL IRON

Half-round
mild steel

25
[1"]

eye

250
[10"]

bolt
to flat

25
[1"]

Lipped iron   Plain iron

FLYING IRONS
('Strap-irons')

Figure 16-16 - MORE STAGE IRONMONGERY
Dimensions are approximate (local custom will dictate).

PICTURE RAIL

CORNICES

two-part moulding

ARCHITRAVES

DADO RAILS

BOLECTION

ASTROGEL

NOSING

SCOTIA

two-part moulding

HANDRAILS

face of door

water runs off here
... and ...
drips-off here.

bottom of door

DOOR DRIP

PANEL MOULDINGS

STAFF BEAD

OVOLO

PARTING BEAD

some skirtings have moulded sections at both ends - to give a choice.

HALF-ROUND

QUADRANT

DOWEL

SASH BAR

OUTSIDE   INSIDE

putty ...

glass

SKIRTINGS

SASH STILE

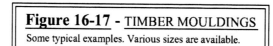

Figure 16-17 - TIMBER MOULDINGS
Some typical examples. Various sizes are available.

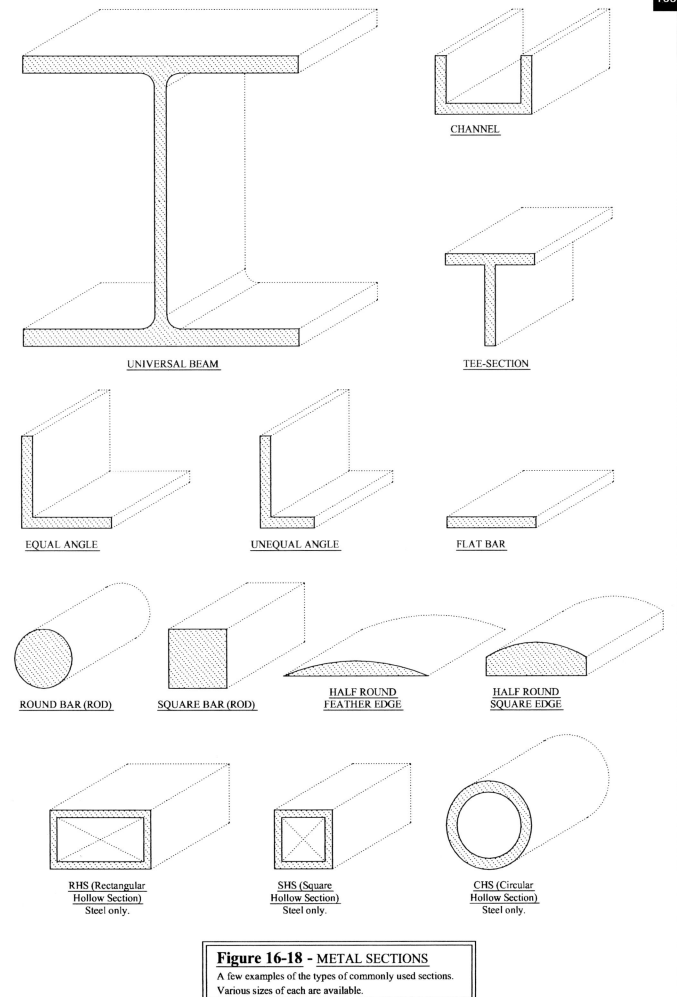

CHANNEL

UNIVERSAL BEAM

TEE-SECTION

EQUAL ANGLE

UNEQUAL ANGLE

FLAT BAR

ROUND BAR (ROD)

SQUARE BAR (ROD)

HALF ROUND
FEATHER EDGE

HALF ROUND
SQUARE EDGE

RHS (Rectangular
Hollow Section)
Steel only.

SHS (Square
Hollow Section)
Steel only.

CHS (Circular
Hollow Section)
Steel only.

Figure 16-18 - METAL SECTIONS
A few examples of the types of commonly used sections.
Various sizes of each are available.

1 - Draw PLAN & ELEVATIONS in relation to the STATION POINT (the point chosen from which the object is to be viewed). Be aware of the CONE OF VISION - which represents the human eye's visual cone. Ideally, this is 45° - if more than 60°, distortion will occur in the final image.   Remember that this cone applies to the side-elevation as well: ensure that the height of the object can be contained within it - move the SP away until all is within these cones.

2 - Locate the PICTURE PLANE (a vertical plane at 90° to the ground plane - imagine it to be glass, and that the final image will be drawn 'upon' it. The picture plane must be at 90° to the plan centre-line of vision. The position of this line ONLY affects the scale - the size - of the final image: the closer it is to the station point, the smaller the image will be; if moved away from the SP, the image will be larger, but still carry the same proportions.

3 - Draw the HORIZON LINE parallel to the picture plane and above it by any convenient distance - the final image is drawn about this line.

4 - Draw the GROUND LINE parallel to the horizon line and below it by the height of the observer's eye above the ground (here, drawn as1600mm). This height is chosen to suit how the object is wanted to be viewed. Here, a standing eye-line has been used, but the observer could well be standing on a step-ladder ... if that is the viewpoint wanted .

5 - From the station point, draw VP LINES to the picure plane that are parallel to the outer plan-view sides of the object. At the picture plane, these lines turn up at 90° to it, and meet the horizon line at points marked as 'VP1' and 'VP2' - these are the two VANISHING POINTS. (VP2 is shown here.)

6 - Extend any convenient side of the object - in plan-view - to meet the picture plane ... and turn the line up at 90° to it. This line is a HEIGHT LINE: known heights are measured UP from the ground line and lines are drawn from the top and bottom back to the relevant VP point ... when extended, these lines become the top and bottom of the object. Height lines are plotted for each plan-view plane (a line in plan), where heights are required.

7 - VISUAL RAYS are drawn from the station point to parts of the object to be drawn ... and they are extended to meet the picture plane ... where they turn up at 90° to it ... and become the vertical lines on the finished perspective drawing.

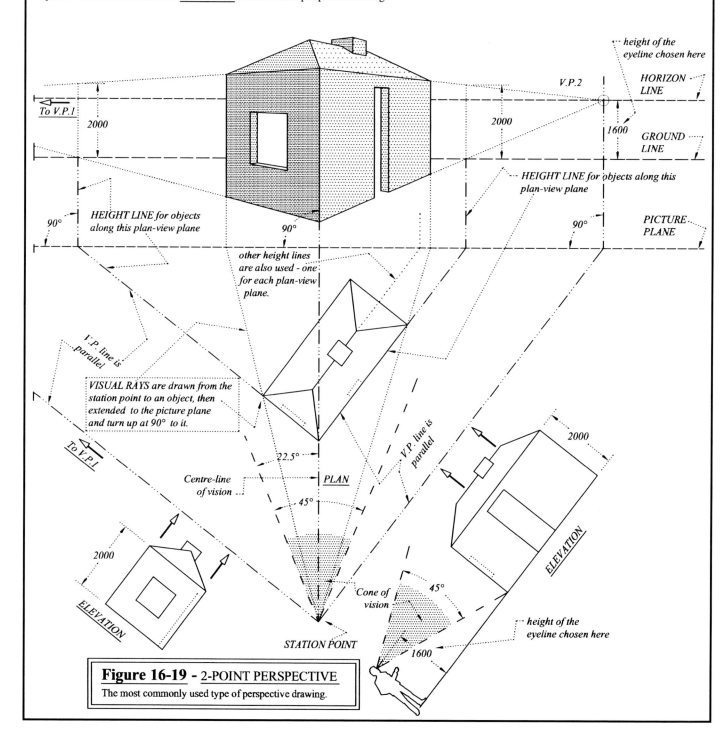

Figure 16-19 - 2-POINT PERSPECTIVE
The most commonly used type of perspective drawing.

Index